W9-CKI-244

DATE DUE

APR 3 0 2001	
AUG 2 9 2002	
OCT 3 0 2002	

GAYLORD   #3523PI   Printed in USA

ANXIETY SENSITIVITY

Theory, Research, and Treatment
of the Fear of Anxiety

The LEA Series in Personality and Clinical Psychology

Irving B. Weiner, Editor

ANXIETY SENSITIVITY

Theory, Research, and Treatment of the Fear of Anxiety

Edited by

Steven Taylor
University of British Columbia

 LAWRENCE ERLBAUM ASSOCIATES, PUBLISHERS
1999   Mahwah, New Jersey   London

RC531 .A638 1999

Anxiety sensitivity :
  theory, research, and

Lawrence Erlbaum Associates, Inc., Publishers
10 Industrial Avenue
Mahwah, New Jersey 07430-2262

Cover design by Kathryn Houghtaling Lacey

Library of Congress Cataloging-in-Publication Data

Anxiety sensitivity : theory, research, and treatment of the fear of
anxiety / edited by Steven Taylor.
        p. cm.
    Includes bibliographical references and index.
    ISBN 0-8058-2865-6 (hardcover : alk. paper)
    1. Anxiety sensitivity. I. Taylor, Steven, 1960–   .
RC531.A638 1998
616.85'223—dc21   98-23956
                                                          CIP

Books published by Lawrence Erlbaum Associates are printed
on acid-free paper, and their bindings are chosen for strength
and durability

Printed in the United States of America
10 9 8 7 6 5 4 3 2 1

Contents

PART III: NEW RESEARCH ON BASIC MECHANISMS: CAUSES AND CONSEQUENCES OF ANXIETY SENSITIVITY

PART IV: NEW DIRECTIONS IN ANXIETY SENSITIVITY RESEARCH

PART V: CONCLUSIONS

Foreword

Stanley Rachman
University of British Columbia

Sensitivity to stress is a perennial and important concept, embedded in all diathesis theories. Plainly, people vary in their sensitivity to stress. In any potentially stressful situation, some people will endure without difficulty while others show signs of acute distress. That said, we need to find out whether the sensitivity is specific to the particular stressor or whether it is a general predisposition, likely to become manifest in a range of situations. Another possibility is that many people harbor a general sensitivity within which specific susceptibilities are nested.

In time, these questions give rise to technical problems: How can we recognize and measure general and specific sensitivities? Is sensitivity unidimensional? How does it develop? Can we construct reliable and valid test-beds without straying over ethical borders? Can we infer sensitivity from the emergence of psychopathology? and so forth. These and many related matters are analyzed and discussed in this timely and useful compendium cum progress report on anxiety sensitivity.

From the time of its introduction by Reiss and McNally in 1985, the concept of *anxiety sensitivity*—the fear of anxiety-related sensations—attracted active attention. In part this attention arose from a recognition that the idea of variable sensitivities has not been adequately explored, even though progress has been made, as in the concepts of *neuroticism*, *trait anxiety*, and so forth. A second reason for the interest in the concept is that its introduction coincided with the first statement of Clark's cognitive theory of panic, and there are obvious links between these two ideas. Third, the growing volume of interest in acute stress disorders and posttraumatic stress disorders inevitably raises, again, the problem of individual sensitivity.

Current interest in anxiety and anxiety disorders can be traced to Pavlov's pioneering research, especially on experimental neuroses, and it will not pass unnoticed that Pavlov described in detail the individual variations in susceptibility observed among the experimental animals. This interest in sensitivity was pursued by Gantt, Liddell, and other scientists and was, of course, a large element in Eysenck's dimensional analysis of personality. The concept of anxiety sensitivity grows out of this earlier work but is distinctly different because of its focus on sensitivity to those sensations that we associate with fear. Given its antecedents, it is no surprise to find that Anxiety Sensitivity Index is indeed related to other and more general forms of sensitivity. However, anxiety sensitivity is peculiarly important at present because of the explosive growth of knowledge about the anxiety disorders, one of the triumphs of modern psychology. Now we need to gain a firmer grasp of susceptibility to anxiety, and find out whether or not it predicts the onset of disorders but not their duration. Or is sensitivity doubly predictive?

Steven Taylor, editor of this book and an active contributor to research on anxiety sensitivity, has recruited leading researchers on this subject and to great effect. There is little on anxiety sensitivity that is not contained here. The book is comprehensively informative, and will also act as a keen stimulant to curiosity about anxiety sensitivity and research into its nature and significance.

Preface

Anxiety sensitivity (AS) is the fear of anxiety-related bodily sensations, which is thought to arise from beliefs that these sensations have harmful somatic, social, or psychological consequences (Reiss & McNally, 1985). To illustrate, palpitations may be feared if the person believes they will lead to cardiac arrest; derealization is feared if the individual believes it is the harbinger of insanity; sweating or trembling are feared if the person believes these reactions will attract ridicule from others.

Since the 1980s, the concept of AS has attracted a great deal of attention from researchers and clinicians. More than 100 peer-reviewed journal articles on AS have been published during this period, and a press conference on AS sponsored jointly by the American Psychological Association (APA) and the Association for Advancement of Behavior Therapy (AABT) was held in 1996. Articles based on the press conference have appeared in *The New York Times*, the *APA Monitor*, and other newspapers. AS has generated a great deal of interest at conferences, as indicated by the numerous symposia and other conference presentations at AABT conventions over the past several years.

Why the growing interest in AS? There are three main reasons: theoretical, empirical, and clinical. First, recent theories of Reiss (e.g., 1991), Clark (1986), and others have postulated that AS and similar constructs play a central role in the etiology and maintenance of fear, anxiety, panic, and related reactions. Second, these theories have stimulated a great deal of research, including experimental, longitudinal, and psychometric studies. The findings of these studies consistently support the etiological importance of AS and show that it is of greater predictive significance than conceptually related variables such as trait anxiety. Evidence also suggests that AS plays a role in a broader range of clinical phenomena than was originally predicted, including depression, substance abuse, and chronic pain. Third, interventions designed to decrease AS have been shown to be effective treatments for panic disorder and may play a role in the treatment of other disorders.

Several reviews of AS have been published in journal articles (e.g., Reiss, 1991; Taylor, 1995). However, none has covered all the domains of the AS literature and there has yet to be a comprehensive survey. The purpose of this volume is to gather experts from a variety of areas to cover the different aspects of theory, research, and treatment of AS. Given that AS is relevant to a wide range of psychopathological phenomena, we hope that this first state-of-the-art review is of interest to clinicians, researchers, their students, and trainees in all the mental health professions.

—*Steven Taylor*

REFERENCES

Clark, D. M. (1986). A cognitive approach to panic. *Behaviour Research and Therapy, 24,* 461–470.

Reiss, S. (1991). Expectancy theory of fear, anxiety, and panic. *Clinical Psychology Review, 11,* 141–153.

Reiss, S., & McNally, R. J. (1985). The expectancy model of fear. In S. Reiss & R. R. Bootzin (Eds.), *Theoretical issues in behavior therapy* (pp. 107–121). New York: Academic Press.

Taylor, S. (1995). Anxiety sensitivity: Theoretical perspectives and recent findings. *Behaviour Research and Therapy, 33,* 243–258.

I

CONCEPTUAL FOUNDATIONS

1

Theoretical Approaches to the Fear of Anxiety

Richard J. McNally
Harvard University

Pathological fears have often been defined by their eliciting stimuli. Nosologists, for example, have traditionally defined *acrophobia* as fear of heights, *claustrophobia* as fear of enclosed spaces, and *agoraphobia* as fear of open, public places. This tradition is notable for its neglect of the *intentionality* of fear. *Intentionality* does not mean deliberateness as in someone doing something intentionally. It refers to the *aboutness* of something (Brentano, 1889/1984). Rather than specify why an agoraphobic person fears shopping malls, subways, and so forth, traditional approaches to nosology merely identify the range of external cues that evoke excessive fear. Yet specifying the intentional object of fear (i.e., what the fear is about), and not merely its eliciting stimuli, has important nosological implications. For example, people with agoraphobia and people with specific flight phobia both nominally fear the same stimuli, yet the motivation for avoidance is entirely different. The intentional object for agoraphobics is panicking while aloft, whereas the intentional object for flight phobics is crashing (McNally & Louro, 1992).

In their landmark article on the reanalysis of agoraphobia, Goldstein and Chambless (1978) departed from the traditional perspective in important ways. Instead of viewing agoraphobia as a fear of stimuli embodied in public places, they emphasized the intentional object of agoraphobic fear—namely, panic and its presumed consequences. They also revived the notion that one's own fear responses could constitute the focus of dread, popularizing the idea that agoraphobia is best conceptualized as a fear of fear itself.

3

The idea that fear can itself be the intentional object of anxiety had been previously expressed by a diverse range of authors. In his essay entitled *Of Fear*, Montaigne (1573/1948) said, "The thing I fear most is fear" (p. 53). He did not elaborate further, and this one sentence paragraph appears somewhat out of the blue. Nearly 400 years later, during the Great Depression, Roosevelt (1933/1965) famously proclaimed in his first Inaugural Address: "So first of all let me assert my firm belief that the only thing we have to fear is fear itself—nameless, unreasoning, unjustified terror which paralyzes needed efforts to convert retreat into advance" (p. 274).

Commentators on the fear of anxiety have not been confined to French essayists of the 16th century or to American politicians of the 20th century. Psychoanalytic theorists have also discussed the concept. Freud's (1895/1962) personal experience with panic attacks may have led him to remark that, "in the case of agoraphobia, etc., we often find *the recollection of an anxiety attack*; and what the patient actually fears is the occurrence of such an attack under the special conditions in which he believes he cannot escape it" (p. 81, italics in original). Likewise, Otto Fenichel (cited in S. Reiss, 1987) proposed that:

> In the first stages, the neurosis may be complicated by a secondary traumatic neurosis, induced by the first anxiety spell which is experienced as a trauma. Many anxiety hysterias develop out of such an experience, *a fear of anxiety*, and simultaneously a readiness to become frightened very easily, which may create a vicious circle. (p. 586)

Psychoanalyst Rosenberg (1949) conceptualized the capacity to tolerate anxiety as an individual difference variable rather than solely as a feature of agoraphobia. But veering off on a weird theoretical tangent, she then traced the fear of anxiety to its presumptive roots in unconscious aggressive and sexual impulses.

In his comprehensive historical review, Reiss (1987) observed that theorists of nearly every school of clinical psychology have addressed the fear of anxiety. The chief difference among them concerned whether they viewed it mainly as a facet of agoraphobia or whether they believed it relevant to a wide range of neurotic disturbances. Thus, Freud (1895/1962) held the former view, whereas Ellis (1978) expressed the latter view in his theory of discomfort anxiety. Reiss (1987) defended a hybrid perspective, noting that the fear of anxiety has implications for psychopathology in general, but acknowledging its special relevance for understanding agoraphobia.

Concluding his article with a call for more research, Reiss (1987) sketched an agenda for the study of the fear of anxiety. During the next 10 years, investigators have tackled many of the topics he mentioned. Much of this work concerned the relationship between the fear of anxiety and panic disorder (and agoraphobia; see, e.g., chaps. 6 and 10, this volume). However, recent studies have addressed topics unforeseen by Reiss (1987), such as the connection between anxiety sensitivity and essential hypertension (Pagotto, Fallo, Fava, Boscaro, & Sonino, 1992), asthma (Carr, Lehrer, Rausch, & Hochron, 1994), and chronic pain (Asmundson & Norton, 1995; see chap. 12, this volume).

The purpose of this introductory chapter is to provide a comparative analysis of the three main approaches to the fear of anxiety: (a) Pavlovian interoceptive conditioning, (b) catastrophic misinterpretation of bodily sensations, and (c) anxiety sensitivity. Because of its historical importance, panic disorder figures prominently in the discussion.

PAVLOVIAN INTEROCEPTIVE CONDITIONING

Goldstein and Chambless (1978) persuasively argued that agoraphobia is best conceptualized as a fear of fear and not as a fear of public places. They also suggested that such fear might develop through processes akin to Pavlovian interoceptive conditioning:

> Having suffered one or more panic attacks, these people become hyperalert to their sensations and interpret feelings of mild to moderate anxiety as signs of oncoming panic attacks and react with such anxiety that the dreaded episode is almost invariably induced. This is analogous to the phenomenon described by Razran (1961) as interoceptive conditioning in which the conditioned stimuli are internal bodily sensations. In the case of fear of anxiety, a client's own physiological arousal becomes the conditioned stimuli for the powerful conditioned response of a panic attack. (p. 55)

Accordingly, just as an external cue (e.g., tone) can be established as a conditioned stimulus (CS) if it predicts an aversive unconditioned stimulus (US), so might an internal cue (e.g., dyspnea) be established as a CS if it predicts panic.

Although many theorists agree that interoceptive conditioning may figure in the genesis of panic disorder (e.g., Barlow, 1988; Seligman, 1988; Wolpe & Rowan, 1988), others have been skeptical (e.g., Clark, 1988; McNally, 1990; Reiss, 1988). Critics have noted that, although Razran's (1961) widely cited article described many Pavlovian interoceptive conditioning preparations (see e.g., McNally, 1990), none involved aversive learning that might provide a plausible model for panic attacks. Moreover, the conceptual clarity of the laboratory preparations is lost once one attempts to map interoceptive conditioning concepts onto the phenomenon of panic. For example, Goldstein and

Chambless (1978) suggested that bodily sensations function as CSs that elicit the conditioned response (CR) of panic. Yet because these sensations are partly constitutive of panic itself, it is unclear which ones count as the CS and which ones count as the CR. Does a "dizziness CS" elicit a "palpitation CR" or vice versa? Distinctions become vague if one defines the CS and CR as two points on a continuum of arousal (i.e., CS = a little arousal, CR = a lot of arousal). That is, the phenomenon assigned the conceptual role of CS (e.g., an increase in heart rate) is the same as that assigned the conceptual role of CR (e.g., a further increase in heart rate).

Identifying the US and unconditioned response (UR) also presents problems. Because certain bodily perturbations are classified as CSs, they must, by definition, have been established as such via their association with a US. But what is the US and what UR does it evoke? The individual's first panic is often viewed as the US. Unfortunately, the bodily sensations associated with panic have already been identified with both the CS and CR. Some theorists maintain that panic is the UR (e.g., Wolpe & Rowan, 1988), but this would imply that an event (i.e., panic as US) causes its own occurrence (i.e., panic as UR). Moreover, the interoceptive conditioning account of panic is based on a contiguity model whereby stimuli present during an attack become established as CSs. But the contiguity model has long been abandoned in favor of information-processing models of Pavlovian conditioning, which describe how organisms learn predictive relations among events (Reiss, 1980).

There was more to the Goldstein and Chambless (1978) theory than just the postulate about Pavlovian interoceptive conditioning (Chambless & Goldstein, 1988). They also emphasized that people with agoraphobia held beliefs about the catastrophic consequences of feared bodily sensations in addition to exhibiting Pavlovian CRs to these sensations. To measure these aspects of the syndrome, Chambless and her colleagues developed the Body Sensations Questionnaire (BSQ) and the Agoraphobic Cognitions Questionnaire (ACQ; Chambless, Caputo, Bright, & Gallagher, 1984).

CATASTROPHIC MISINTERPRETATION
OF BODILY SENSATIONS

Purely biological approaches to panic disorder had become increasingly dominant until the publication of Clark's (1986) influential article, "A Cognitive Approach to Panic." In this article, Clark showed how his model could account for findings adduced in support of various biological theories. The core idea was that panic attacks "result from the catastrophic misinterpretation of certain bodily sensations" (p. 461). Accordingly, an individual might misinterpret dizziness as an impending faint, derealization as impending insanity, or palpitations as an impending heart attack. Initiating a positive feedback loop, these misinterpretations worsen anxiety and intensify bodily sensations until full-blown panic results. Although the misinterpreted bodily sensations may arise from anxiety, they may be associated with other emotional (e.g., anger) or nonemotional (e.g., caffeine ingestion) states as well. Regardless of their source, bodily sensations will not lead to panic unless they are misinterpreted as harbingers of imminent danger.

Reviewing Clark and Beck's theories, Alford and Beck (1997) noted an "identity of conceptualization, even though different words are used" (p. 123). Clark's model was foreshadowed by Beck, Emery, and Greenberg (1985), who stated that "her [the person experiencing a panic] interpretation of sudden uncontrollable symptoms as signs of impending physical or mental disaster then accelerates the process until a full-blown panic occurs" (p. 136). Theoretical resemblances notwithstanding, Clark's (1986) version of the cognitive approach to panic was remarkably influential. Indeed, Clark's article was the second most frequently cited one in the entire field of psychology among the more than 50,000 articles published during the years 1986 through 1990 (Garfield, 1992).

Clark's theory stimulated a series of critiques and rejoinders (for a review, see McNally, 1994). A few are discussed next. One issue concerned whether catastrophic interpretations are causally implicated in the genesis of panic or whether they are merely epiphenomenal correlates of an unfolding, autonomous biological process. For example, Wolpe and Rowan (1988) noted that their patients reported experiencing catastrophic thoughts after their panic attacks were well underway.

Another issue concerned whether catastrophic misinterpretations are necessary for panic to occur. Several studies suggest that full-blown panics may occur in the apparent absence of antecedent catastrophizing (e.g., Aronson, Whitaker-Azmitia, & Caraseti, 1989; Rachman, Lopatka, & Levitt, 1988), and as Teasdale (1988) pointed out, just because some attacks are preceded by catastrophic misinterpretation of bodily sensations, one cannot conclude that all panics are so initiated.

The occurrence of panic attacks that erupt during nondreaming sleep pose another challenge to Clark's central hypothesis. In addressing this anomaly, Clark (1988) suggested that panic patients might nevertheless monitor, detect, and catastrophically misinterpret bodily sensations while sleeping, thereby awakening in the midst of a full-blown attack. Further elaborating his theory,

Clark endeavored to account for panics that did not seem preceded by cata-strophic cognition: "In patients who experience recurrent attacks, catastrophic misinterpretations may be so fast and automatic that patients may not always be aware of the interpretive process" (p. 76).

The postulation of unconscious catastrophic misinterpretation, however plausible, posed thorny problems. Retrospective self-reported thoughts of dying, going crazy, and so forth provided the best evidence for catastrophic misinterpretation. But if the interpretive process were not necessarily accessible to introspection, how could one tell whether the process had in fact occurred? To ensure the testability of the catastrophic misinterpretation process, one would need to devise measures of interpretation that were distinct from meas-ures of panic itself. Otherwise it would be impossible to test whether these cognitive events are, indeed, necessary for the occurrence of panic.

Clark (1988) categorically stated that, "catastrophic misinterpretation of certain bodily sensations is a *necessary* condition for the production of a panic attack" (p. 84, italics added). However, he subsequently revised his views. Noting that it is "unlikely that there is a single explanation" (Clark & Ehlers, 1993, p. 132) for all unexpected panic attacks, such as the occasional ones that occur in the general population, he emphasized that "catastrophic misinterpre-tation of bodily sensations plays a causal role in the production of *recurrent* panic attacks" (Clark & Ehlers, 1993, p. 132, italics added).

Clark's acknowledgment that not all unexpected panic attacks arise because of catastrophic misinterpretation of bodily sensations reflects an important change in the theory. Occasional out-of-the-blue attacks not preceded by catastrophizing (e.g., the occasional sleep panic) would no longer count as evidence against the revised cognitive approach.

The revised theory implies that evidence of catastrophic misinterpretation should be greater in people with recurrent attacks than in people with isolated attacks. Interestingly, Seligman (1988) implicitly defended the opposite hy-pothesis. He thought it especially surprising that people who have survived recurrent attacks would continue to misinterpret bodily sensations catastrophi-cally. If the cognitive theory were correct, Seligman argued, then catastrophic beliefs should have long been refuted for people who have had many attacks yet no catastrophes.

One possible explanation for this apparent paradox is that patients often do not consider the failure of their worst fears to materialize as disconfirmation of their catastrophic beliefs. As Salkovskis, Clark, and Gelder (1996) discovered, panic patients report engaging in avoidance behaviors, some subtle, which they believe prevented the disaster just in the nick of time. Thus, a patient who dreads impending collapse will never learn that panic does not lead to collapse if he or she always sits down in the midst of an attack. Relatedly, patients often seem to exhibit a negative form of the *gambler's fallacy*. In the positive version, the gambler acts as if the dice *know* he has had a streak of bad luck and therefore owe him a few good rolls. Likewise, panic patients often act as if, after surviving a series of bad attacks, their good luck is about to run out and the next attack will have dire consequences.

ANXIETY SENSITIVITY

People vary greatly in their proneness to experience anxiety. Some experience anxiety symptoms with minimal provocation, whereas others become anxious only under the most stressful circumstances. The construct of trait anxiety denotes these individual differences in anxiety proneness. Just as people vary in their proneness to experience anxiety symptoms, so do they vary in their fear of these symptoms. Whereas most people regard anxiety as merely unpleasant, others regard it with dread. The construct of *anxiety sensitivity* (AS) denotes these individual differences in the fear of anxiety (Reiss & McNally, 1985). More specifically, AS refers to fears of anxiety symptoms that are based on beliefs that these symptoms have harmful consequences. Thus, an individual with high AS may believe that heart palpitations signify an impending heart attack, whereas an individual with low AS is likely to regard these sensations as merely unpleasant. The Anxiety Sensitivity Index (ASI; Peterson & Reiss, 1992; Reiss, Peterson, Gursky, & McNally, 1986) has been the principal measure of AS.

Following the first wave of studies, critics questioned whether anxiety sensitivity was distinguishable from trait anxiety. Lilienfeld, Jacob, and Turner (1989) held that phenomena attributed to AS can best be explained by "the more parsimonious hypothesis that the ASI simply measures trait anxiety" (p. 101). The critiques of Lilienfeld and his colleagues (Lilienfeld, 1996a, 1996b; Lilienfeld et al., 1989; Lilienfeld, Turner, & Jacob, 1993, 1996) stimulated rejoinders and conceptual refinement (McNally, 1989, 1996a; 1996b; Taylor, 1995, 1996) as well as new studies designed to adjudicate these debates empirically (e.g., Rapee & Medoro, 1994).

A consensus emerged that AS does indeed denote an individual difference variable that is empirically and conceptually distinct from trait anxiety. Trait anxiety is a higher order construct that denotes a general tendency to respond fearfully to stressors, whereas AS is a lower order construct that denotes a specific tendency to respond fearfully to one's own anxiety symptoms (Lilienfeld, 1996b;

McNally, 1989). In Lilienfeld's (1996a) view, AS is a facet of trait anxiety—a suggestion that accounts for the modest correlation between measures of anxiety sensitivity and those of trait anxiety. The construct of *trait anxiety*, however, has its own conceptual and empirical difficulties (see Reiss, 1997).

Lilienfeld et al. (1989) also pointed out that AS was variously described as reflecting *fears* of anxiety symptoms, *beliefs* about the harmfulness of anxiety symptoms, or fears based on beliefs about the harmfulness of symptoms. They asked whether the construct was intended to be cognitive or affective. There is little question that anxiety sensitivity researchers tend to use these construct descriptors interchangeably, and certainly the wording of many ASI items does not explicitly ask about beliefs. However, AS researchers implicitly assumed that statements like "It scares me when my heart beats rapidly" imply beliefs about the negative consequences of rapid heart rate. Whether this assumption is warranted remains an empirical question.

Evidence for the construct validity of AS has been reviewed elsewhere (McNally, 1994, 1996a) and in other chapters in this volume (e.g., see chap. 4 and 6). Rather than summarize these findings here, I instead conclude this introductory chapter by comparing and contrasting the three main approaches to the fear of anxiety.

PERSPECTIVES ON THE FEAR OF ANXIETY: SIMILARITIES AND DIFFERENCES

Origins of the Fear of Anxiety

Theorists differ on the origins of the fear of anxiety. Some hold that it results from panic attacks, whereas others hold that it may develop in ways other than through direct experience with panic. The Pavlovian interoceptive formulation implied that the fear of anxiety is mainly a consequence of panic attacks (Goldstein & Chambless, 1978). That is, after having had experiences with panic, the individual reflexively responds with fear to symptoms that have preceded full-blown attacks in the past.

In a recent review article, Clark and Ehlers (1993) noted that an enduring tendency to misinterpret sensations catastrophically might arise either from learning experiences that predate the first panic or from the way that the person and health professionals respond to this panic. The first alternative is consistent with an AS perspective (Reiss & McNally, 1985) and with retrospective accounts of panic patients describing how their parents had suffered attacks and modeled illness-related behavior (Ehlers, 1993). The second alternative would involve patients failing to receive an adequate explanation for the perplexing and frightening symptoms associated with their first unexpected panics. Lacking noncatastrophic explanations, these individuals may assume the worst.

According to the AS perspective, just as people can acquire fears through verbal and observational routes as well as through direct conditioning (Rachman, 1977), so might they acquire a fear of anxiety in ways other than solely through direct experience with panic (McNally, 1990). To be sure, spontaneous panic attacks are likely to worsen AS. But one need not have experienced either unexpected (e.g., Donnell & McNally, 1990) or expected (e.g., Cox, Endler, Norton, & Swinson, 1991) panic attacks to score high on the ASI.

Because elevated AS can precede the occurrence of panic, it may constitute a cognitive risk factor for anxiety disorders in general (Reiss & McNally, 1985) and panic disorder in particular (McNally & Lorenz, 1987). Confirming this hypothesis in a landmark longitudinal study, Schmidt, Lerew, and Jackson (1997) demonstrated that scores on the ASI predicted the occurrence of spontaneous panic attacks in cadets at the U.S. Air Force Academy (see chap. 10, this volume).

State Versus Trait

Another difference among the three main approaches to the fear of anxiety concerns the distinction between occurrent and dispositional concepts (Fridhandler, 1986; Ryle, 1949). AS is a dispositional (traitlike) concept, whereas Pavlovian interoceptive fear responses and catastrophic misinterpretations are occurrent (statelike) concepts. AS denotes the tendency to respond fearfully if and when the person experiences anxiety-related symptoms. That is, the disposition is realized (rendered manifest) under conditions involving the experience of anxiety. The dispositional concept of AS is also distinguishable from the occurrent concept of anticipatory anxiety (cf. Beck, 1996); the latter denotes state anxiety evoked by the expectation of threat.

Because Reiss and McNally (1985) conceptualized AS as a traitlike, individual difference variable, they and their colleagues readily developed a questionnaire to measure it (Reiss et al., 1986). State variables that denote online, real-time processes, such as Pavlovian interoceptive CRs and catastrophic misinterpretations, are not as readily assessable as are trait variables. However, Clark et al. (1997) developed and validated the Body Sensations Interpretation Questionnaire (BSIQ) as an index of the disposition to misinterpret bodily sensations catastrophically.

Specificity for Panic Disorder

As noted by Reiss (1987), theorists have differed regarding the specificity of the fear of anxiety for panic disorder (and agoraphobia). The Pavlovian interoceptive account was advanced explicitly to explain panic attacks in agoraphobia (Goldstein & Chambless, 1978). But subsequent research by Chambless and Gracely (1989) indicated that people with anxiety disorders other than agoraphobia also tended to score high on measures of the fear of fear, although not as high as people with agoraphobia. Chambless and Gracely concluded that fear of anxiety symptoms is not unique to agoraphobia, although it is most prominent in this syndrome.

Chambless and Gracely's (1989) results are consistent with those of researchers who used the ASI rather than the BSQ and ACQ to measure the fear of anxiety symptoms (Reiss et al., 1986; Taylor, Koch, & McNally, 1992). With the exception of specific phobia, people with anxiety disorders tend to score high on the ASI and those with panic disorder (and agoraphobia) tend to score highest. Clark et al. (1997) designed the BSIQ to focus specifically on catastrophic misinterpretations of cardiorespiratory and related sensations. In contrast to other broader fear of anxiety scales, the BSIQ does seem relatively specific to people with panic attacks.

Treatment Implications

Despite its conceptual ambiguities, the Pavlovian interoceptive conditioning account of the fear of anxiety has inspired effective treatments for panic disorder (e.g., Barlow, Craske, Cerny, & Klosko, 1989). Structured, prolonged exposure to feared bodily sensations associated with anxiety is an effective means of treating panic disorder. Likewise, the idea that catastrophic misinterpretations underlie the fear of anxiety has also led to treatments that abolish panic attacks by correcting this cognitive abnormality (e.g., Clark et al., 1994).

The AS construal of the fear of anxiety has not directly led to new treatments. The ASI, however, has been increasingly used as an outcome variable in panic disorder treatment studies (e.g., Telch et al., 1993), and it predicts outcome, as does the BSIQ (Clark et al., 1994). For example, Bruce, Spiegel, Gregg, and Nuzzarello (1995) found that the ASI was the only significant predictor of stable withdrawal from alprazolam among panic disorder patients.

CONCLUSIONS

People can fear anxiety-related sensations for several reasons. Some people fear them because they misinterpret them as harbingers of imminent physical or mental disaster. Others may fear them because of social evaluation concerns that are not directly linked to genuine catastrophes. Whether the fear of anxiety is narrowly or broadly conceptualized, its importance for the field of psychopathology is undeniable. The remaining chapters in this volume document this assertion.

REFERENCES

Alford, B. A., & Beck, A. T. (1997). *The integrative power of cognitive therapy*. New York: Guilford.

Aronson, T. A., Whitaker-Azmitia, P., & Caraseti, I. (1989). Differential reactivity to lactate infusions: The relative role of biological, psychological, and conditioning variables. *Biological Psychiatry, 25*, 469–481.

Asmundson, G. J. G., & Norton, G. R. (1995). Anxiety sensitivity in patients with physically unexplained chronic back pain: A preliminary report. *Behaviour Research and Therapy, 33*, 771–777.

Barlow, D. H. (1988). *Anxiety and its disorders*. New York: Guilford.

Barlow, D. H., Craske, M. G., Cerny, J. A., & Klosko, J. S. (1989). Behavioral treatment of panic disorder. *Behavior Therapy, 20*, 261–282.

Beck, A. T., Emery, G., & Greenberg, R. L. (1985). *Anxiety disorders and phobias*. New York: Basic Books.

Beck, J. G. (1996). The crescendo of fear [Review of the book *Panic disorder: A critical analysis*]. *Contemporary Psychology, 41*, 262–263.

Brentano, F. (1984). On the origin of our knowledge of right and wrong. In C. Calhoun & R. C. Solomon (Eds.), *What is an emotion?* (pp. 205–214). New York: Oxford University Press. (Original work published 1889)

Bruce, T. J., Spiegel, D. A., Gregg, S. F., & Nuzzarello, A. (1995). Predictors of alprazolam discontinuation with and without cognitive behavior therapy in panic disorder. *American Journal of Psychiatry, 152*, 1156–1160.

Carr, R. E., Lehrer, P. M., Rausch, L. L., & Hochron, S. M. (1994). Anxiety sensitivity and panic attacks in an asthmatic population. *Behaviour Research and Therapy, 32*, 411–418.

Chambless, D. L., Caputo, G. C., Bright, P., & Gallagher, R. (1984). Assessment of fear of fear in agoraphobics: The Body Sensations Questionnaire and the Agoraphobic Cognitions Questionnaire. *Journal of Consulting and Clinical Psychology, 52*, 1090–1097.

Chambless, D. L., & Goldstein, A. J. (1988). Fear of fear: A reply to Reiss. *Behavior Therapy, 19*, 85–88.

Chambless, D. L., & Gracely, E. J. (1989). Fear of fear and the anxiety disorders. *Cognitive Therapy and Research, 13*, 9–20.

Clark, D. M. (1986). A cognitive approach to panic. *Behaviour Research and Therapy, 24,* 461–470.

Clark, D. M. (1988). A cognitive model of panic attacks. In S. Rachman & J. D. Maser (Eds.), *Panic: Psychological perspectives* (pp. 71–89). Hillsdale, NJ: Lawrence Erlbaum Associates.

Clark, D. M., & Ehlers, A. (1993). An overview of the cognitive theory and treatment of panic disorder. *Applied & Preventive Psychology, 2,* 131–139.

Clark, D. M., Salkovskis, P. M., Hackmann, A., Middleton, H., Anastasiades, P., & Gelder, M. (1994). A comparison of cognitive therapy, applied relaxation and imipramine in the treatment of panic disorder. *British Journal of Psychiatry, 164,* 759–769.

Clark, D. M., Salkovskis, P. M., Öst, L.-G., Breitholtz, E., Koehler, K. A., Westling, B. E., Jeavons, A., & Gelder, M. (1997). Misinterpretation of body sensations in panic disorder. *Journal of Consulting and Clinical Psychology, 65,* 203–213.

Cox, B. J., Endler, N. S., Norton, G. R., & Swinson, R. P. (1991). Anxiety sensitivity and nonclinical panic attacks. *Behaviour Research and Therapy, 29,* 367–369.

Donnell, C. D., & McNally, R. J. (1990). Anxiety sensitivity and panic attacks in a nonclinical population. *Behaviour Research and Therapy, 28,* 83–85.

Ehlers, A. (1993). Somatic symptoms and panic attacks: A retrospective study of learning experiences. *Behaviour Research and Therapy, 31,* 269–278.

Ellis, A. (1978). A note on the treatment of agoraphobics with cognitive modification versus prolonged exposure in vivo. *Behaviour Research and Therapy, 17,* 162–164.

Freud, S. (1962). Obsessions and phobias: Their psychical mechanism and their aetiology. In J. Strachey (Ed. & Trans.), *The standard edition of the complete psychological works of Sigmund Freud* (Vol. 3, pp. 74–82). London: Hogarth. (Original work published 1895)

Fridhandler, B. M. (1986). Conceptual note on state, trait, and the state-trait distinction. *Journal of Personality and Social Psychology, 50,* 169–174.

Garfield, E. (1992). A citationist perspective on psychology: Part 1. Most-cited papers, 1986–1990. *APS Observer, (6),* 8–9.

Goldstein, A. J., & Chambless, D. L. (1978). A reanalysis of agoraphobia. *Behavior Therapy, 9,* 47–59.

Lilienfeld, S. O. (1996a). Anxiety sensitivity is not distinct from trait anxiety. In R. M. Rapee (Ed.), *Current controversies in the anxiety disorders* (pp. 228–244). New York: Guilford.

Lilienfeld, S. O. (1996b). Another look at the relation between anxiety sensitivity and trait anxiety: Reply to McNally. In R. M. Rapee (Ed.), *Current controversies in the anxiety disorders* (pp. 249–252). New York: Guilford.

Lilienfeld, S. O., Jacob, R. G., & Turner, S. M. (1989). Comment on Holloway and McNally's (1987) "Effects of anxiety sensitivity on the response to hyperventilation." *Journal of Abnormal Psychology, 98,* 100–102.

Lilienfeld, S. O., Turner, S. M., & Jacob, R. G. (1993). Anxiety sensitivity: An examination of theoretical and methodological issues. *Advances in Behaviour Research and Therapy, 15,* 147–183.

Lilienfeld, S. O., Turner, S. M., & Jacob, R. G. (1996). Further comments on the nature and measurement of anxiety sensitivity: A reply to Taylor. *Journal of Anxiety Disorders, 10,* 411–424.

McNally, R. J. (1989). Is anxiety sensitivity distinguishable from trait anxiety? A reply to Lilienfeld, Jacob, and Turner (1989). *Journal of Abnormal Psychology, 98,* 193–194.

McNally, R. J. (1990). Psychological approaches to panic disorder: A review. *Psychological Bulletin, 108,* 403–419.

McNally, R. J. (1994). *Panic disorder: A critical analysis.* New York: Guilford.

McNally, R. J. (1996a). Anxiety sensitivity is distinguishable from trait anxiety. In R. M. Rapee (Ed.), *Current controversies in the anxiety disorders* (pp. 214–227). New York: Guilford.

McNally, R. J. (1996b). Reply to Lilienfeld: Toward a resolution of the anxiety sensitivity versus trait anxiety debate. In R. M. Rapee (Ed.), *Current controversies in the anxiety disorders* (pp. 245–248). New York: Guilford.

McNally, R. J., & Lorenz, M. (1987). Anxiety sensitivity in agoraphobics. *Journal of Behavior Therapy and Experimental Psychiatry, 18*, 3–11.

McNally, R. J., & Louro, C. E. (1992). Fear of flying in agoraphobia and simple phobia: Distinguishing features. *Journal of Anxiety Disorders, 6*, 319–324.

Montaigne, M. (1573). Of fear. In D. M. Frame (Ed. & Trans.), *The complete essays of Montaigne* (pp. 52–53). Stanford, CA: Stanford University Press. (Original work published 1573)

Pagotto, U., Fallo, F., Fava, G. A., Boscaro, M., & Sonino, N. (1992). Anxiety sensitivity in essential hypertension. *Stress Medicine, 8*, 113–115.

Peterson, R. A., & Reiss, S. (1992). *Anxiety Sensitivity Index Manual* (2nd ed.). Worthington, OH: International Diagnostic Systems.

Rachman, S. (1977). The conditioning theory of fear–acquisition: A critical examination. *Behaviour Research and Therapy, 15*, 375–387.

Rachman, S., Lopatka, C., & Levitt, K. (1988). Experimental analyses of panic: II. Panic patients. *Behaviour Research and Therapy, 26*, 33–40.

Rapee, R. M., & Medoro, L. (1994). Fear of physical sensations and trait anxiety as mediators of the response to hyperventilation in nonclinical subjects. *Journal of Abnormal Psychology, 103*, 693–699.

Razran, G. (1961). The observable unconscious and the inferable conscious in current Soviet psychophysiology: Interoceptive conditioning, semantic conditioning, and the orienting reflex. *Psychological Review, 68*, 81–147.

Reiss, S. (1980). Pavlovian conditioning and human fear: An expectancy model. *Behavior Therapy, 11*, 380–396.

Reiss, S. (1987). Theoretical perspectives on the fear of anxiety. *Clinical Psychology Review, 7*, 585–596.

Reiss, S. (1988). Interoceptive theory of the fear of anxiety. *Behavior Therapy, 19*, 84–91.

Reiss, S. (1997). Trait anxiety: It's not what you think it is. *Journal of Anxiety Disorders, 11*, 201–214.

Reiss, S., & McNally, R. J. (1985). Expectancy model of fear. In S. Reiss & R. R. Bootzin (Eds.), *Theoretical issues in behavior therapy* (pp. 107–121). San Diego, CA: Academic.

Reiss, S., Peterson, R. A., Gursky, D. M., & McNally, R. J. (1986). Anxiety sensitivity, anxiety frequency and the prediction of fearfulness. *Behaviour Research and Therapy, 24*, 1–8.

Roosevelt, F. D. (1965). First inaugural address. In R. D. Heffner (Ed.), *A documentary history of the United States* (rev. ed., pp. 274–278). New York: Mentor Books. (Original work published 1933)

Rosenberg, E. (1949). Anxiety and the capacity to bear it. *International Journal of Psycho-Analysis, 30*, 1–12.

Ryle, G. (1949). *The concept of mind.* New York: Penguin.

Salkovskis, P. M., Clark, D. M., & Gelder, M. G. (1996). Cognition-behaviour links in the persistence of panic. *Behaviour Research and Therapy, 34*, 453–458.

Schmidt, N. B., Lerew, D. R., & Jackson, R. J. (1997). The role of anxiety sensitivity in the pathogenesis of panic: Prospective evaluation of spontaneous panic attacks during acute stress. *Journal of Abnormal Psychology, 106*, 355–364.

Seligman, M. E. P. (1988). Competing theories of panic. In S. Rachman & J. D. Maser (Eds.), *Panic: Psychological perspectives* (pp. 321–329). Hillsdale, NJ: Lawrence Erlbaum Associates.

Taylor, S. (1995). Issues in the conceptualization and measurement of anxiety sensitivity. *Journal of Anxiety Disorders, 9,* 163–174.

Taylor, S. (1996). Nature and measurement of anxiety sensitivity: Reply to Lilienfeld, Turner, and Jacob (1996). *Journal of Anxiety Disorders, 10,* 425–451.

Taylor, S., Koch, W. J., & McNally, R. J. (1992). How does anxiety sensitivity vary across the anxiety disorders? *Journal of Anxiety Disorders, 6,* 249–259.

Teasdale, J. (1988). Cognitive models and treatments for panic: A critical evaluation. In S. Rachman & J. D. Maser (Eds.), *Panic: Psychological perspectives* (pp. 189–203). Hillsdale, NJ: Lawrence Erlbaum Associates.

Telch, M. J., Lucas, J. A., Schmidt, N. B., Hanna, H. H., Jaimez, T. L., & Lucas, R. A. (1993). Group cognitive-behavioral treatment of panic disorder. *Behaviour Research and Therapy, 31,* 279–287.

Wolpe, J., & Rowan, V. C. (1988). Panic disorder: A product of classical conditioning. *Behaviour Research and Therapy, 26,* 441–450.

2

The Expectancy Theory of Fear, Anxiety, and Panic: A Conceptual and Empirical Analysis

Steven Taylor
Ingrid C. Fedoroff
University of British Columbia

Anxiety sensitivity (AS)—the fear of anxiety-related sensations—has been the center of many debates in recent years. These include debates regarding the measurement of AS, its factor structure and relationship to trait anxiety, and its relationship to panic attacks (e.g., Lilienfeld, 1996a, 1996b; Lilienfeld, Turner, & Jacob, 1993, 1996, 1998; McNally, 1966a, 1996b; Reiss, 1997; Taylor, 1955a, 1995b, 1996). These and related issues are reviewed in various chapters in this volume (see chaps. 4–7). An important area that has escaped critical scrutiny is Reiss' expectancy theory (Reiss, 1980, 1991; Reiss & McNally, 1985). This oversight is surprising because the expectancy theory provides an important theoretical context for AS. The theory was developed to explain how and why AS could cause fear, anxiety, panic, and avoidance behavior. This chapter examines the expectancy theory and reviews its empirical support. It also suggests several conceptual extensions of the theory and some new directions for future investigation.

FUNDAMENTAL FEARS

Central to Reiss' theory is the notion of fundamental fears (sensitivities). Reiss (1991) proposed that there are three fundamental fears: AS; fear of illness,

17

injury, and death; and fear of negative evaluation. In a subsequent revision to the theory, Reiss and Havercamp (1996, 1997) expanded their list of fundamental fears (see chap. 3). However, the basic idea remains the same: Reiss proposed that a small set of fundamental fears contribute to or amplify fear, anxiety, and panic. Theoretically, AS continues to hold the status of a fundamental fear (Reiss & Havercamp, 1996), although it is currently unclear whether it is distinct from other putative fundamental fears such as the fear of pain (see chap. 3).

Reiss (1991) distinguished fundamental fears from common fears. Examples of the latter include fears of harmless animals, situational fears (e.g., fear of heights, fear of enclosed spaces), and social fears (e.g., fear of public speaking, fear of eating in public). Two criteria distinguish fundamental fears from common fears. First, fundamental fears are said to be fears of stimuli that are inherently aversive, at least for most people. In comparison, common fears are not inherently aversive. Second, common fears can be logically reduced to fundamental fears. That is,

> Fundamental fears provide reasons for fearing a wide range of stimuli, whereas ordinary fears do not have this characteristic. For example, consider the rational relationships among three different fears: (a) the fear of snakes; (b) the fear of heights; and (c) the fear of anxiety. Fears of snakes and heights are rationally unrelated to one another in the sense that having one of the fears is not a reason for having the other fear. It makes no sense for a person to say, "I'm afraid of heights *because* I am afraid of snakes." On the other hand, the fear of anxiety is rationally related to the fear of snakes and heights. A rational person might say, "I am afraid of snakes and heights *because* I am afraid I would have a panic attack if I encountered those stimuli." A person who is unusually afraid of…the possibility of a panic attack [i.e., has high AS] holds a reason for potentially fearing snakes, heights, or any other situations that might be expected to lead to panic. (Reiss, 1991, p. 147)

Fundamental fears may interact with specific learning experiences to increase the risk of acquiring common fears and to increase the intensity of fears that have already been acquired. (Learning experiences are presumably the source of danger and anxiety expectancies, as described later.) Three types of learning appear important: traumatic conditioning experiences, observational learning, and receipt of threat-relevant verbal information (Rachman, 1990). To illustrate, dog phobia may arise from specific learning experiences with dogs, such as being mauled by a dog. This experience serves to link one of the fundamental fears (illness/injury/death sensitivity) with dogs and related stimuli. In other words, dogs become conditioned to, or representative of, this fundamental fear. Other fundamental fears may also contribute to or amplify this fear. Fear evoked by a dog could be amplified by AS (i.e., fear is amplified when a person has high AS because the person is not only afraid of the dog, but also frightened of the anxiety evoked by the dog). Similarly, fears can be amplified by fear of negative evaluation (a dog phobic with high fear of negative evaluation would become frightened of the dog and then become further alarmed that others might ridicule him or her for having such a fear).

Several published examples show how common fears can be reduced to fundamental fears. McNally and Steketee (1985) found that some animal phobics were frightened of animals primarily because of fear of having panic attacks (i.e., high AS), which were triggered by exposure to animals. McNally and Louro (1992) found that people with a specific phobia of flying were frightened of air travel mainly because they feared that the plane might crash (i.e., illness/injury/death sensitivity). In comparison, people with agoraphobia reported that they were frightened of flying primarily because of fear of panicking during the flight (AS).

The concept of fundamental fears can account for some rare and otherwise baffling fears (Taylor, 1995a). Consider the case of Mrs. V., described by Rachman and Seligman (1976). Mrs. V. presented for treatment of severe compulsive rituals associated with an intense fear of chocolate. She displayed extreme fear when confronted with chocolate or with any object or place associated with chocolate. She avoided brown objects such as brown furniture and avoided stores that sold chocolate. Her fear began shortly after the death of her mother, to whom she was closely attached. Prior to her mother's death, Mrs. V. consumed chocolate with enjoyment. Rachman and Seligman's account suggest that Mrs. V.'s fear of chocolate arose from an intense illness/injury/death sensitivity:

> It is barely possible that the fear of chocolate had as its origin a strong emotional reaction to the death of her mother during which time she [the patient] had been obliged to observe the coffin containing the body. The patient believes that this coffin was dark brown in colour and that it may have contributed to the association which she had between death and chocolate. Even more telling, she feels sure that she saw a bar of chocolate in the room containing the coffin. This symbolic connection between death, the colour brown and chocolate might be based on too fanciful an interpretation but we did obtain evidence of her fear of death scenes. During a behavioral avoidance test she displayed an inability to approach funeral parlours and considerable fear was aroused during the attempt. (p. 336)

IS ANXIETY SENSITIVITY
A FUNDAMENTAL FEAR?

The first of Reiss' (1991) criteria for fundamental fears is that they are fears of stimuli that are inherently aversive, at least for most people. It appears that AS meets this criterion. Studies using the Anxiety Sensitivity Index (ASI; Peterson & Reiss, 1987) indicate that most people have at least some fear of anxiety and very few people report no fear of anxiety. To illustrate, in a sample of 818 university students, only 4 (0.5%) reported a score of zero on the ASI (Stewart, Taylor, & Baker, 1997). Anxiety sensations were feared to some extent by almost everyone, although there were marked individual differences in the extent to which people feared those sensations. Most people had mild or moderate levels of AS, whereas a smaller proportion had high levels of AS.

Reiss' second criterion for fundamental fears concerns the logical reductions among fears. As mentioned earlier, common fears can be logically reduced to fundamental fears, but fundamental fears cannot be logically reduced to common fears. Reiss (e.g., 1991) and others (e.g., McNally & Louro, 1992) offered illustrative examples, such as those described earlier in this chapter.

Reiss' second criterion entails two important corollaries: (a) that AS is distinct from other fundamental fears (i.e., AS may not be a basic or fundamental fear if it is not distinct from other fears), and (b) that AS cannot be reduced to more basic fears (AS would not be fundamental if it could be logically reduced to more basic fears). Recent findings provide mixed support for these corollaries. Consistent with the first corollary, a factor analytic study using a sample of community volunteers found that AS was factorially distinct from illness/injury/death sensitivity and from fear of negative evaluation (Taylor, 1993). In terms of Reiss' expanded list of sensitivities (Reiss & Havercamp, 1996, 1997), factor analytic studies of responses from mentally retarded samples indicate that AS is factorially distinct from other fundamental fears (see chap. 3). In other samples, however, AS merges with the fear of pain (see chap. 3). Thus, factor analytic studies provide mixed support for the notion that AS is distinct from other putative fundamental fears.

According to the second corollary, AS can be said to be fundamental only if it cannot be reduced to more basic fears. A growing number of studies fail to support this corollary; they show that AS is composed of at least three correlated factors: (a) fear of somatic sensations, (b) fear of cognitive dyscontrol, and (c) fear of publicly observable anxiety reactions (see chap. 5 for a detailed review of the factor analytic literature). It may be that these factors can be reduced to even more basic fears, such as the fear of death, insanity, and negative evaluation.

In summary, there is reason to believe that AS may not be a fundamental fear. Further research is required to determine the most basic fears that underlie AS. These basic fears should not only contribute to AS, but should also contribute to (e.g., amplify) common fears. These hypotheses merit empirical evaluation.

DANGER AND ANXIETY EXPECTANCIES

The construct of AS was developed as part of a broader theoretical framework—the expectancy theory—in which Reiss attempted to account for individual differences in the tendency to acquire common fears and related phenomena (i.e., anxiety, panic, avoidance behavior; Reiss, 1980, 1991; Reiss & McNally, 1985). Reiss proposed that AS can explain individual differences in the conditioning of fears and related reactions. Here, conditioning refers to the processes described by neoconditioning theorists (e.g., Davey, 1992; Rescorla, 1988). Links are established (conditioned) between a potential conditioned stimulus (CS) and an unconditioned stimulus (US) once the organism learns that the CS is predictive of the US. In other words, the CS elicits the expectation that the US will occur. This model "places emphasis not on direct conditioning experiences per se, but on the acquisition of outcome expectancies" (Davey, 1992, p. 53). Neoconditioning theory, with its emphasis on expectations, shares many features with cognitive approaches to fear (Rachman, 1991). Accordingly, the role of AS (as a US) is not limited to classically conditioned fears; it also may play a role in fears arising from observational learning (modeling) or from the acquisition of threat-relevant verbal information.

Reiss (1980, 1991; Reiss & McNally, 1985) extended the neoconditioning approach to develop his expectancy theory. His theory describes how AS and expectancies work together to create fear-related responses (including anxiety, panic, avoidance, and escape behavior). Equation 1 in Table 2.1 presents a formal statement of the theory. The theory specifies only three fundamental fears (sensitivities) and therefore represents a simplified form of the current version of the sensitivity theory (see chap. 3 for a list of other sensitivities). The focus of the present chapter is primarily on the role of AS in this theory.

Equation 1 in Table 2.1 shows that fear responding is a function of expectations and sensitivities. *Expectations* refer to "what the person thinks will happen when the feared object/situation is encountered (e.g., 'I expect the plane will crash', 'I expect to have a panic attack during the flight,' 'I expect other people will notice my fear of flying')" (Reiss, 1991, p. 142). *Sensitivities* (fundamental fears) refer to "the reasons a person holds for fearing the anticipated event (e.g., 'I can't stand the thought of being handicapped,' 'Panic attacks cause heart

TABLE 2.1

Reiss' Expectancy Theory

Let $F(S_1)$	=	Fear response to an ordinary (common or nonreinforcing) situation, S_1 (e.g., fear of flying).
Let k	=	Objective disasters that can be associated with fear situation, S_1 (e.g., wings falling off plane, landing gear failing to operate).
Let j	=	Components of anxiety reaction that can be associated with fear situation, S_1(e.g., shaking, rapid heart beating).
Let I	=	Social disasters that can be associated with feared stimulus, S_1 (e.g., rejection by other passengers).

Then,

$$F(S_1) = \alpha \sum_k (E_k . S_d) + \beta \Sigma(E_j . AS) + \lambda \Sigma(E_i . S_{fne}) \qquad (1)$$

Where,

E_k	=	the individual's expectancy of objective disaster, k, given S_1
E_j	=	the individual's expectancy of anxiety component, j, given S_1
E_i	=	the individual's expectancy of social disaster, i, given S_1
S_d	=	the individual's sensitivity to injury/illness/death
AS	=	the individual's sensitivity to anxiety
S_{fne}	=	the individual's sensitivity to negative evaluation (e.g., criticism)
α, β, λ	=	unknown weights

Notes.

1. S_d is estimated by the Injury Sensitivity Index (ISI).

2. AS is estimated by the Anxiety Sensitivity Index (ASI).

3. S_{fne} is estimated by the Fear of Negative Evaluation (FNE) scale.

4. Gursky and Reiss (1987) developed measures of E_k (danger expectancy) and E_j (anxiety expectancy) for fears of snakes, heights, and public speaking.

5. Technically, "fear" means "avoidance motivation" or "reason to avoid."

6. Ordinary fears, $F(S_n)$'s, are fears of nonreinforcing stimuli; sensitivities (S_d, AS, S_{fne}) are fears of negatively reinforcing stimuli.

7. The total score on a fear survey schedule is $\Sigma_n F(S_n)$.

From S. Reiss. (1991). Expectancy model of fear, anxiety, and panic. *Clinical Psychology Review, 11,* 141–153. Copyright © 1991. Reprinted with permission of Elsevier Science Ltd.

attacks')" (p. 142). Reiss' theory proposes that there are broad individual differences in sensitivities and that "danger and anxiety expectancies are situation-specific factors, whereas anxiety sensitivity is a person-specific factor" (Reiss & McNally, 1985, p. 112).

Fear, Anxiety, and Avoidance

In Equation 1, *fear* is defined as avoidance motivation or reasons to avoid (Reiss, 1991). Thus, if a person has high AS and expects that a given stimulus will create anxiety, the person is strongly motivated to avoid the stimulus. Apart from accounting for avoidance behavior, Reiss' model also states that the total scores on fear survey schedules represent the sum of fears [i.e., $\Sigma_n F(S_n)$] as assessed by fear survey schedules. The most widely used schedules are the Fear Survey Schedule-II (Geer, 1965) and Fear Survey Schedule-III (Wolpe & Lang, 1969). Both assess how disturbed or fearful respondents are of a variety of stimuli. Thus, Reiss implied that Equation 1 applies not only to avoidance motivation, but also to subjective experience of fear. This is consistent with the view that emotions represent action tendencies (Izard, 1977) and fear represents the particular tendency to escape or avoid noxious stimuli.

In summary, Equation 1 states that common fears (e.g., fear of heights) are determined by six variables, which form three interaction terms. The variables are (a) the expectancy of objective danger or disaster (e.g., "I could fall if I look over the cliff edge"), (b) anxiety expectancy ("I will panic"), (c) expectancy of social disaster ("People will laugh at me if they see that I'm frightened of heights"), (d) sensitivity to injury/illness/death ("It would be horrible to fall"), (e) sensitivity to anxiety ("I could die or go crazy if my anxiety gets too intense"), and (f) sensitivity to negative evaluation ("It would be awful to be ridiculed").

As noted earlier, Equation 1 has been used to account for avoidance behavior (Reiss, 1991). We note that the equation also applies to related phenomena, such as anticipatory anxiety. The latter is anxiety [i.e., $F(S_1)$] that a person experiences when anticipating an encounter with S_1. As suggested in the equation, anticipatory anxiety may be partly determined by the interaction between AS and E_j, where E_j represents the person's expectancy about the anxiety sensations that will be experienced when S_1 is actually encountered.

How does Equation 1 account for fear (or anxiety) experienced when the person actually encounters S_1? The equation suggests that the degree of fear or anxiety, $F(S_1)$, is partly determined by the interaction between AS and E_j. What does E_j represent when S_1 is actually encountered? In other words, what does the anxiety expectancy refer to when the person is exposed to S_1 and is currently experiencing anxiety? Reiss' theory is unclear on this point. We suggest that E_j represents the person's expectation about the level of anxiety or fear that will be experienced if he or she continues to be exposed to S_1 (e.g., "If I continue to stay in this situation then my anxiety will become extremely intense").

Panic Attacks

According to the expectancy theory, AS plays an important role in the etiology and maintenance of anxiety disorders, particularly panic disorder: "Anxiety sensitivity can precede panic attacks and may be a risk factor for anxiety disorders and panic attacks" (Reiss, 1991, p. 149), and "high anxiety sensitivity should be associated with both the occurrence of panic attacks and with the severity of panic symptoms" (Peterson & Reiss, 1987, p. 11). Reiss (1991) implied that Equation 1 can account for panic attacks, including spontaneous (unexpected) panics, which are the hallmark of panic disorder (American Psychiatric Association, 1994). However, the expectancy theory fails to spell out how AS might cause unexpected panic attacks.

We propose that the expectancy theory can account for panic attacks in the following manner. Reiss (e.g., 1991) regarded AS as an anxiety amplification factor. Clark's model describes the process by which fear of anxiety sensations could cause these sensations to be amplified into panic. Thus, the mechanisms described in Clark's (1986) cognitive model of panic can be incorporated into the expectancy theory (Taylor, 1995a). According to Clark, panic attacks arise from the catastrophic misinterpretation of anxiety-related bodily sensations. That is, when a person experiences anxiety-related bodily sensations (due to any of a variety of causes; e.g., stress-induced palpitations), he or she may catastrophically misinterpret the sensations (i.e., misinterpret the sensations as signs of impending death, insanity, or loss of control). This causes the person to become anxiously aroused and thereby increases the intensity of the feared sensations (e.g., stronger palpitations). This leads the person to become further alarmed (i.e., he or she becomes convinced that a catastrophe is imminent). In turn, this increases the intensity of the anxiety sensations, and so on, in a vicious cycle culminating in a panic attack. This model assumes that people prone to panic disorder have an enduring tendency to make such misinterpretations. In terms of Reiss' (1991) theory, these people have elevated AS.

Is Clark's vicious cycle model consistent with Equation 1? If $F(S_1)$ represents a panic attack, what is S_1? Presumably it is the feared catastrophic consequences of panic (i.e., death, insanity, or loss of control). Assuming this is the case, panic is a function of $\beta\Sigma_j(E_j \cdot AS)$, where E_j is the person's expectancy that he or she will experience arousal-related bodily sensations (i.e., anxiety or panic symptoms). This model seems capable of accounting for cued panic attacks (i.e., panics triggered by exposure to a feared stimulus, such as a spider in the case of spider phobia). How would the formula account for spontaneous panic attacks? Those panics are characterized by their subjectively unexpected occurrence—they seem to strike the person out of the blue.

One could argue that Equation 1 cannot account for unexpected panic attacks because expectations of panic (E_js?) do not occur. In response, we propose that the E_js are triggered by arousal-related bodily sensations that occur just before the panic attack. This proposal is derived from Clark's (1986) model, which states that spontaneous panics are triggered by the detection of benign bodily sensations. Such sensations include faintness caused by rapidly changing posture (postural hypotension), derealization caused by fatigue or bright fluorescent lights, and palpitations caused by mild exertion. Once these sensations are triggered and detected, the person with high AS tends to catastrophically misinterpret their significance and thereby enters the vicious cycle of panic. Thus, in terms of Equation 1, arousal-related bodily sensations (occurring for any of a variety of reasons) trigger E_js, which interact with AS to create intense fear of imminent death, insanity, or loss of control. This creates anxiety and associated bodily sensations, thereby leading the person into the vicious cycle of panic.

EMPIRICAL TESTS
OF THE EXPECTANCY THEORY

The expectancy theory assumes that AS can be distinguished from anxiety, fear, and panic. Several studies support this distinction (e.g., Reiss, Peterson, & Gursky, 1988; Reiss, Peterson, & Gursky, & McNally, 1986). These are reviewed elsewhere (e.g., Taylor, 1995a, 1995b, 1996; chaps. 4 and 6). The expectancy theory further states that,

> people who are afraid of anxiety should develop a fear of any situation in which there is even a small chance/expectation of becoming anxious; because there are many such situations, people who are extremely sensitive to anxiety should develop fears of many situations. (Reiss, 1991, p. 147)

This suggests that the severity of AS should be correlated with measures of the intensity and number of fears that a person holds. Such findings have been reported in several studies (see chap. 6). Similarly, several studies suggest that AS plays a role in panic attacks (e.g., see chap. 10). The results of these studies are important in that they are consistent with the view that AS is a diathesis for fear, anxiety, and panic (Taylor, 1996). However, the studies do not represent tests of expectancy theory, as expressed in Equation 1 (Lilienfeld et al., 1996). To test the expectancy theory, one must show that fear, anxiety, and panic are predicted by the interaction between AS and anxiety expectancies. Such tests have been reported in only a handful of studies. These and other tests of the expectancy theory are reviewed next.

An assumption in Equation 1 is that danger expectancies are empirically distinct from anxiety expectancies. This assumption was tested by Gursky and Reiss (1987), who constructed a scale to assess danger expectancies and a scale to assess anxiety expectancies for each of three fears: fears of flying, heights, and public speaking (Study 1). The six scales were then completed by 135 college students (Study 2). For each fear, the items from the danger expectancies scale and those from the anxiety expectancies scale were pooled and factor analyzed. A two-factor solution was obtained for each fear, with danger and anxiety expectancies representing separate factors. Thus, one of the main assumptions in Equation 1 was supported.

Three studies provide data relevant to the assumption that fear arises from the interaction between expectancies and sensitivities. Schoenberger, Kirsch, and Rosengard (1991) asked 94 snake-fearful college students to approach and (if possible) touch a live, harmless snake. Measures of danger sensitivity (i.e., illness/injury/death sensitivity) and AS were completed and subjects made ratings of danger expectancy (expectancy of objective disaster), anxiety expectancy, and self-reported fear. Hierarchical regression analyses were conducted to predict self-reported fear. The main effects for sensitivity and expectancy measures were entered first as predictors (i.e., anxiety sensitivity, danger sensitivity, anxiety expectancy, and danger expectancy). Two interactions were entered in the second step: (a) the interaction between AS and anxiety expectancy, and (b) the interaction between danger sensitivity and danger expectancy. The danger sensitivity-by-danger expectancy interaction was significant ($p <$ .02), and there was a trend toward significance for the AS-by-anxiety expectancy interaction ($p < .06$).

To examine the nature of the danger sensitivity-by-danger expectancy interaction, Schoenberger et al. (1991) conducted a series of regression analyses in which danger sensitivity was used to predict self-reported fear. This was computed for each of three different levels of danger expectancy (low, medium, and high). Results indicate that the higher the subjects' danger sensitivity scores, the smaller the regression coefficient (beta weight) for expected danger. Schoenberger et al. did not report the regression coefficient (beta weight) for the danger sensitivity-by-danger expectancy interaction. However, the fact that the partial beta weights declined with increasing danger sensitivity suggests that beta weight for the interaction term would have been negative. Thus, the authors concluded that, "these results are directly opposite to those predicted by Reiss' expectancy theory" (Schoenberger et al., 1991, p. 8). Unfortunately, Schoenberger et al. did not report the regression coefficient for the AS-by-anxiety expectancy interaction and so we do not know whether this trend was in the predicted direction.

Valentiner, Telch, Ilai, and Hehmsoth (1993) tested the expectancy theory in a study of 117 college students who feared enclosed spaces. Each student was asked to walk down a long, narrow, darkened dead-end corridor. Danger expectancy, anxiety expectancy, and the interaction between AS and anxiety expectancy were significant predictors of avoidance behavior (as measured by the amount of time spent in the corridor). However, these variables did not predict heart rate reactivity or self-reports of fear. Thus, the expectancy theory was only partially supported. A limitation of this study is that Valentiner et al. tested an old version of the theory (i.e., the version described by Reiss, 1980; Reiss & McNally, 1985), which states that fear is determined by the main effect for danger expectancy and the AS-by-anxiety expectancy interaction. A more recent version of the theory (Reiss, 1991, Equation 1) states that fear is a function of three expectancy-by-sensitivity interactions. Even with this limitation, the Valentiner et al. results provide limited support for the view that fear responding is a function of the interaction between AS and anxiety expectancy.

Telch and Harrington (1994) investigated the interaction between AS and anxiety expectancy (defined as expectedness of arousal) by asking 39 high-AS and 40 low-AS college students to inhale a mixture of 35% CO_2 and 65% O_2. This harmless compound produces arousal-related bodily sensations and is a potent panicogen for people with high AS (McNally, 1994). Subjects were either told that the inhalation would produce a state of relaxation (expectancy of low arousal) or that it would produce a state of arousal (expectancy of high arousal). Arousal expectancy (low vs. high) was factorially crossed with AS level (low vs. high). Contrary to Equation 1, inhalation-induced panic attacks were most frequent among high-AS subjects in the expect-relaxation condition (52%) compared with high-AS subjects in the expect-arousal condition (17%). Panic frequency was uniformly low for low-AS subjects in each expectancy condition (5% in each condition). Similar findings were obtained for ratings of inhalation-induced fear. Thus, there was a negative interaction between AS and anxiety expectancy, which is directly opposite to that predicted by the expectancy theory.

In summary, only a handful of studies have tested the expectancy theory and none has tested the full theory (as described in Equation 1). Even so, available studies raise doubts about the adequacy of the theory. Telch and Harrington (1994) found that the anxiety expectancy-by-AS interaction was in the opposite direction to that predicted by Reiss' theory. Schoenberger et al. (1991) similarly found that the danger expectancy-by-danger sensitivity was in the opposite direction to that predicted by the theory. Schoenberger et al. reported a trend toward significance for the anxiety expectancy-by-AS interaction, but it is not known whether the interaction was in the predicted direction. Valentiner et al. (1993) found that the anxiety expectancy-by-AS interaction predicted avoidance but not fear.

These findings raise the question of whether other theories provide a better explanation of the data. In future studies, it would be useful to investigate whether the expectancy theory outperforms other models of fear, anxiety, and panic, particularly models that do not postulate AS. For example, the expectancy theory could be contrasted with Bandura's (1988) self-efficacy model and with biological models of panic, such as Klein's (1993) suffocation false-alarm theory of panic. The importance of AS's role would be bolstered by finding that models that include AS, compared with models that do not, are better predictors of fear, panic, and related phenomena.

CONCEPTUAL DEVELOPMENTS AND DIRECTIONS FOR FUTURE RESEARCH

Match and Mismatch in Expectations

The findings of Telch and Harrington (1994) raise the possibility that the degree of error in one's anxiety expectations influences the severity and probability of fear and panic. The results suggest that the probability of panic is increased when one underestimates the probability of arousal, compared with when one has an accurate estimation. Thus, it may be that the expectancy theory needs to be revised to take into consideration the match or mismatch between what is expected and what actually occurs (cf. Gray, 1982). To illustrate, the comparison between expected and actual anxiety could be expressed as Equation 2, which may replace $\beta\Sigma j$ (E_j . AS) in Equation 1:

$$F(S_1) = f\{AS . \Sigma j[\varphi I_j / (\delta E_j + \gamma)]\} \tag{2}$$

Where I_j is the perceived intensity of anxiety sensation j, E_j is the extent to which the person expects sensation j to occur, φ and δ are unknown weights, and γ is a non-zero constant. The latter is included so that Equation 2 is defined when $\delta E_j = 0$.

Observe that $\varphi I_j > (\delta E_j + \gamma)$ represents the situation where unexpected anxiety sensations occur, as in Telch and Harrington's (1994) study. Conversely, $\varphi I_j < (\delta E_j + \gamma)$ represents an overprediction of anxiety. Equation 2 predicts that for a given level of AS, the person's level of fear [i.e., $F(S_1)$] will be high when anxiety is unexpected, moderately high when anxiety is accurately expected, and mild when anxiety is overpredicted. Note that the match–mismatch of expected and experienced anxiety is moderated by AS. Thus, the model simulates the results of Telch and Harrington (1994). It remains to be seen how well it performs on a new data set.

Note that I_j in Equation 2 appears on both sides of the equation because it is implicit in $F(S_1)$. This is not a redundancy because it appears as the sum of a set of ratios on the right-hand side of the equation [i.e., $\Sigma_j[\varphi I_j/(\delta E_j + \gamma)]$]. The inclusion of I_j on both sides of the equation suggests that fear, anxiety, or panic may tend to be self-amplifying, especially when unexpected. Presumably, there is a decay function associated with I_j so that fear, panic, and so on do not self-amplify indefinitely.

Versions of Equation 2 also could be developed for the other components of the expectancy theory in Equation 1—that is, the interaction between expectancy and sensitivity for objective disaster [$\alpha\Sigma_k (E_k . S_d)$], and the interaction between expectancy and sensitivity for social disaster [$\lambda\Sigma_i (E_i . S_{fne})$]. Given the poor performance of Equation 1, as noted in the previous section, it is of interest to determine whether Equation 2 performs any better.

Anxiety Sensitivity: State and Trait?

Equations 1 and 2 assume that fear-relevant variables (fear, anxiety, panic, avoidance, etc.) are best predicted by a trait form of AS. Indeed, most theorists and researchers have considered only this form of AS. However, just as there are state and trait versions of anxiety (Spielberger, 1983), there may be state and trait versions of AS. Although there is a good deal of evidence that AS—as assessed by the ASI—is relatively stable over time (e.g., Reiss, 1991), there also may be statelike fluctuations in AS. To illustrate, for a person with high trait-AS, state-AS may be transiently evoked by exposure to anxiety sensations or by exposure to information pertaining to anxiety or related phenomena (e.g., reading a description of someone having a panic attack). To investigate the possible distinction between state-AS and trait-AS it is first necessary to develop a scale to measure state-AS. This is a task for future research.

A question for future investigation is whether state-AS is superior to trait-AS in the prediction of fear and related phenomena. It may be that the person's current level of fear, anxiety, and so on is best predicted by statelike measures, such as state-AS and current anxiety expectancies. Conversely, trait-anxiety or traitlike forms of fear (fear proneness) may be best predicted by traitlike measures, such as trait-AS and traitlike measures of anxiety expectancies (i.e., the tendency to expect to experience anxiety). Investigation of these possibilities may enhance our understanding of the causes of fear, anxiety, panic, and avoidance.

Dimensions of Anxiety Sensitivity

Equations 1 and 2 assume that AS is a unitary construct. Yet there is growing evidence to suggest that AS is composed of multiple dimensions, such as fear of somatic sensations, fear of cognitive dyscontrol, and fear of publicly observable anxiety sensations (see chap. 5). These dimensions tend to be correlated with one another and thereby represent lower order factors that load on a unitary higher order AS factor. A question for further investigation is which level of the hierarchy has the greatest power in predicting fear and related phenomena. The expectancy theory (as represented in Equation 1) suggests that the higher order factor interacts with anxiety expectancies to produce fear, panic, and so on. However, it may be that fear and related phenomena are better predicted by the interaction between each lower order factor and its corresponding anxiety expectancy. For example, fear of somatic sensations may interact with the person's expectation that he or she will experience somatic sensations. Similarly, fear of cognitive dyscontrol may interact with expectancies that one will experience cognitive symptoms of anxiety. Fear of publicly observable anxiety reactions may interact with expectations that one will blush, tremble, sweat, and so on. These interaction terms may be superior to the interaction between anxiety expectancies and the higher order AS factor (as expressed in either Equations 1 or 2) in the prediction of fear, anxiety, panic, and avoidance. This possibility merits investigation. Finally, as suggested in the preceding section, it may be that the state versions of the lower-order factors are better predictors of state fears, whereas the trait versions of the factors are better predictors of trait fears.

CONCLUSIONS

Reiss' expectancy theory is an attempt to account for individual differences in the acquisition and amplification of fears and related phenomena. Given the wealth of research on AS, it is surprising that there have been few tests of the expectancy theory. It appears that the theory suffers from several conceptual problems. Although most people find anxiety to be aversive, it seems unlikely that AS is a fundamental fear. AS may be composed of more basic fears such as fear of death, insanity, and negative evaluation. Investigation into the causes of AS will help enhance an understanding of the determinants of common and fundamental fears.

Although there have been only a handful of studies of the expectancy theory, available findings cast doubt on the adequacy of the theory. Indeed, some studies have obtained results that are directly opposite to those predicted by Equation 1. Modifications to this equation may be necessary. We have proposed one modification, which was designed to account for recent findings (e.g., Telch & Harrington, 1994). However, it remains to be seen whether our modified equation outperforms Equation 1 when new data sets are used. Also, to determine whether AS is a critical variable, the predictive power of these equations should be directly compared to those of other models, including models that do not include AS as a variable. Such empirically based comparisons should advance our understanding of the role of AS in anxiety disorders and subsequently direct effective treatment strategies.

ACKNOWLEDGMENTS

Preparation of this chapter was supported in part by a grant from the British Columbia Health Research Foundation.

REFERENCES

American Psychiatric Association. (1994). *Diagnostic and statistical manual of mental disorders* (4th ed.). Washington, DC: Author.

Bandura, A. (1988). Self-efficacy conceptions of anxiety. *Anxiety Research, 1*, 77–98.

Clark, D. M. (1986). A cognitive approach to panic. *Behaviour Research and Therapy, 24*, 461–470.

Davey, G. C. L. (1992). Classical conditioning and the acquisition of human fears and phobias: A review and synthesis of the literature. *Advances in Behaviour Research and Therapy, 14*, 29–66.

Geer, J. H. (1965). The development of a scale to measure fear. *Behaviour Research and Therapy, 3*, 45–53.

Gray, J. A. (1982). *The neuropsychology of anxiety.* Oxford: Oxford University Press.

Gursky, D. M., & Reiss, S. (1987). Identifying danger and anxiety expectancies as components of common fears. *Journal of Behavior Therapy and Experimental Psychiatry, 18*, 317–324.

Izard, C. E. (1977). *Human emotions.* New York: Plenum.

Klein, D. F. (1993). False suffocation alarms, spontaneous panics, and related conditions: An integrative hypothesis. *Archives of General Psychiatry, 50*, 306–317.

Lilienfeld, S. O. (1996a). Anxiety sensitivity is not distinct from trait anxiety. In R. M. Rapee (Ed.), *Current controversies in the anxiety disorders* (pp. 228– 244). New York: Guilford.

Lilienfeld, S. O. (1996b). Another look at the relation between anxiety sensitivity and trait anxiety: Reply to McNally. In R. M. Rapee (Ed.), *Current controversies in the anxiety disorders* (pp. 249–252). New York: Guilford.

Lilienfeld, S. O., Turner, S. M., & Jacob, R. G. (1993). Anxiety sensitivity: An examination of theoretical and methodological issues. *Advances in Behaviour Research and Therapy, 15*, 147–183.

Lilienfeld, S. O., Turner, S. M., & Jacob, R. G. (1996). Further comments on the nature and measurement of anxiety sensitivity: A reply to Taylor. *Journal of Anxiety Disorders, 10*, 411–424.

Lilienfeld, S. O., Turner, S. M., & Jacob, R. G. (1998). Déjà vu all over again: Critical misunderstandings concerning anxiety sensitivity and constructive suggestions for future research. *Journal of Anxiety Disorders, 12*, 71–82.

McNally, R. J. (1994). *Panic disorder: A critical analysis*. New York: Guilford.

McNally, R. J. (1996a). Anxiety sensitivity is distinguishable from trait anxiety. In R. M. Rapee (Ed.), *Current controversies in the anxiety disorders* (pp. 214–227). New York: Guilford.

McNally, R. J. (1996b). Reply to Lilienfeld: Toward a resolution of the anxiety sensitivity versus trait anxiety debate. In R. M. Rapee (Ed.), *Current controversies in the anxiety disorders* (pp. 245–248). New York: Guilford.

McNally, R. J., & Louro, C. E. (1992). Fear of flying in agoraphobia and simple phobia: Distinguishing features. *Journal of Anxiety Disorders, 6*, 319–324.

McNally, R. J., & Steketee, G. S. (1985). The etiology and maintenance of severe animal phobias. *Behaviour Research and Therapy, 23*, 431–435.

Peterson, R. A., & Reiss, S. (1987). *Anxiety Sensitivity Index Manual*. Orland Park, IL: International Diagnostic Systems.

Rachman, S. (1990). *Fear and courage*. New York: Freeman.

Rachman, S. (1991). Neo-conditioning and the classical theory of fear acquisition. *Clinical Psychology Review, 11*, 155–173.

Rachman, S., & Seligman, M. E. P. (1976). Unprepared fears: "Be prepared." *Behaviour Research and Therapy, 14*, 333–338.

Reiss, S. (1980). Pavlovian conditioning and human fear: An expectancy model. *Behavior Therapy, 11*, 380–396.

Reiss, S. (1987). Theoretical perspectives on the fear of anxiety. *Clinical Psychology Review, 7*, 585–596.

Reiss, S. (1991). Expectancy model of fear, anxiety, and panic. *Clinical Psychology Review, 11*, 141–153.

Reiss, S. (1997). Trait anxiety: It's not what you think it is. *Journal of Anxiety Disorders, 11*, 201–214.

Reiss, S., & Havercamp. S. H. (1996). The sensitivity theory of motivation: Implications for psychopathology. *Behaviour Research and Therapy, 34*, 621–632.

Reiss, S., & Havercamp, S. H. (1997). Sensitivity theory and mental retardation: Why functional analysis is not enough. *American Journal of Mental Deficiency, 101*, 553–556.

Reiss, S., & McNally, R. J. (1985). Expectancy model of fear. In S. Reiss & R. R. Bootzin (Eds.), *Theoretical issues in behavior therapy* (pp. 107–121). San Diego, CA: Academic Press.

Reiss, S., Peterson, R. A., & Gursley, D. M. (1988). Anxiety sensitivity, injury sensitivity, and individual differences in fearfulness. *Behaviour Research and Therapy, 26*, 341–345.

Reiss, S., Peterson, R. A., Gursky, D. M., & McNally, R. J. (1986). Anxiety sensitivity, anxiety frequency and the prediction of fearfulness. *Behaviour Research and Therapy, 24*, 1–8.

Rescorla, R. A. (1988). Pavlovian conditioning: It's not what you think it is. *American Psychologist, 43*, 151–160.

Schoenberger, N. E., Kirsch, I., & Rosengard, C. (1991). Cognitive theories of human fear: An empirically derived integration. *Anxiety Research, 4*, 1–13.

Spielberger, C. D. (1983). *Manual for the State-Trait Anxiety Inventory (Form Y)*. Palo Alto, CA: Consulting Psychologists Press.

Stewart, S. H., Taylor, S., & Baker, J. M. (1997). Gender differences in dimensions of anxiety sensitivity. *Journal of Anxiety Disorders, 11*, 179–200.

Taylor, S. (1993). The structure of fundamental fears. *Journal of Behavior Therapy and Experimental Psychiatry, 24*, 289–299.

Taylor, S. (1995a). Anxiety sensitivity: Theoretical perspectives and recent findings. *Behaviour Research and Therapy, 33*, 243–258.

Taylor, S. (1995b). Issues in the conceptualization and measurement of anxiety sensitivity. *Journal of Anxiety Disorders, 9*, 163–174.

Taylor, S. (1996). Nature and measurement of anxiety sensitivity: Reply to Lilienfeld, Turner, and Jacob (1996). *Journal of Anxiety Disorders, 10*, 425–451.

Telch, M. J., & Harrington, P. J. (1994, November). *Anxiety sensitivity and expectedness of arousal in mediating affective response to 35% carbon dioxide inhalation.* Paper presented at the 28th meeting of the Association for Advancement of Behavior Therapy, San Diego, CA.

Valentiner, D. P., Telch, M. J., Ilai, D., & Hehmsoth, M. M. (1993). Claustrophobic fear behavior: A test of the expectancy model of fear. *Behavior Research and Therapy, 31*, 395–402.

Wolpe, J., & Lang, P. J. (1969). *Fear survey schedule*. San Diego, CA: EdITS.

3

The Sensitivity Theory of Aberrant Motivation

Steven Reiss
The Ohio State University

In 1985, Richard McNally and I introduced the concept of anxiety sensitivity to explain data pertaining to the treatment of anxiety disorders. In 1996, Susan Havercamp and I generalized certain aspects of that concept—individual differences in sensitivity to a universally reinforcing stimulus—into a comprehensive theory of human motivation called *sensitivity theory*. This generalized theory is expounded and updated in this chapter, with particular attention paid to the concept of aberrant motivation and implications for psychopathology.

INTRINSIC MOTIVATION

All motives can be classified as either extrinsic (means) or as intrinsic (ends). The number of extrinsic motives is potentially limitless. A central issue for behavioral science is to identify and classify the intrinsic motives (end purposes) of behavior.

Motives are organizing forces relevant to understanding how "behavior, cognition, and affect function as coordinated, interacting systems" (Dweck, 1992, p. 166). Two types of motives are goals and sensitivities—people seek goals and avoid sensitivities. Any given goal or sensitivity may be analyzed as either intrinsic or extrinsic motivation. The distinction is based on the purpose of the behavior. As defined here, *intrinsic motivation* is indicated when a person engages in a behavior for no apparent reason "except the activity itself" (Deci, 1975, p. 23) or when a person avoids an aversive activity to minimize discomfort. Examples of intrinsic motivation include a child's playing ball for physical exercise, a student's reading a book out of curiosity, and a person's avoiding dental treatment to avoid pain. In each of these examples, the purpose of the behavior is to obtain reinforcement (physical exercise, learning, or pain avoidance) inherent to the behavior. In contrast, extrinsic motivation is indicated when a person performs an act for its instrumental value; that is, the purpose is to obtain a reinforcement that is not inherent to the behavior or activity. Examples include a professional athlete playing ball to obtain a high salary, a student studying for good grades, and a person avoiding the dentist to save money. In each of these examples, the goal (high salary, good grades, and savings) is reinforcing because it provides a means of obtaining some other reinforcer. For example, a person might seek a high salary as a means of obtaining power, enhancing social status, benefiting family, providing early retirement, or some other reinforcer.

An analysis of many behaviors may identify a chain of extrinsic (instrumental) purposes, but eventually there must be an intrinsic purpose at the end of the chain. For example, a person may take a second job for the extra salary (extrinsic or instrumental motive), desire the extra salary to purchase health care (extrinsic or instrumental motive), and desire the health care to benefit his or her family (intrinsic or end goal). By definition, intrinsic motivation is end motivation. The following comments concern the concepts of intrinsic and extrinsic motivation:

1. Instead of statements such as, "Sally is an intrinsically motivated student and Sherry is an extrinsically motivated student," sensitivity theorists make statements such as, "Sally is highly motivated by curiosity and enjoys academics, whereas Sherry is highly motivated by family and enjoys homemaking." Both Sally's interest in academics and Sherry's interest in family are seen as intrinsic motives (end purposes). There is no implicit value judgment suggesting that Sally's goals are higher or preferable to Sherry's, as sometimes occurs when students are classified as intrinsically versus extrinsically motivated.

2. An inherently reinforcing activity can be intrinsically or extrinsically motivating, depending on the person's end purpose. For example, a person might seek power either for its intrinsic reinforcing value or as an extrinsic means to gratify some other intrinsic goal, such as social status. Similarly, a person might seek social status for its own sake or as a means to obtain power.

3. Sensitivity theory holds that intrinsic and extrinsic motives are sometimes compatible with one another so that both can contribute to the total motivation of the same behavior. For example, a person might attend college both for the intrinsic goal of enjoyment of learning and for the extrinsic goal of enhancing his or her potential for a high-paying job. A person might delay going to the dentist both for the intrinsic goal of avoiding the pain and for the extrinsic goal of saving money. In holding that intrinsic and extrinsic motivation are compatible, sensitivity theorists do not embrace the early statements of overjustification theory (Lepper, Greene, & Nisbett, 1973), which held that these motives interact (see Reiss & Sushinsky, 1975). Although sensitivity theory holds that compatible intrinsic and extrinsic motives are additive, this does not imply that extrinsic motives are necessarily as effective as intrinsic motives. Incentives are much more effective when they are used to teach people to enjoy activities than when they are used in conflicted situations that pressure people into unpleasant, distracting, or anxious situations (Reiss & Sushinsky, 1975).

4. Scientists should identify and classify intrinsic motives. The number of extrinsic motives is potentially limitless, whereas the number of intrinsic motives is likely to be small. How many intrinsic motives are needed to explain human behavior? What do people fundamentally want from their lives?

PLEASURE VERSUS FULFILLMENT

Two types of theories have been advanced concerning the end purposes of human behavior: pleasure and fulfillment theories. Pleasure theories hold that the end purposes of all human behavior are to maximize positive feelings and minimize negative feelings. Fulfillment theories give emphasis to enduring strivings such as love, self-determination, and psychological growth. Sensitivity theory recognizes both pleasure and fulfillment as significant human desires.

Many psychological theories of human motivation can be classified into two categories: those emphasizing the pleasures of the senses versus those emphasizing the strivings of the soul. In this chapter, the former group of theories is called *pleasure theory*, and the latter group is called *fulfillment theory*. Pleasure theory holds that all intrinsic motivation maximizes positive feelings or minimizes negative feelings. According to this view, people read books because they derive pleasure from reading, people engage in physical exercise because that is how they obtain pleasure, and people seek vengeance because revenge is sweet. According to Ryff (1989), pleasure theory implies that happiness is everything.

There are many examples of pleasure theory in psychology. For example, Freud (1916/1963) held that all behavior is motivated by needs to discharge sexual or aggressive tension. Thorndike's (1911) Law of Effect held that behavior is strengthened by the pleasurable effect of rewards (satisfaction) not by the rewards themselves. Bradburn (1969) and colleagues defined *psychological well-being* as a balance between positive and negative feelings.

Pleasure theory is invalid. It implies a unitary concept of pleasure and a unitary concept of discomfort. For example, Klein (1987) noted that Freud's concept of libido implies that all behavior is motivated by pleasure and that all pleasures are the same libidinal phenomenon. Is the pleasure derived from sex the same as the pleasure derived from solving a puzzle? Klein questioned this assumption of equivalence because it suggests that there is but one depressive illness, whereas he suspects several based on individual differences in reaction to antidepressant medications.

Another problem with pleasure theory is suggested by the lack of enthusiasm many people have for pleasure-enhancing drugs. Suppose a drug were developed that guaranteed the maximum amount of positive feelings that is physiologically possible. Pleasure theory implies that everybody would freely choose to experience the drug every minute of their remaining lives, but many people would pass at the opportunity to become a mass of feel-good protoplasm. People might desire pleasure sometimes, but few people seek pleasure as the only end purpose (meaning) in their lives. For example, many parents would not trade the pleasures of watching their children grow up for a drug that directly induced even greater positive feelings. For many parents, children and family are end purposes (intrinsic motives) for a lot of what they do, regardless of how much or little feel-good pleasure is derived. Many parents have given their lives to protect their children or have accepted a life of hard work to pay for them. There is something fundamentally wrong with any theory that equates this parental motivation with the pleasures of a heroin addict.

Yet another problem with pleasure theory is that it implies that everybody is equally motivated to avoid anxiety and other aversive states. Reiss (1997) referred to this view as the idea that anxiety is a psychological monster. The assumption has been held so consistently that Bandura (1986) once wondered whether psychologists could explain the behavior of a relief pitcher. Typically the relief pitcher is called into a baseball game during periods of stress when the outcome is in doubt and his team is in a jam. If all other factors were equal, almost all important psychological theories imply that the relief pitcher should run away from the game to avoid anxiety and stress. Although there are a number of incentives that might explain why a relief pitcher does not run away but instead enters a stressful ball game, Bandura's example reminds us that approaching anxiety-ridden situations is an everyday occurrence.

Rejecting the view that everybody is equally motivated to avoid experiencing anxiety, anxiety sensitivity theorists proposed significant individual differences in the fear of anxiety (McNally, 1994; Reiss & McNally, 1985). People with high anxiety sensitivity believe that anxiety is personally harmful, whereas those with low anxiety sensitivity believe that anxiety is (at least for them) a harmless nuisance that readily dissipates once the source of stress is removed. All other factors being equal, people with high anxiety sensitivity are much more likely to avoid stressful situations than are people with low anxiety sensitivity.

These considerations suggest significant shortcomings in pleasure theories of motivation. There is no evidence that pleasure is a unitary phenomenon—the fun experienced at parties may be psychologically and physiologically different from the intellectual pleasure experienced from mathematics. In their everyday lives, many people are not seeking pleasure in any obvious way. It is not obvious how soldiers who give their lives for their countries or parents who deny themselves for their children are always behaving in ways that are intended to maximize their own personal experiences of pleasure. Aside from a research psychologist who ascribes to pleasure theory, who would look at a busy office or bustling airport terminal and suggest that all of the people are pursuing the same goal of maximizing pleasure? Pleasure theory is far from proved and does not hold up well when considered in depth.

Fulfillment Theory

As early as Plato, Western philosophers argued that the satisfactions of the soul are more important than the pleasures of the senses (see Russell, 1945). This suggests a fundamental distinction between the two sorts of motivations, which forms the historical roots of a number of psychological theories of motivation. For example, Deci's (1975) position that intrinsic motivation arises from the central nervous system, whereas extrinsic motivation arises from tissue needs, is similar to the idea that intrinsic motivation concerns satisfactions of the intellect or soul, whereas extrinsic motivation concerns biological needs and the pleasures of the senses.

Whereas pleasure theory holds that the only end purposes of all behavior are maximizing pleasure and minimizing pain, fulfillment theory gives emphasis to motives that are "enduring life challenges such as having a sense of purpose and direction, achieving satisfying relationships with others, and gaining a sense of self-realization" (Ryff, 1989, p. 1077). For example, Murray (1938) posited 20 psychological needs, including achievement, affiliation, autonomy, and nurturance. Rogers (1961) held that self-actualization is a fundamental desire to realize one's potential. Berlyne (1960) argued that the desire to explore novel stimuli is an intrinsic motive (end purpose) that cannot be explained as drive reduction. Hebb (1946) suggested that people seek an optimal level of cortical arousal. Maslow (1954) proposed a hierarchy of human strivings. Deci (1975) held that self-determination (independence) is the primary source of intrinsic motivation. Bandura (1977) argued that people strive for self-efficacy as a means of overcoming fear. Ryff (1989) proposed that psychological well-being is related to self-acceptance, positive relationships with others, autonomy, environmental mastery, purpose in life, and personal growth.

Fulfillment theorists have noted that higher strivings are intrinsic motives (end purposes) that people pursue even when the effort does not maximize positive feelings and minimize negative feelings. Realizing one's higher strivings may not be easy and can require discipline and effort, which at times may be at odds with short-term pleasure. For example, the pursuit of a college diploma typically involves a considerable amount of test anxiety and frustration. If the only intrinsic motives were to maximize pleasure and minimize discomfort, people probably would not pursue college diplomas. Yet people are willing to endure the stress of college exams because obtaining a college diploma satiates the end desires of achievement and status.

With the notable exception of research on well-being (e.g., Ryff, 1989), research on fulfillment theory consists mostly of the study of a single motive in isolation from other motives. For example, some research studies addressed play (e.g, Lepper, Greene, & Nisbett, 1973), others addressed learning (e.g., Dweck, 1992), and still others addressed self-efficacy (Bandura, 1977). Surprisingly few research efforts have been conducted to study motivation comprehensively by assessing a wide range of motives in the same investigation. How do individuals prioritize various fulfillment motives? How do such motives interact with one another? What accounts for *motivation switching*, in which a person is motivated by curiosity one moment and by a need for physical exercise the next. What determines which motives influence behavior at any moment in time? These and many other questions require a comprehensive approach to motivation rather than the piecemeal approach in which only one motive is studied in any given investigation.

FUNDAMENTAL MOTIVATION

Fundamental motives (a) are end purposes (intrinsic motives), (b) are universally motivating, and (c) account for a significant amount of everyday behavior.

Reiss and Havercamp (1996) introduced the concept of fundamental motivation partially because of ambiguities in the concept of intrinsic motivation. In the past, researchers have applied the term *intrinsic motivation* to personality, motives, and tasks. They have defined *intrinsic motivation* in terms of pleasure, end purpose (performing a behavior for its own sake), and specific motives. For example, Deci (1975) defined *intrinsic motivation* as engaging in an activity for its own sake and then suggested that self-determination is the one true intrinsic motive. In contrast, sensitivity theory holds that the number of end purposes for human behavior is about 25, not 1 (Reiss & Havercamp, 1996). To make this point explicit, Reiss and Havercamp used the term *fundamental motivation* rather than intrinsic motivation.

By definition, *fundamental motives* are universally motivating. For example, sex, food, family, pain, stress, attention, and social contact motivate virtually everybody. Some people crave attention, others avoid it, but virtually everybody is motivated by attention one way or another. Most people seek sex, a few are disgusted by it, but almost nobody is indifferent to (unmotivated by) sex. Interestingly, most or all fundamental motives for humans also serve as fundamental motivators for many animal species.

Some end purposes, such as food and sex, account for a considerable amount of everyday behavior and play a central role in theories of eating and sex disorders. Other end purposes, such as thirst, account for relatively little everyday behavior. In an effort to shorten the list of fundamental motives initially considered by sensitivity theory, only those intrinsic motives most significant for psychological research and explanation are considered to be fundamental. Accordingly, food and sex were defined as fundamental motives, whereas thirst was defined as a nonfundamental motive.

The following additional comments concern the concept of fundamental motivation:

1. Sensitivity theory addresses the study of human motivation in a comprehensive fashion. The theory recognizes both pleasure and fulfillment as significant intrinsic motives (end purposes) affecting the everyday behavior of a great many people. On the one hand, sensitivity theory recognizes that maximizing pleasure and minimizing discomfort are end goals of human behavior. On the other hand, sensitivity theory rejects the suggestion that feel-good happiness is the only end purpose of human behavior. Additionally, sensitivity theory holds that family, social status, independence, power, learning, and order are end purposes that motivate human behavior. Thus, sensitivity theory combines elements of both pleasure and fulfillment theories. A major purpose of sensitivity theory is to encourage researchers to identify the intrinsic

motives (end purposes) of human behavior. What are the goals of human behavior? What end events provide the purpose for human behavior? In part, sensitivity theory is a call for research to address these issues broadly, recognizing the potential role of both pleasure and fulfillment.

2. Initially, sensitivity theory did not address the question of origin of fundamental motivation. However, Reiss and Havercamp (in press) recently suggested a genetics-behavior-cognitive model. According to this model, variations in genetic factors cause some people to experience an end motive such as sex as more pleasurable than do others. Beliefs about the personal consequences of the end motive, as well as other learning experiences, may add or subtract from the individual's total enjoyment. For example, both the belief that sex is sin, and past punishment of sexual behavior, should subtract from the person's overall enjoyment of sex. The net effect is the strength of sex as an end motive for the person.

3. Fundamental reinforcers are not necessarily primary reinforcers. In operant conditioning, primary reinforcers are unlearned sources of motivation and secondary reinforcers are learned sources of reinforcement. Generally, food is thought of as a primary reinforcer, whereas attention and the desire for social status are considered secondary reinforcers. Because sensitivity theory holds that both food and attention are fundamental reinforcers, the concept of fundamental reinforcement cannot be equated with the concept of primary reinforcement. Once a newborn is more than a few days old, it might be argued that no reinforcer is 100% primary or 100% secondary. This assumption limits the applicability of the concept of primary reinforcement in explanation of everyday human behavior. For example, an individual's desire for food may be influenced by physiological factors affecting appetite, self-image concepts such as desirable weight, and cultural factors such as religious beliefs. Thus, the reinforcing value of the food is partially a function of innate biological needs and partially a function of learned attitudes and acquired values.

INDIVIDUAL DIFFERENCES

Sensitivity theory posits stable individual differences, called *set points*, in the effectiveness or strength of each fundamental motive. These differences are expressed as differences in desired amounts of reinforcement, efforts in seeking reinforcement, and rates of satiation.

According to sensitivity theory, the strength of each fundamental motive varies considerably from one person to the next. For example, people show significant differences in how much they like to eat. All people are, to some degree, motivated to eat. However, the amount of time, effort, and persistence devoted to the pursuit of food varies significantly from one individual to the next. The amount of food required for satiation varies considerably from one person to the next, even when deprivational factors are held constant. This is recognized in everyday life by references to some people as being *good eaters* or having *hearty appetites*. These phrases suggest recognition among lay people that there are stable individual differences in the motivational strength of rewards such as food. The plain fact is that some people just like eating much more than other people.

Individuals show important differences in the strength of the various intrinsic motives other than food. Some people are extremely interested in learning, whereas others have only minimal curiosity. Some people panic in stressful situations, whereas others show little overt anxiety. American football players withstand much more physical pain that most people. Some people are much more interested than others in their families.

In sensitivity theory, the concept of set point refers to stable individual differences in fundamental motivation. Set points indicate either the usual amount of reward an individual desires or the strength of an aversive stimulus that an individual usually tolerates. For example, consider individual differences in how much social contact people seek in their everyday lives. People with high set points seek a great deal of social contact, whereas those with low set points prefer to be alone quite a bit.

Depending on one's set point, a reinforcer may lead to pleasant or annoying consequences. For example, moderate amounts of attention can be positively reinforcing for some (show-offs) and punishing for others (shy people). According to sensitivity theory, show-offs have high set points for attention. That is, they require large amounts of attention before satiating. In contrast, shy people have low set points for attention; they desire small amounts of attention and find large amounts annoying.

The concept of set point is relevant to the distinction between gluttony and hunger. A glutton is a person who has a high set point for food and habitually has a hearty appetite and overeats for pleasure. Because gluttony is a trait concept, it only applies to some people. In contrast, hunger is a temporary situational state related mostly to how long it has been since one's last meal; the term *hunger* is not a personality trait and potentially applies to anyone who has not eaten in a while. Our concept of a set point does not apply to hunger.

Sensitivity theory holds that gluttony and hunger refer to different phenomena. Gluttony is inferred when a person has both a history of above-average consumption of food and a future propensity for above-average consumption. Hunger is inferred when the future propensity to consume an above-average amount of food is associated with recent deprivation of food. Sensitivity theory is concerned with personality concepts such as gluttony, not with deprivational concepts such as hunger.

The concept of set point should not be confused with the concept of establishing operations (Keller & Schoenfeld, 1950). These operations are used in operant conditioning to establish an effective reinforcer. For example, deprivation establishes food as an effective reinforcer. When applied behavior analysts use establishing operations to induce motivations, they pay little or no attention to individual differences in reaction to these procedures. In contrast, sensitivity theory gives emphasis to individual differences in reaction to establishing operations. For example, when social isolation is used to establish the reinforcing effectiveness of social contact, the effect should occur much more quickly and powerfully for children with high set points for attention than for those with low set points. Furthermore, food deprivation should induce hunger more quickly and more powerfully in gluttons than in other people.

Resistance to Satiation

Set points have implications for rates of satiation. People with high set points satiate slowly, whereas those with low set points satiate quickly. One difference between motivational states such as hunger and motivational traits such as gluttony lies in the speed with which satiation is acquired and period of time in which a person remains satiated. People who are deprived of food readily satiate when they eat a full meal. In contrast, gluttons are quick to crave food again even after eating a meal. A high reinforcement sensitivity for food, as in gluttony and other conditions such as Prader Willi Syndrome (a rare condition associated with hypotonia, hypergonadism, extreme obesity, and sometimes mental retardation), implies resistance to satiation and a relatively quick reinstatement of motivational states following the consumption of reinforcement.

Reinforcing Effectiveness

The term *reinforcing effectiveness* refers to the motivational strength of a particular reinforcer for a particular individual. The more effective a given reinforcer, the stronger (higher) is the person's motivation to obtain that reinforcer. High set points imply highly effective reinforcers. Theoretically, the more effective a reward is for a particular person, (a) the larger is the amount of reinforcement needed to satiate the person, (b) the more intense and persistent is the person's seeking of reinforcement, (c) the more impatient the person is in waiting for reinforcement, and (d) the lower is the minimal amount of reward that can function as reinforcement for instrumental behavior. The more effective a given aversive stimulus is for a particular person, (a) the lower is the person's threshold for performing coping/avoidance responses, (b) the more intense and persistent is the person's performance of coping/avoidance responses, (c) the more quickly the person will perform coping/avoidance responses, and (d) the lower is the minimal amount of aversive stimulation that can function as negative reinforcement for instrumental behavior.

To illustrate, consider the behavior of a child with mental retardation who has a high set point for adult attention. This child should appear to be very needy, often approaching and interrupting adults and demanding a large amount of attention. Even when a great deal of attention is given, the child should be slow to satiate and slow to move on to other interests. The child's demands for attention may be frequent and persistent; at times it may appear that the child is single-mindedly determined to obtain adult attention. The child should be impatient waiting for attention and demand that attention be given immediately. When the child is alone, he or she may become frustrated because attention cannot be obtained. Moreover, the child's behavior is reinforced by amounts of attention so minimal that even negative forms of attention, such as criticism or reprimands, may function as positive reinforcement strengthening instrumental behavior. In contrast, the child with a low sensitivity for adult attention may appear to be almost indifferent to this reinforcer; he or she may be perfectly comfortable playing alone for sustained periods of time.

There are many other everyday examples of these principles. For example, people with a low threshold for pain put off going to a dentist as long as they can and jump at the most minimal sensations when the dentist begins drilling. Gluttons become impatient waiting for dinner. People who are hungry will work to obtain small amounts of food if that is all that is available. A person with high anxiety sensitivity shows anxiety or panic when biologically challenged (Holloway & McNally, 1987). People with high anxiety sensitivity avoid situations in which even minimal anxiety is expected.

PSYCHOLOGICAL ASSESSMENT

Sensitivity theory can be tested using two recently developed psychometric instruments called the *Reiss Profiles*. These measures can be thought of as motivational personality tests. Essentially, the tests ask people how much they like stimuli that are liked by virtually everybody and how much they dislike stimuli that are disliked by virtually everybody.

As Ryff (1989) noted, researchers interested in testing fulfillment theory have been "immobilized" (p. 1070) because of the lack of objective measures.

Researchers used the Thematic Apperception Test (TAT; Murray, 1943), but there are concerns about the validity of this measure (Zubin, Eron, & Schumer, 1965). Today, the Jackson Personality Inventory (Jackson, 1985) provides a validated measure for testing Murray's theory, but with 440 items the inventory is too lengthy for use in many investigations. Furthermore, the Jackson Personality Inventory is not a pure measure of motivation because a significant number of items assess habits or nonmotivational personality traits.

Two psychometric instruments have been developed to assess fundamental motivation and test sensitivity theory. These instruments are called the *Reiss Profile of Fundamental Goals and Motivational Sensitivities* and the *Reiss Profile of Fundamental Goals and Motivational Sensitivities—MR/DD*. The latter was designed to assess people with mental retardation or developmental disabilities (MR/DD). As shown in Table 3.1, the former is a self-report instrument intended for use with the general population, whereas the latter is an informant ratings instrument intended for use with people who have a developmental disability. Both instruments are suitable for use with adolescents or adults.

The development of these instruments began with a comprehensive list of motivational items (Reiss & Havercamp, 1998). Each item concerned a person's desires, wants, likes, dislikes, enjoyment, needs, priorities, or hatreds. Ideas for items were obtained from psychology textbooks, the fourth edition of

TABLE 3.1
Sample Items From Reiss Profiles

Instrument	Items
General	My word is my bond
	I love to eat
	Sex is very important to me
	I have a "thirst for knowledge"
	I am happiest when I am physically active
	I love parties
Mental Retardation/ Developmental Disability	More than most people, seeks attention
	Strong desire to help others
	Hates interruptions
	Enjoys learning
	Very happy when others do well
	Strong desire for autonomy

the *Diagnostic and Statistical Manual of Mental Disorders* (*DSM–IV*; American Psychiatric Association, 1994), Murray's (1938) personality theory, and suggestions from about 20 people, including colleagues, spouses, children, and friends. After elimination of redundancies, the initial lists consisted of 328 self-report items and 167 MR/DD items (ratings).

The experimental instruments were administered to various research samples and data were submitted to exploratory factor analyses. The instruments were then revised to support emerging factors. The maximum likelihood oblique method of factor analysis was used to test the fit of various factor models. The self-report instrument was administered to four independent samples and the data were submitted to three exploratory and one confirmatory factor analyses. The MR/DD ratings instrument was administered to two independent samples and data were submitted to exploratory and confirmatory factor analyses. Six independent samples were used ($N = 2,548$).

Because large, heterogeneous samples are needed for a stable factor structure, each research sample consisted of between 341 and 515 people. The participants were sampled from diverse walks of life, including human service agencies, members of church clubs, members of a community service organization (Kiwanis club), soldiers in military reserve units, high school students, dental students, physical therapy students, secretaries, business school students, employees of fast food restaurants, and elderly residents of nursing homes. The college students were from private institutions, large state universities, and community colleges. Data were collected from 24 U.S. states and 2 Canadian provinces (Ontario and Quebec).

For each instrument, 15 factors were interpreted and confirmed. Different research samples were used for exploratory and confirmatory factor analyses. Although self-report and informant-rated measures sometimes produce significantly different factor structures (Aman, 1991), the two instruments have similar factor structures. Thirteen of 15 factors on the self-report instrument have corresponding factors on the MR/DD instrument. The main differences are these. The self-report instrument has a scale for power not found on the MR/DD instrument. Also, the MR/DD instrument provides separate scales for anxiety, frustration, and pain sensitivity, whereas the self-report instrument has a single (combined) scale. Otherwise, the two instruments have corresponding scales. The factors for the self-report instrument are shown in Table 3.2. This is a minimal list of fundamental motives that might be expanded with future research.

TABLE 3.2

Fundamental Motives

Motive	Description
Curiosity	Usual strength of the individual's desire to learn
Family	Usual strength of the individual's desire to spend time with own children
Food	Usual strength of the individual's desire to eat
Honor	Usual strength of the individual's desire to behave in accordance with a code of conduct
Independence	Usual strength of the individual's desire to make own decisions
Order	Desired amount of organization (routines, structure) in daily life
Power	Usual strength of the individual's desire to be influential or lead
Physical exercise	Usual strength of the individual's desire for physical exercise
Rejection sensitivity	Usual strength of the individual's fear of being rejected
Sensation sensitivity	Usual strength of the individual's fear of anxiety and pain sensations
Sex	Usual strength of the individual's desire for sexual gratification
Social contact	Usual strength of the individual's desire to be with other people
Social idealism	Usual strength of the individual's desire to contribute to society
Social status	Usual strength of the individual's desire to be admired based on social standing
Vengeance	Usual strength of the individual's desire to get even with people who offend

APPLICATIONS

Aberrant motives are indicated by high set points, expressing either desires for large amounts of reinforcement or hypersensitivities to aversive stimuli. Theoretically, aberrant motives are risk factors for psychopathology.

Because motivation is of general significance in explaining human behavior, sensitivity theory potentially has broad applications. The applications discussed here, however, are limited to research on psychopathology and related phenomena.

Motivational Profiles

Many clinical observers have suggested that psychopathology is associated with strong or intense desires (Carr, 1977; Ellis, 1993; Klein, 1987; Murray,

1938). For example, Ellis (1993) observed that some of his patients believe that they must behave in a certain way. Carr (1977) observed that self-injurious behavior is often associated with excessive irritability (task demands) or strong desires for attention. Zigler and Burack (1989) observed unusual reinforcement preferences in children with both MR/DD and behavior disorders. Bihm, Poindexter, Kienlen, and Smith (1992) found differences in reinforcer preferences among persons with MR/DD who scored high versus low on the Aberrant Behavior Checklist (Aman, Singh, Stewart, & Field, 1985). These observations support the hypothesis that many people who have a significant behavioral or psychiatric disorder also show significant aberrations in the nature or intensity of their motives.

Figure 3.1 shows the Reiss Profile results for two individuals: one with mental retardation (MR) and autism (upper profile) and another with MR and major depression (lower profile). The figure shows how set points can be profiled, not as new data pertaining to the validity of the instrument. The profiles reveal that the individual with autism has a low set point for social contact and a high set point for order. This suggests intolerance of social contact and craving for order, which are consistent with clinical descriptions of autism. The individual with major depression generally has low set points, indicating a lack of interest in fundamental reinforcers. This profile is consistent with clinical descriptions of major depression as a loss of interest in enjoyable activities.

Future researchers should determine the extent to which the profiles shown in Fig. 3.1 are characteristic of the respective diagnostic conditions or specific to the two patients. Future researchers also should test large numbers of patients with various disorders to determine if certain motivations are more prominent in some disorders than in others. Positive findings might be used to help diagnose difficult cases, test various theories of psychopathology, or evaluate treatment outcomes.

Aberrant Motivation

Sensitivity theory holds that a high score (high set point) on any one of the scales of the Reiss Profile of Fundamental Goals and Motivational Sensitivities indicates the presence of aberrant motivation. Sensitivity theory further holds that aberrant motivation is a risk factor for the development of psychopathology. The higher the score on any single scale on the Reiss Profile and the greater the number of scales with high scores, the more aberrant is the person's motivation and the greater is the predicted probability that the person shows aberrant behavior now or will develop a mental disorder at some point in the future.

Person with Autism

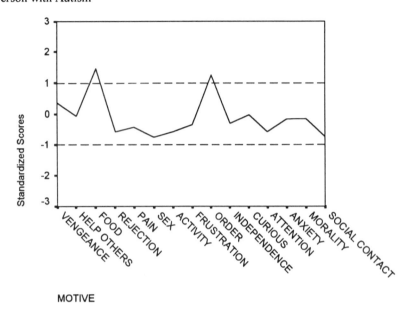

MOTIVE

Person with Mental Retardation and Major Depression

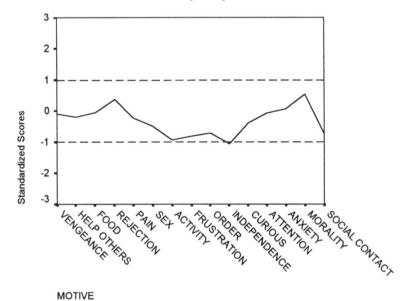

MOTIVE

FIG. 3.1. Reiss profile of two individuals with mental retardation (MR). The upper profile is from an adult with MR and autism and the lower profile is from an adult with MR and major depression.

Research is needed to empirically determine how high a score must be to indicate significant risk for aberrant behavior, but a minimum expectation would be more than 1.0 standard deviation. More likely, scores of about 1.5 to 2.0 standard deviations above norms would indicate significant risk for psychopathology. Research is also needed to verify the hypothesis that a high score on any Reiss motivation scale indicates risk for psychopathology. It may be that risk is predicted from high scores on only some of the Reiss scales. Furthermore, a high score on some scales may indicate risk for a particular category of psychopathology rather than risk for psychopathology generally. For example, high scores on the Anxiety Sensitivity Index (Peterson & Reiss, 1992) indicate increased risk for panic attacks (McNally, 1994; Schmidt, Lerew, & Jackson, 1997; Taylor, 1995; Telch & Harrington, 1994).

Why is aberrant motivation considered a risk factor for aberrant behavior? By definition, *aberrant motivation* implies strong desires for large amounts of reinforcement. In general, socially appropriate behavior does not produce the large amounts of reinforcement needed to gratify aberrant desires. On the contrary, socially inappropriate behavior may offer the best chance of obtaining a large quantity of reinforcement. For example, suppose that a man who craves social status believes that he needs a lot of money to get it. Because the man cannot become rich by going to work and earning a salary, he is tempted to resort to theft as his best chance of obtaining a large sum of money quickly. Although the odds may be high that theft will lead to a jail term, the person still may think that theft offers the best chance of becoming rich quickly.

Children seeking large amounts of adult attention may develop conduct problems as a means of gratifying this desire. In general, socially appropriate behavior leads to moderate amounts of attention, not high amounts. For children who crave high amounts of attention, inappropriate conduct may offer the best chance for obtaining what they want, even though the attention may be negative. Suppose that a psychologist were asked to identify a preschool child who shows no conduct problems today but who is likely to show such problems within 5 years. How should the psychologist proceed? According to sensitivity theory, the psychologist should ask the preschool teacher which child craves the most attention. Sooner or later this child might develop conduct problems as a means of obtaining a great deal of attention.

Researchers should conduct longitudinal studies to test the hypothesis that aberrant motivation is a risk factor for psychopathology. Aberrant motives can be measured in adolescents and perhaps childhood to predict psychopathology in adulthood. (Researchers may need to develop child motivation instruments to conduct this research, although the new Reiss instruments can be used with adolescents as young as age 12.) The significance of such research is that positive findings may offer clues to the causes of psychopathology. Furthermore, the prediction of risk improves early identification—an initial step in primary prevention.

Some evidence has been obtained supporting the hypothesis that aberrant motivation is associated with aberrant behavior. Table 3.3 shows the mean differences in standard scores on the Reiss Profile—MR/DD. The scores shown are the difference in means between two groups—a dual diagnosis group (both mental retardation and mental illness) and a group with mental retardation alone. The scores were significantly different on 13 of 15 fundamental motives, and all differences were in the direction of higher aberrant motivation for the dual diagnosis group. These data provide initial support for the concept of aberrant motivation. In interpreting these data, we need to keep in mind that these differences were obtained by averaging scores from people with various diagnostic conditions; even larger differences might be obtained if specific diagnostic conditions were examined.

TABLE 3.3

Differences Between Mean Standardized Scores: Scores From People With a Dual Diagnosis (Mental Retardation and Mental Illness: DD) (N = 596) Minus Scores From People With Mental Retardation Only (MR) (N = 345)

Scale	Mean Difference	$F(1,939)$	p
Attention	0.4	26.4	<.001
Curiosity	-0.3	17.1	<.001
Help others	-0.4	30.6	<.001
Independence	0.0	0.4	>.1
Morality	-0.5	52.1	<.001
Order	0.3	24.5	<.001
Social contact	-0.3	25.5	<.001
Vengeance	0.6	80.5	<.001
Activity	0.0	0.2	>.1
Food	0.4	18.9	<.001
Sex	0.2	10.1	<.002
Anxiety sensitivity	0.7	74.7	<.001
Frustration sensitivity	0.8	162.0	<.001
Pain sensitivity	0.2	8.3	<.03
Rejection sensitivity	0.3	18.9	<.001

Note. Shown are the 15 confirmed factors for the MR/DD instrument. As many as 13 of these factors have a corresponding factor on the self-report instrument (see Table 3.2). The main differences are these: The self-report instrument has scales for power and citizenship not on the MR/DD instrument. The MR/DD instrument has separate scales for anxiety, frustration, and pain sensitivity, whereas the self-report instrument has a single (combined) scale for these sensitivities.

Person Versus Environmental Determinants

The Reiss motivation instruments may be helpful in assessing the extent to which psychopathology is associated with factors in the person versus factors in the environment. To make such assessments, Reiss and Havercamp (1997) discussed the concept of aberrant environments. These environments do not provide opportunities to gratify ordinary motivational needs (Smull & Harrison, 1992). For example, when a father is uninterested in his daughter, the daughter cannot gratify her desire for an ordinary amount of acceptance. According to sensitivity theory, aberrant environments create risk for psychopathology because people resort to extreme strategies (aberrant behavior) to obtain modest amounts of reinforcement or they may protest or exhibit emotional behavior. For example, people who cannot gratify ordinary needs for acceptance may be at risk to become depressed.

Psychological intervention strategies should vary depending on the extent to which the problem is related to aberrant environments. When aberrant environments contribute significantly to aberrant behavior, the goal should be to change the environment or remove the person from the environment. The goal should not be to change the person. When aberrant motivation contributes significantly to the problem, psychotherapy, cognitive-behavior therapy, or pharmacotherapy may be needed to help the person adjust to environments. Future research is needed to evaluate the validity of the distinction between aberrant environment and aberrant motivation in making these strategic clinical decisions.

Many psychologists have recognized that aberrant behavior can be induced by aberrant environments. For example, many developmental psychologists have noted the effects of extreme family dysfunction on children's mental health. In the field of mental retardation, many observers have cited large congregate care facilities (institutions) as causes of aberrant behavior (Smull & Harrison, 1992). One strategy for addressing such situations is improving the environment (e.g., family therapy, efforts to improve institutional care); another is to remove the child or person (e.g., foster care, closure of institutions). Generally, therapists do not attempt to teach people to adjust to aberrant environments.

Preventing Therapy Relapse

Sensitivity theory holds that the level of aberrant motivation at the end of therapy is predictive of the durability and generalized nature of therapy outcomes. The higher the level of aberrant motivation at the end of therapy, the more likely is a future deterioration in the patient's clinical status. For example, researchers have found that anxiety sensitivity levels at the end of treatment for panic disorder predict future clinical status, including recurrence of spontaneous panic attacks (Jones & Barlow, 1991). This prediction may have special relevance for applied behavior analysis, where nondurable and nongeneralized treatment outcomes are common. Reiss and Havercamp (1997) argued that an integration of applied behavior analysis with sensitivity theory is essential to producing more durable and generalized treatment outcomes from applied behavior analysis. If applied behavior analysts wish to produce more durable and generalized treatment outcomes, they need to find some way to alter the motivational value of the reinforcers maintaining aberrant behavior as opposed to using highly motivating reinforcers to teach appropriate behavior.

The need to treat aberrant motivation applies to all clinical approaches, not just applied behavior analysis. When aberrant motivation is associated with mental disorder, drugs need to reduce the aberrant motivation to have general effectiveness. Cognitive therapy offers some of the most promising strategies for treating aberrant motivation because this approach may directly alter people's attitudes and beliefs about specific fundamental purposes in their lives. Future researchers should evaluate all therapies for their effects on aberrant motivation, with particular attention to the role of aberrant motivation in the probability of treatment relapse. Sensitivity theory holds that aberrant motives are difficult to change, although this is not to say that change is impossible. Motivational traits can be modified by a variety of processes, such as associative learning, cognitive restructuring, and psychoactive drugs.

CONCLUSIONS

Sensitivity theory suggests an enormous amount of new research on human motivation generally and on aberrant motivation specifically.

Sensitivity theorists analyze motivation into instrumental means (extrinsic motivation) and end purposes (intrinsic motivation). Although the number of instrumental motives is potentially limitless, the number of significant end purposes is small. Sensitivity theory is a call for research to identify significant end motives and study the role of such motives in psychopathology.

Sensitivity theory represents a unique combination of three approaches in the study of human motivation. First, sensitivity theory provides a comprehensive approach to the study of human motivation. This means that a number of significant motives are observed in a single investigation, as opposed to the piecemeal approach in which only one significant motive is examined in any given investigation. Second, sensitivity theory gives emphasis to motives as person-specific traits rather than as situation-specific states. For example, sensitivity theory is concerned with the study of gluttony (a future propensity for vigorous eating associated with a history of overeating) rather than the study of hunger (a future propensity for vigorous eating associated with recent deprivation of food). Third, sensitivity theory provides an empirical approach to the study of motivation. This means that standardized measures are used to study motivational traits, as opposed to anecdotal interviews, historical inquiries, or philosophical methods. Although other theories have incorporated one or two of these principles in the study of motivation, sensitivity theory may be unprecedented in combining all three.

Two psychometric instruments, the Reiss Profiles, have been developed to assess fundamental motives and test sensitivity theory. These are perhaps the first standardized instruments that provide a comprehensive assessment of the strength of various fundamental (intrinsic) motives. Factor analytic research on 2,548 people from diverse backgrounds has identified and confirmed 15 fundamental motives: curiosity, family, food, independence (self-reliance), honor (morality), physical exercise, order, sensitivity to rejection, sensation sensitivity, sex, social contact, social idealism, power, social status, and vengeance. Sensitivity theory holds that these end purposes motivate a significant amount of everyday behavior.

Essentially, the Reiss Profiles ask people the extent to which they like stimuli that are liked by virtually everybody and dislike stimuli that are disliked by virtually everybody. It is easy to appreciate why nobody has thought to do this in the past—there is a strong initial presumption that if everybody likes something, there seems to be little point in asking people if they also like it. However, the reality here is not what it seems to be at first look. Everybody likes food, but individual differences in appetite are such that some people overeat and others do not. Nearly everybody likes sex, but some people are hedonists and others are not. People dislike anxiety, but some people fear anxiety much more than others. There are enormous individual differences in the strength of attractions and aversions to universally motivating end purposes. Sensitivity theory suggests that researchers measure these individual differences and study their role in a variety of significant phenomena.

Sensitivity theory is a call for scientific research. An important purpose of any scientific theory is to highlight previously understudied issues, providing future researchers with a conceptual road map for generating new factual information. Because sensitivity theory offers an original perspective on human motivation, it suggests that a number of research questions may be more important than previously supposed or that certain aspects of these questions need a second look. For example, sensitivity theory encourages the following types of research:

1. Researchers can use the new Reiss instruments to develop motivational profiles of various diagnostic conditions.
2. Sensitivity theory has implications for longitudinal research in developmental psychopathology. The theory posits a host of new risk factors that may predict mental disorders in adulthood based on the presence of aberrant motivation in adolescents or children. Positive findings may facilitate early detection of certain mental disorders, which is an important step toward primary prevention.
3. Investigators should study the durability of treatment outcomes. To what extent does the level of aberrant motivation at the end of therapy predict the recurrence of aberrant behavior?
4. Sensitivity theory provides a basis for strengthening applied behavior analysis. The combined approach may lead to more effective clinical techniques for those populations for whom applied behavior analysis is still widely used, such as people with mental retardation. Furthermore, the integration of sensitivity theory and applied behavior analysis may provide a basis for re-building some bridges between this valuable approach and the larger field of clinical psychology.

REFERENCES

Aman, M. G. (1991). *Assessing psychopathology and behavior problems in persons with mental retardation: A review of available instruments.* Rockville, MD: U.S. Department of Health and Human Services.

Aman, M. G., Singh, N. N., Stewart, A. W., & Field, C. J. (1985). The Aberrant Behavior Checklist: A behavior rating scale for the assessment of treatment effects. *American Journal of Mental Deficiency, 89,* 492–502.

American Psychiatric Association. (1994). *Diagnostic and statistical manual of mental disorders* (4th ed.). Washington, DC: Author.

Bandura, A. (1977). Self-efficacy: Toward a unifying theory of behavioral change. *Psychological Review, 84,* 191–215.

Bandura, A. (1986). Fearful expectations and avoidant actions as coeffects on perceived self-efficacy. *American Psychologist, 41,* 1390–1391.

Berlyne, D. E. (1960). *Conflict, arousal and curiosity.* New York: McGraw-Hill.

Bihm, E. M., Poindexter, A. R., Kienlen, T., & Smith, B. L. (1992). Staff perceptions of reinforcer responsiveness and aberrant behavior in people with mental retardation. *Journal of Autism and Developmental Disorders, 22,* 83–93.

Bradburn, N. M. (1969). *The structure of psychological well-being.* Chicago: Aldine.

Carr, E. G. (1977). The motivation of self-injurious behavior: A review of some hypotheses. *Psychological Bulletin, 84,* 800–816.

Deci, E. L. (1975). *Intrinsic motivation*. New York: Plenum.

Dweck, C. S. (1992). The study of goals in psychology. *Psychological Science, 3*, 165–167.

Ellis, A. (1993). Fundamentals of rational-emotive therapy for the 1990s. In. W. Dryden & L. K. Hill (Eds.), *Innovations in rational-emotive therapy* (pp. 1–32). Newbury Park, CA: Sage.

Freud, S. (1916/1963). *Introductory lectures on psycho-analysis*. London: Hogarth Press. (Original work published 1916)

Hebb, D. O. (1946). On the nature of fear. *Psychological Review, 53*, 259–276.

Holloway, W., & McNally, R. J. (1987). Effects of anxiety sensitivity on the response to hyperventilation. *Journal of Abnormal Psychology, 96*, 330–334.

Jackson, D. N. (1985). *Personality Research Form*. Ontario: Research Psychologist Press.

Jones, J. C., & Barlow, D. H. (1991, November). *The relationship between fear of fear/anxiety, diagnosis, and treatment outcomes*. Paper presented at the annual meeting of the Association for Advancement of Behavior Therapy, New York.

Keller, F. S., & Schoenfeld, W. N. (1950). *Principles of psychology*. New York: Appleton-Century-Crofts.

Kipfer, B. A. (Ed.). (1993). *Roget's 21st century thesaurus in dictionary form*. New York: Dell.

Klein, D. F. (1987). Depression and anhedonia. In D. C. Clark & J. Fawcett (Eds.), *Anhedonia and affect deficit states* (pp. 1–14). New York: PMA Publishing.

Lepper, M. R., Greene, D., & Nisbett, R. E. (1973). Undermining children's intrinsic interest with extrinsic rewards: A test of the overjustification hypothesis. *Journal of Personality and Social Psychology, 28*, 129–137.

Maslow, A. H. (1954). *Motivation and personality*. New York: Harper.

McNally, R. J. (1994). *Panic disorder: A critical analysis*. New York: Guilford.

Murray, H. A. (1938). *Explorations in personality*. New York: Oxford University Press.

Murray, H. A. (1943). *Manual of the Thematic Apperception Test*. New York: Oxford University Press.

Peterson, R. A., & Reiss, S. (1992). *Anxiety Sensitivity Index manual* (2nd ed.). Worthington, OH: International Diagnostic Systems.

Reiss, S. (1997). Trait anxiety: It's not what you think it is. *Journal of Anxiety Disorders, 11*, 201–214.

Reiss, S., & Havercamp, S. H. (1996). The sensitivity theory of motivation: Implications for psychopathology. *Behaviour Research and Therapy, 34*, 621–632.

Reiss, S., & Havercamp, S. H. (1997). Sensitivity theory and mental retardation: Why functional analysis is not enough. *American Journal of Mental Deficiency, 101*, 553–556.

Reiss, S., & Havercamp, S. M. (1998). Toward a comprehensive assessment of fundamental motivation: Factor structure of the Reiss profiles. *Psychological Assessment, 10*, 97–106.

Reiss, S., & McNally, R. J. (1985). Expectancy model of fear. In S. Reiss & R. R. Bootzin (Eds.), *Theoretical issues in behavior therapy* (pp. 107–121). San Diego, CA: Academic Press.

Reiss, S., Peterson, R.A., Gursky, D. M., & McNally, R. J. (1986). Anxiety sensitivity, anxiety frequency, and the prediction of fearfulness. *Behaviour Research and Therapy, 24*, 1–8.

Reiss, S., & Sushinsky, L. W. (1975). Overjustification, competing responses, and the acquisition of intrinsic interest. *Journal of Personality and Social Psychology, 31*, 1106–1115.

Rogers, C. R. (1961). *On becoming a person*. Boston: Houghton Mifflin.

Russell, B. (1945). *History of Western philosophy*. New York: Simon & Shuster.

Ryff, C. D. (1989). Happiness is everything, or is it? Explorations on the meaning of psychological well-being. *Journal of Personality and Social Psychology, 57*, 1069–1081.

Schmidt, N. B., Lerew, D. R., & Jackson, R.L. (1997). The role of anxiety sensitivity in the pathogenesis of panic: Prospective evaluation of spontaneous panic attacks during acute stress. *Journal of Abnormal Psychology, 106*, 355–364.

Smull, M. W., & Harrison, S. B. (1992). *Supporting people with severe reputations in the community*. Alexandria, VA: National Association of State Mental Retardation Program Directors.

Taylor, S. (1995). Anxiety sensitivity: Theoretical perspectives and recent findings. *Behaviour Research and Therapy, 33*, 243–258.

Thorndike, E. L. (1911). *Animal intelligence: Experimental studies*. New York: Macmillan.

Telch, M. J., & Harrington, P. J. (1994, November). *The role of anxiety sensitivity and expectedness of arousal in mediating emotional response to inhalation of 35% carbon dioxide*. Paper presented at the annual meeting of the Association for Advancement of Behavior Therapy, San Diego, CA.

Zigler, E., & Burack, J. A. (1989). Personality development and the dually diagnosed person. *Research in Developmental Disabilities, 10*, 225–240.

Zubin, J., Eron, L. D., & Schumer, F. (1965). *An experimental approach to projective techniques*. New York: Wiley.

II

PSYCHOMETRIC FOUNDATIONS

4

Measuring Anxiety Sensitivity

Rolf A. Peterson
Kirsten Plehn
George Washington University

The concept of anxiety sensitivity (AS) was first described by Reiss and McNally (1985). It was later elaborated by Reiss (1987, 1991) to specify various theoretical predictions. Theoretically, AS is predictive of behavior and the development of anxiety reactions in all disorders, which, in part, involve escalating anxiety or escape from or avoidance of AS as part of the pathology. Therefore, AS predicts behaviors that involve escape from and avoidance of anxiety symptoms in a variety of situations and disorders (Reiss, 1991). The instrument used to measure AS should be related to behaviors and adjustment in all disorders or subtypes of disorders in which anxiety arousal, high physiological arousal, or the presence of strong negative, anxiety-like physiological sensation (e.g., pain sensations) is a component. Thus, measurement of AS needs to be accomplished by an instrument that is predictive across the range of behaviors and disorders that may involve an overreaction to anxiety-like symptoms, escape from anxiety arousal, and avoidance of anxiety arousal.

The Anxiety Sensitivity Index (ASI; Peterson & Reiss, 1992) was developed to test anxiety sensitivity theory. The first published use of the ASI was in 1986 involving a study that tested the prediction that the number of fears a person holds would be correlated with his or her level of anxiety sensitivity (Reiss, Peterson, Gursky, & McNally, 1986). Since then, a large literature has developed that relates the ASI to a range of anxiety disorders. The ASI has also been used to predict the development of anxiety and panic attacks; ASI scores have been found to be correlated with maladaptive behaviors and poor adjustment in such disorders as chronic pain and drug and alcohol abuse. This extensive literature is discussed in detail in the other chapters of this book (see chaps. 6, 10, 12, 13).

Prior to the development of the ASI, Chambless, Caputo, Bright, and Gallagher (1984) developed a set of similar measures to measure fear of anxiety sensations. Two measures—the Body Sensations Questionnaire (BSQ) and Agoraphobic Cognitions Questionnaire (ACQ)—were developed within the context of the theory of fear of fear (Goldstein & Chambless, 1978). AS and fear of fear are similar concepts. However, unlike anxiety sensitivity theory (Reiss, 1991), which postulates that individuals differ in sensitivity prior to the experience of panic attacks, Goldstein and Chambless (1978) postulated that high fear of fear resulted from the panic experience and could lead to the development of agoraphobia (Goldstein & Chambless, 1978). Although based on two different theories in terms of the development of anxiety disorders, the ASI and the combination of the BSQ and ACQ are the primary measures of anxiety sensitivity or fear of fear.

The ASI, BSQ, and ACQ have received much attention as measures of beliefs associated with panic and agoraphobia. The National Institute of Mental Health Consensus Development Conference on the Treatment of Panic Disorder recommended the ASI and the combined measures of the ACQ and BSQ as measures of the fear of body sensations component of anticipatory anxiety (Shear & Maser, 1994). The fear of body sensations associated with anxiety was considered an essential aspect in the assessment of panic disorder. Measurement of beliefs about the negative consequences of anxiety is important to the assessment of panic as well as the assessment of any disorder involving anxiety arousal and/or high avoidance of anxiety arousal.

The goal of this chapter is to review the psychometric properties and measurement issues (norms, reliability, and factor structure) of the measures of AS and related concepts. Factor-analytic studies are not reviewed in depth because they are reviewed in chapter 5. Validity studies are not discussed in detail because other chapters in this book deal with a range of concurrent validity, predictive laboratory challenge validity, and general predictive validity studies of the ASI and related measures. The primary focus of the chapter is on the ASI, the most commonly used measure of AS and the most studied measure of AS in terms of psychometric properties.

ANXIETY SENSITIVITY INDEX

The ASI is a 16-item measure asking about the extent to which a person finds anxiety-related sensations to be fearful or catastrophic in outcome (Peterson & Reiss, 1992). Items are presented in Table 4.1. The items are answered on a

TABLE 4.1

Items of the Anxiety Sensitivity Index

1. It is important to me not to appear nervous.
2. When I cannot keep my mind on a task, I worry that I might be going crazy.
3. It scares me when I feel "shaky" (trembling).
4. It scares me when I feel faint.
5. It is important to me to stay in control of my emotions.
6. It scares me when my heart beats rapidly.
7. It embarrasses me when my stomach growls.
8. It scares me when I am nauseous.
9. When I notice that my heart is beating rapidly, I worry I might have a heart attack.
10. It scares me when I become short of breath.
11. When my stomach is upset, I worry that I might be seriously ill.
12. It scares me when I am unable to keep my mind on a task.
13. Other people notice when I feel shaky.
14. Unusual body sensations scare me.
15. When I am nervous, I worry that I might be mentally ill.
16. It scares me when I am nervous.

Note. Reprinted for academic purposes only with permission of the International Diagnostic Systems Publishing Corporation. Not to be reproduced for clinical use.

five-choice format ranging from 0 *very little* to 4 *very much*. The language level is geared to be readable to most high school students.

Most ASI items deal with fear of physical sensations (sensations such as feeling shaky or faint, experiencing a rapid heartbeat, stomach growling, being nauseous or short of breath, and unusual body sensations). Some items deal with beliefs about mental control (effects of being nervous, inability to concentrate) and the effects of nervousness being observed by others (worry that others will notice nervousness or shakiness). In other words, the items focus on being scared of, worried about, or believing in highly negative consequences in regard to the range of experiences associated with high anxiety or anxiety-like symptoms.

Norms

A range of normative data is now available on the ASI. Normative data reported in the 1992 manual (Peterson & Reiss, 1992) included 4,517 subjects gathered from a combination of 12 studies. For the general population, the overall mean was 19.01 with a standard deviation of 9.11. Individual studies cited in the manual report normative sample means varying from 14.2 to 22.5. For diagnostic groups, typically the highest mean scores are associated with agoraphobia (Stoler & McNally, 1991). Panic disorder and panic disorder with agoraphobia obtain ASI mean scores significantly higher than generalized anxiety and social phobia groups (Taylor, Koch, & McNally, 1992a). For U.S. samples reported by Peterson and Reiss (1992), the mean scores for panic disorder with agoraphobia ranged from 32.1 to 46.7 and mean scores for panic disorder ranged from 30.5 to 36.4. Mean scores for Vietnam veterans with posttraumatic stress disorder (PTSD) ranged from 30.6 to 32.1; the mean for social phobia was 24.9 and the mean for specific phobia was 16.1.

Karp and Peterson (1997) reported a mean ASI score of 29.2 (*SD* = 13.2) for a sample of 100 male veterans receiving treatment for alcohol problems. Surprisingly, the mean for alcoholics is quite similar to that reported for panic patients. Further, Asmundson and Norton (1995) reported a mean ASI score of 15.2 (*SD* = 8.6) for a sample of disabled patients with chronic pain, which is similar to the normative sample mean. Sufficient sample size for norms for normative college samples and anxiety disorder samples are available, but more data from other clinical and medical populations need to be obtained before cutoff scores for classification can be developed.

Sex Differences

Findings have been inconsistent regarding sex differences in ASI scores. As reported in the manual (Peterson & Reiss, 1992), when samples were collapsed to compare sex differences, females obtained a mean of 19.8 (*N* = 1,974) compared with 17.6 for males (*N* = 1,762). Stewart, Taylor, and Baker (1997) compared the ASI scores for 528 female and 290 male undergraduates from Dalhousie University and found significant sex differences (female mean = 17.4, *SD* = 9.4; male mean = 14.6, *SD* = 8.7). Thus, among general college populations, which was composed of the majority of subjects in the original normative data, it appears females generally score slightly but significantly higher than males on the ASI. This suggests that future research with nonclinical samples should control for or assess the effects of sex differences when ASI scores are being related to other measures or defined as the independent or dependent variable in the research design.

There may also be sex differences across the factors (subdomains) of the ASI. Stewart et al. (1997) conducted a hierarchical factor analysis that resulted in a general anxiety sensitivity higher order factor and three lower order factors (representing physical concerns, mental incapacitation concerns, and social concerns). The factor structure was the same for females and males. Females obtained significantly higher scores on the physical concerns factor, but no sex differences were found on the other factors. Thus, for the total ASI score, college females may score higher than males because the former score higher on items assessing perceived negative outcomes of physical sensations.

Blais et al. (1997) examined the scores for a combined sample of 340 psychiatric outpatients and 50 college students. The psychiatric outpatients included participants with the diagnosis of panic disorder, major depression, or social phobia. For this sample, Blais et al. (1997) found the ASI had a four-factor structure. Furthermore, they found that women scored significantly higher on the factor that appears to measure the belief that AS will make them worry they are mentally ill. Thus, in contrast to findings from the Stewart et al. (1997) sample of college students, the Blais et al. clinical sample suggested that the sex difference in ASI scores was due to beliefs that anxiety symptoms lead to mental illness.

In summary, the ASI factor structure is essentially the same for males and females, although there may be sex differences in mean scores on some of the factors. These sex differences have not been demonstrated to influence the ability of the ASI total score to classify or predict criteria outcomes. Until further evidence is available, analysis by sex as well as total group is recommended when using the total score or factor scores to predict outcomes.

Norms for Special Groups and Conditions

Normative Samples.   Schmidt, Lerew, and Jackson (1997) examined whether scores on the ASI predict the occurrence of panic attacks during basic training at the U.S. Air Force Academy. For their group of 1,401 cadets, the mean ASI score prior to basic training was 4.0 (SD = 2.9). This is an extremely low mean score compared with the mean total score for normative college samples (cf. Peterson & Reiss, 1992). It suggests that if the ASI is used with samples that are self-selected and screened for possible psychiatric problems, then general normative data for classification may be inappropriate. Military cadets, fire fighters, and police may be groups in which people even moderately high in AS are unlikely to seek membership. Additionally, situations that involve screening for membership or employment may result in participants purposely denying problems with AS in an effort to improve their presentation. It is unlikely that scores were suppressed in the normative samples insofar as individuals completed the ASI anonymously and therefore had little motivation to alter their answers. Despite the differences from the norm group, a low mean group score does not mean anxiety sensitivity will not be predictive. As Schmidt et al. (1997) reported, ASI scores predicted panic attacks, anxiety symptoms, functional impairment, and disability among the cadets during the 5-week basic training experience (see chap. 10). Thus, it appears that, within groups with a low mean ASI score, the ASI is still predictive of anxiety and panic.

Medical Patients.   Asmundson and Norton (1995) reported that their chronic pain patients had a mean ASI score of 15.2 (*SD* = 8.6). Although this suggests a normal level of AS, classification of the sample into high, medium, and low ASI groups revealed that the high ASI group had significantly more negative reactions to pain than the medium and low AS groups. Likewise, Carr, Lehrer, Rausch, and Hochron (1994) reported an ASI mean of 17.2 (*SD* = 7.9) for an asthmatic sample, which is in the normal range. When Carr et al. (1994) compared asthmatics with panic versus those without panic, the ASI discriminated among the groups. Thus, with medical patient samples, although mean ASI score may fall within the normal range, comparisons between high and low ASI groups may provide important information regarding psychological and behavioral functioning.

Cultural and Language Effects.   ASI means have been reported for several diagnostic groups and normative samples from European populations. Sandin, Chorot, and McNally (1996) reported scores for a Spanish version of the ASI that was administered to normal and anxiety-disordered samples. The reported means (and standard deviations) were as follows: panic disorder 32.8 (*SD* = 10.7), generalized anxiety disorder 19.7 (*SD* = 10.1), simple phobia 14.6 (*SD* = 5.4), and normal controls 8.2 (*SD* = 5.1). For an Italian version of the ASI, Saviotti et al. (1991) found the means (and standard deviations) were as follows: panic disorder with agoraphobia 31.5 (*SD* = 13.5) and normal controls 11.2 (*SD* = 6.4). In both studies, scores for panic-disordered patients were at the lower end of the expected mean score range for panic disorders samples from the United States and Canada. Similarly, scores for normal controls were at the lower end of the mean range reported for normals from the United States and Canada (Peterson & Reiss, 1992). The normative samples obtained by Sandin et al. and Saviotti et al. may have been uniquely healthy samples; both were composed of hospital or university staff and therefore may not be representative of the adult populations of Spain and Italy (Sandin et al., 1996; Saviotti et al., 1991). These differences may also be due to the effects of translation, language, and cultural differences. Results of studies using translated versions of the ASI with European samples highlight the need to develop norms that are language and country specific. This is true for diagnostic groups as well as normative samples.

Racial/Ethnic Differences.   At this time, insufficient data are available to delineate any differences in norms for U.S. racial and ethnic groups. Additional normative information is needed to determine whether different racial/ethnic groups tend to score higher or lower as a group on the ASI.

Reliability

Internal Consistency. With college student samples, internal consistency (Cronbach's alpha) for the ASI total scale has been reported at .88 (Peterson & Heilbronner, 1987) and .82 (Telch, Shermis, & Lucas, 1989), and .84 for spider-phobic college students (Taylor, Koch, & Crockett, 1991). For mixed normative and psychiatric samples, alphas of .87 (Cox, Endler, Norton, & Swinson, 1991), .91 (Taylor et al., 1991), and .88 (Blais et al., 1997) have been reported. This is consistent with past reports of good inter-item correlations (Reiss et al., 1986) and a reported Guttman split-half reliability coefficient of .85 (Peterson & Heilbronner, 1987). The consistently high internal reliability reported in the literature suggests the ASI is an internally consistent measure.

Based on factor analysis, Zinbarg, Barlow, and Brown (1997) reported that ASI items had moderate-to-high loadings on a general anxiety sensitivity factor (range of: .33–.66), except the item "it embarrasses me when my stomach growls," which loaded .19. Zinbarg et al. (1997) concluded that the ASI total score is an interpretable measure of a general factor of AS. They suggested that the lower order factors labeled *physical concerns, mental incapacitation concerns,* and *social concerns* are also replicable and provide additional interpretative information. In terms of internal reliability, the presence of the general AS factor and relatively high correlations between lower order factors (Zinbarg et al., 1997) suggests good internal reliability for the scale as a whole.

In contrast to these findings, Blais et al. (1997) reported that, based on adjusted item-total correlations, three ASI items fail to show an adequate level of correlation (i.e., "It is important to me not to appear nervous," "It is important to me to stay in control of my emotions," "It embarrasses me when my stomach growls"). Blais et al. suggested these items not be scored as part of the ASI total score. These conclusions may reflect the sample makeup in the Blais et al. study. Of the 340 psychiatric outpatients, 152 had a diagnosis of panic disorder and 142 had a diagnosis of depression. Only 46 patients had a diagnosis of social phobia and the 50 controls were college students. The overwhelming presence of panic disorder and depression may have reduced the correlation of the two emotional control items with the total scale. The removal of these items may restrict the measure in terms of its usefulness with the general AS dimension.

Additionally, other studies have found these three items correlated with the total scale (see Taylor, Koch, McNally, & Crockett, 1992b; Zinbarg et al., 1997). Further research is needed before investigators and clinicians should exclude ASI items, except in the case of experimental comparison of scores in research projects. Although the item "It embarrasses me when my stomach growls" is consistently poorly or unrelated to the higher order AS factor and secondary factors (Blais et al., 1997; Taylor et al., 1992b; Zinbarg et al., 1997), it should be left in the total score until new norms developed without the item are available. For clinical purposes, it can be noted that the item is probably not a good measure of AS.

In summary, available research indicates that the ASI has good internal consistency. This is true both in terms of the total scale and factor-analytically derived subscales (including the higher order anxiety sensitivity dimension). Although factor scores may provide additional information in some cases, this issue needs further research before factor scores are recommended for clinical use. The total score provides a broad-band measure of AS and should continue to be used in research and clinical practice. Other chapters in this book provide strong evidence of the predictive and group discrimination criterion validity of the ASI (e.g., chaps. 6 and 10).

Test–Retest Reliability.   Scores on the ASI appear to be quite stable over time. In a sample of college students, Reiss et al. (1986) reported a 2-week test–retest correlation of .75. Maller and Reiss (1992) report a 3-year test–retest correlation of .71 for college students. Schmidt et al. (1997) reported a 5-week test–retest correlation of .65, although participants had participated in 5 weeks of highly stressful military training during the interim. Research results suggest the ASI is a highly stable measure of AS, which is consistent with the view that AS level is a highly stable, enduring characteristic of individuals.

Clinical Use of the ASI Factors

The factor structure of the ASI and the concept of AS as a single dimension or constellation of separate factors is discussed in detail in chapter 5. It appears that the best factor fit for the ASI is a combination of a general AS factor with three lower order factors. The lower order factors identified by Zinbarg et al. (1997) were labeled *physical concerns* (e.g., "It scares me when my heart beats rapidly," "It scares me when I am short of breath"), *mental incapacitation concerns* (e.g., "When I cannot keep my mind on a task, I worry that I might be going crazy"), and *social concerns* (e.g., "It is important to me not to appear nervous").

The formal use of proposed ASI factors depends on the extent to which future research can demonstrate that the factor(s) provide additional information and validity above and beyond the total score. For clinical use, it is recommended that the total score be used for screening and overall evaluation, but that the answers to particular factor or individual items be used to help design treatment programs.

Any particularly strong negative beliefs about anxiety consequences need to be addressed in therapy to assure that any core problem with AS is changed.

Distinctions Between the ASI and Anxiety Measures

There has been an ongoing debate on the difference or lack thereof between AS and anxiety. A pertinent question is whether the ASI measures AS as distinct from anxiety (e.g., Lilienfeld, 1996; Lilienfeld, Jacob, & Turner, 1989; Lilienfeld, Turner, & Jacob, 1993, 1996; McNally, 1989, 1996; Reiss, 1991, 1997; Taylor, 1995a, 1995b, 1996). We do not discuss the issue of theoretical differences between AS and anxiety, because that is discussed in other chapters (e.g., see chaps. 1, 2, and 7). However, we comment on the ASI as a measure distinct from traditional anxiety measures, especially the State–Trait Anxiety Inventory (STAI; Spielberger, 1983).

One important measurement issue is the relation between anxiety measures such as the STAI and the ASI. Certainly the content of the items are different between the two measures. The STAI addresses the presence of anxiety symptoms, whereas the ASI asks about worry and negative consequences of anxiety symptoms. One indicator of the extent to which the measures can be said to measure the same variable is the degree of correlation between measures. Reiss (1991) reported that the correlations between trait anxiety measures and the ASI, across 11 different samples, had R^2s ranging from 0 to .36. In other words, the measures tended to share a third or less of their variance. This level of association between measures strongly suggests that trait anxiety measures and the ASI measure distinct variables.

Challenge studies using such techniques as CO_2-induced panic indicate that ASI scores are more predictive of panic outcome than trait anxiety level and history of panic (McNally, 1989; Taylor, 1996). For example, Telch and Harrington (1994) demonstrated that ASI scores predicted CO_2-induced panic in nonclinical subjects with no previous history of panic. Moreover, Schmidt et al. (1997) found that ASI scores predicted panic attacks during basic military training, even when controlling for previous panic attacks and trait anxiety (see chap. 10). The finding that ASI scores predict panic above and beyond trait anxiety in reaction to real-life acute stress strongly suggests that the ASI measures something distinct from anxiety level. Further, when the ASI-by-STAI interaction was entered in the regression to predict panic, after entering the ASI and STAI, the interaction failed to account for significant variance (Schmidt et al., 1997). This finding is consistent with Taylor's (1995a) view that ASI and STAI scores do not interact to predict common fears.

The evidence to date demonstrates that the ASI and trait measures of anxiety assess distinct variables, which in turn strongly suggests that the concept of anxiety sensitivity is distinct from that of anxiety. Furthermore, research clearly supports that the ASI measures the theoretical concept of AS.

Clinical Use of the ASI

The primary recommended use of the ASI is as a screening measure for AS among self- or other-referred clients who may have a highly negative set of beliefs about the consequences of anxiety. The measure has strong validity in relation to identifying belief systems relevant to panic disorder, agoraphobia, and other anxiety disorders. Additionally, high scores may indicate AS problems among other disorders such as chronic pain or alcoholic patients. It is important to identify high levels of AS in the evaluation and treatment of all clients to determine whether AS is an important component of the individual's functioning, and thus an important focus of treatment.

In terms of cutoff scores for self-referred individuals with anxiety problems, a score of 25 or above suggests possible problems with AS; a score of 30 and above may indicate a diagnosis of panic disorder, agoraphobia, PTSD, or other severe psychopathology. To be cautious, it is suggested that, for all individuals receiving scores of 25 or greater, a detailed interview about the catastrophic beliefs of particular anxiety-like symptoms be part of the follow-up diagnostic evaluation of the client.

Clinicians may also want to review the individual items on the ASI or its factors (physical, mental, and social concerns) to determine the focus of the interview. The information obtained from the ASI and follow-up interviews will be particularly important in developing treatment strategies, particularly in developing treatment strategies for reducing AS.

In rare cases, the ASI may not accurately reflect the client's level of AS, even in self-referred clients. In a case seen at George Washington University's Department of Psychology Clinic, a self-referred client sought exposure treatment for multiple phobias. The client reported that previous exposure therapy had resolved the problem, but that the positive effects were now disappearing. This client received a score of 19 on the ASI—a score consistent with a phobia diagnosis and indicating no significant AS problems. After the client refused to elicit anxiety-provoking thoughts during imaginal practice and would only endure therapist-assisted in vivo exposure for brief periods of time, it began to appear that a high level of AS was present.

We discovered that the client had learned a sort of *mental freezing* coping response in which she would make her mind go blank to be unaware of the anxiety-arousing cues. It became clear that she wanted training in being able to *freeze* and not be aware of the anxiety-arousing situation rather than actual exposure to anxiety. The client later reported extremely strong beliefs that anxiety arousal (e.g., heart beating too fast, light headedness) would result in a heart attack or total loss of physical control resulting in self-injury. This case illustrates that a relatively low ASI score may signal problems when a strong motivation exists to avoid anxiety arousal even in therapy. Thus, in all cases in which high avoidance exists, the clinician must constantly evaluate AS through interviews and during the therapy process, even if the ASI does not indicate AS problems.

Clinically, the ASI would seem to produce few false positives in a self-referred population. The frequency of false negatives has not been examined and must be evaluated carefully by the clinician. As mentioned earlier, special group and cultural norms are needed before cutoffs for AS problems are developed. With some groups such as military cadets, a relatively low score may signal problems (Schmidt et al., 1997), which may need to be addressed by interventions to reduce AS.

The ASI has been used successfully to assess acute treatment effects (i.e., changes from pre- to posttreatment) and is recommend for therapy effectiveness research with anxiety and anxiety-related disorders. Clinically, clients reporting high ASI scores at the end of treatment should receive additional treatment to reduce AS. Little data are available on the use of the ASI to predict relapse, but high ASI scores at the end of treatment would suggest high vulnerability to future anxiety-arousing situations (high stressors) and possible development of new problems or relapse. This would appear to be especially true among groups with high AS (e.g., panic and agoraphobia; see chap. 14). Overall, the ASI appears to be an adequate measure of AS for diagnostic and treatment evaluation use.

NEW MEASURES OF ANXIETY SENSITIVITY

Taylor and his colleagues have been involved in developing and testing new, longer measures of AS. Taylor and Cox (in press) suggested that factor-analytic studies of the ASI may not adequately reveal all the lower order factors because16 items may not be sufficient to measure all the factors. The Anxiety Sensitivity Profile (ASP), a 60-item measure that includes items similar to the ASI, contains groups of 10 items to measure six previously identified domains. These domains represent fears of the following symptoms: cardiovascular, respiratory, gastrointestinal, publicly observable anxiety reactions, dissociative and neurological symptoms, and cognitive dyscontrol. An exploratory factor analysis on a sample of 349 college students indicated a single higher order factor with four lower order factors, each of which contain unique variance (Taylor & Cox, in press). The lower order factors were named *fear of respiratory distress, fear of cognitive dyscontrol, fear of gastrointestinal symptoms,* and *fear of cardiac symptoms.*

A second new measure is the revised Anxiety Sensitivity Index (ASI–R; Cox, Taylor, Borger, Fuentes, & Ross, 1996). This measure includes 10 of the original ASI items along with 26 additional items, which were written to measure the same domains as the ASP. Taylor and Cox (1997) conducted an exploratory factor analysis of ASI–R responses from 155 psychiatric outpatients. Results indicate a four-factor structure similar to the ASP, except that a *fear of publicly observable anxiety reactions* factor emerged instead of the *gastrointestinal* factor reported for the ASP. Each of the four factors was significantly correlated with measures of anxiety and depression, with the *cognitive dyscontrol* factor correlating most highly with depression. Panic-disordered patients scored higher on each factor, compared with patients with other anxiety disorders and patients with nonanxiety disorders (e.g., mood disorders). This suggests that the factors are discriminating disorders as expected and consistent with discriminations provided by the ASI.

The ASP and ASI–R need further factor-analytic studies with normative and clinical populations as well as studies of their reliability and validity before their utility can be assessed. The expansion of items written to measure domains that have been indicated as present in the ASI, but not always factorially demonstrated in the original scale, may be able to provide a more comprehensive assessment of the factors involved in AS. As research on additional AS measures develops, one important question for these new measures will be whether they have utility (e.g., predictive ability) above and beyond the ASI.

FEAR OF FEAR MEASURES

The Agoraphobic Cognitions Questionnaire (ACQ) is a 14-item scale containing items that assess "what the person thinks they will do when anxious" (e.g., "I am going to throw up," "I will not be able to control myself;" Chambless et al., 1984). The items are conceptualized to assess six behavioral/social outcomes (e.g., to act foolishly or hurt someone) and eight physiological outcomes (e.g., to throw up or have a heart attack). The 14-item scale was derived after a series of additions and deletions from an initial test scale. Chambless et al. (1984) reported that scores on the ACQ are stable over an average 8-day test–retest interval, $r = .86$, and that the ACQ has adequate internal consistency (Cronbach's $\alpha = .80$). An orthogonal factor analysis indicated that items generally loaded on the two expected factors of behavioral/social and physiological consequences.

The Body Sensations Questionnaire (BSQ) is a 17-item scale that assesses fear of various physiological anxiety reactions. The reported alpha was .87 and the test–retest reliability was $r = .67$ (during a retest interval with a median of 31 days) (Chambless et al., 1984).

Moderate correlations were obtained between the ACQ and the Mobility Inventory (.21), Beck Depression Inventory (.38), and the trait version of the STAI (.35). For the BSQ, the respective correlations were .17, .36, and .21. The BSQ and ACQ were correlated .34 for a sample of 95 agoraphobic clients and .67 for a normal sample. The low correlation between the BSQ and ACQ within the agoraphobic sample is inconsistent with the notion that fear of body sensations and beliefs of dangerousness about such sensations are highly associated and are related components of the same AS dimension (Taylor, 1995a, 1995b). Chambless et al. (1984) suggested the two scales provide independent information, but these authors did not comment on how the scales may be related to or form components of a single *fear of fear* dimension. Both scales significantly discriminated between clinical and normal samples, and both measures showed highly significant changes with treatment (Chambless et al., 1984).

In a second study, Chambless and Gracely (1989) administered the ACQ and BSQ to 271 outpatients with diagnoses of agoraphobia with panic, panic disorder, generalized anxiety disorder, social phobia, obsessive–compulsive disorder, or depression. Agoraphobics scored significantly higher on the BSQ than all other groups. The ACQ scores were also significantly higher for all clinical groups as compared with normals, but surprisingly agoraphobics were not significantly different from other diagnostic groups. Both the ACQ and BSQ were significantly related to self-reported avoidance behavior even after trait anxiety was partialed out.

A third major study on the ACQ and BSQ was carried out by Arrindell (1993a) on a sample of 47 patients with agoraphobia (with or without panic disorder). The participants were in a controlled clinical trial and were assessed over a 3-month treatment-free interval. The 3-month test–retest correlation was .79 for the total ACQ, .85 for the Social/Behavioral Concerns subscale, and .81 for the Physical Concerns subscale. For the BSQ the test-retest correlation was .92. These results show high stability among diagnosed patients who do not receive treatment. Also, scores on the ACQ and BSQ at the first assessment point predicted avoidance behavior 3 months later, even when controlling for scores at the first assessment point on measures of avoidance, neuroticism, and anxiety/panic. Thus, the scales demonstrated predictive power of future avoidant behavior among agoraphobic patients.

Using confirmatory factor analysis, Arrindell (1993b) found support for the combined ACQ/BSQ as a three-factor structure, with the factors corresponding to the BSQ and two ACQ subscales. Because Arrindell did not test other models, it is not known whether a higher order or general AS factor was present (Arrindell, 1993b). The correlations reported by Chambless et al. (1984) suggest that, among agoraphobic patients, the ACQ and BSQ assess relatively unrelated dimensions of fear of fear.

Schmidt and Telch (1994) studied the effects of hyperventilation in nonclinical college students using the BSQ. High and low BSQ score groups were formed. The high BSQ group showed a greater subjective fear and reported more physical symptoms during hyperventilation than the low BSQ group. This result is similar to the results of biological challenge studies using the ASI to classify groups as high or low AS. Additionally, when Schmidt, Lerew, and Trakowski (1997) used the BSQ as their measure of AS, they found it was related to level of body vigilance. Further, the pretreatment BSQ was related to changes in body vigilance post-treatment. Thus, the BSQ, as a measure of AS, has produced results consistent with AS theory (Reiss, 1991), when AS has been defined by the fear of physical symptoms and body sensations.

The studies reviewed suggest that the ACQ and BSQ scores are strongly associated with agoraphobic beliefs and behavior. In effect, the measures appear to measure the belief system that is characteristic of agoraphobic patients and adds to the understanding of agoraphobia. What remains unknown is the extent to which the ACQ and BSQ can predict future agoraphobic behavior (in patients who currently have panic disorder without agoraphobia) and whether these scales predict naturally occurring or experimentally inducted anxiety and panic attacks among normal samples. Schmidt and Telch's (1994) study provides initial evidence that the BSQ can predict reactions to arousal induced by biological challenges administered to college students.

At this time, the ACQ and BSQ are known to measure beliefs relevant to agoraphobia, but more evidence is needed to determine whether these scales measure the full range of AS beliefs, including those found in the general population. More data are needed on diagnostic groups and normal samples to provide norms (e.g., means and standard deviations) that could be used for diagnostic classification.

Clinical Use of the ACQ and BSQ

Both the ACQ and BSQ have demonstrated validity as measures of reported beliefs during anxiety and fear of physical symptoms among agoraphobic patients. As part of the overall assessment of agoraphobic and panic patients, the ACQ and BSQ can be used to assess beliefs and fears. The measures also appear to be appropriate measures of pre-and posttreatment effects (Arrindell, 1993a). Regardless of treatment type, if a high level of negative beliefs still exists after treatment, additional treatment may be necessary. More work is needed to assess the ability of the ACQ and BSQ as predictors of relapse, but, clinically, high scores at the end of treatment suggest a less than successful outcome.

Because the ACQ and BSQ were developed to measure particular beliefs and fears that occur while the individual is highly anxious, these scales may not measure all aspects of AS. The beliefs about the consequences of anxiety are present prior to anxiety arousal and may be an important dimension of agoraphobic-avoidance behavior. The ASI and ACQ/BSQ are not highly correlated, which suggests that the ASI should be included in the assessment of agoraphobic patients. The extent to which each measure can provide unique information for predictions among agoraphobic patients has not yet been determined.

Relationship Between the ASI and ACQ/BSQ

Asmundson, Norton, Lanthier, and Cox (1996) assessed a sample of college students who either had a history of panic attacks ($N = 48$) or no history of panic ($N = 48$). Asmundson et al. found relatively low correlations between the ASI and ACQ/BSQ measures. Within the panickers, the ASI correlated .38 with ACQ-Total, .19 with ACQ-Physical Concerns subscale, .40 with ACQ-Social/Behavioral Concerns subscale, and .38 with the BSQ. For the nonpanickers, the respective correlations were .44, .34, .43, and .38. These correlations are moderate and suggest the ASI and ACQ/BSQ are not measuring the same dimension.

In the panickers, the ACQ-Total score and BSQ were correlated .61, suggesting a strong common component between the two measures for that sample. For the nonpanickers, however, the correlation between the ACQ-Total and BSQ was only .20, suggesting that beliefs and fear of physical symptoms were unrelated. In contrast, Chambless et al. (1984) found a much higher correlation between the measures for the normals compared with agoraphobic samples. Part of the reason for this inconsistency, and a general issue in regard to what is measured by the ACQ, is that the ACQ asks individuals to rate how frequently they experience thoughts when they are anxious. Thus, the ACQ may be a measure of actual experienced thoughts under extreme anxiety conditions (panic or agoraphobia) rather than beliefs about the consequences of anxiety (Taylor, 1995a).

How the ACQ relates to anxiety and AS remains an open question. It is interesting that in the Asmundson et al. (1996) report, the ACQ, particularly the Social/Behavioral Concerns subscale, appeared to be more strongly associated with trait anxiety (anxiety proneness) than with the ASI. It appears that trait anxiety is related to reports of the presence of Social/Behavioral Concerns when anxious, but trait anxiety was unrelated to fear of physical symptoms (Asmundson et al., 1996).

The ACQ subscale and BSQ intercorrelations with the panicker sample (Asmundson et al., 1996) suggest the subscales are measuring a common factor among those who have experienced panic, but the scales have not been combined into a single total score or submitted to factor analysis that would allow one to investigate the presence of a single general factor. Also, it is unclear why the ACQ and BSQ appear to relate to each other differently depending on the presence or absence of panic attacks. In people who have never had panic attacks, the ACQ and BSQ may not be measuring a single dimension of AS.

Asmundson et al. (1996) also used a number of variables to discriminate between panickers and nonpanickers. The ASI was found to be the best single predictor of group membership. The ACQ-Physical Concerns and BSQ did contribute a significant but small amount of additional variance to the ability to discriminate between groups. The reason this result is somewhat surprising is that the ACQ and BSQ focus on beliefs that are experienced during high anxiety (or panic), suggesting a strong association with panic status. It appears that sensitivity to anxiety, as compared with thoughts experienced during anxiety, is more associated with the panic experience. This is consistent with the findings reported in other chapters in this book, in which ASI level prior to arousal-inducing biological challenge conditions is predictive of subjective emotional reactions and symptom reporting.

RELATED MEASURES OF PANIC
AND AGORAPHOBIA

A large number of self-report measures have been developed to assess panic, many of which are relevant to the assessment of AS. Bouchard, Pelletier, Gauthier, Cote, and Laberge (1997) reviewed several global measures of panic, including the National Institute of Mental Health Panic Questionnaire (Scupi, Maser, & Uhde, 1992), the Panic and Agoraphobia Scale (Bandelow, 1995), the Panic-Associated Symptoms Scale (Argyle et al., 1991), and the Panic Attack Questionnaire (Norton, 1989; Norton, Harrison, Hauch, & Rhodes, 1985). Also reviewed were measures of beliefs (or other cognitions) relevant to panic and agoraphobia. These included the ACQ, BSQ, and ASI, as well as the Agoraphobic Cognitions Scale (Hoffart, Friis, & Martinsen, 1992), the Catastrophic Cognitions Questionnaire (Khawaja, Oei, & Baglioni, 1994), the Panic Appraisal Inventory (Telch, Brouillard, Telch, Agras, & Taylor, 1989), the Panic Attack Cognition Questionnaire (Clum, Broyles, Borden, & Watkins, 1990), the Panic Attack Symptoms Questionnaire (Clum et al., 1990), the Panic Belief Questionnaire (Greenberg, 1988), and the Self-Efficacy to Control Panic Attacks Questionnaire (Gauthier, Bouchard, Cote, Laberge, & French, 1993; cited in Bouchard et al., 1997).

The global measures of panic focus mainly on panic attack characteristics. However, some measures (e.g., the Panic and Agoraphobia scale) include items about avoidance, the presence of particular beliefs while anxious, and AS. These items have not been used to predict panic attacks, but are related to measures such as anxiety and avoidance. Their utility in assessing AS remains to be further investigated.

The belief measures focus primarily on beliefs expressed by panic and agoraphobic patients. The scales reviewed by Bouchard et al. (1997) all show some evidence of diagnostic discrimination or sensitivity to detecting treatment effects and appear useful in assessing panic and agoraphobia (see Bouchard et al., 1997, for details of scale validities). What remains to be determined is how well the general concept of AS or fear of fear across normative and other anxiety samples is measured by these instruments. In general, panic attack frequency and beliefs during panic do not fully explain future reactions to stress or biological challenges (e.g., CO_2 inhalation). The ASI has consistently been found to predict panic or anxiety reactions to these challenges, above and beyond that accounted for by previous panic attack experience (McNally, 1989; Taylor, 1996; Telch & Harrington, 1994; also see chap. 9).

All of these measures focus on disorder-specific characteristics. Because panic and agoraphobic cognitions are similar to the beliefs assessed in the ASI, some overlap in measurement should occur. The key difference that distinguishes the ASI from panic-assessment measures is that the ASI focuses on AS rather than disorder-specific beliefs.

CONCLUSIONS

The ASI is the most widely used measure of AS. Scores for a large normative sample can be found in Peterson and Reiss (1992). Internal consistency analyses and test–retest results suggest excellent reliability. The factor structure of the ASI still requires investigation, but there is growing support for a higher order factor with three lower order factors. The large number of validity studies based on the total score for the original 16-item scale suggests that the ASI is a highly valid measure of AS. New developments include subscales based on ASI factor scores, modified ASI scales with items removed, and new, expanded scales. For each of these measures, more research is needed on their psychometric properties; norms need to be established before being adopted for clinical use.

It is important to note that the ASI is not just a measure of panic or agoraphobia. As a measure of the continuum of AS across normal and clinical populations, the ASI appears to measure the general dimension of AS. Consistent with this view, the ASI predicts anxiety-related behavior among normal as well as clinical samples. The ASI discriminates diagnostic groups (especially anxiety disorders) from normal controls in theoretically expected ways. The ASI has also been shown to provide important information in the study of chronic pain and drug and alcohol abuse. Theoretically, other measures of AS should be performed in a similar fashion, although this remains to be seen. At this time, only the ASI has research support as a well-normed, reliable, and valid measure of the general dimension of AS.

REFERENCES

Argyle, N., Deltito, J., Allerup, P., Maier, W., Albus, M., Nutzinger, D., Rasmussen, S., Ayuso, J. L., & Beech, P. (1991). The Panic-Associated Symptom Scale: Measuring the severity of panic disorder. *Acta Psychiatrica Scandinavica, 83*, 20–26.

Arrindell, W. A. (1993a). The fear of fear concept: Stability, retest, artifact and predictive power. *Behaviour Research and Therapy, 31*, 139–148.

Arrindell, W. A. (1993b). The fear of fear concept: Evidence in favour of multidimensionality. *Behaviour Research and Therapy, 31*, 507–518.

Asmundson, G. J. G., & Norton, C. R. (1995). Anxiety sensitivity in patients with physically unexplained chronic back pain: A preliminary report. *Behaviour Research and Therapy, 33*, 771–777.

Asmundson, G. J. G., Norton, G. R., Lanthier, N. J., & Cox, B. (1996). Fear of anxiety: Do current measures assess unique aspects of the construct? *Personality and Individual Differences, 20*, 607–612.

Bandelow, B. (1995). Assessing the efficacy of treatments for panic disorder and agoraphobia: II. The Panic and Agoraphobia Scale. *International Clinical Psychopharmacology, 10*, 73–81.

Blais, M. A., Otto, M. W., Zucker, B. G., McNally, R. J., Fava, M., & Pollack, M. H. (1997). *Structure of the Anxiety Sensitivity Index: I. Suggestions for scale refinement based on item and factor analyses.* Manuscript in preparation.

Bouchard, S., Pelletier, M. H., Gauthier, J. G., Cote, G., & Laberge, B. (1997). The assessment of panic using self-report: A comprehensive survey of validated instruments. *Journal of Anxiety Disorders, 11*, 89–111.

Carr, R. E., Lehrer, P. M., Rausch, R. L., & Hochron, S. M. (1994). Anxiety sensitivity and panic attacks in an asthmatic population. *Behaviour Research and Therapy, 32*, 411–418.

Chambless, D. L., Caputo, G. C., Bright, P., & Gallagher, R. (1984). Assessment of fear of fear in agoraphobics: The Body Sensations Questionnaire and the Agoraphobic Cognitions Questionnaire. *Journal of Consulting and Clinical Psychology, 52*, 1090–1097.

Chambless, D. L., & Gracely, E. J. (1989). Fear of fear and the anxiety disorders. *Cognitive Therapy and Research, 13*, 9–20.

Clum, G. A., Broyles, S., Borden, J., & Watkins, P. L. (1990). Validity and reliability of the Panic Attack Symptoms and Cognitions Questionnaire. *Journal of Psychopathology and Behavioral Assessment, 12*, 233–245.

Cox, B. J., Endler, N. S., Norton, G. R., & Swinson, R. P (1991). Anxiety sensitivity and non-clinical panic attacks. *Behaviour Research and Therapy, 29*, 367–369.

Cox, B. J., Taylor, S., Borger, S., Fuentes, K., & Ross, L. (1996, November). *Development of an expanded Anxiety Sensitivity Index: Multiple dimensions and their correlates.* In S. Taylor (Chair), "New studies on the psychopathology of anxiety sensitivity." Symposium presented at the 30th annual meeting of the Association for Advancement of Behavior Therapy, New York.

Goldstein, A. J., & Chambless, D. L. (1978). A reanalysis of agoraphobia. *Behavior Therapy, 9*, 47–59.

Greenberg, R. L. (1988). Panic disorder and agoraphobia. In J. M. G. Williams & A. T. Beck (Eds.), *Cognitive therapy in clinical practice: An illustrative casebook* (pp. 25–49). London: Routledge.

Hoffart, A., Friis, S., & Martinsen, E.W. (1992). Assessment of fear of fear among agoraphobic patients: The Agoraphobic Cognitions Scale. *Journal of Psychopathology and Behavioral Assessment, 14*, 175–187.

Karp, J., & Peterson, R. A. (1997). *The alcohol expectancy and anxiety sensitivity relationship among alcoholics.* Unpublished manuscript, George Washington University, Washington, DC.

Khawaja, N. G., Oei, T. P. S., & Baglioni, A. J. (1994). Modification of the Catastrophic Cognitions Questionnaire (CCQ-M) for normals and patients: Exploratory and LISREL analyses. *Journal of Psychopathology and Behavioral Assessment, 16*, 325–342.

Lilienfeld, S.O. (1996). Anxiety sensitivity is not distinct from trait anxiety. In R. M. Rapee (Ed.), *Current controversies in the anxiety disorders* (pp. 228–244). New York: Guilford.

Lilienfeld, S. O., Jacob, R. G., & Turner, S. M. (1989). Comment on Holloway and McNally's "Effects of anxiety sensitivity on the response to hyperventilation." *Journal of Abnormal Psychology, 98*, 100–102.

Lilienfeld, S. O., Turner, S. M., & Jacob, R. G. (1993). Anxiety sensitivity: An examination of theoretical and methodological issues. *Advances in Behaviour Research and Therapy, 15*, 147–183.

Lilienfeld, S. O., Turner, S. M., & Jacob, R. G. (1996). Further comments on the nature and measurement of anxiety sensitivity: A reply to Taylor (1995b). *Journal of Anxiety Disorders, 10*, 411–424.

Maller, R. G., & Reiss, S. (1992). Anxiety sensitivity in 1984 and panic attacks in 1987. *Journal of Anxiety Disorders, 6*, 241–247.

McNally, R. J. (1989). Is anxiety sensitivity distinguishable from trait anxiety? Reply to Lilienfeld, Jacob, & Turner (1989). *Journal of Abnormal Psychology, 98*, 193–194.

McNally, R. J. (1996). Anxiety sensitivity is distinguishable from trait anxiety. In R. M. Rapee (Ed.), *Current controversies in the anxiety disorders* (pp. 214–227). New York: Guilford.

Norton, G. R. (1989). Panic Attack Questionnaire. In M. Hersen & A. Bellack (Eds.), *Dictionary of behavioral assessment techniques* (pp. 332–334). New York: Pergamon.

Norton, G. R., Harrison, B., Hauch, J., & Rhodes, L. (1985). Characteristics of people with infrequent panic attacks. *Journal of Abnormal Psychology, 94*, 216–221.

Peterson, R. A., & Heilbronner, R. L. (1987). The Anxiety Sensitivity Index: Construct validity and factor analytic structure. *Journal of Anxiety Disorders, 1*, 117–121.

Peterson, R. A., & Reiss, S. (1992). *Anxiety Sensitivity Index Revised Manual.* Worthington, OH: International Diagnostic Systems Publishing Corporation.

Reiss, S. (1987). Theoretical perspectives on the fear of anxiety. *Clinical Psychology Review, 7*, 585–596.

Reiss, S. (1991). Expectancy model of fear, anxiety, and panic. *Clinical Psychology Review, 11*, 141–153.

Reiss, S. (1997). Trait anxiety: It's not what you think it is. *Journal of Anxiety Disorders, 11*, 201–214.

Reiss, S., & McNally, R. J. (1985). Expectancy model of fear. In S. Reiss & R. R. Bootzin (Eds.), *Theoretical issues in behavior therapy* (pp. 107–121). San Diego, CA: Academic Press.

Reiss, S., Peterson, R. A., Gursky, D. M., & McNally, R. J. (1986). Anxiety sensitivity, anxiety frequency and the prediction of fearfulness. *Behaviour Research and Therapy, 24*, 1–8.

Sandin, B., Chorot, P., & McNally, R. J. (1996). Validation of the Spanish version of the Anxiety Sensitivity Index in a clinical sample. *Behaviour Research and Therapy, 34*, 283–290.

Saviotti, F. M., Grandi, S., Savron, G., Ermentini, R., Bartolucci, G., Conti, S., & Fava, G.A. (1991). Characterological traits of recovered patients with panic disorder and agoraphobia. *Journal of Affective Disorders, 23*, 113–117.

Schmidt, N. B., Lerew, D. R., & Jackson, R. J. (1997). The role of anxiety sensitivity in the pathogenesis of panic: Prospective evaluation of spontaneous panic attacks during acute stress. *Journal of Abnormal Psychology, 106*, 355–364.

Schmidt, N. B., Lerew, D. R., & Trakowski, J. H. (1997). Body vigilance in panic disorder: Evaluating attention to bodily perturbations. *Journal of Consulting and Clinical Psychology, 65*, 214–220.

Schmidt, N. B., & Telch, M. J. (1994). Role of fear of fear and safety information in moderating the effects of voluntary hyperventilation. *Behavior Therapy, 25*, 197–208.

Scupi, B. S., Maser, J. D., & Uhde, T. W. (1992). The National Institute of Mental Health Panic Questionnaire: An instrument for assessing clinical characteristics of panic disorder. *Journal of Nervous and Mental Disease, 180*, 566–572.

Shear, M. K., & Maser, J. D. (1994). Standardized assessment for panic disorder research: A conference report. *Archives of General Psychiatry, 51*, 346–354.

Spielberger, C. D. (1983). *Manual for the State-Trait Anxiety Inventory (Form Y).* Palo Alto, CA: Consulting Psychologist's Press.

Stewart, S. H., Taylor, S., & Baker, J. M. (1997). Gender differences in dimensions of anxiety sensitivity. *Journal of Anxiety Disorders, 11*, 179–200.

Stoler, L. S., & McNally, R. J. (1991). Cognitive bias in symptomatic and recovered agoraphobics. *Behaviour Research and Therapy, 29*, 529–545.

Taylor, S. (1995a). Anxiety sensitivity: Theoretical perspectives and recent findings. *Behaviour Research and Therapy, 33*, 243–258.

Taylor, S. (1995b). Issues in the conceptualization and measurement of anxiety sensitivity. *Journal of Anxiety Disorders, 9*, 163–174.

Taylor, S. (1996). Nature and measurement of anxiety sensitivity: Reply to Lilienfeld, Turner, and Jacob (1996). *Journal of Anxiety Disorders, 10*, 425–451.

Taylor, S., & Cox, B. J. (1997). *An expanded Anxiety Sensitivity Index: Evidence for a hierarchic structure in a clinical sample.* Manuscript submitted for publication.

Taylor, S., & Cox, B. J. (in press). Anxiety sensitivity: Multiple dimensions and hierarchic structure. *Behaviour Research and Therapy.*

Taylor, S., Koch, W. J., & Crockett, D. J. (1991). Anxiety sensitivity, trait anxiety, and the anxiety disorders. *Journal of Anxiety Disorders, 5,* 292–311.

Taylor, S., Koch, W. J., & McNally, R. J. (1992a). How does anxiety sensitivity vary across the anxiety disorders? *Journal of Anxiety Disorders, 6,* 249–259.

Taylor, S., Koch, W. J., McNally, R. J., & Crockett, D. J. (1992b). Conceptualizations of anxiety sensitivity. *Psychological Assessment, 4,* 245–250.

Telch, M. J., Brouillard, M., Telch, C. F., Agras, W. S., & Taylor, C. B. (1989). Role of cognitive appraisal in panic related avoidance. *Behaviour Research and Therapy, 27,* 373–383.

Telch, M. J., & Harrington, P. J. (1994, November). *Anxiety sensitivity and expectedness of arousal in mediating affective response to 35% carbon dioxide inhalation.* Paper presented at the 28th meeting of the Association for Advancement of Behavior Therapy, San Diego, CA.

Telch, M. J., Shermis, M. D., & Lucas, J. A. (1989). Anxiety sensitivity: Unitary personality trait or domain specific appraisals? *Journal of Anxiety Disorders, 3,* 25–32.

Zinbarg, R. E., Barlow, D. H., & Brown, T. A. (1997). Hierarchical structure and general factor saturation of the Anxiety Sensitivity Index: Evidence and implications. *Psychological Assessment, 9,* 277–284.

5

Dimensions of Anxiety Sensitivity

Richard E. Zinbarg
Jan Mohlman
Nicholas N. Hong
University of Oregon

Reiss and colleagues (Reiss, 1987, 1991; Reiss & McNally, 1985; Reiss, Peterson, Gursky, & McNally, 1986) defined *anxiety sensitivity* (AS) as the fear of anxiety and anxiety-related sensations arising from beliefs that anxiety and related sensations have harmful consequences. Theoretical and empirical work over the past two decades accords AS and closely related constructs (such as the fear of fear) a central role in the nature and etiology of the anxiety disorders in general and panic disorder in particular (e.g., Barlow, 1988, 1991; Clark, 1986; Goldstein & Chambless, 1978; McNally, 1990; Reiss, 1991; Reiss & McNally, 1985; Reiss, Peterson, Gursky, & McNally, 1986).

Given the prominent role of the AS construct in current models of panic disorder and other anxiety disorders, it is important to critically examine the validity of the AS construct and the psychometric instruments devised to measure it. The primary purpose of this chapter is to review the literature bearing on the dimensionality of AS and the factor structure of the measures used as putative indicators of AS. This is an important undertaking for two reasons. First, an examination of dimensionality is one of the critical steps in the construct validation process within any given domain. Second, although consensus is beginning to emerge in this literature, the dimensionality of AS has been a controversial issue in the past. At the one extreme pole of this debate, some researchers hypothesized AS to be a unidimensional construct (e.g., McNally, 1996; Reiss, 1991). At the opposite pole, other researchers hypothesized that there are several specific AS dimensions with no underlying unitary construct (e.g., Telch, Shermis, & Lucas, 1989). To complicate matters even more, the empirical evidence has appeared to be inconsistent with respect to the number of AS dimensions and has not provided unequivocal support for either one of these extreme positions over the other. Much of our attention in this chapter is devoted to the description and evaluation of a proposed synthesis of these opposing views that was first articulated by Lilienfeld, Turner, and Jacob (1993). This synthesis holds that the structure of AS is organized hierarchically and, as is seen shortly, is capable of explaining many of the inconsistencies in the literature on the dimensionality of AS.

THE ANXIETY SENSITIVITY INDEX

Clearly the most widely used measure of AS is the Anxiety Sensitivity Index (ASI; Reiss et al., 1986). The ASI consists of 16 items that tap fears of anxiety (e.g., "It scares me when I am nervous") and anxiety-related sensations (e.g., "It scares me when my heart beats rapidly"), as well as concerns about possible negative consequences of anxiety (e.g., "When I am nervous, I worry that I might be mentally ill") and anxiety-related sensations (e.g., "When I notice my heart is beating rapidly, I worry that I might have a heart attack"). The test–retest reliability, internal consistency, and predictive validity of the ASI have been demonstrated in more than 100 peer-reviewed journal articles (for reviews, see Peterson & Reiss, 1992; Reiss, 1991; chap. 4, this volume).

Factor Structure of the ASI

We begin our examination of the dimensionality of AS with a review of the literature on the structure of the ASI, given that it is the foremost measure of AS. There have been 12 published studies examining the factor structure of the ASI and at least two other unpublished factor-analytic studies of the ASI. Table 5.1 summarizes these 14 studies. As noted in several earlier reviews of this literature (Lilienfeld, Turner, & Jacob, 1993; McNally, 1996; Taylor, 1995a, 1995b), Table 5.1 reveals inconsistent results across studies: Some researchers claim support for a unidimensional structure, whereas other researchers claim support for multidimensional structures, including as many as four factors. Taylor (1995a, 1995b) suggested three possible explanations for these inconsistent results. First, the ASI may not have a stable factor structure. Second, the ASI may have a stable structure within specific populations but the structure may vary across different populations. Third, inappropriate methods of analysis

TABLE 5.1

Factor Analytic Studies of the Anxiety Sensitivity Index

Author(s)	Sample	Method of Factor Extraction	Method of Factor Rotation	Criterion for Number of Factors	Number of Factors
Cox, Parker, & Swinson (1996)	365 college students	CFA			4
	216 panic disorder outpatients	CFA			4
Cox, Taylor, Borger, Fuentes, & Ross (1996)	315 college students	PCA	Orthogonal	Scree test & Kaiser's criterion	3
Peterson & Heilbronner (1987)	122 college students	PCA	Oblique	Kaiser's criterion	4
Reiss, Peterson, Gursky, & McNally (1986)	49 college students	PCA		Kaiser's criterion	1
	98 college students	PCA		?	1
Sandin, Chorot, & McNally (1996)	126 anxiety disorder outpatients	PCA		Scree test & simple structure	1
Stewart, Dubois-Nguyen, & Pihl (1990)	216 college students	PCA		Scree	1
Stewart, Taylor, & Baker (1997)	818 college students	PCA	Oblique	Parallel analysis interpretability, & replicability	3
Taylor (1996)	144 community volunteers	PCA		Parallel analysis	1
	199 outpatients with panic disorder and/or major depression and 19 subclinical panickers[a]	PCA	Oblique	Parallel analysis	3
Taylor, Koch, & Crockett (1991)	142 spider-fearful college students	PCA		Scree test & simple structure	1
	93 anxiety disorder outpatients	PCA		Scree test & simple structure	1

(continues)

TABLE 5.1 (continued)

Author(s)	Sample	Method of Factor Extraction	Method of Factor Rotation	Criterion for Number of Factors	Number of Factors
Taylor, Koch, McNally, & Crockett (1992)	327 anxiety disorder out-patients[b]	CFA			1
	142 spider-fearful college students[c]	CFA			1
Taylor, Koch, Woody, & McLean (1996)	135 outpatients with panic disorder and/or major depression	PCA	Oblique	Parallel analysis	3
Telch, Shermis, & Lucas (1989)	840 college students	PCA	Ortho-gonal	Kaiser's criterion	4
Wardle, Ahmad, & Hayward (1990)	160 agoraphobic out-patients	PCA	Ortho-gonal	Kaiser's criterion	4
	120 normal controls	PCA	Ortho-gonal	Kaiser's criterion	4
Zinbarg, Brown, & Barlow (1997)	432 anxiety disorder out-patients	PAF & CFA	Oblique	Replicability	3

Note. PCA = principal components extraction; PAF = principal axis factor extraction; CFA = confirmatory factor analysis; ? indicates that the study was not reported in sufficient detail to allow for an unambiguous determination of the particular method used; Kaiser's criterion = the eigenvalue greater than one rule. The methods of factor rotation for exploratory factor analyses in which only a single factor was extracted and confirmatory factor analyses are meaningless and were therefore omitted.

[a]These patients include the 135 patients comprising the sample obtained by Taylor et al. (1996). [b]These patients include 73 of the individuals included in the sample of 93 patients obtained by Taylor et al. (1991). [c]This is the same sample as the spider-fearful sample analyzed by Taylor et al. (1991).

result in overextraction of factors in the studies reporting evidence putatively supporting multidimensionality (for a similar argument, see McNally, 1996). Of course, to construct an exhaustive list of the possibilities, one should add two more possible explanations for the inconsistencies in this literature to the three suggested by Taylor. Thus, a fourth explanation is that inappropriate methods of analysis result in underextraction of factors in the studies reporting evidence putatively supporting unidimensionality. The fifth and final possible explanation, originally put forth by Lilienfeld et al. (1993), is that the ASI has a hierarchical factor structure containing several first-order factors and a single second-order factor. We explore the plausibility of each of these five possible explanations in turn.

Is the Factor Structure of the ASI Inherently Unstable?

The evidence strongly suggests that this hypothesis—that the factor structure of the ASI is inherently unstable—is implausible. If the factor structure of the ASI were inherently unstable, we might expect each study to result in a different structure; we certainly would not expect to find more than chance levels of convergence of results across studies. In fact, there is much more order in the results than this. The various studies claiming support for a single factor structure (e.g., Peterson & Hielbronner, 1987; Reiss, Peterson, & Gursky, 1988; Reiss, Peterson, Gursky, & McNally, 1986; Taylor, Koch, & Crockett, 1991; Taylor, Koch, McNally, & Crockett, 1992) have obviously converged on a highly similar structure. Moreover, although it is not as immediately transparent, the various studies claiming support for a multidimensional structure (e.g., Cox, Parker, & Swinson, 1996; Cox, Taylor, Borger, Fuentes, & Ross, 1996; Stewart, Taylor, & Baker, 1997; Taylor, 1996; Taylor, Koch, Woody, & McLean, 1996; Telch, Shermis, & Lucas, 1989; Wardle, Ahmad, & Hayward, 1990; Zinbarg, Barlow, & Brown, 1997) have also converged on a highly similar structure. Several investigators (e.g., Stewart et al., 1997; Taylor, 1996; Zinbarg & Barlow, 1996; Zinbarg et al., 1997) have noted that three factors appear to be replicable across the studies reporting multidimensional structures and that the content tapped by these three factors corresponds to fears of physical sensations, mental incapacitation, and public observation of anxiety and anxiety-related sensations.

Zinbarg et al. (1997) named the three replicable factors, in order, AS–Physical Concerns, AS–Mental Incapacitation Concerns, and AS–Social Concerns. In addition, these investigators tested the degree to which these factor names reflect shared meaning versus the degree to which they reflect meaning that is entirely subjective and idiosyncratic to the authors. They did so by asking 12 judges who were not involved in the factor-naming process to match the factor names with the item sets comprising the factors. The 12 judges included seven doctoral-level psychologists with expertise in clinical psychology, two doctoral-level psychologists with expertise in personality and factor analysis, and three graduate students in clinical psychology who had just completed an anxiety assessment and treatment practicum. The judges achieved perfect matching performance in this task, indicating that the factor names derived by the authors communicated valid intersubjective knowledge.

For this chapter, we computed coefficients of congruence (Burt, 1948; Gorsuch, 1983) to quantify the degree of convergence across the multidimensional solutions obtained by Cox et al. (1996), Peterson and Heilbronner (1987), Stewart et al. (1997), Taylor (1996), Telch et al. (1989), Wardle et al. (1990), and Zinbarg et al. (1997). In comparing our results with those reported by Wardle et al. (1990), we only used the results from their sample of individuals with agoraphobia given that these authors concluded that "the item structure had little obvious psychological meaning" (Wardle et al., 1990, p. 332) in their normal sample. Table 5.2 presents the congruence coefficients for corresponding factors across studies and provides fairly strong evidence that the AS–Physical Concerns, AS–Mental Incapacitation Concerns, and AS–Social Concerns factors are the same or at least highly similar across the various multidimensional solutions that have been reported. The mean congruence coefficient across the three patient samples equaled .91 for AS–Physical Concerns, .92 for AS–Mental Incapacitation Concerns, and .90 for AS–Social Concerns (and the medians equaled .93, .92, and .89, respectively). The mean congruence coefficient among the four nonpatient samples equaled .84, .87, and .80 (and the medians equaled .87, .88, and .81). The mean congruence coefficient aggregating across all seven samples equaled .85, .88, and .81 (and the medians equaled .87, .88, and .82). The convergence of the three factors across studies is particularly impressive considering that the studies not only differed in the nature of the samples studied but also in the factor extraction (principal components vs. principal axis factors) and factor rotation (oblimin vs. varimax) techniques used by the investigators. In contrast, the coefficients of congruence between the noncorresponding factors across studies were much lower, as shown in Table 5.3.

Furthermore, Table 5.2 shows that when a fourth factor is extracted, it shows much less evidence of convergence across studies. The mean congruence coefficient for an additional factor beyond the AS–Physical Concerns, AS–Mental Incapacitation Concerns, and AS–Social Concerns factors across the four studies in which a fourth factor was examined equaled only .39 (and

TABLE 5.2

Coefficients of Congruence Between Corresponding Anxiety Sensitivity Index Factors From Different Studies

	w1	w2	w4	w3	ta1	ta2	ta3	te1	te2	te3	te4	p3	p1	p2	p4	c1	c2	c3	s1	s2	s3
z1	.95				.93			.77				.85				.87			.94		
z2		.92				.96			.91				.93				.75			.93	
z3			.93				.87			.80								.81			.90
z4				.81							.33				.12						
w1					.86			.72				.78				.85			.87		
w2						.88			.92				.88				.88			.92	
w4							.89			.82								.82			.83
w3											.40				.41						
ta1								.81				.89				.87			.95		
ta2									.84				.89				.67			.88	
ta3										.70								.78			.69
te1												.63				.97			.89		
te2													.92				.87			.96	
te3														.89				.75			.81
te4															.25						
p3																.69			.87		
p1																	.80			.88	
p2																		.78			.88
p4																					
c1																			.93		
c2																				.82	
c3																					.68

Note. z = Zinbarg, Barlow, & Brown (1997); w = Wardle, Ahmad, & Hayward (1990); ta = Taylor (1996); te = Telch, Shermis, & Lucas (1989); p = Peterson & Heilbronner (1987); c = Cox, Taylor, Borger, Fuentes, & Ross (1996); s = Stewart, Taylor, & Baker (1997).

TABLE 5.3
Coefficients of Congruence Between Noncorresponding Anxiety Sensitivity Index Factors From Different Studies

	w1	w2	w4	w3	ta1	ta2	ta3	te1	te2	te3	te4	p3	p1	p2	p4	c1	c2	c3	s1	s2	s3
z1		.31	.21	.49	.15	.00	.38	.20	.41	.09	.84		.27	.17	.50		.58	.29		.23	-.1
z2	.28		.29	.36			.26			.13	.16	.00		.11	.20	.23		.59	.12		.04
z3	.28	.31		.39	.14	.21		.47	.32		.08	.00	.10		.50	.47	.15		.31	.36	
z4	.30	.24	-.1		.64	.25	-.2	.34	.33	-.1		.52	.46	.00		.43	.14	.51	.22	-.2	.54
w1						.14	.54	.58	.17	.85		.38	.21	.60		.70	.45			.44	.00
w2					.32		.42	.29	.39	.30	.43	.28	.28	.20	.35		.71	.31			.12
w4					.14	.26		.47	.50		.03	.03	.21		.50		.51		.31	.43	.24
w3								.80				.52	.49			.49	.15	.48	.68	.39	
ta1									.40	.10	.81		.34	.18	.40	.49	.61	.27		.22	-.1
ta2								.17		.05	.06	.03		.14	.10	.15		.59	.04		.11
ta3								.44	.48	.11	.10	.18		.70	.54	.30	.38			.49	
te1										.26			.32	.41	.60		.42	.46		.28	.29
te2												.26	.16	.48	.51	.65	.39				.06
te3												.00	.05		.10	.20	.07	.19		.21	
te4												.90	.24			.63	.71	.32	.79	.28	-.2
p3														.09			.59	.21			
p1																.33	.52	.26		.10	.17
p2																.37	.08		.32	.19	-.1
p4																.70	.30	.40	.50	.40	.30
c1																				.35	
c2																			.55	.40	.23
c3																			.38	.70	-.2

Note. z = Zinbarg, Barlow, & Brown (1997); w = Wardle, Ahmad, & Hayward (1990); ta = Taylor (1996); te = Telch, Shermis, & Lucas (1989); p = Peterson & Heilbronner (1987); c = Cox, Taylor, Borger, Fuentes, & Ross (1996); s = Stewart, Taylor, & Baker (1997).

the median equaled .36). Thus, the results from the congruence coefficients indicate that the ASI contains three first-order factors in samples of outpatients with anxiety disorders and in nonclinical samples of college students (we emphasize that these factors are first-order factors because the evidence also indicates that the ASI contains a second-order factor, as is discussed in detail later).

Given that item-level factor analyses are notoriously vulnerable to artifactual influences, such as categorization effects (Bernstein & Teng, 1989) and "difficulty factors" (e.g., Ferguson, 1941; McDonald, 1965; Wherry & Gaylord, 1944), it is important to consider the possibility that the three replicable ASI factors are primarily artifactual in nature. Even if the three ASI factors are not based entirely on methodological artifact and tap partially distinct substantive constructs, the question arises as to whether it is meaningful to distinguish among the three first-order factors in terms of predicting variables of theoretical or clinical import.

To address the issues of methodological artifact and the importance of distinguishing among the three first-order ASI factors, it is crucial to examine their construct validity. In fact, preliminary evidence that the three first-order factors display differential concurrent validity has been reported by Stewart et al. (1997), Taylor, Koch, Woody, and McLean (1996), Zinbarg and Barlow (1996), and Zinbarg et al. (1997). Stewart et al. found that the three first-order ASI factors show different patterns of sex differences. Their results show that women score significantly higher than men only on the AS–Physical Concerns factor. They also found that women score significantly higher on the AS–Physical Concerns factor than they do on the other two factors, whereas men score significantly lower on the AS-Physical Concerns relative to their scores on the other two factors.

Taylor et al. (1996) reported that the AS–Physical Concerns and AS–Social Concerns factors tended to significantly correlate with anxiety-related but not with depression-related measures. In contrast, AS–Mental Incapacitation Concerns showed the converse pattern, tending to correlate significantly with depression-related but not with anxiety-related measures. Consistent with these correlational analyses, Taylor et al. also found that the presence of a diagnosis of major depression was associated with the highest scores on the AS–Mental Incapacitation Concerns factor.

Zinbarg and Barlow (1996) performed scale-level factor analyses that included ASI subscales corresponding to the three first-order ASI factors, in addition to measures of other key features of the anxiety disorders. In these scale-level analyses, the AS–Social Concerns subscale had its highest loading on a factor defined primarily by scales tapping social anxiety. In addition, whereas both the AS–Physical Concerns and AS–Mental Incapacitation Concerns subscales had their highest loadings on a factor defined primarily by them, the AS–Mental Incapacitation Concerns subscale was the only one of the three subscales to show a salient loading on a Generalized Dysphoria factor defined primarily by measures of generalized anxiety, tension, and depressed mood.

Finally, Zinbarg et al. (1997) found that the three first-order ASI factors differentiate among different anxiety disorders (defined in terms of principal diagnosis) in a manner consistent with their content (principal diagnosis being defined as the diagnosis associated with the greatest clinical severity on the basis of symptom severity, degree of distress, and impairment). That is, as expected, individuals with a principal diagnosis of panic disorder showed the highest scores on the AS–Physical Concerns factor and individuals with a principal diagnosis of social phobia showed the highest scores on the AS–Social Concerns factor. Although we did not have strong expectations regarding which group would show the greatest elevation on the AS–Mental Incapacitation Concerns factor, this factor did show a different pattern of relations with principal diagnosis than did the other two factors. That is, Zinbarg et al. found that only the AS–Mental Incapacitation Concerns factor did not significantly discriminate a group with principal diagnoses of simple phobia from the no mental disorder group. The evidence of differential concurrent validity reported by Stewart et al. (1997), Taylor et al. (1996), Zinbarg and Barlow (1996), and Zinbarg et al. (1997) leads us to conclude that the three first-order ASI factors should not be interpreted entirely as methodological artifacts and that it is indeed important to distinguish between them.

Does the Factor Structure of the ASI Vary Across Different Populations?

The evidence similarly suggests the implausibility of the hypothesis that the factor structure of the ASI is stable within a specific population but varies across different populations. If this hypothesis were valid, we should expect to find convergence of results only among studies drawing their samples from similar populations; studies sampling from dissimilar populations should find discrepant results. In fact, the discrepancies across studies do not seem to be a simple function of differences in sampling strategy. Among the studies concluding that the ASI is unidimensional, some sampled from college students (e.g., Reiss et al., 1986; Taylor, 1996, Sample 1; Taylor et al., 1991) whereas others sampled from anxiety-disordered outpatients (Sandin, Charot, & McNally, 1996; Taylor et al., 1992). Similarly, among the studies concluding that the ASI is multidimensional, some were sampled from college students (e.g., Cox et al., 1996; Stewart et al., 1997; Telch et al., 1989) whereas others were sampled from anxiety-disordered outpatients (e.g., Cox et al., 1996; Taylor, 1996, Samples 2 & 3; Wardle et al., 1990; Zinbarg et al., 1997). The facts that (a) there is a great deal of evidence of convergence across different populations, and (b) there are some instances of discrepant results despite using similar populations are inconsistent with the notion that the factor structure of the ASI varies across populations.

Have Inappropriate Methods of Analysis Resulted in Overextraction of Factors in the Studies Reporting Evidence Putatively Supporting Multidimensionality?

According to this hypothesis, the factor structure of the ASI is unidimensional and all of the studies concluding that the structure is multidimensional were mistaken. Taylor (1995a, 1995b; see also McNally, 1996) suggested this hypothesis based on his observation that the only multidimensional solutions published prior to the time of his reviews used Kaiser's "eigenvalues greater than one" criterion to determine the number of factors to extract. Simulation studies have shown that this criterion often extracts an excessive number of factors (Hakstian, Rogers, & Cattell, 1982; Revelle & Rocklin, 1979; Velicer & Jackson, 1990; Zwick & Velicer, 1986). Although this hypothesis was plausible at the time that Taylor suggested it, more recent studies suggest that it can be rejected. That is, several studies using more accurate criteria for the number of factors to extract, such as the scree test and parallel analysis, have since obtained evidence for the multidimensionality of the ASI (e.g., Stewart et al., 1997; Taylor, 1996, samples 2 & 3; Taylor et al., 1996; Zinbarg et al., 1997; see also Cox et al. 1996).

Have Inappropriate Methods of Analysis Resulted in Underextraction of Factors in the Studies Reporting Evidence Putatively Supporting Unidimensionality?

In essence, this hypothesis states the converse of the previous hypothesis. According to this hypothesis, the factor structure of the ASI is multidimensional and all of the studies concluding that the structure is unidimensional were mistaken. The logic behind this hypothesis stems from the considerations that almost all of the studies of the factor structure of the ASI based their determination of the number of factors to extract on results from a single sample. Some researchers (e.g., Cudeck & Browne, 1983; Everett, 1983; Watson et al., 1995) suggested using factor replicability across samples as a basis for determining the number of factors to extract. One could argue that, in fact, replicability is what we should be most interested in. Following this argument, the various single sample statistical procedures can be seen as attempts to predict which factors will be replicable when we do not have multiple samples in hand to more directly assess replicability.

Although the various single sample statistical procedures may accurately predict replicability under many conditions, it is important to recognize that there will be some limitations to these predictions. Essentially, most of the single sample statistical criteria for the number of factors to extract (scree test, parallel analysis, etc.) simply tell us whether a given factor accounts for more item variance than what could be expected due to chance alone. If a given factor is larger than what could be expected due to chance alone, it tells us that the factor in question taps variance above and beyond that which can be attributed to chance. What if a given factor is not larger than what can be expected due to chance alone? Does this tell us that the factor in question is also a random factor? We do not think so; it merely does not allow us to rule out the possibility that the factor is a random factor. If we have only one sample in hand, then by all means we should not accept a factor that is not larger than what can be expected due to chance and therefore cannot be distinguished from a random factor. If we have more than one sample, however, we have the opportunity to investigate the possibility that a small factor might tap meaningful and systematic variance, although it may run through few enough items that it is no larger than a factor produced by chance alone. How can we distinguish between a small but systematic factor from a factor arising from capitalization on error? A small but systematic factor should replicate across samples, a random factor (by definition) should not.

In fact, the results presented in Table 5.2 and reviewed earlier provide strong evidence that at least three factors do replicate across samples (Cox et al., 1996; Stewart et al., 1997; Taylor, 1996; Zinbarg et al., 1997). This evidence suggests that the advocates of a unidimensional structure of the ASI were, strictly speaking, mistaken. As discussed in the next section, however, the rejection of a unidimensional model of the ASI should not necessarily be equated with the rejection of a unitary AS construct. As is argued next, the best available evidence suggests that the multidimensional structure underlying the ASI is hierarchical in nature. More specifically, we interpret the best available evidence as suggesting the existence of a single, second-order factor in addition to the presence of several first-order factors underlying the ASI.

Does the ASI Have a Hierarchical Structure Consisting of Several First-Order Factors and a Single Second-Order Factor?

Before we discuss the evidence testing the validity of a hierarchical model of the ASI, it may be useful to articulate how the hypothesis of a hierarchical structure is capable of explaining the inconsistencies in the extant literature. As noted by Goldberg and Digman (1994), inconsistencies in the number of factors extracted across studies are to be expected when (a) a hierarchical structure is present, and (b) investigators' procedures for deciding on the optimal number of factors are not guided by the distinction between higher and lower level factors. Given that the hypothesis that the factor structure of the ASI is hierarchical was first articulated fairly recently (i.e., Lilienfeld et al., 1993), it should not be surprising that most studies in this area have not been explicitly guided by the distinction between higher and lower level factors. Thus, a hierarchical model of the ASI, if valid, is capable of integrating many of the apparently discrepant findings in the literature; it suggests that those investigators (e.g., Telch et al., 1989; Wardle et al., 1990) who advocated a multifactor solution had a tacit focus on the lower level of the hierarchy, whereas those (e.g., Reiss et al., 1986; Taylor et al., 1991, 1992) who advocated a single-factor solution had a tacit focus on the higher level.

Given the potential of a hierarchical model for resolving and explaining the inconsistencies in the ASI literature, we believe that researchers in this area should evaluate the validity of the hypothesis that the ASI contains a hierarchical structure. The hierarchical nature of the factor structure of an instrument can be tested in at least two ways. Within an exploratory factor-analytic approach, the most widely used strategy is to use an oblique rotation and observe the size of the estimated factor intercorrelations. Moderate to large factor intercorrelations (e.g., .30 to .60) would suggest the presence of at least one higher order factor and would warrant a higher order factor analysis of the correlations among the first-order factors. Within a confirmatory factor-analytic approach, one can compare the goodness of fit of a hierarchical model (or a multidimensional oblique model, in which the first-order factors are free to correlate) with two comparison models: (a) a single-factor model, and (b) a multidimensional model in which the number of factors equals the number of first-order factors in the hierarchical model but the factors are constrained to be orthogonal.

Studies testing the hierarchical nature of the factor structure of the ASI have applied both exploratory and confirmatory factor-analytic strategies as described earlier. Regrettably, two of the earliest exploratory factor-analytic studies (e.g., Telch et al., 1989; Wardle et al., 1990) reporting support for multidimensional structures used orthogonal rotations, forcing the factors obtained to be uncorrelated. Thus, it is impossible to say whether the evidence from these studies suggests the presence of higher order factors. Fortunately, Peterson and Heilbronner (1987) and several of the more recent factor-analytic studies have used methods that permit the testing of the hierarchical nature of the ASI. Peterson and Heilbronner used an oblique rotation in their exploratory factor analysis and found moderate correlations among their first-order factors. Taylor et al. (1996) also performed an exploratory factor analysis using an oblique rotation and obtained weak to moderate correlations among their three first-order factors. Although he did not report the relevant results in his 1996 article, S. Taylor (personal communication, January 27, 1997) obtained similar results when he analyzed data from a sample that included 64 new patients in addition to the 135 patients included in the original analyses performed by Taylor et al. The correlations among the first-order factors in each of these studies suggest the presence of a second-order factor. Stewart et al. (1997) not only reported that their three first-order factors were moderately correlated but also conducted a higher order factor analysis of the correlations among their first-order factors. The results of this higher order analysis supported a single second-order factor. When the authors related the items directly to the second-order factor, it became clear that this second-order factor was a general factor because all 16 items had salient loadings on it.

Three confirmatory factor analyses of the ASI have been published to date. On the basis of their confirmatory factor analyses, Taylor et al. (1992) stated that their

> oblique solution could be seen as part of hierarchical factor structure in which all the oblique factors load on a superordinate factor. The oblique factors, however, are intercorrelated to such an extent that they are more appropriately regarded as facets of a single construct (p. 250)

They went on to conclude that the ASI is best regarded as unifactorial. As noted by Zinbarg et al. (1997), however, Taylor et al. did not perform the appropriate statistical test to warrant their conclusion. This would have involved testing the differences in fit between their oblique multidimensional model on the one hand and their one-factor model and orthogonal multidimensional model on the other. Given that the only two appropriate confirmatory factor-analytic studies of the ASI obtained results consistent with a hierarchical structure (discussed later), we strongly suspect that if Taylor et al. had performed the appropriate statistical tests they would have also obtained results consistent with a hierarchical structure.

Cox et al. (1996) performed a series of confirmatory factor analyses in both a panic-disorder patient sample and a college student sample. These investigators compared a unidimensional model and several four-factor models based on the results of Peterson and Heilbronner (1987), Telch et al. (1989) and Wardle et al. (1990). For each of the four-factor models, Cox et al. tested both oblique and orthogonal solutions. They found that the orthogonal four-factor models could not be fitted to either their patient or student data, and the unidimensional model did not display adequate levels of fit in either sample. The only models that displayed acceptable levels of fit were the oblique four-factor models. In addition, the oblique four-factor models provided significantly better fits to both the patient and student data than the unidimensional models.

Given that oblique factors imply the presence of higher order factors (Gorsuch, 1983), the results of Cox et al. (1996) demonstrating the superiority of oblique multidimensional models provide evidence supporting the hierarchical nature of the factor structure of the ASI. That is, the Cox et al. results suggest that the factor structure of the ASI consists of several first-order factors in addition to at least one second-order factor. Although Cox et al. did not perform a higher order factor analysis of the correlations among their first-order factors, we factor analyzed the correlations among the factors for the oblique (Peterson & Heilbronner, 1987) four-factor model reported by Cox et al. Our reanalyses of their data indicate a single second-order factor in both the patient sample (the eigenvalues equaled 2.85, .73, .28, and .13) and the student sample (the eigenvalues equaled 2.72, .66, .47, and .15). The loadings of the first-order factors on the second-order factor revealed that the second-order factor was quite strong with the smallest of these four loadings, equaling .60 in the patient sample and .52 in the student sample.

Zinbarg et al. (1997) compared a unidimensional model, a model with three orthogonal factors corresponding to AS–Physical Concerns, AS–Mental Incapacitation Concerns, and AS–Social Concerns, and a hierarchical model comprised of the same three factors that each loaded on a single second-order factor rather than being constrained to be orthogonal. In their sample of anxiety disordered outpatients, the hierarchical model provided a significantly better fit to the data than did either the single-factor model or the model with the three first-order factors constrained to be orthogonal. The factor loadings obtained by Zinbarg et al. on the second-order factor and the three residualized first-order factors after a Schmid–Leiman transformation was applied to the factor pattern matrix are shown in Table 5.4. Table 5.4 clarifies that the second-order factor is a general factor because 15 of the 16 ASI items have a loading of .30 or greater on it (see Stewart et al., 1997, for almost identical results).

TABLE 5.4

Anxiety Sensitivity Index Factor Pattern Matrix After Oblimin Rotation and Schmid–Leiman Transformation

Item	General	Factor 1	Factor 2	Factor 3
6. It scares me when my heart beats rapidly.	**.61**	**.56**	-.08	.09
10. It scares me when I am short of breath.	**.57**	**.53**	-.04	.03
9. When I notice that my heart is beating rapidly, I worry that I might have a heart attack	**.51**	**.53**	.04	-.14
4. It scares me when I feel faint.	**.58**	**.47**	-.09	.20
14. Unusual body sensations scare me.	**.62**	**.43**	.16	.01
3. It scares me when I feel "shaky" (trembling).	**.66**	**.38**	.06	.28
11. When my stomach is upset, I worry that I might be seriously ill.	**.44**	**.30**	.21	-.09
8. It scares me when I am nauseous.	**.46**	.28	.14	.06
2. When I cannot keep my mind on a task, I worry that I might be going crazy.	**.52**	-.01	**.62**	.01
15. When I am nervous, I worry that I am mentally ill.	**.53**	.02	**.54**	.07
12. It scares me when I am unable to keep my mind on a task.	**.56**	.03	**.56**	.07
16. It scares me when I am nervous.	**.39**	.18	.29	.27
1. It is important to me not to appear nervous.	**.40**	-.08	.06	**.61**
5. It is important to me to stay in control of my emotions.	**.42**	.07	.03	**.45**
13. Other people notice when I feel shaky.	**.33**	-.01	.07	**.39**
7. It embarrasses me when my stomach growls.	.19	.04	-.03	.23

Note. Values ≥1.30l are listed in boldface. General = the unitary, second-order factor underlying the Anxiety Sensitivity Index; Factor 1 = the first-order factor labeled AS–Physical Concerns; Factor 2 = the first-order factor labeled AS–Mental Incapacitation Concerns; Factor 3 = the first-order factor labeled AS–Social Concerns. From "The Hierarchical Structure and General Factor Saturation of the Anxiety Sensitivity Index: Evidence and implications" by R. E. Zinbarg, T. A. Brown, & D. H. Barlow, 1997. *Psychological Assessment, 9,* pp. 277–284. Copyright 1997 by the American Psychological Association. Reproduced with permission.

Considering the results reported by Cox et al. (1996), Peterson and Heilbronner (1987), Stewart et al. (1997), Taylor (1996), Taylor et al. (1996), and Zinbarg et al. (1997), together with the congruence coefficient results presented in Table 5.2, we draw the following three conclusions. First, the ASI has a hierarchical factor structure consisting of three partially distinct first-order factors and one general, second-order factor. Second, the three first-order factors correspond to AS–Physical Concerns, AS–Mental Incapacitation Concerns, and AS–Social Concerns. Finally, this hierarchical structure appears to be highly similar across the two populations—anxiety-disordered outpatients and college students—in which the ASI has been most frequently studied.

OTHER MEASURES OF AS
AND CLOSELY RELATED CONSTRUCTS

Although the ASI is the most widely used and studied measure in this area, several other measures have been developed to measure AS and closely related constructs. These include the Agoraphobic Cognitions Questionnaire (ACQ), Body Sensations Questionnaire (BSQ; Chambless, Caputo, Bright, & Gallagher, 1984), the Agoraphobic Cognitions Scale (ACS; Hoffart, Friis, & Martinsen, 1992), the Anxiety Sensitivity Beliefs Scale (ASBS; Kenardy, Evans, & Oei, 1992), the Panic Consequences subscale of the Panic Appraisal Inventory (PAI; Telch, 1987; Telch, Brouillard, Telch, Agras, & Taylor, 1989), and the Beliefs About Negative Consequences Inventory (BANCI; Lilienfeld & Jones, 1992). Each of these alternative measures is purported to tap aspects of the overall AS construct. Because analyses on the factor structure of the BANCI have not yet been conducted, it is not discussed further in this chapter.

Agoraphobic Cognitions Questionnaire
and Body Sensations Questionnaire

The ACQ and BSQ were developed by Chambless et al. (1984) as companion measures to address fear of fear in agoraphobic patients. Because the measures were meant for use with a limited population, the researchers conceptualized AS as the fear of panic attacks rather than the fear of a broad spectrum of anxiety symptoms. Thus, the ACQ and BSQ do not purport to measure a general AS construct. Chambless et al. noted that the ACQ and BSQ address "panic-associated concerns" (p. 1097) or "two aspects of fear of fear" (p. 1095). Content of the 14-item ACQ includes thoughts about the negative consequences of anxiety that typically occur during episodes of high arousal and panic ("I will choke to death," "I will not be able to control myself"). The measure has a 5-point Likert scale whose anchors reflect the frequency of thoughts, ranging from 1 (*thought never occurs*) to 5 (*thought always occurs*). The ACQ is composed of items intended to form two rationally derived subscales, corresponding to fears about sensations and fears of social and behavioral consequences of anxiety. The BSQ is a measure of the degree to which physical sensations associated with anxiety and arousal are feared ("heart palpitations," "feeling disoriented and confused"). The BSQ has 15 items and a 5-point Likert scale measuring severity of fear about the symptom also ranging from 1 (*not frightened or worried by this sensation*) to 5 (*extremely frightened by this sensation*). Thus, the ACQ can be construed as a measure of frequency of a set of specific thoughts, whereas the BSQ measures severity of fear of a set of specific sensations. Both measures have shown sensitivity to treatment.

The ACQ and BSQ represent an attempt to tease apart the respective contributions of frequency of AS-related thoughts and perceived severity of sensations. As noted by Chambless et al. (1984), although the utility of the ACQ and BSQ has been established in patients with panic disorder with agoraphobia, the measures await further validation in samples of patients with other disorders.

Factor Structure of the ACQ and BSQ.   Factor analyses of the ACQ have consistently revealed multifactor solutions (e.g., Arrindell, 1993a; Chambless et al., 1984; Marks, Basoglu, Alkubaisy, Sengun, & Marks, 1991), although both two- and three-factor solutions have been suggested. From a theoretical standpoint, the two-factor solution would be favored over other multifactorial models because the ACQ was designed with two rationally derived subscales in mind: fears about sensations and fears about the social and behavioral consequences of anxiety.

Chambless et al. (1984) administered the ACQ to 88 panic-disordered patients and found a two-factor solution corresponding to the rationally derived subscales. The ACQ's physical and social-behavioral factors were correlated .26, and total ACQ scores correlated .34 and .67 with total BSQ scores in two different samples (*ns* = 95 and 50, respectively). The BSQ was not factor analyzed but appeared to show good internal consistency in a sample of 53 patients (α = .87).

Arrindell (1993a) investigated the structure of the ACQ and BSQ with confirmatory factor analysis. It was expected that the three-factor model would fit the data, corresponding to the two rationally derived ACQ subscales and to the BSQ, which he purported to be unifactorial. Arrindell administered the measures to 94 patients with panic disorder or agoraphobia, and results indicate acceptable congruence coefficients between the predicted and observed models. However, Taylor (1996) argued that Arrindell may have ignored alternative solutions to the three-factor model that may have also fit the data. Regardless of this potential weakness in Arrindell's work on the measures, he also reported that the three ACQ and BSQ factors were moderately intercorrelated, suggesting a hierarchical structure.

Marks et al. (1991) extracted three factors in a principal components analysis of the ACQ, which was administered to 140 anxiety patients. Their solution was composed of one physical fears factor and two factors pertaining to social-behavioral consequences of anxiety. Because there was no clear theoretical distinction between the two social and behavioral factors, Taylor (1996) suggested that the third factor may have been the result of overextraction, resulting from the eigenvalues greater than 1 extraction rule used by the researchers. Although the results of this analysis are not in complete accordance with those of the previous two, all three studies suggest the presence of multiple lower order factors. Because Marks et al. used an orthogonal rotation, their analysis did not allow for the emergence of a higher order construct. Thus, their study does not constitute a test of the hierarchical AS model.

Considered together, the results obtained by Arrindell (1993a), Chambless et al. (1984), and Marks et al. (1991) strongly suggest that the ACQ is multifactorial. Chambless et al. hypothesized the BSQ to be unifactorial, although appropriate analyses have not yet been conducted on the BSQ to provide the necessary empirical support. Thus, the analyses of the ACQ and BSQ suggest that there are at least three first-order AS factors. Both Chambless et al. and Arrindell reported moderate correlations among them, consistent with a hierarchical model of AS.

Agoraphobic Cognitions Scale

Like Chambless et al. (1984), Hoffart et al. (1992) developed their measure of AS, the ACS, to reflect two conceptual components of AS: the response aspect (the extent to which sensations are feared) and the belief aspect (beliefs about the catastrophic consequences of anxiety). The ACS is a 10-item measure with 8 items representing agoraphobic fears, 1 item addressing social fears, and 1 item addressing general fear of fear. Items are rated on a 5-point scale measuring severity of fear (0 = *no fear*, 4 = *fear very much*). Hoffart et al. found the measure to have acceptable validity, internal consistency, and sensitivity to treatment effects.

Factor Structure of the ACS.   The ACS was factor analyzed with oblique rotation by its developers, Hoffart et al. (1992). Data were collected from two samples. The first was a heterogeneous group of patients ($n = 139$) who met criteria for panic disorder with agoraphobia ($n = 67$), social phobia ($n = 16$), generalized anxiety ($n = 10$), or depression ($n = 46$). The second sample consisted of 14 patients who met criteria for panic disorder with agoraphobia. The participants in the heterogeneous sample who received an agoraphobia diagnosis were not asked about other anxiety symptoms, thus the existence of possible subgroups within the agoraphobic group was not clearly established or ruled out. Three-factor solutions were revealed in both analyses, which, according to the researchers, suggests that the solution found in the heterogeneous sample was probably not an artifact of subgroups of patients who endorsed items differentially. However, without firmly establishing the presence of disorders in addition to agoraphobia in the agoraphobic participants, it is still possible that the current results were artifactual, resulting from diagnoses secondary to agoraphobia.

The three factors found by Hoffart et al. (1992) were named fear of bodily incapacitation, fear of losing control, and fear of embarrassing action. They closely resemble the three replicable first-order factors of the ASI discussed earlier in the chapter. Factor intercorrelations were moderate, ranging from .29 to .38 in the heterogeneous sample, and therefore suggest the existence of a common higher order construct.

Anxiety Sensitivity Beliefs Scale

The Anxiety Sensitivity Beliefs Scale (ASBS), developed by Kenardy et al. (1992) also purports to measure AS. The ASBS items were partly derived from an earlier measure, the Agoraphobia Behavior Survey Schedule (AgBSS; Cautela, 1981), which included retrospective questions from several domains (anxiety, public places, traveling, medical history, onset, and problem-solving attempts). The majority of items were borrowed from the AgBSS, with the remaining items added by Kenardy et al. to reflect commonly reported beliefs of anxiety patients. AgBSS items that were not considered to be typical of anxiety patients (e.g., "I fear that I will scream") were eliminated from the new measure. ASBS items comprise 16 anxiety symptoms, including those that appear as *DSM–III–R* criteria for panic attacks, ("lightheadedness," "palpitations") and five fears about the consequences of anxiety and panic ("feelings of unreality," "fears of losing control").

Factor Structure of the ASBS.   Kenardy et al. (1992) examined ASBS data from 390 patients using principal components analysis with oblique rotation; they found that a four-factor solution best fit the data. The factors corresponded to vestibular symptoms ("dizziness," "fear of fainting"), respiratory symptoms ("difficulty breathing," "tightness or pain in chest"), psychological threat ("surroundings seem unreal," "fear of losing control"), and autonomic arousal ("sweating," "hot/cold flushes"). The latter are also called *sociality fears* (Beck, Emery, Greenberg, 1985). These factors closely resemble those obtained in the analysis of the ASI reported by Telch et al. (1989) and certainly suggest a multidimensional AS construct. Moreover, Kenardy et al. found factor intercorrelations ranging from .29 to .55, indicating the presence of at least one higher order factor.

These results support a hierarchical model; however, they are not without limitation. As noted by Taylor (1995), the ASBS contains only five items that measure fears of sensations and their consequences; the remaining items measure the intensity of bodily sensations irrespective of whether they are feared. Taylor further noted four out of the five items assessing fear of sensations and their consequences loaded on the same factor (psychological threat). Thus, "the remaining factors were primarily or entirely measures of the *intensity* of bodily sensations, not the *fear* of these sensations" (p. 247).

Panic Appraisal Inventory

The Panic Appraisal Inventory (PAI) was developed by Telch et al. (1989) to investigate a set of proposed cognitive predictors of avoidance in agoraphobic patients. The measure consists of three separate dimensions representing proposed predictors: panic consequences, panic coping, and anticipated panic. The measure consists of 35 items, with 10 items each on the anticipated panic and panic coping scales and 15 on the panic consequences scale. Telch et al. reported that the three scales have acceptable test–retest reliability and internal consistency. Because the anticipatory panic and panic coping scales are not directly related to the structure of AS, they are not discussed further here.

The panic consequences scale includes 15 items that describe various thoughts related to panic attacks (e.g., "I may die," "I may scream"). Items load on three subscales representing physical concerns, social concerns, and lack of control concerns. Participants rate the degree to which each thought would concern or trouble them during a panic attack (0 = *not at all concerned*, 100 = *extremely concerned*). The three subscale scores and the total index have shown good internal consistency.

Factor Structure of the PAI Panic Consequences Scale. Telch et al. (1989) factor analyzed the scale and found three separate factors with five items each: loss of control concerns ("I may go insane"), physical concerns ("I may suffocate"), and social concerns ("People may think I'm weird"). These factors are similar in content to the three replicable factors found in analyses of the ASI, suggesting again the existence of three first-order AS factors. Factor intercorrelations for the three subscales of the PAI were not reported. Thus, it is not possible to conclude whether evidence exists for a hierarchical model of AS based on these analyses.

An expanded 45-item version of the PAI was psychometrically tested by Feske and DeBeurs (1996, 1997). Their sample consisted of 46 patients with panic disorder, 42 with agoraphobia and 4 without agoraphobia. The panic consequences scale was not modified in the 45-item version, thus these analyses can be viewed as a direct replication of those conducted on this scale by Telch et al. (1989). The three subscales and the overall index showed good internal consistency and all demonstrated sensitivity to treatment effects. Feske and DeBeurs (1996) reported that the three-factor structure obtained by Telch et al. (1989) replicated despite their small sample. Pearson correlations between the panic consequences subscales were .15 for physical–social, .16 for physical–loss of control, and .59 for social–loss of control. Although the study's small sample size should be kept in mind when interpreting these results, the fact that two of the three correlations are somewhat weak certainly cannot be considered strong evidence for a higher order unitary AS construct.

Summary of the Evidence Regarding the Factor Structure of Measures of AS Other Than the ASI

All seven studies reported to date, including three studies of the ACQ and BSQ (Arrindell, 1993a; Chambless et al., 1984; Marks et al., 1991), one of the ACS (Hoffart et al., 1992), one of the ASBS (Kenardy et al., 1992), and two of the PAI (Feske & DeBeurs, 1996; Telch et al., 1989), support the multidimensionality of AS. Four of the five studies that included tests of the hierarchical nature of AS reported results supporting a hierarchical model. On the one hand, the results of any one of these studies does not allow for firm conclusions because we do not have a great deal of evidence regarding the construct validity of any of the measures involved. On the other hand, we are impressed with the degree to which the results converge across these studies. We are also impressed with the degree to which the results of these studies converge with those from studies of the factor structure of ASI.

One should not underestimate the theoretical import of the convergence of results from the ASI with those from the preliminary studies of the ACQ and the BSQ, ACS, ASBS, and PAI. The convergence suggests that it is not just a specific measure (e.g., the ASI) that has a hierarchical structure. Rather, the convergence of results across different measures strongly suggests that the underlying domain of AS possesses a hierarchical structure.

IMPLICATIONS OF THE HIERARCHICAL MODEL OF ANXIETY SENSITIVITY

The hierarchical model of AS adopted here has implications for theory, research, and clinical practice. Beginning with the theoretical implications, the evidence supporting a hierarchical model of AS shows that the formulation advanced by McNally (1996) and Reiss (1991; see also Reiss & McNally, 1985), in which AS is seen as unidimensional, is mistaken and should be rejected. That is, the evidence clearly indicates that AS is multi-faceted; there are several first-order AS dimensions that are at least partially distinct. In contrast to earlier multidimensional models of AS (Peterson & Heilbronner, 1987; Telch et al., 1989; Wardle et al., 1989), however, our review suggests three first-order AS factors rather than four. Although we reject a unidimensional model of AS, we do not reject a unitary AS construct. To the contrary, we conclude that the earlier formulation articulated by Telch et al. (1989), in which it is posited that there are several specific AS factors with no underlying unitary construct, is also mistaken and should be rejected. The evidence from those studies that used appropriate methodology (e.g., oblique rotations, higher order exploratory factor analyses, confirmatory factor analyses of higher order models) consistently supports the existence of a unitary, higher order AS construct.

Although the evidence reviewed here is consistent with the broadly stated hypothesis articulated by Lilienfeld et al. (1993)—that AS is hierarchically structured—the evidence does not support all details of the particular hierarchical model of AS more specifically hypothesized by Lilienfeld et al. That is, although there is considerable empirical support for two of the first-order AS factors included in their model, the evidence does not support their other two first-order factors. On the one hand, the evidence does support the two first-order factors labeled by Lilienfeld et al. as concern for physical sensations and concern regarding mental/cognitive incapacitation and labeled by Zinbarg et al. (1997) as AS–Physical Concerns and AS–Mental Incapacitation Concerns. On the other hand, the evidence does not support first-order factors labeled by Lilienfeld et al. as concern regarding loss of control and concern regarding heart/lung failure. Rather, the analysis of factor replicability across studies reported here suggests only three replicable first-order factors with the third factor being labeled by Zinbarg et al. as AS–Social Concerns.

When interpreting the theoretical implications of the hierarchical model of AS presented here (see also Stewart et al., 1997; Zinbarg et al., 1997), one should consider Taylor's (1995a) suggestion that Reiss' (1987, 1991; Reiss & McNally, 1985) original definition of AS is too broad; it blurs the distinction between AS and negative evaluation sensitivity (NES). Taylor asked us to consider the following question: "If anxiety sensations are feared because of anticipated social consequences (e.g., rejection or censure), then how is this different from fear of negative evaluation?" (p. 246). He went on to suggest a narrower definition of AS that eliminates the overlap between AS and fear of negative evaluation. Given this definition, the factor named AS–Social Concerns corresponds entirely to NES but not at all to AS, and its covariation with the other two AS factors must be attributable entirely to trait anxiety (or some other construct hypothesized to operate at an even higher level than AS).

Evidence reported by Zinbarg and Barlow (1996) provides more support for Reiss' broad definition of AS than Taylor's narrow definition. Zinbarg and Barlow found that the ASI–Social Concerns subscale had a secondary loading (.26) on a factor defined primarily by the other two ASI subscales, although its highest loading was on a factor defined primarily by scales tapping NES. This secondary loading suggests that AS–Social Concerns is a blend of AS and NES. Therefore, the distinction between AS and NES is inherently somewhat blurry as is typical of distinctions between constructs at the lowest and intermediate levels in hierarchical structures (see the following discussion regarding the hypothesized position of AS and NES in a hierarchical model of trait anxiety).

The distinction between our broad definition of AS and NES is as follows. NES is associated with the social consequences of a wide range of behavior (including the social consequences of one's own emotional reactions). In contrast, to the extent that it is associated with social concerns, AS is associated with the more specific tendency to be concerned with the social consequences of one's own anxiety. Someone who is high on AS and AS–Social Concerns but low on NES will not be concerned about social performance if confident that he or she will not be anxious in that social situation. The person who is high on NES will experience apprehension about social performance even if he or she could be guaranteed to be relatively calm in the situation (e.g., "I'll say something stupid," "I won't know what to say" or "I am unattractive").

The final theoretical implication of the hierarchical model of AS considered here is that the model raises questions about the relationship between AS and trait anxiety. That is, if anxiety sensitivity really is a higher order construct related to multiple first-order factors, what is left for trait anxiety? Lilienfeld et al. (1993) suggested a hierarchical model of trait anxiety that provides a plausible answer to this question. These authors proposed that trait anxiety is a third-order factor that may be "conceptualized as a general tendency to react anxiously to potentially anxiety-provoking stimuli, whereas AS is a more specific tendency to react anxiously to one's own anxiety and anxiety-related sensations" (p. 171). These authors proposed other specific forms of anxiety-proneness that co-exist with AS at the second-order level, including Reiss' (1987, 1991; Reiss & McNally, 1985) factors of injury sensitivity and NES. These second-order sensitivities are hypothesized to covary as a result of their loadings on the third-order trait anxiety factor. Lilienfeld et al. suggested that AS is divisible into still lower order factors. We and others (Stewart et al., 1997; Taylor, 1996; Taylor et al., 1996; Zinbarg et al., 1997) have argued that these lowest-order factors are AS–Physical Concerns, AS–Somatic Embarrassment, and AS–Mental Incapacitation.

Given the broad scope of the model proposed by Lilienfeld et al. (1993), which also included a fourth-order factor labeled *negative emotionality*, it is difficult if not impossible to adequately test in the context of any single study. Much more data are necessary before the model can be thoroughly evaluated. However, the preliminary evidence is consistent with the model. McNally (1996) and Reiss (1991) reviewed 11 studies that included correlations between the ASI and trait anxiety measures and concluded that trait anxiety and AS are related but separable constructs. This conclusion is consistent with the hierarchical structure proposed by Lilienfeld et al. Chambless et al. (1984) also found evidence that AS and trait anxiety are related but separable constructs using the ACQ and BSQ rather than the ASI. Preliminary factor analytic evidence reported by Taylor (1995a) and Zinbarg and Barlow (1996) is also consistent with the hypotheses of trait anxiety as a third-order factor and AS as one of several second-order factors that can be decomposed into first-order AS factors. (For related discussions of the relation between AS and superordinate constructs such as trait anxiety and neuroticism, see Arrindell, 1993b; chap. 7, this volume; Lilienfeld et al., 1996; Reiss, 1997; Taylor, 1995b, 1996.)

The hierarchical model of AS also has implications for research and methodology in this area. It is important to note that acceptance of a hierarchical model of AS raises important questions about the construct validity of total scores derived from the ASI and other measures of AS (Lilienfeld et al., 1993; Taylor et al., 1992; Taylor, 1996; Telch et al., 1989). The mere demonstration that a higher order, general factor exists does not constitute sufficient psychometric justification for deriving a total score from an item set. Instead, as cogently argued by Cronbach (1951), what is required is an examination of the scale's general factor saturation, which is the proportion of variance in the total scores accounted for by the general factor (see also Revelle, 1979; Zinbarg, 1997). Zinbarg et al. (1997) performed such an analysis for the ASI and estimated that the second-order, general factor accounts for roughly 60% of the variance in ASI total scores. This finding suggests that the ASI total score does provide an interpretable measure of the unitary AS construct. Thus, the preliminary findings do provide justification for the common practice of deriving a total score from the ASI. However, it must be noted that these preliminary findings for the ASI are in need of replication. Furthermore, there are no available estimates of general factor saturation for any of the other measures in this area (e.g., ACQ, ACS, ASBS, PAI). Thus it is entirely unclear at this time whether the practice of obtaining total scores from these measures is justifiable.

When interpreting the methodological implications of the hierarchical model of AS, it is also important to remember that the most widely used measure in this area is the ASI. Unfortunately, the vast majority of studies in this area have used only ASI total scores and have not used subscales corresponding to the first-order AS factors (for exceptions, see Stewart et al., 1997; Taylor et al., 1996; Zinbarg et al., 1997). Therefore, it is unclear whether the significant relations between ASI total scores and various criteria that have been demonstrated in these previous studies should be attributed to the second-order, general AS factor or to one or more of the first-order factors.

Similarly, it is unclear how to interpret studies showing that ASI total scores have incremental validity, predicting various criteria even after controlling for trait anxiety (for reviews, see Lilienfeld, 1996; Lilienfeld et al., 1993; McNally, 1989, 1996; Reiss, 1991). Given that these studies did not include subscales corresponding to the lower order AS factors, it is impossible to determine whether they demonstrate the incremental validity of the second-order, general factor or of one or more of the first-order AS factors (a similar limitation applies to a study by Chambless and Gracely, 1989, demonstrating incremental validity using the ACQ and BSQ). Reanalyses of previous studies using the ASI are needed in which subscales corresponding to the first-order AS factors are calculated and analyzed in addition to total scores to determine which level of the AS hierarchy contributes to a given phenomenon. To prevent such interpretive ambiguities from recurring, researchers would be well advised to plan for similar analyses when designing new studies in this area.

Finally, the hierarchical model of AS has clinical implications as well. The findings of Taylor et al. (1996) and Zinbarg et al. (1997) suggest that examining an individual's profile across the three first-order AS factors has some potential to be a useful aid for assessment. For example, the findings of Zinbarg et al. suggest that individuals with a principal diagnosis of social phobia would be more likely to have a higher elevation on AS–Social Concerns than on AS–Physical Concerns, whereas those with a principal diagnosis of panic disorder would be more likely to have a higher elevation on AS–Physical Concerns. Similarly, the results of Taylor et al. suggest that the presence of major depression in the absence of panic disorder should be associated with a higher elevation on AS–Mental Incapacitation Concerns than on either of the other two factors. Thus, examining the degree of match between an individual's AS profile and his or her principal diagnosis, rather than simply deriving his or her total AS score, has the potential to provide a more detailed assessment that could have important implications for our confidence in that principal diagnosis. For example, if an individual received a principal diagnosis of panic disorder, we would have more confidence in that diagnosis if his or her highest elevation were on AS–Physical Concerns than if it were on AS–Social Concerns. In addition, as noted by Zinbarg et al. (1997), such profiles have the potential to identify themes in patients' concerns other than those related to their diagnoses.

Limitations in the Existing Literature on the Dimensionality of AS and Directions for Future Research

Little work has examined the dimensionality of AS in children. To date, the only measure of AS in children is the Child Anxiety Sensitivity Index (CASI: Silverman, Fleisig, Rabian, & Peterson, 1991), which is an 18-item modification of the ASI (for details on item content and reliability and validity of the CASI, see chap. 11, this volume). W. K. Silverman (personal communication, July 4, 1997) used confirmatory factor analysis to test various models of the structure of the CASI. She reported preliminary evidence supporting multidimensionality of AS in both child patients and nonpatients, suggesting that the factors resemble the three first-order AS factors included in the hierarchical model of AS adopted here. Unfortunately, information regarding the correlation among these factors was not available to us when we were writing this chapter. Additional data on the factor structure of the CASI should be available soon (Robin A. Weill from the University of Southern Mississippi recently collected CASI data and is currently examining its factor structure). In addition, the third author of this chapter is planning to conduct factor structure investigations of the CASI.

Even less research has examined the dimensionality of AS in older adults than in children. The second author of this chapter recently collected data on the ASI from a group of over 300 community volunteers ages 65 to 97 and plans to commence data analyses shortly. However, we are not aware of any previous reports on the structure of AS in this population.

Although the initial evidence supports the construct validity of the three first-order AS factors, it must be acknowledged that it is not yet known whether the subscales display differential predictive validity with such clinically important variables as response to panic provocation procedures, treatment response, and course of disorder. Thus, there is still much work ahead of us before we can firmly conclude that the three first-order AS factors not only represent three partially distinct substantive constructs, but that it is clinically important to distinguish among these constructs. Together with David Barlow and his colleagues, we are currently in the process of reanalyzing data from earlier studies of panic provocation and panic control therapy to provide such tests of the importance of distinguishing among the three first-order AS factors.

Finally, a limitation of several of the available measures of AS is that they contain too few markers of some of the first-order AS factors to measure them reliably. For example, the small number of items constituting the AS–Social Concerns and AS–Mental Incapacitation Concerns subscales of the ASI suggest that the reliability of these subscales may be suspect. Indeed, Zinbarg and Barlow (1996) reported that coefficient alpha is substantially lower for the AS–Social Concerns subscale (.62) than for the AS–Physical Concerns (.89) and AS–Mental Incapacitation Concerns (.85) subscales. Expanding the ASI by writing more items to tap the AS–Social Concerns and AS–Mental Incapacitation Concerns subscales is likely to enhance the reliability of these subscales; it may also produce even stronger evidence for the replicability of the three first-order AS factors across samples. Both our lab group and a group led by Brian Cox and Steven Taylor are currently working on expanding the ASI along these lines.

CONCLUSIONS

The evidence reviewed here provides strong support for a hierarchical model of AS among both outpatients with anxiety disorders and college students. This evidence consists primarily of factor analyses of the ASI, but also includes converging evidence from the available studies of the factor structure of the other published scales in this area—namely, the ACQ and the BSQ, ASBS, ACQ, and PAI. The lower level of the AS hierarchy consists of three group factors that Zinbarg et al. (1997) labeled AS–Physical Concerns, AS–Mental Incapacitation Concerns, and AS–Social Concerns. All three group factors load on a general factor consistent with the existence of a unitary, higher order AS construct. The two levels of the AS hierarchy should be viewed as complementary phenomena because the general variance representing the second-order, unitary AS construct co-exists with the more specific variance representing more differentiated facets of AS at the first-order level. Researchers and clinicians alike would do well to keep the distinction between the two levels of the hierarchy in mind. Teasing apart the contributions of the two levels of the hierarchy to AS-related phenomena should facilitate the clarification of theoretical relations in this area and has the potential to assist in clinical assessment.

REFERENCES

Arrindell, W. A. (1993a). The fear of fear concept: Evidence in favour of multidimensionality. *Behaviour Research and Therapy, 31*, 507–518.

Arrindell, W. A. (1993b). The fear of fear concept: Stability, retest artefact and predictive power. *Behaviour Research and Therapy, 31*, 139–148.

Barlow, D. H. (1988). *Anxiety and its disorders: The nature and treatment of anxiety and panic.* New York: Guilford.

Barlow, D. H. (1991). Disorders of Emotion. *Psychological Inquiry, 2*, 58–71.

Beck, A.T., Emery, G., & Greenberg, R.L. (1985). *Anxiety disorders and phobias: A cognitive perspective.* New York: Basic Books.

Bernstein, I. H., & Teng, G. (1989). Factoring items and factoring scales are different: Spurious evidence for multidimensionality due to item categorization. *Psychological Bulletin, 105*, 467–477.

Burt, C. L. (1948). The factorial study of temperamental traits. *British Journal of Psychology, 1*, 178–203.

Cautela, J.R. (1981). *Behavior analysis forms for clinical intervention* (Vol. 2). Champaign, IL: Research Press.

Chambless, D. L., Caputo, G. C., Bright, P., & Gallagher, R. (1984). Assessment of fear in agoraphobics: The body sensation questionnaire and the agoraphobic cognitions questionniare. *Journal of Consulting and Clinical Psychology, 52*, 1090–1097.

Chambless, D. L., & Gracely, E. J. (1989). Fear of fear and the anxiety disorders. *Cognitive Therapy and Research, 13*, 9–20.

Clark, D. M. (1986). A cognitive approach to panic. *Behaviour Research and Therapy, 24*, 461–470.

Cox, B. J., Parker, J. A., & Swinson, R. P. (1996). Anxiety sensitivity: Confirmatory evidence for a multidimensional construct. *Behaviour Research and Therapy, 34*, 591–598.

Cox, B. J., Taylor, S., Borger, S., Fuentes, K., & Ross, L. (1996, November). Development of an expanded Anxiety Sensitivity Index: Multiple dimensions and their correlates. In S. Taylor (Chair), *New studies on the psychopathology of anxiety sensitivity.* Symposium presented at the 30th annual meeting of the Association for Advancement of Behavior Therapy, New York, NY.

Cronbach, L. J. (1951). Coefficient alpha and the internal structure of tests. *Psychometrika, 16*, 297–334.

Cudeck, R., & Browne, M. W. (1983). Cross-validation of covariance structures. *Multivariate Behavioral Research, 18*, 147–167.

Everett, J. (1983). Factor comparability as a means of determining the number of factors and their rotation. *Multivariate Behavioral Research, 18*, 197–218.

Ferguson, G. A. (1941). The factorial interpretation of test difficulty. *Psychometrika, 6*, 323–329.

Feske, U., & DeBeurs, E. (1996, November). *The Panic Appraisal Inventory: Psychometric properties*. Poster presented at the annual meeting of the Association for the Advancement of Behavior Therapy, New York.

Feske, U., & DeBeurs, E. (1997). The Panic Appraisal Inventory: Psychometric properties. *Behaviour Research and Therapy, 35*, 875–882.

Goldberg, L. R., & Digman, J. M. (1994). Revealing structure in the data: Principles of exploratory factor analysis. In S. Strack & M. Lorr (Eds.), *Differentiating normal and abnormal personality* (pp. 216–242). New York: Springer.

Goldstein, A. J., & Chambless, D. L. (1978). A reanalysis of agoraphobia. *Behavior Therapy, 9*, 47–59.

Gorsuch, R. L. (1983). *Factor analysis*. Hillsdale, NJ: Lawrence Erlbaum Associates.

Hakstian, A. R., Rogers, W. T., & Cattell, R. B. (1982). The behavior of number-of-factors rules with simulated data. *Multivariate Behavioral Research, 18*, 197–218.

Hoffart, A., Friis, S., & Martinsen, E. W. (1992). Assessment of fear of fear among agoraphobic patients: The Agoraphobics Cognitions Scale. *Journal of Psychopathology and Behavioral Assessment, 14*, 175–187.

Kenardy, J., Evans, L., & Oei, T.P.S. (1992). The latent structure of anxiety symptoms in anxiety disorders. *American Journal of Psychiatry, 149*, 1058–1061.

Lilienfeld, S. O. (1996). Anxiety sensitivity is not distinct from trait anxiety. In R. Rapee (Ed.), *Current controversies in the anxiety disorders* (pp. 228–244). New York: Guilford.

Lilienfeld, S. O., & Jones, J. C. (1992). *The Beliefs About Negative Consequences Inventory (BANCI)*. Unpublished manuscript, University at Albany, State University of New York.

Lilienfeld, S. O., Turner, S. M., & Jacob, R. G. (1993). Anxiety sensitivity: An examination of theoretical and methodological issues. *Advances in Behaviour Research and Therapy, 15*, 147–183.

Lilienfeld, S. O., Turner, S. M., & Jacob, R. G. (1996). Further comments on the nature and measurement of anxiety sensitivity: A reply to Taylor (1995b). *Journal of Anxiety Disorders, 10*, 411–424.

Marks, M., Basoglu, M., Alkubaisy, T., Sengun, S., & Marks, I. M. (1991). Are anxiety symptoms and catastrophic cognitions directly related? *Journal of Anxiety Disorders, 5*, 247–254.

McDonald, R. P. (1965). Difficulty factors and non-linear factor analysis. *British Journal of Mathematical and Statistical Psychology, 18*, 11–23.

McNally, R. J. (1989). Is anxiety sensitivity distinguishable from trait anxiety? Reply to Lilienfeld, Jacob and Turner (1989). *Journal of Abnormal Psychology, 98*, 193–194.

McNally, R. J. (1990). Psychological approaches to panic disorder. *Psychological Bulletin, 101*, 283–303.

McNally, R. J. (1996). Anxiety sensitivity is distinguishable from trait anxiety. In R. Rapee (Ed.), *Current controversies in the anxiety disorders* (pp. 214–227). New York: Guilford.

Peterson, R. A., & Heilbronner, R. L. (1987). The anxiety sensitivity index: Construct validity and factor analytic structure. *Journal of Anxiety Disorders, 1*, 117–121.

Peterson, R. A., & Reiss, S. (1992). *Anxiety sensitivity index manual* (2nd ed.). Worthington, OH: International Diagnostic Systems.

Reiss, S. (1987). Theoretical perspectives on the fear of anxiety. *Clinical Psychology Review, 7*, 585–596.

Reiss, S. (1991). The expectancy model of fear, anxiety and panic. *Clinical Psychology Review, 11*, 141–153.

Reiss, S. (1997). Trait anxiety: It's not what you think it is. *Journal of Anxiety Disorders,* *11*, 201–214.

Reiss, S., & McNally, R. J. (1985). Expectancy model of fear. In S. Reiss & R. R. Bootzin (Eds.), *Theoretical issues in behavior therapy* (pp. 107–121). San Diego, CA: Academic Press.

Reiss, S., Peterson, R. A., & Gursky, D. M. (1988). Anxiety sensitivity, injury sensitivity, and individual differences in fearfulness. *Behaviour Research and Therapy, 26,* 341–345.

Reiss, S., Peterson, R. A., Gursky, D. M., & McNally, R. J. (1986). Anxiety sensitivity, anxiety frequency, and the prediction of fearfulness. *Behaviour Research and Therapy, 24,* 1–8.

Revelle, W. R. (1979). Hierarchical cluster analysis and the internal structure of tests. *Multivariate Behavioral Research, 14,* 57–74.

Revelle, W. R. , & Rocklin, T. (1979). Very simple structure: An alternative procedure for estimating the optimal number of interpretable factors. *Multivariate Behavioral Research, 14,* 403–414.

Sandin, B., Chorot, P., & McNally, R. J. (1996). Validation of the Spanish version of the Anxiety Sensitivity Index in a clinical sample. *Behaviour Research and Therapy, 34,* 283–290.

Silverman, W. K., Fleisig, W., Rabian, B., & Peterson, R. A. (1991). Child Anxiety Sensitivity Index. *Journal of Clinical Child Psychology, 20,* 162–168.

Stewart, S. H., Taylor, S., & Baker, J. M. (1997). Gender differences in dimensions of anxiety sensitivity. *Journal of Anxiety Disorders, 11,* 179–200.

Taylor, S. (1995a). Anxiety sensitivity: Theoretical perspectives and recent findings. *Behaviour Research and Therapy, 33,* 243–258.

Taylor, S. (1995b). Issues in the conceptualization and measurement of anxiety sensitivity. *Journal of Anxiety Disorders, 9,* 163–174.

Taylor, S. (1996). Nature and measurement of anxiety sensitivity: Reply to Lilienfeld, Turner, and Jacob (1996). *Journal of Anxiety Disorders, 5,* 425–451.

Taylor, S., Koch, W. J., & Crockett, D. J. (1991). Anxiety sensitivity, trait anxiety, and the anxiety disorders. *Journal of Anxiety Disorders, 5,* 293–311.

Taylor, S., Koch, W. J., McNally, R. J., & Crockett, D. J. (1992). Conceptualizations of anxiety sensitivity. *Psychological Assessment, 4,* 245–250.

Taylor, S., Koch, W. J., Woody, S., & McLean, P. (1996). Anxiety sensitivity and depression: How are they related? *Journal of Abnormal Psychology, 105,* 474–479.

Telch, M.J. (1987). *The Panic Appraisal Inventory.* Unpublished manuscript, University of Texas, Austin.

Telch, M.J., Brouillard, M., Telch, C.F., Agras, W.S., & Taylor, C.B. (1989). Role of cognitive appraisal in panic-related avoidance. *Behaviour Research and Therapy, 27,* 373–383.

Telch, M. J., Shermis, M. D., & Lucas, J. A. (1989). Anxiety sensitivity: Unitary personality trait or domain-specific appraisals? *Journal of Anxiety Disorders, 3,* 25–32.

Velicer, W. F., & Jackson, D. N. (1990). Components analysis vs. common factor analysis: Some issues in selecting an appropriate procedure. *Multivariate Behavioral Research, 25,* 1–28.

Wardle, J., Ahmad, T., & Hayward, P. (1990). Anxiety sensitivity in agoraphobia. *Journal of Anxiety Disorders, 4,* 325–333.

Watson, D., Clark, L. A., Weber, R., Assenheimer, J.S., Strauss, M. E., & McCormick, R. A. (1995). Testing a tripartite model: II. Exploring the symptom structure of anxiety and depression in student, adult and patient samples. *Journal of Abnormal Psychology, 104,* 15–25.

Wherry, R. I., & Gaylord, R. H. (1944). Factor pattern of test items and tests as a function of the correlation coefficient: Content, difficulty and constant error factors. *Psychometrika, 9,* 237–244.

Zinbarg, R. E. (1997). *General factor saturation and the internal structure of tests.* Manuscript submitted for publication.

Zinbarg, R. E., & Barlow, D. H. (1996). The structure of anxiety and the anxiety disorders: A hierarchical model. *Journal of Abnormal Psychology, 105,* 181–193.

Zinbarg, R. E., Barlow, D. H., & Brown, T. A. (1997). The hierarchical structure and general factor saturation of the Anxiety Sensitivity Index: Evidence and implications. *Psychological Assessment, 9,* 277–284.

Zwick, W. R., & Velicer, W. F. (1986). Comparison of five rules for determining the number of components to retain. *Psychological Bulletin, 99,* 432–442.

6

Anxiety Sensitivity and Emotional Disorders: Psychometric Studies and Their Theoretical Implications

Brian J. Cox
Sharon C. Borger
Murray W. Enns
University of Manitoba

The purpose of this chapter is to provide an overview and commentary concerning the relationship between anxiety sensitivity (AS) and emotional disorders. We do this in large part by documenting studies that have used the Anxiety Sensitivity Index (ASI) in various clinical samples. We also document several studies that have compared the ASI to different measures of psychopathology in clinical and nonclinical samples. Throughout the chapter, we attempt to understand the mechanisms responsible for observed relations between AS and emotional disturbances. As part of this task, we critically examine the nature of the AS construct and the ASI. Where appropriate we refer to results obtained from a large college student data set that is currently being prepared for publication submission. These results have only appeared previously as different conference presentations (Borger, Cox, Fuentes, & Ross, 1996; Cox, 1997; Cox, Fuentes, Ross, Borger, & Taylor, 1996; Cox, Taylor, Borger, Fuentes, & Ross, 1996). *Disorder* is treated in a broad sense in this chapter. The recent editions of the *DSM* serve as the standard in our discussion, but other types of maladaptive psychological functioning are also discussed.

In regard to clinical phenomena, Reiss (1991) proposed that AS is a predisposing personality factor in the development of anxiety disorders. Reiss also related AS to other problems such as insomnia and stress-related illnesses (in addition to posttraumatic stress disorder [PTSD]). However, AS has come to be treated by many investigators as a cognitive risk factor for panic disorder in particular. McNally (1994) noted that "preexisting beliefs" about certain bodily sensations may "predispose" people to respond to them fearfully, and thereby panic, and that this possibility is embodied in the AS hypothesis (p. 116). Thus, AS could serve as a useful construct for understanding several forms of psychopathology. It may exacerbate a number of clinical disorders; in the case of panic disorder, it may actually serve as a psychological risk factor. At least three assumptions are made in AS theory and research: (a) it concerns anxiety-related sensations, (b) it refers to a belief system, and (c) it is a predisposition rather than a correlate of panic attacks and panic disorder. The validity of these three interrelated assumptions is discussed throughout this chapter. All of this research has assessed AS using the ASI.

Table 6.1 presents the findings of several studies that have administered the ASI to different clinical samples. Our intention in presenting this table is to provide representative ASI scores for various clinical disorders. Therefore, weighted means are also presented in Table 6.1. Studies of AS and chronic pain and AS and alcohol use and abuse are not included in this list because they are reviewed elsewhere in this volume (see chaps 12 and 13).

Several general observations about AS research can be drawn from this table. Panic disorder has attracted the most research attention, whereas other conditions such as specific phobia have received less attention. The latter is surprising given that AS is supposedly a fundamental fear that can amplify other fears (see chap. 2). This paucity of research is contrasted with the number of studies on AS and major depression. Although not originally implicated in AS theory, depression has been more intensely scrutinized. The table further shows that there has been little research on other clinical problems implicated in AS theory (e.g., Reiss, 1991), such as insomnia and stress-related disorders. Although hypochondriasis is not purported to be a result of AS, there is considerable phenomenological overlap between AS and hypochondriasis (as is discussed later). The lack of ASI data on clinical samples with primary hypochondriasis is noteworthy. A final point is that the Sandin et al. study reported many of the lowest scores for most of the disorders, but this study was based on a Spanish version of the ASI.

Representative studies of normative data on the ASI are also presented in Table 6.1. The mean ASI scores for the clinical samples can be compared to these studies, which show nonclinical samples (mostly college students) score 20 or lower on the ASI (also see chap. 4). Adults recruited from the community

TABLE 6.1
Anxiety Sensitivity Index Scores in Various Clinical Samples

Study	Sample (and Comments on Sample Characteristics)	N	Mean	SD
	Panic Disorder, Agoraphobia, or Both Disorders			
Apfeldorf et al. (1994)		93	38.4	11.6
Ball et al. (1995)		22	34.7	12.1
Baranyai (1991)		50	40.1	11.5
Brown et al. (1995)	With comorbid disorders	64	37.0	11.6
Brown et al. (1995)	With no additional disorder	23	30.2	10.2
Calamari et al. (1996)		33	41.6	11.7
Cox et al. (1996)		216	37.4	12.2
Ehlers (1995)	Those who sought treatment	22	31.6	—
Ehlers (1995)	Those not seeking treatment	17	23.4	—
Ehlers & Margraf (1993)	Sample 1	63	22.4	11.0
Ehlers & Margraf (1993)	Sample 2	56	25.1	11.4
Furer et al. (1997)	With hypochondriasis	10	37.2	—
Furer et al. (1997)	Without hypochondriasis	11	29.8	—
Hazen et al. (1995)		47	33.8	8.9
Hecker et al. (1996)		16	33.4	15.3
Maidenberg et al. (1996)		15	33.2	9.5
Marks et al. (1988)		45	36.0	—
McNally & Foa (1987)		9	46.7	—
McNally & Lorenz (1987)		48	36.3	11.9
Otto et al. (1992)		50	30.5	11.2
Rapee et al. (1988)		18	36.1	—

(continues)

TABLE 6.1 (continued)

Study	Sample (and Comments on Sample Characteristics)	N	Mean	SD
Reiss et al. (1986)	Study 2	9	38.2	—
Sandin et al. (1996)		35	32.8	10.7
Stewart et al. (1992)		23	30.0	12.5
Taylor et al. (1992)		151	36.6	12.3
Taylor et al. (1996)	Without major depression	52	31.4	9.6
Taylor et al. (1996)	With major depression	37	40.3	11.3
Wardle et al. (1990)		160	41.0	10.6
Zeitlin & McNally (1993)		27	37.0	10.2
Weighted Mean	(weighted for sample size, based on 29 means)		35.5	
Posttraumatic Stress Disorder				
Taylor et al. (1992)		32	31.6	12.8
Obsessive–Compulsive Disorder				
Calamari et al. (1996)		72	26.8	13.1
Sandin et al. (1996)		26	16.2	17.3
Taylor et al. (1992)		67	25.4	12.4
Zeitlin & McNally (1993)		31	27.9	11.7
Weighted Mean	(weighted for sample size, based on 4 means)		25.1	
Generalized Anxiety Disorder				
Sandin et al. (1996)		30	19.7	10.1
Taylor et al. (1992)		17	26.2	10.9
Weighted Mean	(weighted for sample size, based on 2 means)		22.1	
Social Phobia				
Asmundson & Stein (1994)		24	27.6	7.4
Ball et al. (1995)		50	28.0	10.9
Ball et al. (1995)	With comorbid panic disorder	14	34.8	10.7
Ball et al. (1995)	With comorbid major depression or dysthymia	16	35.0	10.6

Reference	Description	n	M	SD
Hazen et al. (1995)		47	26.0	10.0
Maidenberg et al. (1996)		15	34.1	7.6
Marks et al. (1988)		15	34.0	—
Orsillo et al. (1994)		62	23.0	9.3
Sandin et al. (1996)		15	19.9	5.4
Taylor et al. (1992)		23	24.9	12.3
Weighted Mean	(weighted for sample size, based on 10 means)		27.2	
	Specific Phobia			
Marks et al. (1988)		29	18.0	—
Sandin et al. (1996)		20	14.6	7.4
Taylor et al. (1992)		23	16.1	8.1
Weighted Mean	(weighted for sample size, based on 3 means)		16.5	
	Major Depression			
Otto et al. (1995)	Study 1	15	25.3	12.5
Otto et al. (1995)	Study 2: Without a comorbid anxiety disorder	63	25.2	11.9
Otto et al. (1995)	Study 2: With a nonpanic anxiety disorder	53	28.5	12.2
Otto et al. (1995)	Study 2: With comorbid past or present panic disorder	19	31.2	13.0
Taylor et al. (1996)		46	22.1	10.6
Weighted Mean	(weighted for sample size, based on 5 means)		26.0	
	Somatoform Disorders			
Cox et al. (1994)	Somatoform pain disorder (with alexithymia)	29	29.5	12.9
Cox et al. (1994)	Somatoform pain disorder (without alexithymia)	16	14.8	8.5
Weighted Mean	(weighted for sample size, based on 2 means)		24.3	
	Normative Samples			
Asmundson & Stein (1994)	Community sample matched for age and gender to patient sample	20	12.9	8.1

(continues)

TABLE 6.1 (continued)

Study	Sample (and Comments on Sample Characteristics)	N	Mean	SD
Borger et al. (1996)	College students	320	19.7	93
Cox et al. (1991)	College students	265	22.5	10.1
Lilienfeld (1997)	College students	252	19.1	8.6
Peterson (1986)	Community college students: females	227	18.2	8.8
Peterson (1986)	Community college students: males	120	18.6	8.3
Peterson & Heilbronner (1987)	College students: females	[a]	23.6	10.9
Peterson & Heilbronner (1987)	College students: males	[a]	19.7	9.6
Reiss et al. (1986)	College students: females	80	20.5	10.2
Reiss et al. (1986)	College students: males	67	15.4	8.1
Seidenberg & Peterson (1986)	Medical students	147	14.4	7.2
Stewart et al. (1997)	College students: females	528	17.4	9.4
Stewart et al. (1997)	College students: males	290	14.6	8.7
Stewart & Zeitlin (1995)	College students	314	18.7	9.9
Telch et al. (1989)	College students (with no history of panic attacks)	745	18.5	8.7
Wardle et al. (1990)	Community sample matched for age to patient sample	120	15.0	10.2
Weighted Mean	(weighted for sample size, based on 15 means)		18.3	

— Not reported.

[a] $N = 122$ for combined (males and females). Samples sizes for each gender were not reported.

For the Marks et al. (1988) study, 16 was subtracted from total ASI scores because the ASI was incorrectly scored using a 5-point scale. Spanish and German versions of the ASI were used in the Sandin et al. (1996) and Ehlers and Margraf (1993) studies, respectively. For the Ehlers and Margraf (1993) study, the unpublished panic disorder sample means were provided by Anke Ehlers.

tend to score even lower. In general, the highest mean ASI scores (> 30) have been obtained in panic disorder samples. There is also some suggestion that greater clinical severity in panic disorder (e.g., those with comorbid diagnoses, those who had sought treatment) is associated with higher ASI scores.

There is mixed support for association between AS and agoraphobia. McNally and Lorenz (1987) reported elevated ASI scores in agoraphobics, but this was likely due to the presence of panic attacks (panic was not given prominence over agoraphobia in the psychiatric nomenclature until the *DSM–III–R* was published in 1987). In the case of panic disorder with agoraphobia, some studies failed to find that ASI scores increase with greater severity of agoraphobia (e.g., Cox, Endler, & Swinson, 1995a). When examined simultaneously, panic expectancy variables rather than AS appear to be more important determinants of agoraphobia.

ANXIETY SENSITIVITY AND PANIC DISORDER

Several other lines of evidence demonstrate a link between AS and both panic attacks and panic disorder. Taylor, Koch, and McNally (1992) found that panic disorder patients scored significantly higher on the ASI compared with patients with other anxiety disorders, with the exception of PTSD. AS was found to be the strongest predictor of panic disorder patients' success in discontinuing alprazolam medication and maintaining abstinence, regardless of whether they also received cognitive therapy (Bruce, Spiegel, Gregg, & Nuzzarello, 1995). AS has been shown to mediate responses to panic provocation procedures in individuals without a prior history of panic attacks (see chap. 9). AS has been found to distinguish nonclinical panickers (i.e., people who have panic attacks but not panic disorder) from people who have never had a panic attack (for a review, see Norton, Cox, & Malan, 1992). Reiss' (1991) emphasis on the clinical importance of AS is consistent with the criteria for panic disorder described in the current version of the *DSM* (*DSM–IV*; American Psychiatric Association, 1994). Here the diagnostic criteria are not based on the frequency or severity of panic attacks, but rather on the fear of panic (which arises from the person's beliefs about the implications or consequences of panic attacks). In other words, the *DSM–IV* emphasizes the fear of anxiety rather than the presence of anxiety. Finally, longitudinal studies support the role of AS in the development of panic *attacks*, although the effects have been modest and a prospective link with panic disorder has not yet been established (see chap. 10).

AS theory is similar to Clark's (1986, 1988) cognitive model of panic attacks. Clark proposed that panic attacks arise from the catastrophic misinterpretation of certain bodily sensations. That is, panic attacks arise when the person interprets the sensations as being much more dangerous than they really are. For example, an individual might misinterpret a skipped heartbeat as a sign of an impending heart attack. McNally (1994) contrasted AS theory with Clark's theory by stating that AS is a fear of anxiety or arousal sensations and not a misinterpretation that the sensations are a sign of an imminent catastrophe. McNally claimed that "the anxiety sensitivity hypothesis does not require that patients misconstrue anxiety as something else (e.g., impending heart attack) for panic to be highly aversive" (p. 116).

It is unclear whether individuals who score high on the ASI are fearful of the sensations of anxiety (or other arousal states for that matter) that they do not correctly identify as anxiety. The alternate possibility is that these individuals truly fear anxiety, and are aware that the sensations they fear do, in fact, constitute anxiety. Many of the items that comprise the ASI do not make this distinction, and empirical findings on items most relevant for panic disorder patients are not particularly encouraging for AS theory. In comparing mean item scores for panic disorder patients compared with PTSD patients, Taylor et al. (1992) observed that the largest differences ($ts > 3.0$) were for these items: "It scares me when my heart beats rapidly" and "When I notice that my heart is beating rapidly, I worry that I might have a heart attack." Hazen, Walker, and Stein, (1995) compared panic disorder and social phobia patients on ASI item scores and found that panic disordered patients were characterized by higher scores on two items: "It scares me when my heart beats rapidly" and "It scares me when I am short of breath." Similarly, Apfeldorf, Shear, Leon, and Portera (1994) identified four items that best discriminated panic disorder patients from patients with other anxiety disorders. The items referred to feeling shaky, feeling faint, rapid heart rate, and shortness of breath. In significant contrast, none of these studies found that the two ASI items that explicitly refer to a fear of anxiety ("It scares me when I am nervous," "When I am nervous I worry that I might be mentally ill") were particularly salient for panic disorder patients. Taken together, these findings are more consistent with Clark's model of catastrophic misinterpretation of bodily sensations rather than a fear of anxiety per se.

Cox (1996) attempted to further integrate some aspects of Clark's cognitive process of catastrophic misinterpretation and AS theory. In Clark's model, it is not clear what gives rise to the catastrophic cognitive process other than some type of "enduring tendency," and AS could be an important predisposing factor. Cox viewed AS as a multidimensional trait in which congruence is required between a lower order facet of AS and a trigger stimulus to initiate the catastrophic process described by Clark. To illustrate, a person with an extreme fear of cardiac sensations may panic in response to palpitations, but not in response to a feeling of depersonalization. In comparison, depersonalization could serve as a congruent trigger (i.e., a panic trigger) for an individual with a fear of cognitive dyscontrol. There is evidence from several exploratory and confirmatory factor-analytic studies that the ASI is composed of multiple facets. These lower order facets are likely hierarchically structured within a higher order AS factor (see chap. 5). The lower order AS dimensions most often identified include fear of somatic sensations, fear of cognitive dyscontrol, and fear of publicly observable anxiety symptoms. One of the limitations to date is that the ASI probably contains too few items to reliably identify a multifactor solution. Accordingly, in collaboration with Taylor, we have been conducting factor-analytic studies with an expanded ASI that contains new items referring to proposed lower order facets. We have also developed a completely revised measure of AS, designed for the same purpose, and we have had some success with both of these approaches (e.g., Cox et al., 1996; Taylor & Cox, in press).

If a psychometrically sound, multidimensional measure of AS can be developed, we may be able to test whether Cox's (1996) prediction of an improvement in precision in panic disorder research is a valid one (e.g., whether panic attacks can be more accurately predicted when there is a more precise match between the symptoms evoked by a provocation task and the symptoms a person fears). Further study of the AS dimensions should increase our understanding of which bodily sensations trigger panic attacks in which individuals and why. This suggestion is consistent with the recent empirical findings of McNally and Eke (1996). Using a sample of college students, they found that the fear of dyspnea (a facet of AS) predicted fearful responding to a congruent trigger (carbon dioxide challenge), and this facet of AS was a better predictor than the ASI total score. Research to date suggests that ASI items assessing catastrophic consequences of bodily sensations are more relevant to the assessment of panic disorder. Our emphasis on the importance of catastrophic thinking is again more consistent with Clark's model of catastrophic misinterpretation than it is with AS theory.

ANXIETY SENSITIVITY
AND OTHER ANXIETY DISORDERS

Studies in Table 6.1 indicate that, apart from panic disorder, AS is also elevated in several other anxiety disorders. Although the number of studies is small, research suggests that AS is elevated in PTSD. The mean ASI scores are similar to those obtained in panic disorder. Taylor et al. (1992) speculated that this relation could be due in part to the phenomenological similarity between panic attacks and flashbacks, which are a hallmark feature of PTSD (see chap. 15). This possibility remains untested and more work is needed with PTSD patients, perhaps in the form of a structured interview, to explore the nature of this relation. However, from examining the item responses between PTSD patients and panic disorder patients reported in the Taylor et al. study, it appears that there is a different pattern of ASI responding in PTSD. Whereas cardiorespiratory fears seem to be relevant for panic disorder patients, there was a trend for PTSD patients to score higher on fears of psychological sensations (e.g., "When I cannot keep my mind on a task, I worry that I might be going crazy," "It scares me when I am unable to keep my mind on a task"). A multidimensional measure of AS that better assesses fear of cognitive dyscontrol may help answer the question of whether there is a distinct type of AS that is more germane to PTSD than to panic disorder. Fear of cognitive dyscontrol has also been linked to major depression (to be discussed shortly). Investigation of this AS facet in relation to PTSD with comorbid with depression would therefore be of interest.

In addition, there are other feared types of cognitive dyscontrol that are salient for PTSD patients and are not currently assessed by the ASI (e.g., nightmares). If an expanded ASI could be developed that was more relevant for PTSD, it would be interesting to test its predictive powers in a prospective study of individuals who have been exposed to traumatic events but who have not yet developed PTSD. This type of assessment could serve to screen for people at risk for PTSD. Such people might benefit from early intervention procedures such as critical incident stress debriefing.

Table 6.1 displays evidence that ASI scores are elevated in social phobia, with scores approaching or even exceeding those of panic disorder. Hazen et al. (1995) compared ASI item scores in patients with either panic disorder or social phobia. The results suggest that a different form of ASI responding is operating in social phobia compared with panic disorder. Compared with panic disorder patients, social phobia patients had significantly higher scores on three items ("It is important to me not to appear nervous," "It embarrasses me when my stomach growls," and "Other people notice when I feel shaky"). In contrast, panic disorder patients scored significantly higher mainly on those items referring to cardiorespiratory and other physical sensations. The contents of the three items most relevant for social phobia patients appear to come close to assessing fear of negative evaluation—a proposed fundamental fear that is distinct from AS both theoretically (e.g., Reiss & McNally, 1985) and empirically (Taylor, 1993).

A fear of anxiety symptoms can conceivably be elevated in both social phobia and panic disorder. In social phobia, individuals may fear publicly observable anxiety symptoms (e.g., sweating, blushing, trembling) if they believe these symptoms have harmful social consequences. In panic disorder, as discussed earlier, individuals are more likely to fear cardiac and respiratory anxiety symptoms and believe that these symptoms have harmful physical consequences. These considerations underscore the need for item-level or dimensional analyses in clarifying the nature of AS in various clinical conditions.

In factor-analytic studies of the ASI, a factor representing fear of publicly observable symptoms often emerges. Catastrophic cognitions about the social consequences of anxiety are common in panic disorder and should not be removed from an assessment of one of several possible harmful consequences of anxiety sensations. Yet some of the original ASI items are perhaps too heavily contaminated by fear of negative evaluation. This possibility is empirically supported by a recent factor-analytic study of a revised measure of AS, where a factor representing fear of publicly observable symptoms failed to emerge (Taylor & Cox, in press). It is possible that an expanded or revised measure of AS could still be saturated with fear of negative evaluation, but that it is distributed across all of the items and would therefore not emerge as a separate factor.

Finally, there is some suggestion that the original ASI may be more associated with public speaking and other performance-related fears than with generalized social phobia (Norton, Cox, Hewitt, & McLeod, 1997). Using a sample of college students, Norton et al. found that the ASI was the best predictor of self-reported social performance anxiety, whereas a measure of neuroticism was the best predictor of self-reported social interaction anxiety. However, the ASI was a significant predictor of social interaction anxiety as well and it is not clear whether this is due to some ASI items being too reflective of fear of negative evaluation. Further work with clinical samples appears warranted.

There has been noticeably less systematic research on AS in generalized anxiety disorder (GAD) and obsessive–compulsive disorder (OCD; e.g., item-level comparisons, factor analysis). However, Table 6.1 indicates that some studies have found elevated ASI total scores in these samples. It is not known whether unique ASI patterns of responding would also be true for these samples, but it seems reasonable to predict that this is likely. For example, fear of cognitive dyscontrol, compared with fears of cardiorespiratory or other physical sensations, may be more relevant for OCD and GAD. As with PTSD, future work could involve developing more cognitive dyscontrol items relating to worry and intrusive thoughts/images for these clinical groups. Such items could be useful in predicting onset, exacerbation, and relapse of OCD and GAD. Just as AS is believed to differ from anxiety frequency, so too might sensitivity to episodes of worry differ from worry proneness. Examples of cognitive dyscontrol items include: "It scares me when an unwanted image pops into my mind" (OCD) and "It is frightening when I can't stop myself from worrying" (GAD). Cartwright-Hatton and Wells (1997) developed a new measure to assess beliefs about worry and intrusive thoughts. Their Meta-Cognitions Questionnaire may hold promise for examining the sensitivity to (i.e., fear of) cognitive dyscontrol. (Note that Cartwright-Hatton and Wells do not refer to AS and are instead concerned with cognitive appraisals in GAD and problematic worry.)

Many people in the general population experience unwanted intrusive thoughts, but few develop OCD. A sense of inflated responsibility (Rachman, 1993) for controlling one's mental activities could give rise to a fear of cognitive dyscontrol. This could in turn give rise to subsequent negative appraisals of intrusive thoughts (Salkovskis, 1985) that are characteristic of OCD. As noted by Salkovskis (1996), "the deployment of effortful strategies and attention towards the *control of mental activity* involves a variety of phenomena that all may contribute to the experience of obsessional symptoms and their maintenance" (p. 62). Similarly, Criterion B of the GAD diagnostic criteria in the *DSM–IV* states that the "person finds it difficult to control the worry" (p. 435). Thus, further research on fear of cognitive dyscontrol may shed light on the nature of clinical and nonclinical obsessions and worries.

Reiss and Havercamp (1996) recently proposed several new types of fundamental motives or sensitivities to account for individual differences in the type and amount of reinforcement that people desire from their environment (see chap. 3). Of these fundamental motives, self-control and morality would appear to be good candidates for OCD. Other than AS, it is not immediately clear which other sensitivities listed by Reiss and Havercamp may apply to GAD.

Although limited, available research has not supported the idea that ASI is generally elevated in specific phobia. In discussing this null finding, Taylor et al. suggested that fundamental fears other than AS may be more relevant for certain types of specific phobias (e.g., fear of injury in blood/injury phobia). It is possible that AS, or facets within AS, may still be relevant for some types of specific phobias (e.g., fear of physical sensations may play a role in choking phobia). A recent study did find that the ASI was a significant predictor of accident phobia in a sample of motor vehicle accident survivors (Asmundson, Larsen, Cox, & Frombach, 1997). However, when patients with comorbid PTSD were excluded, the ASI was no longer a significant predictor in the regression equation (G. J. G. Asmundson, personal communication, November 3, 1997).

Further work is needed to determine whether AS can amplify specific fears and phobias. As Reiss (1997) recently stated, "anxiety sensitivity is a fear amplification factor, so that increases in anxiety sensitivity lead to increased fearfulness" (p. 210). However, it seems that what exactly operates as the fundamental fear in this process is not always clear. As an illustration of the AS fear amplification process, Reiss presented an example of a man who was persuaded that his medical condition was so precarious he should avoid excitement lest he have a fatal heart attack. Reiss stated that by definition this would increase the person's AS. Reiss went on to state that prior to acquiring AS, the man may have feared air travel because of a fear of the plane crashing. However, the man would now have the additional fear that worrying about the plane crashing would cause a fatal heart attack. Yet one wonders whether AS truly amplifies other fears in this type of example or whether these fears, including apparent AS, could be reducible to a more fundamental fear—namely, the fear of death or dying (see chap. 2). The man in this case might avoid situations that would make him angry for the same reason, but it is unlikely we would think of him as having anger sensitivity per se. It would seem that if the man were not concerned about dying, he would not acquire the elevated AS or even arousal sensitivity. It is also possible that Reiss chose a less than ideal example because the idea that perceiving anxiety sensations as much more dangerous than they really are is not really true for this case example.

ANXIETY SENSITIVITY AND HYPOCHONDRIASIS

When inspecting the item content of the ASI and when reading cognitive accounts of panic disorder, one cannot help but wonder how much overlap exists between AS and hypochondriasis. The absence of research on primary hypochondriasis (as defined in *DSM–IV*) and AS is a concern because the distinctive and overlapping features of AS and hypochondriasis are not yet well defined. This issue has been the focus of debate in the literature (Otto & Pollack, 1994; Otto, Pollack, Sachs, & Rosenbaum, 1992; Taylor, 1994, 1995b). The debate was sparked by the finding that several subscales of the Illness Attitudes Scale (IAS; Kellner, 1986) were found to significantly correlate with the ASI in a sample of panic disorder patients (Otto et al., 1992).

On a diagnostic level, a recent study by Furer, Walker, Chartier, and Stein (1997) compared panic disorder patients with and without comorbid hypochondriasis and found elevated ASI scores in the former group (see Table 6.1). The difference in scores was not significant, but this may have been due to inadequate statistical power given the small sample size. Alternatively, the comorbid patients tended to score higher on other measures of psychopathology. Thus, it is not clear whether ASI elevations were due to the presence of hypochondriasis specifically or whether these patients represented generally more severe cases of panic disorder.

It would be interesting to conduct ASI item-level comparisons in a larger sample of panic disorder patients with versus without comorbid hypochondriasis as well as patients with a primary diagnosis of hypochondriasis to see whether there are differences in patterns of ASI item scores. Specifically, it would be of interest to determine whether the ASI items that have been found to best discriminate panic disorder from other anxiety disorders would also discriminate panic disorder from primary hypochondriasis.

In the case of the Otto et al. (1992) study, debate has focused on whether the AS/hypochondriasis overlap may be due to limitations of the IAS. AS refers to a fear of anxiety and anxiety obviously involves several physical sensations. Therefore, it is not surprising that individuals with elevated AS would also score high on a measure of fear of physical sensations (as assessed by the IAS). However, high AS individuals would not necessarily fear a wide range of sensations, but rather would fear only arousal-related sensations (e.g., cardiorespiratory distress). This differentiation is consistent with cognitive accounts of panic disorder (Clark, 1988).

In this view, the cognitive processes in panic disorder are focused on autonomic nervous system responses that are exacerbated by anxiety, and the perceived threat is seen as immediate rather than long term. Taylor (1994) suggested that fears of arousal-reactive sensations (e.g., cardiac activity) and fears of arousal-nonreactive symptoms (e.g., rashes) may constitute separate dimensions that distinguish panic disorder (and AS) from hypochondriasis. Taylor also noted that the IAS does not make this important distinction; this could account in part for the significant correlations between IAS subscales and the ASI. However, another limitation that may have actually lowered the correlations is the fact that the two measures are quite different in format. It is for these reasons that our research group sought to further investigate this issue using new ASI-type items with hypochondriacal content as part of a series of studies on the AS construct and the ASI. At this point we introduce this research enterprise.

Using a large sample of college students ($N = 320$), we administered a battery of psychopathology and personality measures. These measures included personality variables assessed by the NEO Personality Inventory (NEO–PI–R; Costa & McCrae, 1992), as well as several Likert-type questions we developed (e.g., items to assess the perceived importance of control over emotions). We also administered an expanded ASI that included an item pool containing the original ASI followed by similarly worded items to assess proposed facets within AS and other variables such as hypochondriasis. We compared subsamples of individuals who scored either one standard deviation above the mean (high AS) or one standard deviation below the mean (low AS) on the original ASI (for the sample of 320 students, the obtained mean of 19.7 and standard deviation of 9.3 are similar to other college student studies; see chap. 4). High and low AS subjects were interviewed using the anxiety disorders, somatoform disorders, and substance use disorders sections of the Structured Clinical Interview for the *DSM–IV* (SCID; First, Spitzer, Gibbon, & Williams, 1995). Subjects answered the SCID screening questions and positive responses were followed by the relevant SCID sections. The interviewer was blind as to subjects' level of AS.

In regard to SCID results, only two subjects met full diagnostic criteria for a somatoform disorder. One subject had somatization disorder and one had pain disorder (both were high AS). People with high AS, compared with those with low AS, were more likely to respond positively to SCID somatoform disorders screening questions. Significantly fewer high AS subjects reported that their physical health was good compared with low AS subjects, and high AS subjects also reported significantly more health worries and physician visits. High AS individuals, compared with those with low AS, were far more likely to meet *DSM–IV* criteria for an anxiety disorder and more likely to respond positively to the SCID panic attack screening question.

As part of the expanded ASI, we created eight items designed to assess hypochondriasis (ASI–H). We tried to focus these items on either nonarousal sensations and/or references to long-term rather than immediate harmful consequences (e.g., "When I have a rash on my skin, I fear it may be skin cancer," "When I get aches or pains, I worry there is something seriously wrong with my health"). A factor analysis was conducted and a two-factor solution was specified to determine whether separate AS and hypochondriasis factors would emerge. This was indeed the case; all eight ASI–H items loaded more than .30 on a distinct factor and did not cross-load on the AS factor. However, some of the ASI items loaded or cross-loaded on the hypochondriasis factor. Two ASI items loaded more than .30 on the hypochondriasis factor and did not load (< .30) on the AS factor ("When I notice that my heart is beating rapidly, I worry that I might have a heart attack," "When my stomach is upset, I worry that I might be seriously ill"). Four other ASI items cross-loaded (> .30) on both factors. Most of these items referred to physical sensations (e.g., shortness of breath, rapid heart rate). The scree plot suggested a four-factor solution: three AS factors and one hypochondriasis factor. In this solution, three ASI items (shortness of breath, rapid heart rate/heart attack, upset stomach/seriously ill) continued to load on a distinct hypochondriasis factor.

Taken together, these new findings indicate that some ASI items are more reflective of hypochondriasis than of a fear of anxiety (an alternate possibility is that fear of anxiety represents a facet of a broader set of hypochondriacal fears). Of particular concern is the fact that almost all of the ASI items most strongly associated with hypochondriasis are the same items that were previously identified as most salient for panic disorder (e.g., rapid heart rate, shortness of breath).

The relationship between hypochondriasis—as a construct and a clinical disorder—and AS clearly warrants further investigation. Even if AS and hypochondriasis are overlapping phenomena that can still be differentiated, both may share a common diathesis. This possibility is supported by a recent study that examined the learning history origins of individuals with different levels of AS (Watt, Stewart, & Cox, in press). This study paralleled the work of Ehlers (1993) on the childhood learning experiences of panic disorder patients and used an expanded version of Ehlers' Learning History Questionnaire. The results indicate that the learning experiences of high AS individuals were not specific to anxiety symptoms, but also involved parental reinforcement of sick-role behavior related to having colds. This was not true for individuals with self-reported panic attacks who reported more learning experiences specific to anxiety symptoms compared with nonpanickers. The authors suggested that AS may arise from learned fears of bodily sensations in general, rather than from learned fears of anxiety symptoms in particular. However, Watt et al. also noted that further work is needed with other types of somatic complaints. These preliminary results provide additional support for the idea that the ASI assesses phenomena that are broader than a fear of anxiety. The results are also consistent with the conclusions of the Cox et al. (1994) study of somatoform disorder. Cox et al. proposed that the ASI may sometimes assess a "fear of unusual physical and emotional sensations that are not necessarily identified as anxiety" (p. 525).

ANXIETY SENSITIVITY AND DEPRESSION

It is not intuitively obvious why there should be a relationship between fear of anxiety (AS) and depression, apart from a general association with negative affectivity. Although AS has been theoretically implicated in a number of forms of psychopathology, depression is not in the list. Therefore, it was somewhat surprising that Otto et al. (1995) found elevated ASI scores in depressed subjects (even in subjects without a comorbid anxiety disorder) and that the scores were similar to those obtained in social phobia, OCD, and GAD samples (see Table 6.1). Not surprisingly, depressed patients with a comorbid anxiety disorder had even higher ASI scores. It was also interesting that, in this case, AS was subject to strong state effects of depression. Otto et al. found that ASI scores declined from a mean of 27.1 to a mean of 20.0 in a group of 86 depressed patients treated with 8 weeks of fluoxetine.

Taylor, Koch, Woody, and McLean (1996) replicated these observations. They also attempted to identify the mechanisms responsible for this elevation by conducting a factor analysis of the ASI in a sample of patients with major depression and/or panic disorder. The analysis yielded a three-factor solution similar to those found in factor analytic studies of AS in other types of samples: fear of publicly observable symptoms (Factor I), fear of cognitive dyscontrol (Factor II), and fear of somatic sensations (Factor III). Factor II showed strong associations with measures of depression severity, but not with measures of anxiety severity, whereas the reverse was true for Factors I and III. Further, a diagnosis of major depression was associated with the highest scores on Factor II.

As with several other types of psychopathology, it appears that only one facet of AS is implicated in depression—namely, phrenophobia (fear of cognitive dyscontrol). Taylor et al. described this facet as a "depression-specific form of anxiety sensitivity" (p. 478). However, in this case, depression (rather than anxiety) may be amplified by fear of loss of cognitive control. In other words, it seems that phrenophobia does not simply reflect worry about depression symptoms or an anxious depression. The fact that in the Taylor et al. study, phrenophobia was associated with indexes of depression severity, but not anxiety severity, supports this assertion.

As discussed earlier in sections on PTSD, OCD, and GAD, it is likely that phrenophobia is not depression-specific. It may be important in other disorders as well. However, depression sensitivity (fear of depression) may have a broader scope than simply phrenophobia. There may be other associated features of depression (e.g., sleep disruption, fatigue) that depression-sensitive individuals could catastrophically interpret as indicators of harmful consequences (e.g., impending major depressive episode), thereby worsening depressive symptoms or causing them to persist. This may be particularly meaningful for those individuals who have recovered from a major depressive episode and are concerned about relapse (a form of the *scar hypothesis*[1]).

There has been some work along these lines, such as Taylor and Rachman's (1991) fear of sadness construct and Nolen-Hoeksema's (1991) rumination hypothesis, in which rumination about depressed mood causes persistence of

---

[1]The *scar hypothesis* posits that depressive episodes, particularly when chronic or recurrent, may result in relatively permanent personality or cognitive changes that render the individual vulnerable to future episodes of depression (Lewinsohn, Steinmertz, Larson, & Franklin, 1981).

symptoms. In the latter case, depression sensitivity may help explain why some individuals are prone to engage in rumination. However, there is no specific model or measure that focuses on depression sensitivity; it is not mentioned in the new Reiss–Havercamp list of sensitivities (see chap. 3). We propose that depression sensitivity is a predisposition to react to depressed mood and/or other depressive symptoms (e.g., impaired concentration) in a manner that results in amplification of depression symptoms. This reaction is hypothesized to arise because depressive symptoms are catastrophically interpreted as evidence of impending or irreversible depression, cognitive incapacitation, or personal inadequacy.

It is not currently clear whether individuals with a supposed depression sensitivity would correctly identify depressed moods as such but simply find them intolerable, or whether a catastrophic misinterpretation is involved. Drawing on cognitive accounts of panic disorder (Clark, 1986) and OCD (Salkovskis, 1985), individuals scarred from a major depressive episode may catastrophically misinterpret normal episodes of fatigue, memory lapses, sadness, and so on as signs of an impending relapse into another major depressive episode, rather than as transient, unpleasant events that are part of the human experience. (Such a catastrophic tendency could be an important target in relapse prevention in cognitive-behavioral treatment approaches.)

In other cases, the misinterpretation might relate to different catastrophic outcomes. For example, an individual with clinical depression might misinterpret concentration difficulties as a sign of brain damage and impending dementia rather than as a symptom of depression, and may actually be reassured that it is a case of the latter rather than the former. Either scenario could result in an elevation in the phrenophobia facet of the ASI. This stresses the need for future research to clarify the nature of the association between depression and fear of cognitive dyscontrol (which was only comprised of three ASI items in the Taylor et al. study).

Research by Williams, Chambless, and Ahrens (1997) also extended the fear of fear construct to include fear of loss of one's control of emotions (in general), including fear of depressed mood. Williams et al. demonstrated that fear of emotion (fear of depression, anger, and positive emotions) predicted fear of laboratory-induced bodily sensations in a group of subjects with no history of panic attacks. One wonders whether the depressed mood subscale (sample item: "Depression is scary to me—I am afraid that I could get depressed and never recover") may tap a tendency to react catastrophically to the experience of normal depressed mood (sadness) and thereby produce further depression. A limitation of this measure for the purposes of assessing depression sensitivity is that it concentrates on the emotion of depression and does not include depression-related sensations or symptoms, such as fatigue, insomnia, and so on, which could also be catastrophically misinterpreted.

Other research has shown that the ASI predicts depressed mood in nonclinical individuals. Schmidt, Lerew, and Jackson's (1997) prospective study found that, in addition to predicting the occurrence of panic attacks, the ASI was also a significant (but not powerful) predictor of scores on the Beck Depression Inventory (BDI). Catanzaro (1993) also provided evidence that the ASI is associated with depressed mood. He found that an interaction between the ASI and a measure of negative mood regulation expectancy was a significant predictor of BDI scores (in addition to the main effects of each variable). Individuals with high levels of anxiety sensitivity and weak beliefs in their ability to regulate negative moods reported the most emotional distress.

Finally, in our expanded ASI item pool, we developed eight items regarding beliefs about emotions (e.g., "Powerful emotions scare me"), as well as items regarding emotional control ("It scares me when I can't control how I feel"). We developed these items to help further explore the hypothesized emotion regulation component of the ASI (i.e., the ASI contains an item stating that "It is important to me to stay in control of my emotions"). A factor analysis specifying a two-factor solution revealed that separate factors emerged for AS and beliefs/control concerning emotions. However, the ASI item assessing the importance of emotional control and another item ("It is important to me not to appear nervous") loaded on the emotions factor and did not cross-load on the AS factor. ASI items relating to "Keeping my mind on a task," "Nervous/mentally ill," and "It scares me when I am nervous" also cross-loaded (loadings .30 on each factor).

In addition, we questioned subjects about how important it was for them to be in control of their emotions and how much they currently perceived themselves as being in control of their emotions. We then computed the difference between these two ratings. The difference score was a significant predictor of ASI scores, even when a number of other NEO–PI personality facets (including trait anxiety) were entered in a regression analysis. Taken together, these results suggest that there is an element of emotion regulation associated with or contained in the ASI. Sensitivity about negative emotions and perceived control over emotions warrant further study in relation to emotional distress (including depression).

RELATIONS BETWEEN THE ASI
AND SELF-REPORT MEASURES
OF PSYCHOPATHOLOGY

Table 6.2 presents correlations between the ASI and a number of different self-report measures. Most studies in Table 6.2 used college student samples, but the results are generally consistent with the clinical observations reviewed in the previous sections of this chapter. The relations between the ASI and measures of fears and trait anxiety/negative affectivity have been the subject of several published reviews (e.g., Lilienfeld, Turner, & Jacob, 1993; McNally, 1996; Reiss, 1997; Taylor, 1995a, 1996) and are also discussed elsewhere in this book (see chap. 7). Therefore, this work is only summarized here; we did not include correlations with the State-Trait Anxiety Inventory in Table 6.2.

The ASI can be distinguished from measures of other proposed fundamental fears, and it predicts variance in common fears (mostly agoraphobia). Research also indicates that AS is not simply a form of trait anxiety or neuroticism, although there is support for the view that AS is a lower order factor that is hierarchically nested in these higher order factors (see chaps. 5 and 7). In fact, the studies cited in Table 6.2 show that, although the ASI is correlated with a number of different measures and some of these correlations can be considered large ones, the ASI seems to assess a distinct individual difference variable that is not better accounted for by related measures. Hence, in none of the cases did the percent of shared variance exceed 50%. Further, although some of the highest correlations have been observed between the ASI and fear inventories, Taylor's (1993) factor-analytic study clearly demonstrated that the ASI loads separately from other measures of proposed fundamental fears. Although AS has often been associated with panic attacks and panic disorder, Table 6.2 shows that the correlations between the ASI and the Beck Anxiety Inventory (which assesses a number of panic attack symptoms) were not excessive (i.e., less than 50% shared variance). This finding is consistent with a factor analytic investigation of ASI items and panic symptom severity ratings in panic disorder patients. Despite some overlap, ASI items and panic attack symptoms loaded on separate factors (Cox, Endler, & Swinson, 1995b).

Interestingly, Table 6.2 shows that, although the ASI is correlated with other measures of fear of anxiety—the Agoraphobic Cognitions Questionnaire (ACQ) and the Body Sensations Questionnaire (BSQ)—the correlations are not as large as one might expect given that these measures are ostensibly assessing the same underlying construct. However, the ACQ/BSQ and the ASI are not identical in format. Asmundson, Norton, Lanthier, and Cox (1996) have noted

TABLE 6.2
Correlations Between the Anxiety Sensitivity Index and Psychopathology Measures

Study	Sample	Measure	r
		Agoraphobic Cognitions Questionnaire	
Asmundson et al. (1996)	College students: panickers (*n* = 48)	Total score	.38
"	College students: nonpanickers (*n* = 48)	"	.44
"	College students: panickers (*n* = 48)	Social behavioral subscale	.40
"	College students: nonpanickers (*n* = 48)	"	.43
"	College students: panickers (*n* = 48)	Physical concerns subscale	.19
"	College students: nonpanickers (*n* = 48)	"	.34
Lilienfeld (1997)	College students (*n* = 220)	Total score	.59
McNally & Lorenz (1987)	Agoraphobics (*n* = 48)	"	.66
Borger et al. (1996); Cox et al. (1996)	College students (*n* = 320)		.53
		Beck Anxiety Inventory	
Schmidt et al. (1997)	Air Force cadets (*n* = 472)	"	.30
Catanzaro (1993)	College students (*n* = 502)		.39
		Beck Depression Inventory	
McNally & Lorenz (1987)	Agoraphobics (*n* = 48)	"	.63
Schmidt et al. (1997)	Air Force cadets (*n* = 472)	"	.24
		Body Sensations Questionnaire	
Asmundson et al. (1996)	College students: Panickers (*n* = 48)		.38
"	College students: Nonpanickers (*n* = 48)	"	.38
Edelmann & Skov (1993)	College students (*n* = 82)	"	.59
Lilienfeld (1997)	College students (*n* = 220)	"	.63
McNally & Lorenz (1987)	Agoraphobics (*n* = 48)	"	.64

(continues)

TABLE 6.2 (continued)

Study	Sample	Measure	r
		Fear Survey Schedule (FSS: Versions II or III)	
Baranyai (1991)	Patients with agoraphobia, other anxiety disorders, or chronic headache (n = 150)	FSS–III: Agoraphobia subscale	.48
"	"	FSS–III: Social subscale	.35
"	"	FSS–III: Blood/injury subscale	.36
Ehlers & Margraf (1993)	Patients with panic disorder (± agoraphobia) (n = 241)	FSS–III total	.64
McNally & Lorenz (1987)	Agoraphobics (n = 48)	FSS–II total	.65
Reiss et al. (1986), Study 1	College students (n = 49)	"	.59
Reiss et al. (1986), Study 2	College students (n = 98)	"	.71
Reiss et al. (1988)	College students (n = 147)	Dissimilar Fear Survey (adapted from FSS–II)	.52
Taylor (1996), Sample 1	Community volunteers (n = 144)	FSS–III: Agoraphobia subscale	.45
"	"	FSS–III: Social subscale	.50
"	"	FSS–III: Blood/injury subscale	.41
"	"	FSS–III: Animals subscale	.35
		Fear Questionnaire	
McNally & Lorenz (1987)	Agoraphobics (n = 48)	Total score	.47
Taylor (1996), Sample 3	People with recurrent unexpected panic attacks (e.g., full or subclinical panic disorder) (n = 83)	Agoraphobia subscale	.34
"	"	Social phobia subscale	.33
Ehlers & Margraf (1993)	Patients with panic disorder (± agoraphobia) (n = 241)	Agoraphobia subscale	.52

Illness Attitudes Scales

Study	Sample	Scale	
Borger et al. (1996); Cox et al. (1996)	College students (*n* = 320)	Total score (sum of scale scores)	.43
"	"	Worry about illness	.37
"	"	Concern about pain	.32
"	"	Hypochondriacal beliefs	.26
"	"	Thanatophobia	.35
"	"	Disease phobia	.30
"	"	Bodily preoccupation	.39
"	"	Effects of symptoms	.39
Otto et al. (1992)	Patients with panic disorder (± agoraphobia) (*n* = 50)	Worry about illness	.43
"	"	Concern about pain	.42
"	"	Thanatophobia	.49
"	"	Disease phobia	.32
"	"	Bodily preoccupation	.49

Subscales of the Mobility Inventory for Agoraphobia

Study	Sample	Scale	
Ehlers & Margraf (1993)	Patients with panic disorder (± agoraphobia) (*n* = 241)	Avoidance when alone	.61
Taylor (1996), Sample 2	Patients with panic disorder, major depression, or both (*n* = 135)	"	.42
"	"	Avoidance when accompanied	.35
Taylor (1996), Sample 3	People with recurrent, unexpected panic attacks (e.g., full or subclinical panic disorder) (*n* = 83)	Avoidance when alone	.32

Taylor Manifest Anxiety Scale

Study	Sample		
McNally & Lorenz (1987)	Agoraphobics (*n* = 48)		.46
Reiss et al. (1986), Study 1	College students (*n* = 49)	"	.43
Reiss et al. (1986), Study 2	College students (*n* = 98)	"	.50

(continues)

TABLE 6.2 (continued)

Study	Sample	Measure	r
		Miscellaneous Scales	
Baranyai (1991)	Patients with agoraphobia, other anxiety disorders, or chronic headache (n = 150)	Zung Depression Scale	.45
"	"	Eysenck Personality Questionnaire –Neuroticism scale	.56
Edelmann & Skov (1993)	College students (n = 82)	Blushing Propensity Scale	.42
Ehlers & Margraf (1993)	Patients with panic disorder (± agoraphobia) (n = 241)	Symptom Checklist-90 total score	.57
McNally & Eke (1996)	College students (n = 78)	Profile of Mood States: Tension/anxiety subscale	.33
"	"	Suffocation Fear Scale	.63
"	"	Anxiety Sensations Checklist	.39
Norton et al. (1997)	College students (n = 95)	Social Phobia Scale	.64
"	"	Social Interaction Anxiety Scale	.56
Reiss et al. (1986), Study 1	College students (n = 49)	Anxiety Frequency Checklist	.36
Reiss et al. (1986), Study 2	College students (n = 98)	"	.32
Schmidt et al. (1997)	Air Force cadets (n = 472)	Beck Hopelessness Scale	.10
Stewart et al. (1992)	Clinical panickers, nonclinical panickers, and nonpanicking controls (n = 139)	Interpersonal Dependency Inventory (IDI): total score	.52
"	"	IDI Subscale 1: emotional reliance on another person	.58
"	"	IDI Subscale 2: lack of social self-confidence	.44
Taylor (1996), Sample 2	Patients with panic disorder, major depression, or both (n = 135)	Agoraphobia fear scale from the revised Anxiety Disorders Interview Schedule	.47
Zeitlin & McNally (1993)	Patients with panic disorder (n = 27)	Toronto Alexithymia Scale	.57
"	Patients with obsessive–compulsive disorder (n = 31)	"	.21

Note. A German version of the ASI was used For the Ehlers and Margraf (1993) study.

According to Cohen (1992), correlations of .10, .30, and .50 represent small, medium, and large effect sizes, respectively.

several distinguishing characteristics of the scales, including that the BSQ concentrates on the intensity of fear of specific bodily sensations. In comparison, the ASI also includes cognitive and emotional aspects as well as perceived harmful consequences. On a theoretical level, fear of anxiety is also conceptualized differently in these measures. The ACQ/BSQ assesses a fear of fear that is believed to be a consequence of panic experiences, whereas AS is thought to be more of a predispositional construct. Asmundson et al. found that the ASI was the best single predictor of the presence of unexpected panic attacks in a college student sample.

One of the more surprising findings in the studies listed in Table 6.2 is the observed relation between the ASI and measures of interpersonal or social concerns (e.g., Norton et al., 1997; Stewart, Knize, & Pihl, 1992). For example, Stewart et al. found that the ASI was significantly correlated with two domains of interpersonal dependency: "emotional reliance on another person" and "lack of social confidence." Similarly, Liebman and Allen (1995) found that ASI scores, along with heightened state anxiety, was associated with negative interpersonal perceptions (based on perceived facial emotions in photographs). Liebman and Allen concluded that the ASI "may well be assessing a chronic state of emotional hypervigilence that triggers heightened anxiety and apprehension upon entering ambiguous situations" (p. 264). Part of this association could be because interpersonal concerns and AS both share an element of general distress or negative affectivity. Also, this association may simply indicate that the ASI is highly contaminated with fear of negative evaluation. However, these findings do suggest that the relation between the ASI and control over emotions (discussed earlier) could be particularly relevant for the interpersonal domain.

PSYCHOPATHOLOGY AND LOW LEVELS OF ANXIETY SENSITIVITY

Numerous studies have compared normal subjects with high levels of AS to subjects with medium or low levels of AS. Because of space limitations and because the findings generally parallel clinical observations, these nonclinical studies are not reviewed here. To summarize, panic attacks and distress responses to panic provocation procedures (see chap. 9) have been consistently associated with high levels of AS. Yet, because many studies use low AS subjects as a comparison group, the question arises as to whether low AS truly represents normal functioning.

By definition, subjects who score at least one standard deviation below the mean (a common selection procedure used in AS research) represent an extreme group. It is quite possible that, like anxiety, the relation between AS and abnormal functioning may be a curvilinear one. That is, a moderate amount of AS could be more optimal than having little AS. To illustrate, in a study of people classified as having either low, medium, or high AS, Shostak and Peterson (1990) examined physiological arousal and subjective anxiety following an anxiety-inducing task (mental arithmetic). High AS subjects reported more anxiety symptoms compared with low AS subjects following the task. However, the low AS subjects did show some increases in subjective anxiety and "low ASs reported an increase in anxious mood without the perception of much, if any, physiological anxiety symptoms change even though low AS individuals showed the same level of physiological arousal to the mental challenge as did all AS groups" (p. 518).

Based on this finding, Shostak and Peterson (1990) concluded that "low anxiety sensitivity individuals appeared not just to be a good contrast group to demonstrate high sensitivity effects but, in fact, appeared to be an extreme group that behaves differently than average AS individuals" (p. 520). Shostak and Peterson speculated that low AS may even relate to antisocial personality disorder; people with this disorder may not regard physiological arousal as aversive and, with poor moral development, there could be a failure to inhibit antisocial behavior.

In one of the studies conducted in our lab, the graduate student interviewer was asked to make notes at the end of each interview on the appearance and behavior of the high and low AS subjects. This was done simply for the purpose of hypothesis generation. It was observed in several interviews that low AS subjects seemed to present themselves as super normal and appeared very laid back—to the point of seeming bored or indifferent to the whole process.

In a second college student study recently completed (Werhun & Cox, 1997), we sought to investigate this issue further by examining ASI responses in relation to self-deception and repression. Weinberger, Schwartz, and Davidson (1979) operationalized repression as a low level of reported manifest anxiety and a high level of social desirability. Compared with truly low anxious subjects, Weinberger et al. found that repressors cope ineffectively with psychosocial stressors and experience elevated physiological reactivity. In regard to self-deception, some authors (e.g., Taylor & Brown, 1988) have argued that self-deception is actually adaptive. However, recent empirical work has shown that, when confronted with unambiguous threat (e.g., clear failure, no excuses), individuals with self-deceptive coping styles demonstrate less effective problem solving on subsequent tasks compared with individuals who do not engage in self-deception (Johnson, 1995; Johnson, Vincent, & Ross, 1997).

In a sample of 296 students, we found a medium-size negative correlation between the ASI and a measure of self-deception ($r = -.38$), a small correlation with a measure of denial ($r = -.17$), and almost no relation with a measure of impression management ($r = -.06$). Based on the common cutoff procedure of one standard deviation above or below the mean ASI score, we divided subjects into low ($M = 6.1, SD = 2.0, n = 37$), medium ($M = 18.1, SD = 5.9, n = 214$) and high ($M = 38.4, SD = 6.5, n = 45$) AS groups. Using the Weinberger et al. (1979) operational definition of *repression*, we found that 27% of low AS subjects, but none of the high AS subjects, were classified as repressors. Finally, we found that, in response to a scenario dealing with a hypothetical health concern (a persistent dry cough), low AS subjects were significantly more likely to choose the response that represented denial with rationalization (characteristic of self-deception). In contrast, the majority of both medium and high AS subjects chose the task-oriented response (i.e., address the problem by consulting a physician).

It appears that extremely low levels of AS may represent maladaptive functioning and these individuals could be at risk for problems other than distress disorders (i.e., other than anxiety and depression). The contention that low AS may be maladaptive is also supported by a recent study of drug choice in relation to levels of AS in individuals seeking treatment for substance abuse (Norton et al., 1997). Norton et al. found that, although high ASI scores were associated with a preference for alcohol, men who scored low on the ASI were significantly more likely to prefer marijuana (ASI scores did not predict choice of drug for women).

Finally, it is worth remembering that *low*, *medium*, and *high* AS are relative terms. For example, a recent prospective study found that elevated AS was a significant predictor of spontaneous panic (Schmidt et al., 1997). However, the mean ASI score of subjects who experienced panic attacks in this study was only 7.5 ($SD = 3.6$)—a score that might constitute a low AS group in other studies. This unusual finding may have been due in part to the use of a rather unique sample group in AS research (military recruits undergoing basic training; see chap. 10).

A reasonable hypothesis concerning low AS is that some people truly have low AS, whereas for other individuals with apparently low AS there is a strong self-deception or repression element at work. Given a sufficient stressor, low AS subjects with the latter characteristics may be at greater risk for psychopathology.

IS ANXIETY SENSITIVITY
A COGNITIVE PREDISPOSITION?

A discussion of AS and psychopathology would not be complete without examining this question, especially in regard to explanatory mechanisms. Reiss (1991; Reiss et al., 1986) noted that AS is indicated by beliefs about anxiety. In comparison, McNally (1994) claimed that AS is a fear of anxiety symptoms "based on beliefs" (p. 116). McNally further remarked that "anxiety sensitivity denotes *beliefs* about the harmfulness of bodily sensations, not conditioned *responses* to them...[and that] anxiety sensitivity is a *dispositional*, not an *occurrent*, concept" (p. 117). Reiss (1997) also stated that the nature of this belief system is that "sensations of anxiety are personally harmful" (p. 206). Despite the impressive amount of empirical support for the AS construct, there is a paucity of research that has directly evaluated these theoretical claims.

We attempted to further examine this issue empirically by including an item in our expanded ASI item pool that stated, "I believe that anxiety is harmful to my health" (in our student sample, $M = 1.5, SD = 1.3$). This item was correlated with each of the 16 ASI items as well as the ASI total score. The correlation between this belief item and the ASI total score was only .26. Correlations with this belief item and each of the ASI items ranged from .09 to .22. In contrast to these findings, 13 of the 16 ASI items had item-total correlations at or above .50. We also included an item that read, "I think that fear is a terrible emotion," and the results follow a similar pattern. The correlation with this item and the ASI total score was .33 and the correlations with individual ASI items ranged from .08 to .29. It should be noted that a limitation of these analyses is that they are based on item-level comparisons. Taylor and Cox (in press) found that a new, more cognitively oriented measure of AS did correlate highly (.66) with the ASI. However, in general, neither the item content of the Taylor and Cox measure of AS or the original ASI simultaneously includes: (a) "I believe" types of statements, (b) explicit references to anxiety and not sensations that may be associated with anxiety, and (c) references to harmful consequences of anxiety.

These preliminary results question the idea that AS, at least as measured by the ASI, is a cognitive belief system about anxiety per se (a counterargument is that AS denotes a belief system, but the ASI is not the best way of assessing these beliefs). Rather, the findings are consistent with the idea that the ASI assesses a fear of sensations that is not necessarily identified as anxiety.

A second important assumption in AS theory (McNally, 1994) is that AS represents a dispositional rather than occurrent concept. Unlike other accounts of fear of fear, high AS can occur without prior panic experiences. Also, the ASI can be differentiated from trait anxiety measures (which are based more on frequency of anxiety experiences; see chap. 7). However, the question remains as to whether the ASI items assess beliefs independent of occurrences of relevant fear experiences. More research is needed in this area to determine the strength of AS as a predisposing factor.

For example, if an individual agrees strongly with the ASI item "It scares me when my heart beats rapidly" and then undergoes a provocation challenge procedure that produces a rapid heart rate, should we then be impressed by the finding that the person reports an increase in fear? Does this really support the predictive validity of the ASI or merely its concurrent validity? In other words, this scenario may provide evidence for the occurrent aspect of AS rather than providing support for the idea that AS is a cognitive diathesis (i.e., a predisposing belief system). If this individual's heart is beating rapidly enough and the corresponding fear also increases, the person may experience a panic attack (Reiss has suggested that panic is an intense state of fear). In this type of case, to say that high AS is a cognitive predisposition does not seem to be accurate, even if the person does not have a history of prior panic experiences (i.e., the person nevertheless has a prior fear of cardiac sensations). Perhaps the more interesting question in terms of predisposition is why the individual agrees so strongly with this type of item. Clearly, more research is needed into understanding individuals' subjective meaning of the nature and origins of AS.

It is also worth noting that the ASI instructions are rather ambiguous in terms of differentiating occurrence from predisposition. Respondents are asked to answer the items on the basis of their own experience; if the item content does not represent their personal experience, they are asked to answer on the basis of how they might feel if they had such an experience. In other words, we do not know how much a given ASI score is based on *when* types of statements versus *if* types of statements. The latter would seem to more closely approximate a predisposition rather than an occurrence.

CONCLUSIONS

An impressive amount of research has accumulated on AS and its measurement. This is a testament to the value of this individual difference variable in understanding various forms of psychopathology, particularly panic disorder. However, the fact that AS has been linked to so many clinical disorders should also force us to critically examine this issue, especially in regard to underlying mechanisms responsible for these observations. The research reviewed here strongly suggests that AS, at least as measured by the ASI, is comprised of multiple facets rather than a single construct. Some facets (e.g., fear of cognitive dyscontrol) may be more important for particular disorders (e.g., PTSD, OCD, major depression). Several findings could also be used to assert that the ASI assesses something broader than a fear of anxiety; also, it cannot yet be concluded that the ASI measures beliefs that the experience of anxiety is personally harmful. Many questions remain unanswered (e.g., subjective meaning and origins of AS); the intriguing story of AS is far from complete.

REFERENCES

American Psychiatric Association. (1994). *Diagnostic and statistical manual of mental disorders* (4th ed.). Washington, DC: Author.

Apfeldorf, W. J., Shear, M. K., Leon, A. C., & Portera, L. (1994). A brief screen for panic disorder. *Journal of Anxiety Disorders, 8,* 71–78.

Asmundson, G. J. G., Larsen, D. K., Cox, B. J., & Frombach, I. (1997, November). *Predicting phobia associated with motor vehicle accidents.* Poster presented at the annual meeting of the Association for Advancement of Behavior Therapy, Miami Beach, FL.

Asmundson, G. J. G., Norton, G. R., Lanthier, N. J., & Cox, B. J. (1996). Fear of anxiety: Do current measures assess unique aspects of the construct? *Personality and Individual Differences, 20,* 607–612.

Asmundson, G. J. G., & Stein, M. B. (1994). Selective processing of social threat in patients with generalized social phobia: Evaluation using a dot-probe paradigm. *Journal of Anxiety Disorders, 8,* 107–117.

Ball, S. G., Otto, M. W., Pollack, M. H., Uccello, R., & Rosenbaum, J. F. (1995). Differentiating social phobia and panic disorder: A test of core beliefs. *Cognitive Therapy and Research, 19,* 473–482.

Baranyai, G. (1991, June). *The Anxiety Sensitivity Index: Resolving a conceptual dilemma.* Paper presented at the annual convention of the Canadian Psychological Association, Calgary, AB.

Borger, S. C., Cox, B. J., Fuentes, K., & Ross, L. M. (1996, November). *Anxiety sensitivity and the five-factor model of personality.* Poster presented at the annual meeting of the Association for Advancement of Behavior Therapy, New York, NY.

Brown, T. A., Antony, M. M., & Barlow, D. H. (1995). Diagnostic comorbidity in panic disorder: Effect on treatment outcome and course of comorbid diagnoses following treatment. *Journal of Consulting and Clinical Psychology, 63,* 408–418.

Bruce, T. J., Spiegel, D. A., Gregg, S. F., & Nuzzarello, A. (1995). Predictors of alprazolam discontinuation with and without cognitive behavior therapy in panic disorder. *American Journal of Psychiatry, 152,* 1156–1160.

Calamari, J. E., Wiegartz, P. S., Janeck, A. S., & Heffelfinger, S. K. (1996, November). *Anxiety sensitivity in obsessive-compulsive disorder.* Poster presented at the 30th annual meeting of the Association for Advancement of Behavior Therapy, New York.

Cartwright-Hatton, S., & Wells, A. (1997). Beliefs about worry and intrusions: The Meta-Cognitions Questionnaire and its correlates. *Journal of Anxiety Disorders, 11,* 279–296.

Catanzaro, S. J. (1993). Mood regulation expectancies, anxiety sensitivity, and emotional distress. *Journal of Abnormal Psychology, 102,* 327–330.

Clark, D. M. (1986). A cognitive approach to panic. *Behaviour Research and Therapy, 24,* 461–470.

Clark, D. M. (1988). A cognitive model of panic attacks. In S. Rachman & J. D. Maser (Eds.), *Panic: Psychological perspectives* (pp. 71–89). Hillsdale, NJ: Lawrence Erlbaum Associates.

Cohen, J. (1992). A power primer. *Psychological Bulletin, 112,* 155–159.

Costa, P. T., Jr., & McCrae, R. R. (1992). *Revised NEO Personality Inventory (NEO-PI-R) and NEO Five-Factor Inventory (NEO-FFI) professional manual.* Odessa, FL: Psychological Assessment Resources.

Cox, B. J. (1996). The nature and assessment of catastrophic thoughts in panic disorder. *Behaviour Research and Therapy, 34,* 363–374.

Cox, B. J. (1997, June). *Recent findings on the nature and assessment of anxiety sensitivity.* In S. Bouchard (Chair), "New frontiers in our understanding of the treatment mechanism of panic disorder with agoraphobia." Symposium presented at the annual meeting of the Canadian Psychological Association, Toronto, ON.

Cox, B. J., Endler, N. S., Norton, G. R., & Swinson, R. P. (1991). Anxiety sensitivity and nonclinical panic attacks. *Behaviour Research and Therapy, 29,* 367–369.

Cox, B. J., Endler, N. S., & Swinson, R. P. (1995a). An examination of levels of agoraphobic severity in panic disorder. *Behaviour Research and Therapy, 33,* 57–62.

Cox, B. J., Endler, N. S., & Swinson, R. P. (1995b). Anxiety sensitivity and panic attack symptomatology. *Behaviour Research and Therapy, 33,* 833–836.

Cox, B. J., Fuentes, K., Ross, L., Borger, S. C., & Taylor, S. (1996, May). *Anxiety sensitivity, hypochondriasis, and the somatoform disorders.* Poster presented at the conference "Pain, Disability, & Personal Injury: Scientific and Applied Aspects," Regina, SK.

Cox, B. J., Kuch, K., Parker, J. D. A., Shulman, I. D., & Evans, R. J. (1994). Alexithymia in somatoform disorder patients with chronic pain. *Journal of Psychosomatic Research, 38,* 523–527.

Cox, B. J., Parker, J. D. A., & Swinson, R. P. (1996). Anxiety sensitivity: Confirmatory evidence for a multidimensional construct. *Behaviour Research and Therapy, 34,* 591–598.

Cox, B. J., Taylor, S., Borger, S. C., Fuentes, K., & Ross, L. M. (1996, November). *Development of an expanded Anxiety Sensitivity Index: Multiple dimensions and their correlates.* In S. Taylor (Chair), "New studies on the psychopathology of anxiety sensitivity." Symposium presented at the annual meeting of the Association for Advancement of Behavior Therapy, New York.

Edelmann, R. J., & Skov, V. (1993). Blushing propensity, social anxiety, anxiety sensitivity and awareness of bodily sensations. *Personality and Individual Differences, 14,* 495–498.

Ehlers, A. (1993). Somatic symptoms and panic attacks: A retrospective study of learning experiences. *Behaviour Research and Therapy, 31,* 269–278.

Ehlers, A. (1995). A 1-year prospective study of panic attacks: Clinical course and factors associated with maintenance. *Journal of Abnormal Psychology, 104,* 164–172.

Ehlers, A., & Margraf, J. (1993). Fear of fear: A new concept in the assessment of anxiety disorders. *Verhaltenstherapie, 3,* 14–24.

First, M. B., Spitzer, R. L., Gibbon, M., & Williams, J. B. W. (1995). *Structured clinical interview for DSM-IV Axis 1 disorders.* New York: New York State Psychiatric Institute.

Furer, P., Walker, J. R., Chartier, M. J., & Stein, M. B. (1997). Hypochondriacal concerns and somatization in panic disorder. *Depression and Anxiety, 6,* 78–85.

Hazen, A. L., Walker, J. R., & Stein, M. B. (1995). Comparison of anxiety sensitivity in panic disorder and social phobia. *Anxiety, 1,* 298–301.

Hecker, J. E., Losee, M. C., Fritzler, B. K., & Fink, C.M. (1996). Self-directed versus therapist-directed cognitive behavioral treatment for panic disorder. *Journal of Anxiety Disorders, 10,* 253–265.

Johnson, E. A. (1995). Self-deceptive coping: Adaptive only in ambiguous contexts. *Journal of Personality, 63,* 759–791.

Johnson, E. A., Vincent, N., & Ross, L. (1997). Self-deception versus self-esteem in buffering the negative effects of failure. *Journal of Research in Personality, 31,* 385–405.

Kellner, R. (1986). *Somatization and hypochondriasis.* New York: Praeger.

Lewinsohn, P. M., Steinmertz, J., Larson, D., & Franklin, J. (1981). Depression related cognitions: Antecedents or consequences? *Journal of Abnormal Psychology, 90,* 213–219.

Liebman, S. E., & Allen, G. J. (1995). Anxiety sensitivity, state anxiety and perceptions of facial emotions. *Journal of Anxiety Disorders, 9,* 257–267.

Lilienfeld, S. O. (1997). The relation of anxiety sensitivity and fear of fear to higher- and lower-order personality dimensions: Implications for the etiology of panic attacks. *Journal of Abnormal Psychology, 106,* 539–544.

Lilienfeld, S. O., Turner, S. M., & Jacob, R. G. (1993). Anxiety sensitivity: An examination of theoretical and methodological issues. *Advances in Behaviour Research and Therapy, 15,* 147–183.

Maidenberg, E., Chen, E., Craske, M., Bohn, P., & Bystritsky, A. (1996). Specificity of attentional bias in panic disorder and social phobia. *Journal of Anxiety Disorders, 10,* 529–541.

Marks, M. P., Lindsay, S. J. E., Marks, I. M., & Alkubaisy, T. (1988). *Fear of fear in different phobic groups.* Paper presented at World Congress of Behavior Therapy, Edinburgh, UK.

McNally, R. J. (1994). *Panic disorder: A critical analysis.* New York: Guilford.

McNally, R. J. (1996). Anxiety sensitivity is distinguishable from trait anxiety. In R. M. Rapee (Ed.), *Current controversies in the anxiety disorders* (pp. 214–227). New York: Guilford.

McNally, R. J., & Eke, M. (1996). Anxiety sensitivity, suffocation fear, and breath-holding duration as predictors of response to carbon dioxide challenge. *Journal of Abnormal Psychology, 105,* 146–149.

McNally, R. J., & Foa, E. B. (1987). Cognition and agoraphobia: Bias in the interpretation of threat. *Cognitive Therapy and Research, 11,* 567–581.

McNally, R. J., & Lorenz, M. (1987). Anxiety sensitivity in agoraphobics. *Journal of Behavior Therapy and Experimental Psychiatry, 18,* 3–11.

McNally, R.J., Luedke, D.L., Besyner, J.K., Peterson, R. A., Bohm, K., & Lips, O. J. (1987). Sensitivity to stress-relevant stimuli in posttraumatic stress disorder. *Journal of Anxiety Disorders, 1,* 105–116.

Nolen-Hoeksema, S. (1991). Responses to depression and their effects on the duration of depressive episodes. *Journal of Abnormal Psychology, 100,* 569–582.

Norton, G. R., Cox, B. J., Hewitt, P. L., & McLeod, L. (1997). Personality factors associated with generalized and non-generalized social anxiety. *Personality and Individual Differences, 22,* 655–660.

Norton, G. R., Cox, B. J., & Malan, J. (1992). Nonclinical panickers: A critical review. *Clinical Psychology Review, 12,* 121–139.

Norton, G. R., Rockman, G. E., Ediger, J., Pepe, C., Goldberg, S., Cox, B. J., & Asmundson, G. J. G. (1997). Anxiety sensitivity and drug choice in individuals seeking treatment for substance abuse. *Behaviour Research and Therapy, 35,* 859–862.

Orsillo, S. M., Lilienfeld, S. O., & Heimberg, R. G. (1994). Social phobia and response to challenge procedures: Examining the interaction between anxiety sensitivity and trait anxiety. *Journal of Anxiety Disorders, 8,* 247–258.

Otto, M. W., & Pollack, M. H. (1994). Panic disorder and hypochondriacal concerns: A reply to Taylor. *Journal of Anxiety Disorders, 8,* 101–103.

Otto, M. W., Pollack, M. H., Fava, M., Uccello, R., & Rosenbaum, J. F. (1995). Elevated anxiety sensitivity index scores in patients with major depression: Correlates and changes with antidepressant treatment. *Journal of Anxiety Disorders, 9,* 117–123.

Otto, M. W., Pollack, M. H., Sachs, G. S., & Rosenbaum, J. F. (1992). Hypochondriacal concerns, anxiety sensitivity, and panic disorder. *Journal of Anxiety Disorders, 6,* 93–104.

Peterson, R. A. (1986). [*ASI normative college student study*]. Unpublished raw data, Department of Psychology, George Washington University, Washington, DC.

Peterson, R. A., & Heilbronner, R. L. (1987). The Anxiety Sensitivity Index: Construct validity and factor analytic structure. *Journal of Anxiety Disorders, 1,* 117–121.

Rachman, S. (1993). Obsessions, responsibility and guilt. *Behaviour Research and Therapy, 31,* 149–154.

Rapee, R. M., Ancis, J. R., & Barlow, D. H. (1988). Emotional reactions to physiological sensations: Panic disorder patients and non-clinical Ss. *Behaviour Research and Therapy, 26,* 265–269.

Reiss, S. (1991). Expectancy model of fear, anxiety, and panic. *Clinical Psychology Review, 11,* 141–153.

Reiss, S. (1997). Trait anxiety: It's not what you think it is. *Journal of Anxiety Disorders, 11,* 201–214.

Reiss, S., & Havercamp, S. (1996). The sensitivity theory of motivation: Implications for psychopathology. *Behaviour Research and Therapy, 34,* 621–632.

Reiss, S., & McNally, R. J. (1985). Expectancy model of fear. In S. Reiss & R. R. Bootzin (Eds.), *Theoretical issues in behavior therapy* (pp. 107–121). New York: Academic Press.

Reiss, S., Peterson, R. A., & Gursky, D. M. (1988). Anxiety sensitivity, injury sensitivity, and individual differences in fearfulness. *Behaviour Research and Therapy, 26,* 341–345.

Reiss, S., Peterson, R. A., Gursky, D. M., & McNally, R. J. (1986). Anxiety sensitivity, anxiety frequency and the prediction of fearfulness. *Behaviour Research and Therapy, 24,* 1–8.

Salkovskis, P. M. (1985). Obsessional-compulsive problems: A cognitive-behavioural analysis. *Behaviour Research and Therapy, 25,* 571–583.

Salkovskis, P. M. (1996). The cognitive approach to anxiety: Threat beliefs, safety-seeking behavior, and the special case of health anxiety and obsessions. In P. M. Salkovskis (Ed.), *Frontiers of cognitive therapy* (pp. 48–74). New York: Guilford.

Sandin, B., Chorot, P., & McNally, R. J. (1996). Validation of the Spanish version of the Anxiety Sensitivity Index in a clinical sample. *Behaviour Research and Therapy, 34,* 283–290.

Schmidt, N. B., Lerew, D. R., & Jackson, R. J. (1997). The role of anxiety sensitivity in the pathogenesis of panic: Prospective evaluation of spontaneous panic attacks during acute stress. *Journal of Abnormal Psychology, 106,* 355–364.

Seidenberg, M., & Peterson, R. A. (1986). [*ASI scores in a medical school population*]. Unpublished raw data, Department of Psychology, George Washington University, Washington, DC.

Shostak, B. B., & Peterson, R. A. (1990). Effects of anxiety sensitivity on emotional response to a stress task. *Behaviour Research and Therapy, 28,* 513–521.

Stewart, S. H., Knize, K., & Pihl, R. O. (1992). Anxiety sensitivity and dependency in clinical and non-clinical panickers and controls. *Journal of Anxiety Disorders, 6,* 119–131.

Stewart, S. H., Taylor, S., & Baker, J. M. (1997). Gender differences in dimensions of anxiety sensitivity. *Journal of Anxiety Disorders, 11,* 179–200.

Stewart, S. H., & Zeitlin, S. B. (1995). Anxiety sensitivity and alcohol use motives. *Journal of Anxiety Disorders, 9,* 229–240.

Taylor, S. (1993). The structure of fundamental fears. *Journal of Behavior Therapy and Experimental Psychiatry, 24,* 289–299.

Taylor, S. (1994). Comment on Otto et al. (1992): Hypochondriacal concerns, anxiety sensitivity, and panic disorder. *Journal of Anxiety Disorders, 8,* 97–99.

Taylor, S. (1995a). Anxiety sensitivity: Theoretical perspectives and recent findings. *Behaviour Research and Therapy, 33,* 243–258.

Taylor, S. (1995b). Panic disorder and hypochondriacal concerns: Reply to Otto and Pollack (1994). *Journal of Anxiety Disorders, 9,* 87–88.

Taylor, S. (1996). Nature and measurement of anxiety sensitivity: Reply to Lilienfeld, Turner, & Jacob (1996). *Journal of Anxiety Disorders, 10,* 425–451.

Taylor, S., & Cox, B. J. (in press). Anxiety sensitivity: Multiple dimensions and hierarchic structure. *Behaviour Research and Therapy.*

Taylor, S., Koch, W. J., & McNally, R. J. (1992). How does anxiety sensitivity vary across the anxiety disorders? *Journal of Anxiety Disorders, 6,* 249–259.

Taylor, S., Koch, W. J., Woody, S., & McLean, P. (1996). Anxiety sensitivity and depression: How are they related? *Journal of Abnormal Psychology, 105,* 474–479.

Taylor, S., & Rachman, S. J. (1991). Fear of sadness. *Journal of Anxiety Disorders, 5,* 375–381.

Taylor, S. E., & Brown, J. D. (1988). Illusion and well-being: A social psychological perspective on mental health. *Psychological Bulletin, 103,* 193–210.

Telch, M. J., Shermis, M. D., & Lucas, J. A. (1989). Anxiety sensitivity: Unitary personality trait or domain-specific appraisals? *Journal of Anxiety Disorders, 3,* 25–32.

Wardle, J., Ahmad, T., & Hayward, P. (1990). Anxiety sensitivity in agoraphobia. *Journal of Anxiety Disorders, 4,* 325–333.

Watt, M. C., Stewart, S. H., & Cox, B. J. (in press). A retrospective study of the learning history origins of anxiety sensitivity. *Behaviour Research and Therapy.*

Weinberger, D. A., Schwartz, G. E., & Davidson, R. J. (1979). Low-anxious, high-anxious, and repressive coping styles: Psychometric patterns and behavioral and physiological responses to stress. *Journal of Abnormal Psychology, 88,* 369–380.

Werhun, C. D., & Cox, B. J. (1997). [*Anxiety sensitivity, self-deception, and repression*]. Unpublished raw data, Department of Psychology, University of Manitoba.

Williams, K. E., Chambless, D. L., & Ahrens, A. (1997). Are emotions frightening? An extension of the fear of fear construct. *Behaviour Research and Therapy, 35,* 239–248.

Zeitlin, S. B., & McNally, R. J. (1993). Alexithymia and anxiety sensitivity in panic disorder and obsessive-compulsive disorder. *American Journal of Psychiatry, 150,* 658–660.

7

Anxiety Sensitivity
and the Structure of Personality

Scott O. Lilienfeld
Emory University

The constructs of anxiety sensitivity (AS; Lilienfeld, Turner, & Jacob, 1993, 1996; McNally, 1994; Reiss, 1991; Taylor, 1995a, 1995b) and fear of fear (FOF; Goldstein & Chambless, 1978) have attracted considerable attention in recent research and theorizing on panic disorder and other anxiety disorders. These constructs are closely related conceptually (Reiss, 1987) and refer to individual differences in the tendency to experience fear in response to one's own anxiety symptoms. Because measures of AS and FOF—such as the Anxiety Sensitivity Index (ASI; Reiss, Peterson, Gursky, & McNally, 1986), the Agoraphobic Cognitions Questionnaire (ACQ), and the Body Sensations Questionnaire (BSQ; Chambless, Caputo, Bright, & Gallagher, 1984)—tend to be moderately to highly correlated (Asmundson, Norton, Lanthier, & Cox, 1996; Lilienfeld, 1997; McNally & Lorenz, 1987), they are heretofore regarded as alternative indicators of the AS construct and are referred to as *AS measures* in the remainder of this chapter. However, because different AS measures may assess somewhat different facets of fear of anxiety (e.g., fear of panic; Asmundson et al., 1996), their relations with variables relevant to anxiety disorders should not be expected to be identical.

Despite the considerable research attention accorded to the AS construct in recent years, relatively little is known concerning its relation to the broader personality domain. This chapter examines what is known regarding the association between AS measures and personality traits; it places particular emphasis on the location of the AS construct within hierarchical models of personality

149

structure. This information should provide valuable clues to the etiology of AS and anxiety disorders that may be influenced by AS. First, however, a brief overview of models of personality structure is necessary.

MODELS OF PERSONALITY STRUCTURE: A PRIMER

Although Allport and Odbert (1936) identified approximately 18,000 trait or trait-like adjectives in the English language, it seems likely that the dispositions assessed by this bewildering array of terms can be reduced to a smaller and more comprehensible set of fundamental underlying dimensions. Consequently, two questions have received considerable attention from personality researchers over the past several decades. First, how many major dimensions underlie the variation in human personality? Second, what are these dimensions?

The technique of exploratory factor analysis, which has been the principal means of investigating these questions in the personality domain, offers some guidance with respect to both questions, particularly the first. Nevertheless, because exploratory factor analysis does not provide definitive answers to either question, a number of subjective judgments are required on the part of the investigator (Floyd & Widaman, 1995). Such techniques as inspection of the scree plot of the eigenvalues (Cattell, 1966) offer the researcher some assistance in determining the number of factors underlying a set of correlations, although psychological interpretability is often used as an informal criterion for terminating factor extraction. Because of the well-known "problem of indeterminacy" (Gorsuch, 1983), which refers to the fact that a given data set is mathematically compatible with an infinite number of possible factor-analytic rotations, the nature of the underlying factors cannot be determined by exploratory factor-analytic methods alone. This is because each rotation yields a somewhat different psychological interpretation of these factors (Watson, Clark, & Harkness, 1994). Consequently, the construct validity of the factors derived from factor analysis can be ascertained only by examining their relations with external (i.e., nontest) criteria, such as laboratory data and biological variables (Eysenck, 1993; Lykken, 1971). In somewhat different terms, exploratory factor analyses of personality data are well suited for the *context of discovery* (i.e., hypothesis generation), but poorly suited for the *context of justification* (i.e., hypothesis testing; Reichenbach, 1938).

Although disagreement persists concerning the most veridical model for the underlying structure of personality, there is an emerging consensus that personality traits are hierarchically organized (Watson et al., 1994). In a hierarchical model, traits that are lower in the hierarchy (lower order traits) are more specific and circumscribed than traits that are higher in the hierarchy (higher order traits). Hierarchical models have had a long history of application in the domain of intelligence (Vernon, 1961) and have proved increasingly useful in clarifying questions concerning the structure of personality.

A hierarchical structure is a logical consequence of the fact that lower order traits covary and often give rise to higher order dimensions (Floyd & Widaman, 1995; Watson & Clark, 1992). As Watson et al. (1994) noted, "trait dimensional hierarchies are variance-covariance hierarchies: The covariance of the lower order elements becomes the variance of the higher order elements" (p. 19). Because the covariation between lower order traits is imperfect, these traits possess unique variance that is not shared with the higher order dimension. Hierarchical models provide at least a partial resolution to the question of the number of factors underlying the variation in personality; different levels of a hierarchical structure can be thought of as corresponding to the extraction of different numbers of factors that differ in their generality versus specificity (Watson et al., 1994).

Studies of the personality correlates of AS are necessary for two major reasons. First, such studies may lead to a better understanding of how AS maps onto the factor space defined by the major higher and lower order dimensions of personality. Because some higher order dimensions can be thought of as source traits (Cattell, 1950)—that is, fundamental underlying traits that give rise to more specific surface traits—a better understanding of the relation of AS to higher order dimensions may provide valuable clues to the nature and etiology of AS, as well as to the causes of panic disorder and other anxiety disorders. Although the cognitive model of panic (Clark, 1986) has received considerable attention in recent years, relatively little attention has been devoted to the question of what psychological factors, including stable personality dispositions, might predispose individuals to the catastrophic misinterpretation of ambiguous or unexpected bodily sensations. According to many authors, this process of misinterpretation lies at the core of panic attacks (Barlow, 1988; McNally, 1990).

Moreover, some higher order personality dimensions may bear close ties to major psychobiological systems, such as Gray's (1982) behavioral inhibition system (BIS) and behavioral activation system (BAS), which in turn appear to be associated with major neurotransmitter systems (e.g., Cloninger, 1987; Depue, 1996). Consequently, data on the relations of AS to such systems may hold important implications for the physiological underpinnings of AS and related individual difference dimensions.

Second, higher and lower order personality dimensions can provide competing explanations for certain hypotheses (Watson & Clark, 1992). If a researcher proposes a hypothesis concerning the relation of a lower order dimension to external criteria, but neglects to include a measure of the higher order dimension on which this lower order dimension loads, the researcher may erroneously conclude that the hypothesis has been corroborated. In fact, the observed relation may be attributable to the influence of the unmeasured higher order dimension (e.g., see Watson & Pennebaker, 1989, for an illustration of how the relation between stressful life events and somatic complaints appears to be mediated by the dimension of Negative Emotionality, described later). As Watson and Clark (1992) noted, "to the extent that one level [in the hierarchy] is responsible for these effects, the importance of the other is diminished" (p. 499). Thus, it is essential to examine the extent to which AS relates to more general personality dimensions and to include such dimensions in investigations of the relations between AS and external criteria. Otherwise researchers may arrive at mistaken conclusions regarding the specificity of these relations to AS. A potential case in point concerns the relationship between AS and trait anxiety.

ANXIETY SENSITIVITY AND TRAIT ANXIETY

Although extensive data support the construct validity of measures of AS, including the ASI, Lilienfeld, Jacob, and Turner (1989) argued that at least some of the findings attributed to AS might be accounted for by trait anxiety or related dimensions, which may lie above trait anxiety in the hierarchy of personality traits (see Lilienfeld et al., 1993; Taylor, 1995b, for a hierarchical model in which AS is posited to be a lower order marker of a trait anxiety factor). Indeed, the correlations of the ASI with trait anxiety indexes typically range from $r = .3$ to $.5$ (Lilienfeld et al., 1989). Lilienfeld et al. (1989) suggested, for example, that findings demonstrating that (a) agoraphobics obtain higher ASI scores than normals (Reiss et al., 1986; Taylor, Koch, & McNally, 1992), (b) the posttreatment ASI scores of agoraphobics return to normal limits following cognitive-behavioral therapy (McNally & Lorenz, 1987), and (c) the ASI moderates the controversial association between mitral valve prolapse syndrome and panic disorder (Lyons, Talano, Gitter, Martin, & Singer, 1986) were equally consistent with a trait anxiety explanation as with an AS explanation. Specifically, because measures of AS are moderately correlated with trait anxiety, such findings might be attributable not to AS per se, but to the variance shared by AS with trait anxiety. Lilienfeld et al. (1989, 1993) recommended that researchers who examine the relations between AS and other variables include indexes of trait anxiety in their investigations to examine this competing hypothesis.

The results of several subsequent studies have demonstrated that the ASI possesses incremental validity above and beyond trait anxiety measures in the prediction of self-reported fears (Reiss et al., 1986), anxiety responses to hyperventilation (McNally, 1989; Rapee & Medoro, 1994), hypochondrical fears (Otto, Pollack, Sachs, & Rosenbaum, 1992), and several other criteria relevant to anxiety and anxiety disorders (see McNally, 1996, for a review). In contrast, Brown and Cash (1989) reported that the ASI scores of panic disorder patients and nonpanic patients did not differ after their scores on a trait anxiety index were statistically controlled. However, Taylor et al. (1992) found that ASI scores were associated with several anxiety disorders even after scores on a trait anxiety measure were partialed out. The ACQ and BSQ have similarly been shown to exhibit incremental validity above and beyond a measure of trait anxiety in the prediction of agoraphobic avoidance (Chambless & Gracely, 1989).

Measures of AS, although moderately related to trait anxiety, thus exhibit incremental validity above and beyond trait anxiety for some (but perhaps not all; Brown & Cash, 1990) criteria relevant to panic and other anxiety disorders. Consequently, it is clear that such measures possess reliable variance that is not shared with trait anxiety indexes (Lilienfeld et al., 1993; McNally, 1996). The personality correlates of this unique variance, however, remain to be clarified. I return to the relationship between AS and trait anxiety later in this chapter.

ANXIETY SENSITIVITY AND THE "BIG THREE"

Conceptualizations of the "Big Three"

As noted earlier, the question of the underlying structure of personality remains unresolved (Watson et al., 1994). Proponents of the Big Three (e.g., Eysenck, 1991) argue that much of the common variance in personality can be accounted for by three higher order dimensions. Nevertheless, Big Three proponents have not always agreed on the interpretation of these dimensions. For example, Eysenck (1991; see also Eysenck & Eysenck, 1975) maintained that these three superordinate dimensions are best conceptualized as Extraversion, Neuroticism, and Psychoticism. According to Eysenck, Extraversion reflects the ease of conditionability of the central nervous system (with extraverts being less conditionable than introverts) and is manifested in such lower order traits as sociability, dominance, and assertiveness. Neuroticism, Eysenck maintained, reflects the lability versus stability of the autonomic nervous system (with neurotic individuals being more labile) and is manifested in such lower order traits as trait anxiety, guilt-proneness, and shyness. Because Eysenck (1979) posited that Neuroticism is an amplifier of conditioning, neurotic individuals are hypothesized to be particularly prone to the development of classically conditioned anxiety reactions. Finally, although Eysenck was less explicit concerning the physiological bases of Psychoticism than the other two dimensions, he contended that the lower order traits loading on this dimension include aggressiveness, impulsivity, and callousness. It should be noted, however, that Eysenck's Psychoticism dimension appears to be misnamed because there is relatively little evidence that this dimension measures psychotic symptoms per se (Tellegen & Waller, 1994). Indeed, Zuckerman (1994) suggested that the P in Psychoticism might be better thought of as Psychopathy than Psychoticism because a number (although probably not all; see Harpur, Hare, & Hakstian, 1989) of the traits comprising this dimension are among the core features of psychopathy, as delineated by Cleckley (1982).

In contrast, Tellegen (1978/1982; see also Tellegen & Waller, 1994) argued that the Big Three are best conceptualized as Positive Emotionality (PE), Negative Emotionality (NE), and Constraint (CN). Although these three dimensions bear important conceptual and empirical linkages to those of Eysenck, they also differ from Eysenck's dimensions in several substantial ways. PE is a propensity to experience positive affects of many kinds, including cheerfulness, feelings of social intimacy, achievement strivings, and other lower order traits; it is closely related to, although broader, than Eysenck's Extraversion dimension. NE is a propensity to experience negative affects of many kinds, including trait anxiety, anger, feelings of alienation, and other lower order traits; it is closely related to, although broader, than Eysenck's Neuroticism dimension (Zinbarg & Barlow, 1996). Because PE and NE are essentially orthogonal, individuals can be high on one and not the other, low on both, or high on both. CN is a fearfulness or response inhibition dimension (Tellegen, 1978/1982) that is manifested in such lower order traits as avoidance of harm, impulse control, and traditionalism. CN is closely related to Eysenck's (reversed) Psychoticism dimension (Tellegen & Waller, 1994).

Fowles (1987), Depue (1996), and several other authors have attempted to link some or all of Tellegen's dimensions to the psychobiological systems posited by Gray (1982) to underlie both normal and abnormal personality. For example, PE has been hypothesized by Depue (1996) to be a psychometric marker of Gray's (1982) BAS, a largely dopaminergically mediated mesolimbic and mesocortical system that mediates sensitivity to reward and signals of reward. In contrast, CN has been hypothesized by several authors (e.g., Depue & Spoont, 1987; Fowles, 1987; Spoont, 1992) to be associated with Gray's (1982) BIS—a largely serotonergically mediated system based in the septum, hippocampus, and orbital prefrontal cortex, that mediates sensitivity to signals of danger.

A more recent interpretation of the Big Three was offered by Cloninger (1987), who explicitly cast his interpretation of these dimensions in terms of Gray's (1982) psychobiological systems. Cloninger's dimension of Novelty Seeking reflects individual differences in sensitivity to reward and is hypothesized to be closely aligned with Gray's (1982) BAS. His dimension of Harm Avoidance reflects individual differences in sensitivity to danger and is hypothesized to be closely aligned with Gray's BIS. Cloninger's third major dimension, Reward Dependence, does not bear a clear correspondence to Gray's systems, but is instead believed to reflect individual differences in the maintenance of reinforced behavior in the face of withdrawal of reinforcement (i.e., extinction).

The construct validity of Cloninger's dimensions has been called into question. For example, Waller, Lilienfeld, Tellegen, and Lykken (1991) found that Cloninger's Harm Avoidance dimension was primarily a marker of Tellegen's (1978/1982) dimension of NE rather than CN (although it also was weakly positively related to CN and weakly negatively related to PE), suggesting that Harm Avoidance may not be closely associated with Gray's BIS. In addition, Waller et al. found that Cloninger's Novelty Seeking dimension was primarily associated with Tellegen's dimension of CN, rather than his dimension of PE, suggesting that Novelty Seeking may not be closely associated with Gray's BAS. Nevertheless, because these conclusions presume that the conjectures of Depue (1996) and others regarding the relations of Tellegen's dimensions to Gray's systems are correct, they should be regarded as preliminary.

The relations among these different interpretations of the Big Three, along with influential interpretations of these dimensions by other investigators (e.g., Block, 1965; Gough, 1987), are presented in Table 7.1. In this table, the correspondence among these alternative conceptualizations is based on the best available data (e.g., Tellegen & Waller, 1994; Waller et al., 1991; Watson et al., 1994), but it should be borne in mind that (a) several of the linkages among

TABLE 7.1
Conceptualizations of the Big Three by Various Investigators

Eysenck (1991)	Tellegen (1978/1982)	Cloninger (1987)	Gough (1987)	Block (1965)
Extraversion	Positive emotionality	—	Internality (reversed)	—
Neuroticism	Negative emotionality	Harm Avoidance	Self-Realization (reversed)	Ego Resilience (reversed)
Psychoticism	Constraint (reversed)	Novelty Seeking	Norm-Favoring (reversed)	Ego Control (reversed)

these dimensions (e.g., that between Block's Ego Control dimension and other higher order dimensions) must remain conjectural pending further data, and (b) several of these dimensions (e.g., Cloninger's Harm Avoidance; Waller et al., 1991) may be admixtures of several higher order dimensions. A blank space in the table indicates that the relevant higher order dimension is not explicitly represented in that investigator's model of personality traits.

Studies of the Relations Between Anxiety Sensitivity and the Big Three

Several investigators have examined the relation of AS measures to one or more of the Big Three dimensions. In addition, some of these researchers have examined the relation of AS indexes to lower order dimensions nested within these superordinate dimensions and have therefore provided important information concerning the placement of AS within hierarchical models of personality structure.

Arrindell (1993) administered the following battery to 94 clients (14 males, 80 females) at psychiatric outpatient centers: the ACQ and BSQ in conjunction with the short version of the Eysenck Personality Questionnaire (EPQ; Eysenck & Eysenck, 1975), which assesses Extraversion, Neuroticism, and Psychoticism; and the Revised Symptom Checklist–90 (SCL–90–R; Derogatis, 1977), which assesses a broad spectrum of psychopathological symptoms. Also administered was the Mobility Inventory (Chambless, Caputo, Jasin, Gracely, & Williams, 1985), which assesses agoraphobic avoidance, the Fear Questionnaire (FQ; Marks & Mathews, 1979), the Fear Survey Schedule–III (FSS–III; Wolpe & Lang, 1964), and the Depression Adjective Checklist (DAC; Lubin, 1981). The ACQ was subdivided into social-behavioral fear and physical fear subscales on the basis of a previous factor analysis (Chambless et al., 1984). The FQ contains several rationally derived subscales (e.g., agoraphobic fears, social fears, blood-injury fears), as does the FSS–III (e.g., social anxiety, fear of bodily injury, animal fears).

Arrindell reported that all three AS indexes (the two ACQ subscales and the BSQ) were moderately and significantly correlated with EPQ Neuroticism (rs ranged from .30 to .40), but essentially uncorrelated with EPQ Extraversion and Psychoticism (rs ranged from -.14 to .09). The moderate correlations with EPQ Neuroticism are consistent with previous findings that AS is associated with trait anxiety (Lilienfeld et al., 1989) because trait anxiety is a central lower order component of Eysenck's Neuroticism dimension. The three AS subscales were moderately correlated with virtually all fear and anxiety indexes, including most of the FQ and FSS–III subscales. In addition, the AS measures were moderately and significantly correlated with all SCL–90–R subscales, including anxiety, depression, somatization, anger, interpersonal sensitivity, sleep disturbance, and general psychological distress. This raises the possibility that the ACQ and BSQ are not specific to anxiety disorders but are instead markers of generalized psychopathology. In general, the AS subscales were significantly positively correlated with the DAC trait dysphoria subscale and significantly negatively correlated with the DAC trait euphoria subscale, although most of these correlations were weak or moderate in magnitude. Because indexes of depression tend to be heavily saturated with NE (Watson & Clark, 1984), these findings are broadly consistent with the moderate correlations of the ACQ subscales and BSQ with EPQ Neuroticism. Nevertheless, because many depression measures are a composite of high NE and low PE (Tellegen, 1985; Watson et al., 1994), further examination of the relation of AS measures to PE appears to be warranted.

Principal component analyses conducted by Arrindell yielded four major components. The first component was marked by high loadings on the ACQ subscales and BSQ (range = .59 to .79), as well as high loadings on EPQ Neuroticism, most of the anxiety measures, and all SCL–90–R subscales. As noted by Arrindell, this component reflects pervasive negative affect and maladjustment and appears quite similar to Tellegen's (1978/1982) NE dimension. The second, third, and fourth components were interpreted by Arrindell as Phobic Fears, Positive Affect, and Agoraphobia, respectively. None of these components had salient loadings on any of the AS indexes, although these indexes all exhibited low positive loadings on the Agoraphobia Component (range = .14 to .16). A separate AS component did not emerge in these analyses. Arrindell's results suggest that AS measures are moderately to highly related to Neuroticism and NE, but not to other Big Three dimensions.

The relation of AS indexes to NE was further examined by Zinbarg and Barlow (1996), who administered the ASI and a number of other self-report anxiety measures to 432 outpatients (247 with *DSM–III–R* panic disorder and all but 16 with a *DSM–III–R* anxiety disorder) who were admitted to an anxiety disorders clinic; the comparison sample consisted of 32 individuals with no history of psychiatric disorder. Anxiety disorder diagnoses were established with semistructured diagnostic interviews. Among the questionnaire indexes of anxiety administered were the Fear Survey Schedule–II (Geer, 1965), Penn State Worry Questionnaire (Meyer, Miller, Metzger, & Borkevec, 1990), Maudsley Obsessive–Compulsive Inventory (Hodgson & Rachman, 1977), and two indexes relevant to social anxiety and social phobia: the Social Interaction

Anxiety Scale (Mattick & Clark, 1988) and the Social Phobia Scale (Mattick & Peters, 1988). Several of these measures were in turn subdivided into subscales on the basis of item-level factor analyses (see Zinbarg & Barlow, 1996). For example, the ASI was subdivided into three subscales: Fear of Somatic Sensations, Social Concerns, and Fear of Going Crazy. As Zinbarg and Barlow pointed out, these subscales correspond reasonably well to those identified in previous factor analyses of the ASI (e.g., Taylor, Koch, McNally, & Crockett, 1992b).

Zinbarg and Barlow found that the self-report indexes of anxiety exhibited a perfect pattern of positive manifold, as all 253 intercorrelations (among 23 measures) were positive and statistically significant. Confirmatory factor analyses using LISREL suggested that the model that best fit these correlations was one positing a single higher order factor and six correlated lower order factors. The higher order factor was characterized by moderate to high loadings on virtually all of the anxiety measures and was essentially interpreted by Zinbarg and Barlow as an NE dimension. Two of the ASI subscales—Fear of Somatic Sensations and Fear of Going Crazy—loaded on a lower order fear of fear factor, whereas the ASI Social Concerns subscale loaded on a lower order Social Anxiety factor. Several of the lower order factors, including Fear of Fear, successfully distinguished among different anxiety disorder groups by means of discriminant function analysis. This suggested that Zinbarg and Barlow's findings were not entirely attributable to method covariance (i.e., correlations resulting from the shared use of a self-report format across measures).

Zinbarg and Barlow's findings further support the contention (e.g., Arrindell, 1993) that measures of AS are markers of NE. Because indexes of other higher order factors (e.g., PE) were not administered, however, their results do not exclude the possibility that AS relates to other Big Three dimensions. In addition, Zinbarg and Barlow's results are consistent with a hierarchical model of AS and NE (e.g., see Lilienfeld et al., 1993; Taylor, 1995b) because they suggest that indexes of AS, although highly saturated with NE, possess unique variance of their own. Although their findings suggest that the unique variance of the ASI may be split between two different lower order dimensions (i.e., Fear of Fear and Social Anxiety), further examination of the variance components of AS measures not shared with the higher order NE factor is warranted.

Saviotti et al. (1991) administered the ASI and Cloninger's (1987) Tridimensional Personality Questionnaire (TPQ) to 33 patients who had recovered from panic disorder and 33 nonpatients who were matched for age, gender, and other demographic variables. The TPQ is designed to assess the three higher order dimensions of Cloninger's (1987) model of personality. Saviotti et al. found that the ASI was positively, although not significantly, correlated with TPQ Harm Avoidance in patients ($r = .18$) and nonpatients ($r = .12$). The correlations between the ASI and the other two TPQ dimensions, Novelty Seeking and Reward Dependence, were low and nonsignificant (Novelty Seeking: rs = .22 and .09, for patients and nonpatients, respectively; Reward Dependence: rs = -.02 and .05, respectively; G.A. Fava, personal communication, August 20, 1997). The Saviotti et al. findings raise questions concerning the relation between AS and NE because Cloninger's Harm Avoidance dimension is primarily a marker of NE (Waller et al., 1991; Zinbarg & Barlow, 1996). Nevertheless, because TPQ Harm Avoidance appears to be a composite of high NE, low PE, and high CN (Waller et al., 1991), the implications of their results for the relation between AS and NE per se are somewhat unclear.

In a subsequent study, Fava et al. (1994) examined the relations between the ASI and TPQ among 16 patients with panic disorder and agoraphobia, all of whom had been taking benzodiazepines prior to treatment. Patients were tested both before and after discontinuation from benzodiazepines. At the initial testing, ASI scores were positively and moderately correlated with TPQ Harm Avoidance ($r = .39$), although this correlation fell short of significance. At the second testing, the correlation of the ASI with TPQ Harm Avoidance was again nonsignificant ($r = .19$). The correlations of the ASI with TPQ Novelty Seeking during the two testings were nonsignificant (rs = .15 and .26, respectively), as were the correlations of the ASI with TPQ Reward Dependence (rs = .18 and -.35, respectively; G.A. Fava, personal communication, August 20, 1997).

Lilienfeld (1996) administered the ASI, ACQ, BSQ, and a new index of AS, the Beliefs About Negative Consequences Inventory (BANCI), to 220 under-graduates (118 males, 110 females, and 2 individuals who neglected to report their gender). Measures of anxiety and personality included the FQ, Trait Form of the State–Trait Anxiety Inventory (STAI; Spielberger, Gorsuch, & Lushene, 1970), DSM–III–R version of the Panic Attack Questionnaire (PAQ; Norton, Dorward, & Cox, 1986; see Walker, Norton, & Ross, 1991), and Tellegen's (1978/1982) Multidimensional Personality Questionnaire (MPQ)—a measure designed to assess the principal dimensions of Tellegen's model of personality. Because this study provides detailed information regarding the relation of AS measures to higher and lower order personality dimensions, it is described in detail (see Lilienfeld, 1997, for a description of these findings using a composite measure of AS).

The BANCI was developed by Lilienfeld and Jones (1992) to address the criticism that many ASI items assess emotional responses to, rather than beliefs concerning the harmfulness of, anxiety symptoms (Lilienfeld et al., 1989). The

BANCI consists of 12 items assessing the same content domains as the ASI (e.g., "feeling faint," "becoming short of breath"). On the BANCI, however, respondents are asked to rate the degree to which they believe that each anxiety symptom would result in harmful or dangerous consequences for them.

In addition to the three higher order dimensions of PE, NE, and CN, the MPQ consists of 11 lower order dimensions derived from item-level factor analyses. Well-Being, Social Potency, Social Closeness, and Achievement load primarily on PE. Stress Reaction, Alienation, and Aggression load primarily on NE, and Harm Avoidance, Control (vs. Impulsiveness), and Traditionalism load primarily on CN. Absorption does not load primarily on any single higher order factor, although it typically has low positive loadings on both PE and NE.

Two MPQ lower order scales seem especially relevant to AS. Stress Reaction, which assesses feelings of tenseness, irritability, and moodiness, is similar in content to standard measures of trait anxiety, which are known to overlap with AS measures (Lilienfeld et al., 1989). Harm Avoidance assesses a tendency to avoid physically dangerous experiences and is primarily a measure of fearfulness. Fearfulness differs from trait anxiety in that the former is a sensitivity to signals of impending harm or danger, whereas the latter is a chronic susceptibility to experiencing anxiety (Tellegen, 1978/1982). Unlike Cloninger's Harm Avoidance dimension, which is primarily a marker of NE (Waller et al., 1991), Tellegen's Harm Avoidance is primarily a marker of CN.

Lilienfeld et al. (1993) predicted that AS measures would be associated with the higher order dimensions of NE (and its lower order factor of trait anxiety) and CN. Individuals with high levels of CN might be expected to be particularly vulnerable to experiencing fear in response to unusual or unexpected bodily sensations and thus to developing elevated levels of AS.

Lilienfeld (1996) further hypothesized that AS would be associated with the lower order dimension of Absorption (Tellegen & Atkinson, 1974). Absorption, which overlaps conceptually with Hilgard's (1979) construct of *imaginative involvement* (Roche & McConkey, 1990), reflects a propensity toward immersion in sensory experiences and mental imagery. The MPQ Absorption scale contains such items as, "If I wish I can imagine some things so vividly that they hold my attention as a good movie or story does" and "I can be deeply moved by a sunset." It has been found to be predictive of hypnotic susceptibility (Nadon, Hoyt, Register, & Kihlstrom, 1991; cf. Council, Kirsch, & Hafner, 1986). In addition, this scale correlates moderately with the Openness to Experience dimension featured in five-factor models of personality (Church, 1994; McCrae & Costa, 1985). Absorption has been typically viewed as facilitating pleasurable experiences, such as an enhanced appreciation of art and music (Wild, Kuiken,

& Schopflocher, 1995). Nevertheless, Absorption may also make individuals more attuned to unpleasant or potentially frightening internal sensations and thereby heighten their risk for anxiety disorders (e.g., panic disorder) that are characterized by a hypersensitivity to interoceptive cues.

The correlations among the four AS indexes in the sample were moderately high, significant, and comparable in magnitude (rs ranged from .50 to .63), suggesting that these indexes assess largely overlapping aspects of the same construct. The correlations between the four measures of AS, on the one hand, and the personality and fear measures, on the other, are presented in Table 7.2. Also included in this table are the correlations between the AS measures and two indexes of social desirability/impression management derived from the MPQ: Unlikely Virtues and Desirable Response Inconsistency (DRIN). (See Lilienfeld, 1997; Tellegen, 1978/1982, for information regarding the construction and interpretation of these measures.) These correlations provide information concerning the extent to which scores on AS measures are influenced by social desirability response styles.

As can be seen in Table 7.2, the patterns of correlations between all AS indexes and other measures were, with few exceptions, quite similar. At the higher order level, AS indexes were significantly and moderately correlated with NE, corroborating the findings of Arrindell (1993) and Zinbarg and Barlow (1996). Only the ASI was significantly correlated with CN, although this correlation was low in magnitude. At the lower order level, AS indexes were significantly correlated with Stress Reaction, Alienation, and Absorption. In addition, AS indexes were significantly and moderately correlated with the STAI–Trait Form and the FQ total score. In almost all cases, the correlations of the AS indexes with the three FQ subscales were significant, although several of these correlations were low in magnitude. The AS indices were negligibly correlated with Unlikely Virtues and DRIN, suggesting that these indexes are not substantially contaminated by a social desirability response style.

To further examine the relation of AS indexes to personality dimensions, the AS, personality, fear, and social desirability/impression management measures were submitted to a principal axis factor analysis using orthogonal (Varimax) rotation. An orthogonal rotation was used in light of Tellegen's (1978/1982) assertion that the higher order dimensions of the MPQ are essentially uncorrelated. (An oblique rotation produced results extremely similar to those obtained with Varimax rotation; only the Varimax-rotated solution is presented here.) The lower order, rather than higher order, factors of the MPQ were used in these analyses because the latter only contain the common, but not the unique, variance possessed by lower order factors (Watson et al., 1994).

TABLE 7.2
Correlations Between AS Indexes and Measures
of Personality, Social Desirability, and Fear

Measures	ASI	BANCI	ACQ	BSQ
Multidimensional Personality Questionnaire				
Higher Order Dimensions				
Positive Emotionality	.07	-.04	-.09	.01
Negative Emotionality	.29***	.36***	.30***	.33***
Constraint	.18*	.11	-.01	.12
Lower Order Dimensions				
Well-Being	-.11	-.21***	-.22***	-.10
Social Potency	.01	.01	-.06	.00
Social Closeness	-.10	-.10	-.20**	-.13
Achievement	.12	.01	-.04	.00
Stress Reaction	.38***	.43***	.34***	.34***
Alienation	.16**	.26***	.23***	.23***
Aggression	,.00	.06	.04	.12
Control	.10	.05	-.06	.04
Harm Avoidance	.10	.06	-.06	.10
Traditionalism	.07	.03	-.02	.05
Absorption	.25***	.16*	.23***	.25***
Social Desirability Scales				
Unlikely virtues	.11	-.02	.08	.10
Desirable Response Inconsistency	-.04	-.16*	-.05	.03
State–Trait Anxiety Inventory—Trait Form	.39***	.39***	.38***	.37***
Fear Questionnaire				
Total Score	.42***	.33***	.22***	.39***
Agoraphobia	.35***	.23***	.19**	.31***
Social Phobia	.36***	.32***	.23***	.29***
Blood/Injury Phobia	.30***	.24***	.11	.31***

Note. Ns range from 206 to 220.

* $p < .05$. ** $p < .01$. *** $p < .001$, two-tailed.

ACQ = Agoraphobic Cognitions Questionnaire; ASI = Anxiety Sensitivity Index; BANCI = Beliefs About Negative Consequences Inventory; BSQ = Body Sensations Questionnaire.

Because the MPQ consists of three higher order factors, three factors were extracted. In addition, visual inspection of the scree plot (Cattell, 1966) indicated a fairly clear break in the eigenvalues corresponding to a three-factor solution. The results of the rotated solution are displayed in Table 7.3.

The first factor was marked by salient (i.e., .30 or higher) loadings on the MPQ lower order markers of Stress Reaction, Alienation, and Absorption and appears to represent a NE dimension. All of the AS indexes loaded highly on this factor, as did the STAI–Trait Form and FQ variables. The second factor was bipolar and characterized by salient positive loadings on the MPQ lower order markers of Well-Being, Social Potency, Achievement, and Absorption and appears to represent a PE dimension. Both trait anxiety indexes (i.e., MPQ Stress Reaction and the STAI–Trait Form) exhibited salient negative loadings

TABLE 7.3
Loadings for Three-Factor Solution (Varimax Rotation)

Variable	Factor I	Factor II	Factor III
ASI	**.75**	.13	.08
BANCI	**.64**	.00	-.04
ACQ	**.60**	-.04	-.12
BSQ	**.71**	.11	-.04
Well-Being	-.27	**.72**	.25
Social Potency	.01	**.51**	-.12
Social Closeness	-.12	.26	**.37**
Achievement	.03	**.50**	.25
Stress Reaction	**.64**	**-.34**	.02
Alienation	**.38**	-.14	**-.43**
Aggression	.14	.09	**-.48**
Control	.07	.23	**.55**
Harm Avoidance	.12	-.21	**.58**
Traditionalism	.10	.28	**.33**
Absorption	**.30**	**.34**	-.14
Unlikely Virtues	-.01	.14	-.02
Desirable Response Inconsistency	-.11	.06	-.20
Stait–Trait Anxiety Inventory—Trait Form	**.62**	**-.46**	-.13
Fear Questionnaire—Agoraphobia Scale	**.54**	.03	.11
Fear Questionnaire—Blood-Injury Scale	**.47**	.05	.06
Fear Questionnaire—Social Phobia Scale	**.55**	-.19	.11

Note. Ns range from 206 to 220. Salient (≥ .30) factor loadings are in bold.

ASI = Anxiety Sensitivity Index; BANCI = Beliefs About Negative Consequences Inventory; ACQ = Agoraphobic Cognitions Questionnaire; BSQ = Body Sensations Questionnaire.

TABLE 7.4

Partial Correlations Between AS Indexes and MPQ Alienation and Absorption Scales, Controlling for Trait Anxiety

AS Indices	Controlling for MPQ Stress Reaction		Controlling for Trait Version of STAI	
	Alienation	Absorption	Alienation	Absorption
ASI	.03	.19**	.00	.25**
BANCI	.11	.08	.11	.12
ACQ	.11	.17*	.11	.22**
BSQ	.12	.19**	.12	.24***

Note. Ns range from 206 to 220. * p < 05; ** p < 01; ***p < 001, , two tailed.

ASI = Anxiety Sensitivity Index; ACQ = Agoraphobic Cognitions Questionnaire; BANCI = Beliefs About Negative Consequences Inventory; BSQ = Body Sensations Questionnaire; MPQ = Multidimensional Personality Questionnaire; STAI = State–Trait Anxiety Inventory.

on this factor, whereas the loadings of the AS indexes on this factor were neglible. The third factor, which was also bipolar, was marked by salient positive loadings on the MPQ lower order markers of Social Closeness, Control, Harm Avoidance, and Traditionalism and appears to represent a CN dimension. Both MPQ Alienation and MPQ Aggression exhibited salient negative loadings on this factor. The AS indexes were again neglibly related to this factor.

It might be argued that the correlations between the AS indexes and other personality measures (specifically, Alienation and Absorption) are attributable to the variance that both sets of variables share with trait anxiety. To address this possibility, partial correlation analyses were conducted to ascertain whether the correlations between AS measures, on the one hand, and Alienation and Absorption, on the other, could be accounted for by trait anxiety. In one set of analyses, MPQ Stress Reaction was used as the covariate; in the other set of analyses, the STAI–Trait Form was used as the covariate. The results of these analyses are displayed in Table 7.4.

After controlling for scores on Stress Reaction, the correlations between AS measures and Alienation became nonsignificant and, in the case of the ASI, essentially zero. In contrast, with the exception of the BANCI, the correlations between AS indexes and Absorption remained significant after controlling for scores on Stress Reaction. After controlling for scores on the STAI–Trait Form, the correlations between AS measures and Alienation again became nonsignificant and, in the case of the ASI, zero. Again, with the exception of the BANCI, the correlations between AS measures and Absorption remained significant after controlling for scores on the STAI–Trait Form.

In the next set of analyses, I examined whether the most consistent personality correlates of AS indexes identified in the previous analyses (viz., NE, Alienation, Absorption, and the two trait anxiety measures) differed among participants with versus without a recent history of panic attacks, as assessed by the PAQ. The correlations between AS measures and these personality variables among participants with versus without a history of panic attacks in the past year are shown in Table 7.5.

It can be seen that the correlations among these measures in the two groups were quite similar. Using a test of the difference between independent correlations (Cohen & Cohen, 1983), none of the correlations differed significantly (at $p < .05$) across the two groups. In both groups, AS indexes correlated positively and, in most cases, significantly with the four MPQ variables and the STAI–Trait form, although several of the correlations with the MPQ variables were relatively weak in magnitude. Similar results emerged when comparing participants with versus without a lifetime history of panic attacks (see Lilienfeld, 1997).

TABLE 7.5

Correlations Between Indexes Of NE, Stress Reaction, Alienation, Absorption, and STAI–Trait Form and AS for Participants With Versus Without History of Panic Attacks in the Past Year

Measures	ASI	BANCI	ACQ	BSQ
Participants with a history of panic attacks in past year (n = 74)				
MPQ Variables				
NE	.18	.36**	.18	.24*
Stress Reaction	.28*	.39***	.24*	.24*
Alienation	.04	.25*	.14	.12
Absorption	.23	.08	.21	.27*
STAI–Trait Form	.30*	.29*	.27*	.24
Participants with no history of panic attacks in past year (n = 146)				
MPQ Variables				
NE	.31***	.33***	.23***	.35***
Stress Reaction	.39***	.42***	.36***	.37***
Alienation	.18*	.23**	.23**	.25**
Absorption	.23**	.16	.18*	.19*
STAI–Trait Form	.39***	.41***	.38***	.40***

Note. * $p < .05$. ** $p < .01$. *** $p < .001$, two tailed.

ASI = Anxiety Sensitivity Index; ACQ = Agoraphobic Cognitions Questionnaire; BANCI = Beliefs About Negative Consequences Inventory; BSQ = Body Sensations Questionnaire; MPQ = Multidimensional Personality Questionnaire; NE = Negative Emotionality; STAI = State–Trait Anxiety Inventory.

Finally, incremental validity analyses conducted using hierarchical logistic regression techniques indicated that all of the AS indexes demonstrated incremental validity above and beyond both NE and its lower order markers (e.g., measures of trait anxiety, Alienation) in the prediction of panic attack history. With the exception of the BANCI, the increments in variance accounted for by AS indexes above and beyond measures of NE were statistically significant. These findings corroborate those of other researchers (e.g., Hasten & Stokes, 1987; see Lilienfeld et al., 1993; McNally, 1996, for reviews) who have reported that AS measures, although moderately correlated with NE and trait anxiety, nonetheless possess unique variance related to anxiety and anxiety disorders. Parallel incremental validity analyses indicated that, again with the exception of the BANCI, AS measures exhibited incremental validity above and beyond Absorption in the prediction of panic attack history.

In summary, these findings suggest that AS indexes are highly related to NE and lower order markers of this dimension (e.g., trait anxiety, Alienation), although they contain reliable and psychologically meaningful variance that is not shared with NE. The superficially surprising correlations between AS indexes and Alienation are probably attributable to the latter's heavy saturation with NE (Tellegen & Waller, 1994). With the possible exception of the ASI, AS indexes appear to be neglibly related to CN, suggesting that the construct of AS may not, as initially hypothesized by Lilienfeld et al. (1993), be closely associated with hypersensitivity to signals of threat.

Perhaps most interesting, all AS indexes were significantly correlated with Absorption, although these correlations were relatively low in magnitude. These correlations may reflect a propensity toward internal self-focus and imaginative involvement (e.g., Hilgard, 1979) that is assessed by both AS measures and Absorption. Of greater theoretical importance is the finding that AS indexes were positively and, in most cases, significantly correlated with Absorption even among individuals with no panic attack history. This finding is consistent with the hypothesis that a propensity toward immersion in sensory and imaginative experiences is a diathesis for, rather than simply a consequence of, panic attacks, although longitudinal research examining individuals with differing levels of Absorption will be needed to subject this hypothesis to a more direct test.

Aside from scattered findings of heightened hypnotizability among phobic patients (Frankel & Orne, 1976; cf. Frishholz, Spiegel, Spiegel, Balma, & Markell, 1982), Absorption and related variables have received little attention in the anxiety disorders literature. Such variables may increase individuals' risk for certain anxiety disorders by heightening their self-focus and awareness of potentially frightening physical symptoms. With respect to NE, Pennebaker and Watson (1991) noted that individuals with high levels of this trait "appear to be hypervigilant about their bodies and have a lower threshold for noticing and reporting subtle bodily sensations" (p. 27). Absorption, which correlates with NE, may produce similar effects by increasing individuals' awareness of interoceptive sensations. It is important to note that Absorption correlated significantly with AS indexes even after the effects of trait anxiety were statistically controlled; subsidiary analyses controlling for NE yielded similar results. These findings suggest that, although NE is associated with hypervigilance regarding bodily sensations, Absorption shares unique variance with AS that is not exclusively accounted for by NE.

These results suggest several interesting avenues for further investigation. First, it will be important to examine the relations between Absorption and AS, on the one hand, and hypochondriasis, on the other. Barsky and Klerman (1983) argued that "somatic amplification" (i.e., a tendency toward the heightened perception of physical symptoms) is a key factor in the etiology of hypochondriasis. This propensity toward somatic amplication may help explain the results of Sigmon, Rohan, Fink, and Hotovy (1995), who found that females with high ASI scores reported more intense menstrual symptoms, including headaches, cramps, and water retention, than females with low ASI scores. Moreover, hypochondriasis shares a number of features with panic disorder, particularly a preoccupation with the potentially catastrophic implications of unusual or unexpected physical symptoms. The primary features differentiating the two conditions are the time frame for danger (delayed in the case of hypochondriasis, immediate in the case of panic disorder) and the symptoms that are the focus of apprehension (nonautonomic in the case of hypochondriasis, autonomic in the case of panic disorder; McNally, 1994). Although Otto, Pollack, Sachs, and Rosenbaum (1992) found that the ASI was correlated with the number of hypochondriacal concerns among panic disorder patients, the relation of AS to hypochondriasis per se has yet to be examined.

Second, it will be of interest to examine the relation between Absorption and AS, on the one hand, and relaxation-induced panic attacks, on the other. Many patients with panic disorder are prone to experiencing panic attacks during relaxation exercises, perhaps because such exercises are associated with increased attention to subtle bodily sensations (Barlow, 1988). Therefore, individuals with high levels of Absorption, AS, and similar traits associated with somatic amplification may be particularly susceptible to relaxation-induced panic. A similar analysis may help explain the origin of nocturnal panic attacks (B. J. Cox, personal communication, January 13, 1996). According to the cognitive-behavioral model of nocturnal panic attacks (e.g., Craske & Freed, 1995), noctural panic is triggered by minor changes in physiological activity (e.g., muscle twitches, heart rate increases) among individuals who are hyper-sensitive to interoceptive cues.

Third, the specificity of the present findings to panic attacks and panic disorder remains to be ascertained. For example, because heightened self-focused attention appears to be a correlate of numerous psychological disorders (Ingram, 1990), it might be argued that the correlation between Absorption and panic attack history is a nonspecific reflection of the propensity of individuals with generalized psychopathology to experience high levels of self-preoccupation.

The only findings of the present study that bear on the specificity issue concern the relation between Absorption and unexpected panic attacks. Al-though panic attacks occur in elevated rates in all anxiety disorders (Barlow, 1988), panic disorder is the only diagnosis for which the presence of unexpected panic attacks is a prerequisite. In this study, Absorption was correlated positively ($r = .17$), although nonsignificantly, with a history of unexpected panic attacks. In addition, among participants with a history of unexpected panic attacks, Absorption was correlated positively ($r = .46$, $p < .01$) with the proportion of panic attacks that were unexpected. Although these findings provide prelimi-nary support for the hypothesis that Absorption is a relatively specific risk factor for unexpected panic attacks, and therefore for panic disorder, it might be argued that unexpected panic attacks are indicative of greater severity than are expected panic attacks (B. J. Cox, personal communication, January 13, 1996). According to this alternative explanation, high levels of Absorption are asso-ciated not with panic disorder per se, but with more severe manifestations of many or all anxiety disorders. Further investigations incorporating indexes of other anxiety disorders (e.g., social phobia, obsessive–compulsive disorder) are needed to distinguish between these two possibilities.

ANXIETY SENSITIVITY AND THE "BIG FIVE"

The higher order model of personality that represents the major alternative to the Big Three is the "Big Five" (Goldberg, 1993; Costa & McCrae, 1992), which has received considerable attention over the past decade. The Big Five consists of the dimensions of Extraversion and Neuroticism, which are essen-tially identical to their Big Three counterparts (although Tellegen's NE dimen-sion appears to be an admixture of both Neuroticism and low Agreeableness; Church, 1994), along with Agreeableness, Conscientiousness, and Openness to Experience (the latter is sometimes interpreted as Intellectual Curiosity or Degree of Culture). The Big Five emerged from the lexical approach to personality, which posits that the major individual differences in human personality are encoded in language. The early studies of the Big Five (e.g., Tupes & Cristal, 1958) involved factor analyses of trait terms derived from the dictionary. Although the Big Five has demonstrated impressive consistency across samples and cultures, both its comprehensiveness and validity as a model of personality have not gone unchallenged (see Block, 1995; Waller & Ben-Porath, 1987, for critiques). Unlike most conceptualizations of the Big Three (e.g., Tellegen, 1978/1982), the Big Five is not clearly linked to underlying psychobiological dimensions (Eysenck, 1993) and thus appears to be closer to a taxonomy of surface traits than source traits in Cattell's (1950) terminology.

Borger, Cox, Fuentes, and Ross (1996) examined the relation between the ASI and the Big Five as assessed by the Neuroticism–Extraversion–Openness Personality Inventory–Revised (NEO–PI–R: Costa & McCrae, 1992) among a sample of 320 undergraduates (123 males, 197 females). Both the five higher order dimensions of the NEO–PI–R and their lower order facets (see Costa & McCrae, 1992) were examined. In addition, participants were administered the Death Anxiety scale (Templer, 1970) to examine the relation between AS and pathological fears of death and catastrophic injury, which are common among patients with panic disorder. The correlations between the ASI and Big Five higher and lower order dimensions are displayed in Table 7.6.

At the higher order level, Borger et al. found that the ASI was moderately and significantly related to Neuroticism, weakly but significantly related (negatively) to both Extraversion and Conscientiousness, and essentially unrelated to either Agreeableness or Openness to Experience. In addition, at the lower order level, the ASI was significantly associated with a number of specific facets within these five dimensions. For example, the ASI was moderately positively correlated with the Neuroticism facets of Anxiety and Self-Consciousness and weakly negatively correlated with the Extraversion facets of Assertiveness and Gregariousness and with the Conscientiousness facets of Self-Discipline and Competence. In addition, the ASI was positively and significantly correlated ($r = .29$) with the Death Anxiety scale.

A stepwise multiple-regression analysis indicated that, of the Big Five dimensions, Neuroticism and Extraversion were the only significant predictors of ASI scores. An additional stepwise multiple-regression analysis of the lower order facets within Neuroticism and Extraversion indicated that Anxiety, Self-Consciousness, and Gregariousness were the only significant predictors of ASI scores. Because stepwise multiple-regression analyses are associated with a high rate of Type I error (Cohen & Cohen, 1983), these findings need to be replicated in independent samples.

TABLE 7.6
Correlations Between ASI and Big Five
Higher and Lower Order Dimensions

Dimension	Correlation
Neuroticism	.50***
Anxiety	.51***
Angry Hostility	.24***
Depression	.43***
Self-Consciousness	.49***
Impulsivity	.17**
Vulnerability to stress	.42***
Extraversion	-.26***
Warmth	-.10
Gregariousness	-.23***
Assertiveness	-.27***
Activity	-.17**
Excitement-Seeking	-.18***
Positive emotions	-.17**
Agreeableness	.02
Trust	-.22***
Straitforwardness	.05
Altruism	-.08
Modesty	.15**
Tendermindedness	.08
Conscientiousness	-.17**
Competence	-.24***
Order	.03
Dutifulness	-.06
Achievement-Striving	-.18***
Self-Discipline	-.31***
Deliberation	.02
Compliance	.12*
Openness to Experience	-.08
Fantasy	.03
Aesthetics	-.02
Feelings	.13*
Actions	-.22***
Ideas	-.14*
Values	-.12*

Note. $N = 320$. *$p < .05$. **$p < .01$. ***$p < .001$, two tailed.

The Borger et al. results concerning the moderate association between the ASI and Neuroticism are consistent with those of studies of the Big Three (e.g., Arrindell, 1993). In addition, the significant correlations they reported between the ASI and Extraversion, particularly those facets of Extraversion relating to interpersonal relationships (e.g., Assertiveness and Gregariousness), warrant replication and further examination. These findings differ from those of Arrindell (1993), who reported that AS measures were essentially uncorrelated with Extraversion.

As Borger et al. noted, the AS construct may hold important implications for social functioning. Nevertheless, because individuals with high levels of NE tend to perceive themselves negatively (Watson & Clark, 1984), it is important to rule out the possibility that these results are attributable to the overlap between certain facets of Extraversion and NE. The significant correlations between the ASI and facets of other Big Five dimensions may be largely or entirely due to the saturation of these dimensions with NE. The significant negative correlation of the ASI with the Trust facet of Agreeableness, for example, may reflect the fact that feelings of alienation and mistrust are common characteristics of high NE individuals (Tellegen, 1978/1982). In contrast, the significant negative correlation of the ASI with the Competence facet of Conscientiousness may reflect the fact that high NE individuals tend to view themselves negatively (Watson & Clark, 1984). Future investigators should examine this possibility by statistically controlling for NE (or Neuroticism) when examining the relations between AS measures and Big Five facets.

The low correlation between the ASI and Big Five Openness to Experience dimension is somewhat surprising given that Openness to Experience is moderately correlated with Absorption (Church, 1994), which, as noted earlier, has been found to be associated with measures of AS. Nevertheless, because the correlations between Absorption and AS measures are fairly low in magnitude (Lilienfeld, 1997) and because most of the facets of Openness to Experience do not appear to be closely related to Absorption (see Costa & McCrae, 1992), this low correlation should not be entirely unexpected.

OTHER STUDIES EXAMINING THE RELATION BETWEEN ANXIETY SENSITIVITY AND PERSONALITY

Two other teams of researchers, although not couching their investigations with an explicit framework of personality structure (e.g., Big Three, Big Five), have examined the relations between AS measures and various indexes of normal and abnormal personality. The results of these studies may provide further clues concerning the dispositional underpinnings of AS.

Koszycki, Zacharko, and Bradwejn (1996) administered the ASI and the Minnesota Multiphasic Personality Inventory (MMPI; Hathaway & McKinley, 1940) to 29 patients (8 males, 21 females) with panic disorder with or without agoraphobia. Because only the MMPI Hypochondriasis, Depression, Hysteria, Psychasthenia, Social Introversion, and Anxiety scales (the last a supplemental scale constructed by Welsh, 1956) were hypothesized to be relevant to panic attacks, data on the other MMPI scales were not reported. With the exception of the correlation between the ASI and Social Introversion (r =.26), the correlations between the ASI and other MMPI scales reported were significant (rs ranged from .50 to .79). Nevertheless, because many MMPI scales, particularly Anxiety and Psychasthenia (Watson & Clark, 1984), are heavily saturated with an NE or general maladjustment dimension (Finney, 1985), these correlations may reflect only the shared variance between the ASI and NE. Further research examining the relations between AS measures and MMPI scales that may be less saturated with NE (e.g., Hypomania) is warranted (see Watson & Clark, 1984, for data suggesting that manics may be characterized by normal or low levels of NE).

Stewart, Knize, and Pihl (1992) administered the ASI and Interpersonal Dependency Inventory (IDI; Hirschfeld et al., 1977) to 116 undergraduates (22 of whom had a history of spontaneous panic attacks) and 23 patients with panic disorder with agoraphobia. In the full sample, the ASI correlated significantly with the total IDI score (r=.52). (See also Hoffart & Hedley, 1997, for evidence that scores on the ACQ physical fear subscale predict changes in dependent personality disorder symptoms following psychotherapy.) In addition, the ASI correlated significantly with the IDI emotional reliance on another person (r =.58) and lack of social self-confidence (r=.44) subscales, but not with the IDI assertion of autonomy subscale (r=-.01). Separate correlations of the IDI total score or subscales within the two samples were not reported.

The Stewart et al. findings corroborate those of Borger et al. in suggesting that AS is associated with interpersonal dysfunction, although it is possible that the greater dependency of high AS individuals is a secondary consequence of panic attacks, agoraphobic avoidance, or both. Analyses comparing the correlation between the ASI and IDI among undergraduates with versus without a history of spontaneous panic attacks might have shed light on this possibility. In addition, in future research it will be important to ascertain the extent to which the relation between AS measures and indexes of interpersonal dependency are attributable to NE. Although high NE individuals, compared with low

NE individuals, tend to be more nonconforming and relatively unconcerned about social approval (Watson & Clark, 1984), they also tend to be more self-critical and dissatisfied with their relationships with others (Tellegen & Waller, 1994).

CONCLUSIONS AND FUTURE DIRECTIONS

Until recently, the relation of the AS construct to the broader personality domain has received relatively little attention. Although considerable emphasis has been placed on the question of how AS differs from NE, trait anxiety, and other personality traits (e.g., Reiss, 1997), little emphasis has been placed on the equally important question of how AS is similar to these traits (Lilienfeld, 1996). Data relevant to both questions could provide valuable clues to the etiology of AS, as well as to the etiology of anxiety disorders (e.g., panic disorder) in which AS may play an important causal role.

The findings reviewed here indicate that measures of AS are moderately to highly related to the higher order dimension of NE (or, in Eysenck's scheme, Neuroticism), which reflects a pervasive tendency to experience aversive emotional states of all kinds. Because Eysenck (1979) regarded Neuroticism as an amplifier of conditionability, this finding is broadly consistent with the claim (Reiss, 1991) that AS potentiates anxiety responding. Nevertheless, studies of the incremental validity of AS measures (Lilienfeld, 1997; McNally, 1996) suggest that these measures possess reliable variance not shared with NE.

The data reported here also indicate that, with the possible exception of the ASI, measures of AS are neglibly related to the higher order dimension of CN, which has been posited by a number of authors to be a marker of Gray's (1982) BIS and to reflect a tendency to experience fear in response to danger cues. These findings suggest that high AS individuals may not be excessively fearful of future threat, although they may overreact to threat once it is perceived as inevitable. Alternatively, these findings may suggest that CN does not relate to Gray's BIS as closely as some authors (e.g., Depue & Spoont, 1987) have hypothesized. Future research is needed to distinguish between these two possibilities.

The Borger et al. (1996) findings concerning the relations between the ASI and the Big Five Extraversion and Conscientiousness dimensions, as well as the relations between the ASI and several Big Five lower order facets relevant to interpersonal functioning, merit further examination (see also Stewart et al., 1992). These findings may point to other higher and lower order personality dimensions that might increase risk for panic and other anxiety disorders.

Nevertheless, it is also possible that the interpersonal deficits (e.g., dependency) associated with high levels of AS are not causes, but consequences or complications resulting from AS (e.g., panic attacks, limited symptom attacks). A third possibility, as discussed earlier, is that the relation between AS and interpersonal deficits is mediated by NE. Because NE is a pervasive dimension that affects numerous aspects of self-concept and emotional adjustment (Watson & Clark, 1984), it is important for future researchers to ascertain the extent to which the relations between AS measures and interpersonal dysfunction are attributable to NE.

The findings reported here indicate a significant association between AS and Absorption; although this is intriguing, this association also requires replication. Although secondary analyses suggested that this association was not accounted for entirely by NE, the moderate overlap between Absorption and NE (Tellegen, 1978/1982) suggests that future analyses of the relation between AS and Absorption should be certain to examine the potential mediating role of NE. Nevertheless, longitudinal studies of people at risk for panic attacks should be conducted to investigate the possibility that a propensity toward heightened immersion in sensory experiences (which may be assessed by both Absorption and AS measures) is a risk factor for panic attacks.

Because the data reviewed in this chapter are correlational, they cannot provide definitive information concerning the direction of the relation between AS and personality traits. A source trait perspective (Cattell, 1950) is most compatible with the hypothesis that specific lower order traits such as AS arise from general higher order traits such as NE in interaction with learning experiences (e.g., negative experiences with anxiety, observing others experience panic attacks), information regarding the adverse consequences of anxiety (Rachman, 1977), and other personality traits (e.g., somatic anxiety: Schalling, 1978; Absorption: Tellegen & Atkinson, 1974). Nevertheless, it is possible that the true causal relation runs in the opposite direction (Reiss, 1997) and that AS and related sensitivities (e.g., injury sensitivity: Reiss, 1991; Reiss & Havercamp, 1996) give rise to NE and other higher order dimensions.

In addition to longitudinal and causal modeling (e.g., see Loehlin, 1992) studies of individuals with differing levels of AS, NE, and related dimensions, multivariate behavior-genetic designs can provide useful information concerning the causes of the overlap among these personality traits (Lilienfeld et al., 1996). Such designs permit investigators to determine the extent to which the covariation among traits is attributable to genetic, shared environmental, and nonshared environmental factors. Moreover, the incorporation of direction-of-causation models (Neale & Cardon, 1992) within multivariate behavior-genetic designs may clarify whether NE and trait anxiety (in interaction with environmental factors and other personality traits) give rise to AS, as suggested by Lilienfeld et al. (1993), or whether AS and other traits give rise to NE and trait anxiety, as suggested by Reiss (1997).

The history of science teaches us that many of the most important advances in knowledge stem from the demonstration that constructs previously thought to be distinct or independent are in fact interrelated (Bronowski, 1978; see also Ackerman, 1997). A better understanding of the relation of AS to the personality domain may provide important insights not only into how AS differs from other traits (e.g., trait anxiety, Absorption), but also into the underlying causal processes that mediate the covariation between AS and these traits. A better understanding of these processes may in turn provide important clues to the etiology of panic and other anxiety disorders.

REFERENCES

Ackerman, P. L. (1997). Personality, self-concept, interests, and intelligence: Which construct doesn't fit? *Journal of Personality, 65*, 171–204.

Allport, G. W., & Odbert, H. S. (1936). Trait-names: A psycho-lexical study. *Psychological Monographs, 47*, 1–171.

Arrindell, W. A. (1993). The fear of fear concept: Evidence in favor of multidimensionality. *Behaviour Research and Therapy, 31*, 507–518.

Asmundson, G. J. G., Norton, G. R., Lanthier, N. J., & Cox, B. J. (1996). Fear of anxiety: Do current measures assess unique aspects of the construct? *Personality and Individual Differences, 20*, 607–612.

Barlow, D. H. (1988). *Anxiety and its disorders: The nature and treatment of anxiety and panic.* New York: Guilford.

Barsky, A. J., & Klerman, G. L. (1983). Overview: Hypochondriasis, bodily complaints, and somatic styles. *American Journal of Psychiatry, 140*, 273–283.

Block, J. (1965). *The challenge of response sets.* New York: Appleton-Century-Crofts.

Block, J. (1995). A contrarian view of the five-factor model to personality description. *Psychological Bulletin, 117*, 187–215.

Borger, S. C., Cox, B. J., Fuentes, K., & Ross, L. M. (1996, November). *Anxiety sensitivity and the five-factor model of personality.* Poster presented at the annual meeting of the Association for Advancement of Behavior Therapy, New York.

Bronowski, J. (1978). *The origins of knowledge and imagination.* New Haven, CT: Yale University Press.

Brown, T. A., & Cash, T. F. (1989). The phenomenon of panic in nonclinical populations: Further evidence and methodological considerations. *Journal of Anxiety Disorders, 4*, 15–29.

Cattell, R. B. (1950). *Personality: A systematic, theoretical, and factual study.* New York: McGraw-Hill.

Cattell, R. B. (1966). The scree test for the number of factors. *Multivariate Behavioral Research, 1*, 245–276.

Chambless, D. L., Caputo, G. C., Bright, P., & Gallagher, R. (1984). Assessment of fear of fear in agoraphobics: The Body Sensations Questionnaire and the Agoraphobic Cognitions Questionnaire. *Journal of Consulting and Clinical Psychology, 52*, 1090–1097.

Chambless, D. L., Caputo, G. C., Jasin, S. E., Graceley, E. J., & Williams, C. (1985). The Mobility Inventory for agoraphobia. *Behaviour Research and Therapy, 23*, 35–44.

Chambless, D. L., & Gracely, E. J. (1989). Fear of fear and the anxiety disorders. *Cognitive Therapy and Research, 13*, 9–20.

Church, A. T. (1994). Relating the Tellegen and five-factor models of personality structure. *Journal of Personality and Social Psychology, 67*, 898–909.

Clark, D. M. (1986). A cognitive approach to panic. *Behaviour Research and Therapy, 24*, 461–470.

Cleckley, H. (1982). *The mask of sanity* (6th ed.). St. Louis, MO: Mosby.

Cloninger, R. C. (1987). A systematic method for clinical description and classification of personality variants: A proposal. *Archives of General Psychiatry, 44*, 573–588.

Cohen, J., & Cohen, P. (1983). *Applied multiple regression/correlation analysis for the behavioral sciences*. Hillsdale, NJ: Lawrence Erlbaum Associates.

Costa, P. T., & McCrae, R. R. (1992). *Revised NEO Personality Inventory (NEO-PI-R) and NEO Five-Factor Inventory (NEO-FFI) professional manual*. Odessa, FL: Psychological Assessment Resources.

Council, J., Kirsch, I., & Hafner, L. P. (1986). Expectancy versus absorption in the prediction of hypnotic responding. *Journal of Personality and Social Psychology, 50*, 182–189.

Craske, M. G., & Freed, S. (1995). Expectations about arousal and nocturnal panic. *Journal of Abnormal Psychology, 104*, 567–575.

Depue, R. A. (1996). A neurobiological framework for the structure of personality and emotion: Implications for personality disorders. In J. F. Clarkin & M. F. Lenzenweger (Eds.), *Major theories of personality disorder* (pp. 347–390). New York: Guilford.

Depue, R. A., & Spoont, M. R. (1987). Conceptualizing a serotonin trait: A dimension of behavioral constraint. In J. Mann & M. Stanley (Eds.), *The psychobiology of suicidal behavior* (pp. 47–62). New York: New York Academy of Sciences.

Derogatis, L. R. (1977). *SCL-90: Administration, scoring, and procedures manual-I for the R(evised) version and other instruments of the psychopathology rating series*. Baltimore, MD: Clinical Psychometrics Unit, Johns Hopkins University School of Medicine.

Eysenck, H. J. (1979). The conditioning model of neurosis. *Behavioral and Brain Sciences, 2*, 155–199.

Eysenck, H. J. (1991). Dimensions of personality: 16, 5, or 3? Criteria for a taxonomic paradigm. *Personality and Individual Differences, 12*, 773–790.

Eysenck, H. J. (1993). Comment on Goldberg. *American Psychologist, 48*, 1299–1300.

Eysenck, H. J., & Eysenck, S. B. (1975). *Manual of the EPQ*. San Diego, CA: EdITS.

Fava, G. A., Grandi, S., Belluardo, P., Savron, G., Raffi, A. R., Conti, S., & Saviotti, F. M. (1994). Benzodiazepines and anxiety sensitivity in panic disorder. *Progress in Neuro-Psychopharmacology and Biological Psychiatry, 18*, 1163–1168.

Finney, J. C. (1985). Anxiety: Its measurement by objective personality tests and self-report. In A. H. Tuma & J. D. Maser (Eds.), *Anxiety and the anxiety disorders* (pp. 645–673). Hillsdale, NJ: Lawrence Erlbaum Associates.

Floyd, F. J., & Widaman, K. (1995). Factor analysis in the development and refinement of clinical assessment instruments. *Psychological Assessment, 7*, 286–299.

Fowles, D. C. (1987). Application of a behavioral theory of motivation to the concepts of anxiety and impulsivity. *Journal of Research in Personality, 21*, 417–435.

Frankel, F. H., & Orne, M. T. (1976). Hypnotizability and phobic behavior. *Archives of General Psychiatry, 33*, 1259–1261.

Frishholz, E. J., Spiegel, D., Spiegel, H., Balma, D. L., & Markell, C. S. (1982). Differential hypnotic responsivity of smokers, phobics, and chronic-pain control patients: A failure to confirm. *Journal of Abnormal Psychology, 91*, 269–272.

Geer, J. H. (1965). The development of a scale to measure fear. *Behaviour Research and Therapy, 3*, 45–53.

Goldberg, L. R. (1993). The structure of phenotypic personality traits. *American Psychologist, 48*, 26–34.

Goldstein, A. J., & Chambless, D. L. (1978). A reanalysis of agoraphobia. *Behavior Therapy, 9*, 47–59.

Gorsuch, R. L. (1983). *Factor analysis* (2nd ed.). Hillsdale, NJ: Lawrence Erlbaum Associates.

Gough, H. G. (1987). *California Psychological Inventory [Administrator's Guide]*. Palo Alto, CA: Consulting Psychologists Press.

Gray, J. A. (1982). *The neuropsychology of anxiety*. New York: Oxford University Press.

Harpur, T. J., Hare, R. D., & Hakstian, A. R. (1989). Two–factor conceptualization of psychopathy: Construct validity and assessment implications. *Psychological Assessment, 1*, 6–17.

Hasten, J., & Stokes, J. (1987). *Anxiety sensitivity and negative affectivity*. Unpublished manuscript, University of Illinois at Chicago.

Hathaway, S. R., & McKinley, J.C. (1940). A multiphasic personality schedule (Minnesota): I. Construction of the schedule. *Journal of Psychology, 10*, 249–254.

Hilgard, E. R. (1979). *Personality and hypnosis: A study of imaginative involvement* (2nd ed.). Chicago: University of Chicago Press.

Hirschfeld, R. M. A., Klerman, G. L., Gough, H. G., Barrett, J., Korchin, S. J., & Chodoff, P. (1977). A measure of interpersonal dependency. *Journal of Personality Assessment, 41*, 610–618.

Hodgson, R. J., & Rachman, S. (1977). Obsessive-compulsive complaints. *Behaviour Research and Therapy, 15*, 389–395.

Hoffart, A., & Hedley, L. M. (1997). Personality traits among panic disorder with agoraphobia patients before and after symptom-focused treatment. *Journal of Anxiety Disorders, 11*, 77–87.

Holloway, W., & McNally, R. J. (1987). Effects of anxiety sensitivity on the response to hyperventilation. *Journal of Abnormal Psychology, 96*, 330–334.

Ingram, R. E. (1990). Self-focused attention in clinical disorders: Review and a conceptual model. *Psychological Bulletin, 107*, 156–176.

Koszycki, D., Zacharko, R. M., & Bradwejn, J. (1996). Influence of personality on behavioral response to cholecystokinin-tetrapeptide in patients with panic disorder. *Psychiatry Research, 62*, 131–138.

Lilienfeld, S. O. (1996). Anxiety sensitivity is not distinct from trait anxiety. In R.M. Rapee (Ed.), *Current controversies in the anxiety disorders* (pp. 228–244). New York: Guilford.

Lilienfeld, S. O. (1997). The relation of anxiety sensitivity to higher and lower order personality dimensions: Implications for the etiology of panic attacks. *Journal of Abnormal Psychology, 106*, 539–544.

Lilienfeld, S. O., Jacob, R. G., & Turner, S. M. (1989). Comment on Holloway and McNally's (1987) "Effects of anxiety sensitivity on the response to hyperventilation." *Journal of Abnormal Psychology, 98*, 100–102.

Lilienfeld, S. O., & Jones, J. C. (1992). *Beliefs About Negative Consequences Inventory (BANCI)*. Unpublished manuscript, University at Albany, State University of New York, Albany.

Lilienfeld, S. O., Turner, S. M., & Jacob, R. G. (1993). Anxiety sensitivity: An examination of theoretical and methodological issues. *Advances in Behaviour Research and Therapy, 15*, 147–183.

Lilienfeld, S. O., Turner, S. M., & Jacob, R. G. (1996). Further comments on the nature of measurement of anxiety sensitivity: A reply to Taylor (1995b). *Journal of Anxiety Disorders, 10*, 411–424.

Loehlin, J. C. (1992). *Latent variable models: An introduction to factor, path, and structural analysis* (2nd ed.). Hillsdale, NJ: Lawrence Erlbaum Associates.

Lubin, B. (1981). *Manual for the depression adjective check lists.* San Diego, CA: EdITS.

Lyons, J. S., Talano, J. V., Gitter, H., Martin, G. J., & Singer, D. H. (1986, August). *Mitral valve prolapse and panic disorder.* Paper presented at the annual meeting of the American Psychological Association, Washington, DC.

Lykken, D. T. (1971). Multiple factor analysis and personality research. *Journal of Experimental Research in Personality, 5*, 161–170.

Marks, I. M., & Mathews, A. M. (1979). Brief standard self-rating for phobic patients. *Behaviour Research and Therapy, 17*, 263–267.

Mattick, R. P., & Clark, L. (1988). *Development and validation of measures of social scrutiny fear and social interaction anxiety.* Unpublished manuscript, University of New South Wales, Kensington, Australia.

Mattick, R. P., & Peters, L. (1988). Treatment of severe social phobia: Effects of guided exposure with and without restructuring. *Journal of Consulting and Clinical Psychology, 56*, 251–260.

McCrae, R. R., & Costa, P. T. (1985). Openness to experience. In R. Hogan & W. H. Jones (Eds.), *Perspectives in personality* (Vol. 1, pp. 145–172). Greenwich, CT: JAI.

McNally, R. J. (1989). Is anxiety sensitivity distinguishable from trait anxiety? Reply to Lilienfeld, Jacob, and Turner (1989). *Journal of Abnormal Psychology, 98*, 193–194.

McNally, R. J. (1990). Psychological approaches to panic disorder: A review. *Psychological Bulletin, 3*, 403–419.

McNally, R. J. (1994). *Panic disorder: A critical analysis.* New York: Guilford Press.

McNally, R. J. (1996). Anxiety sensitivity is distinguishable from trait anxiety. In R. M. Rapec (Ed.), *Current controversies in the anxiety disorder* (pp. 214–227). New York: Guilford.

McNally, R. J., & Lorenz, M. (1987). Anxiety sensitivity in agoraphobics. *Journal of Behavior Therapy and Experimental Psychiatry, 18*, 3–11.

Meyer, T. J., Miller, M. L., Metzger, R. L., & Borkevec, T. D. (1990). Development and validation of the Penn State Worry Questionnaire. *Behaviour Research and Therapy, 28*, 487–495.

Nadon, R., Hoyt, I. P., Register, P. A., & Kihlstrom, J. F. (1991). Absorption and hypnotizability: Context effects reexamined. *Journal of Personality and Social Psychology, 60*, 144–153.

Neale, M. C., & Cardon, L. R. (1992). *Methodology for genetic studies of twins and families.* Dordrecht, The Netherlands: Kluwer Academic Publishers.

Norton, G. R., Dorward, J., & Cox, B. J. (1986). Factors associated with panic attacks in nonclinical subjects. *Behavior Research and Therapy, 17*, 239–252.

Otto, M. W., Pollack, M. H., Sachs, G. S., & Rosenbaum, J. F. (1992). Hypochondriacal concerns, anxiety sensitivity, and panic disorder. *Journal of Anxiety Disorders, 6*, 93–104.

Pennebaker, J. W., & Watson, D. (1991). The psychology of somatic symptoms. In L. J. Kirmayer & J. M. Robbins (Eds.), *Current concepts of somatization* (pp. 21–35). Washington, DC: American Psychiatric Press.

Rachman, S. J. (1977). The conditioning theory of fear acquisition: A critical examination. *Behaviour Research and Therapy, 15*, 375–387.

Rapee, R. M., & Medoro, L. (1994). Fear of physical sensations and trait anxiety as mediators of the response to hyperventilation in nonclinical subjects. *Journal of Abnormal Psychology, 103*, 693–699.

Reichenbach, H. (1938). *Experience and prediction*. Chicago: University of Chicago Press.

Reiss, S. (1987). Theoretical perspectives on the fear of anxiety. *Clinical Psychology Review, 11*, 141–153.

Reiss, S. (1991). Expectancy model of fear, anxiety, and panic. *Clinical Psychology Review, 11*, 141–153.

Reiss, S. (1997). Trait anxiety: It's not what you think it is. *Journal of Anxiety Disorders, 11*, 201–214.

Reiss, S., & Havercamp, S. (1996). The sensitivity theory of motivation: Implications for psychopathology. *Behaviour Research and Therapy, 34*, 621–632.

Reiss, S., Peterson, R. A., Gursky, D. M., & McNally, R. J. (1986). Anxiety sensitivity, anxiety frequency, and the prediction of fearfulness. *Behaviour Research and Therapy, 24*, 1–8.

Roche, S. M., & McConkey, K. M. (1990). Absorption: Nature, assessment, and correlates. *Journal of Personality and Social Psychology, 59*, 91–101.

Saviotti, F. M., Grandi, S., Savron, G., Ermentini, R., Bartolucci, G., Conti, S., & Fava, G. A. (1991). Characterological traits of recovered patients with panic disorder and agoraphobia. *Journal of Affective Disorders, 23*, 113–117.

Schalling, D. (1978). Psychopathy-related personality variables and the psychophysiology of socialization. In R.D. Hare & D. Schalling (Eds.), *Psychopathic behaviour: Approaches to research* (pp. 85–106). Chichester, England: Wiley.

Sigmon, S. T., Rohan, K. J., Fink, C. M., & Hotovy, L. A. (1995, November). *Relationship of anxiety sensitivity and menstrual symptoms*. Poster presented at the annual meeting of the Association for Advancement of Behavior Therapy, Washington, DC.

Spielberger, C. D., Gorsuch, R. R., & Lushene, R. E. (1970). *State-trait anxiety inventory test manual for form X*. Palo Alto, CA: Consulting Psychologists Press.

Spoont, M. R. (1992). Modulatory role of serotonin in human information processing: Implications for human psychopathology. *Psychological Bulletin, 112*, 330–350.

Stewart, S. H., Knize, K., & Pihl, R. O. (1992). Anxiety sensitivity and dependency in clinical and non-clinical panickers and controls. *Journal of Anxiety Disorders, 6*, 119–131.

Taylor, S. (1995a). Anxiety sensitivity: Theoretical perspectives and recent findings. *Behaviour Research and Therapy, 3*, 243–258.

Taylor, S. (1995b). Issues in the conceptualization and measurement of anxiety sensitivity. *Journal of Anxiety Disorders, 9*, 163–174.

Taylor, S., Koch, W. J., & McNally, R. J. (1992). How does anxiety sensitivity vary across the anxiety disorders? *Journal of Anxiety Disorders, 6*, 249–259.

Taylor, S., Koch, W. J., McNally, R. J., & Crockett, D. J. (1992b). Conceptualizations of anxiety sensitivity. *Psychological Assessment, 4*, 245–250.

Tellegen, A. (1978/1982). *Brief manual for the Multidimensional Personality Questionnaire*. Unpublished manuscript, University of Minnesota, Minneapolis.

Tellegen, A. (1985). Structure of mood and personality and their relevance to assessing anxiety, with an emphasis on self-report. In A. H. Tuma & J. D. Maser (Eds.), Anxiety and the anxiety disorders (pp. 681–706). Hillsdale, NJ: Lawrence Erlbaum Associates.

Tellegen, A., & Atkinson, G. (1974). Openness to absorbing and self-altering experiences ("absorption"), a trait related to hypnotic susceptibility. *Journal of Abnormal Psychology, 83*, 268–277.

Tellegen, A., & Waller, N. G. (1994). Exploring personality through test construction: Development of the Multidimensional Personality Questionnaire. In S.R. Briggs & J.C. Cheek (Eds.), *Personality measures: Development and evaluation* (Vol. 1, pp. 133–161). Greenwich, CT: JAI.

Templer, D. I. (1970). The construction and validation of a death anxiety scale. *Journal of General Psychology, 82,* 165–177.

Tupes, E. C., & Cristal, R. E. (1958). *Stability of personality trait rating factors under diverse conditions* (USAF WACD Technical Note # 58–61). Lackland Air Force Base, TX: U.S. Air Force.

Vernon, P. E. (1961). *The structure of human abilities* (2nd ed.). London: Methuen.

Walker, J. R., Norton, G. R., & Ross, C. A. (1991). *Panic disorder and agoraphobia: A comprehensive guide for the practitioner.* Pacific Grove, CA: Brooks/Cole.

Waller, N. G., & Ben-Porath, Y. S. (1987). Is it time for clinical psychology to embrace the five factor model of personality? *American Psychologist, 42,* 887–889.

Waller, N. G., Lilienfeld, S. O., Tellegen, A., & Lykken, D. T. (1991). The Tridimensional Personality Questionnaire: Structural validity and comparison with the Multidimensional Personality Questionnaire. *Multivariate Behavioral Research, 26,* 1–23.

Watson, D., & Clark, L. A. (1984). Negative affectivity: The disposition to experience negative emotional states. *Psychological Bulletin, 98,* 219–235.

Watson, D., & Clark, L. A. (1992). Affects separable and inseparable: On the hierarchical arrangement of the negative affects. *Journal of Personality and Social Psychology, 62,* 489–505.

Watson, D., Clark, L. A., & Harkness, A. R. (1994). Structures of personality and their relevance to psychopathology. *Journal of Abnormal Psychology, 103,* 18–31.

Watson, D., & Pennebaker, J. W. (1989). Health complaints, stress, and distress: Exploring the central role of negative affectivity. *Psychological Review, 96,* 234–254.

Welsh, G. S. (1956). Factor dimensions A and R. In G. S. Welsh & G. Dahlstrom (Eds.), *Basic readings on the MMPI in psychology and medicine* (pp. 264–281). Minneapolis, MI: University of Minnesota Press.

Wild, T. C., Kuiken, D., & Schopflocher, D. (1995). The role of absorption in experiental involvement. *Journal of Personality and Social Psychology, 3,* 569–579.

Wolpe, J., & Lang, P. J. (1964). A fear survey schedule for use in behaviour therapy. *Behaviour Research and Therapy, 2,* 27–30.

Zinbarg, R. E., & Barlow, D. H. (1996). Structure of anxiety and the anxiety disorders: A hierarchical model. *Journal of Abnormal Psychology, 105,* 181–193.

Zuckerman, M. (1994). *Behavioral expressions and biosocial bases of sensation seeking.* New York: Cambridge University Press.

III

NEW RESEARCH ON BASIC MECHANISMS: CAUSES AND CONSEQUENCES OF ANXIETY SENSITIVITY

8

Anxiety Sensitivity and Information-Processing Biases for Threat

Richard J. McNally
Harvard University

In his classic article on the two disciplines of psychology, Cronbach (1957) emphasized the complementary strengths of the correlational (e.g., psychometric) and experimental traditions in our field. Most chapters in this volume concern studies conducted in the first tradition. This chapter addresses those conducted in the second—namely, experiments on threat-related cognitive biases in people characterized by high anxiety sensitivity (AS). Most studies on this topic concern panic disorder; patients with this syndrome commonly score high on the Anxiety Sensitivity Index (ASI; McNally & Lorenz, 1987; Reiss, Peterson, Gursky, & McNally, 1986; Taylor, Koch, & McNally, 1992). The chief question is whether people, identified psychometrically as at risk for panic disorder, exhibit the same biases as do those who have developed the disorder.

The theoretical importance of this issue arises because AS is a dispositional variable (McNally, 1989; Reiss & McNally, 1985) whose predictive significance for panic attacks somehow should be rendered manifest in biases that occasion panic attacks. That is, the ASI taps beliefs (explicit and implicit) about the negative valence of certain sensations and these beliefs should influence online processing of these sensations. To illustrate, moment-to-moment interpretation of bodily perturbations may depend on relatively stable AS beliefs. AS beliefs may thereby undergird attentional, memory, and interoceptive biases for threat as well. Which, if any, of these biases are present in psychiatrically healthy people with high AS remains understudied.

Thus, although elevated ASI scores do predict the onset of spontaneous panic attacks (Schmidt, Lerew, & Jackson, 1997), and thus may constitute a cognitive risk factor for panic, there are few data relevant to determining whether information-processing biases are present before the onset of panic. The remainder of this chapter reviews the evidence for cognitive biases in panic disorder (which is characterized by elevated AS) and the growing literature on these biases in people who are psychiatrically healthy but who have elevated AS.

COGNITIVE BIASES IN PANIC DISORDER

Interpretive Bias

Pathological anxiety should be associated with a proneness for disambiguating stimuli as harmful. That is, any bias for interpreting ambiguous input as threatening should increase the frequency of anxiety episodes because stimuli whose meaning is unclear are common in everyday life. To test this hypothesis, McNally and Foa (1987) had agoraphobics, recovered agoraphobics, and healthy control subjects interpret ambiguous scenarios concerning either internal or external events. These were included in a booklet based on one developed by Butler and Mathews (1983). Subjects were asked to write down the first explanation that occurred to them; then they were to turn the page and rank three researcher-provided explanations for the ambiguous event in terms of its probability of coming to mind should the subject encounter a similar situation in everyday life. The results reveal that agoraphobics, compared with recovered agoraphobics and control subjects, tended to exhibit interpretive biases favoring threat. Contrary to expectation, agoraphobics did not exhibit more bias for internal than external scenarios. Interestingly, these patients were characterized by high ASI scores ($M = 46.67$); the mean ASI scores for the recovered agoraphobics was 16.44.

Replicating McNally and Foa's (1987) basic findings, Harvey and her associates found that patients with social phobia exhibited similar interpretive biases to those of panic patients on the scenarios used by McNally and Foa (Harvey, Richards, Dziadosz, & Swindell, 1993). The ASI scores of the social phobia patients ($M = 35.00$), however, were as high as those of the panic disorder group ($M = 39.30$). This suggests that interpretive bias may be more closely linked to anxiety sensitivity than to panic disorder per se.

Two recent studies have clarified interpretive bias in panic disorder. Clark et al. (1997) modified McNally and Foa's (1987) methods and found that panic disorder patients (most nonagoraphobic) interpreted only ambiguous scenarios about abruptly occurring bodily sensations (e.g., heart palpitations) as threatening; they did not do so for ambiguous scenarios about other potentially threatening stimuli. Moreover, biased interpretations of sudden bodily sensations were accompanied by ratings of high belief conviction in the panic disorder group. Clark et al. demonstrated that this interpretive bias was more pronounced among panic patients than among patients with either generalized anxiety disorder or social phobia—two syndromes whose ASI scores are notably lower than those of panic disorder patients (Taylor et al., 1992).

Using the Swedish translation of the Clark et al. (1997) booklet, Westling and Öst (1995) found that panic patients with minimal agoraphobia again demonstrated a specific bias for interpreting sudden bodily sensations in a threatening fashion relative to healthy control subjects. This bias was abolished by both cognitive-behavior therapy and by applied relaxation. Moreover, elimination of panic attacks was strongly related to declines in interpretive bias.

Using different methods to examine interpretive bias, Stoler and McNally (1991) asked agoraphobic, recovered agoraphobic, and healthy control subjects to complete sentence stems with the first thought that came to mind and then write down several additional sentences elaborating on their initial response. The sentence stems were either related or unrelated to threat and were either ambiguous or unambiguous. Thus, for the stem "Knowing that entering the store would produce a sure fit, I...", the word *fit* might refer to either clothes or a panic attack.

The results reveal that agoraphobics exhibited biases for interpreting stems as threatening in contrast to control subjects and that the interpretive patterns of recovered agoraphobics resembled those of symptomatic agoraphobics more than those of the control subjects. However, the additional sentences jotted down by the recovered agoraphobics suggested a tendency to cope adaptively with threatening situations (e.g., applying anxiety management techniques), whereas those of symptomatic agoraphobics did not. Although recovered agoraphobics scored significantly lower than symptomatic agoraphobics on the ASI ($M = 26.33$ vs. $M = 39.07$), they still scored significantly higher than the control subjects ($M = 18.33$).

In a recent investigation, panic/agoraphobic patients (ASI: $M = 40.47$) and normal control subjects (ASI: $M = 16.13$) completed one questionnaire requiring them to interpret scenarios about anxietylike sensations occurring in nonthreatening contexts (Kamieniecki, Wade, & Tsourtos, 1997). For example:

You water the plants and then do some physical exercises for 15 minutes. You then have a glass of cold water, rearrange some magazines on the coffee table and turn on the television. You suddenly realize that you are short of breath and your heart is beating fast. (p. 144)

Subjects were allowed 10 seconds to provide the first interpretation that occurred to them; these were classified as either anxiety related (e.g., imminent panic attack), harm related (e.g., impending stroke), or benign (e.g., exercise induced).

A second questionnaire was composed of scenarios concerning ambiguous internal stimuli such as, "You have just got out of bed in the morning and notice you are trembling and shaking" (p. 145). Scenarios concerning ambiguous external stimuli were modeled on those of McNally and Foa (1987). Subjects were permitted 20 seconds to provide their initial interpretation and then provide any others that came to mind. The authors noted whether any of these alternatives were benign. Subjects also rated the subjective cost (negative valence) of their initial interpretation (i.e., how bad it would be for the subject if the interpretation were true).

Those with panic disorder, in contrast to control subjects, provided fewer benign explanations and more anxiety-related explanations for physical sensations (but not more harm-related ones) on the first questionnaire. On the second questionnaire, 87% of the patients provided a minimum of one costly (negative) anxiety-related interpretation for which they were unable to generate a benign alternative; only 7% of the control subjects were unable to generate innocuous alternatives. That is, the vast majority of patients provided at least one interpretation related to anxiety and rated it as something that would be very bad if it were to occur.

In summary, these studies have repeatedly shown that patients with panic disorder, often agoraphobic, are characterized by biases for interpreting ambiguous information in a threatening manner. Most studies have included ASI scores and these have consistently indicated elevated AS in the panic disorder groups. Recovery from panic disorder is associated with a reduction, and sometimes abolition, of interpretive biases.

Attentional Bias

Because people can only attend to a subset of stimuli at a given moment, any bias for selectively attending to threat should increase the frequency of anxiety episodes (Williams, Watts, MacLeod, & Mathews, 1988, 1997). Researchers have applied several paradigms to test this hypothesis in patients with anxiety syndromes, including those with panic disorder.

Burgess and his colleagues (Burgess, Jones, Robertson, Radcliffe, & Emerson, 1981) published a pioneering study indicating that agoraphobic and social phobic subjects were especially effective in detecting disorder-relevant threat phrases (e.g., *shopping alone*) embedded in the unattended channel during dichotic listening. This finding is consistent with the hypothesis that panic patients have a bias for selectively attending to threat cues. However, some commentators (e.g., MacLeod, 1991) expressed concern over whether such dichotic listening methods were capable of discriminating a genuine attentional bias from a response bias for guessing (sometimes correctly) that a threat target had occurred.

The emotional Stroop color-naming paradigm remains the most commonly applied technique for studying attentional bias for threat in the anxiety disorders. In this paradigm, subjects are shown words of varying emotional significance and are asked to name the colors in which the words appear while ignoring the meanings of the words (Williams, Mathews, & MacLeod, 1996). Stroop interference occurs when the meaning of the word captures the subject's attention, slowing the subject's color-naming response.

Several studies have shown that panic patients tend to exhibit longer color-naming times for threat words, especially those strongly connected to their central preoccupations (e.g., *fatal, collapse*; Ehlers, Margraf, Davies, & Roth, 1988; Hope, Rapee, Heimberg, & Dombeck, 1990; McNally et al., 1994; McNally, Riemann, & Kim, 1990). Ehlers et al. (1988) found that panic patients and nonclinical panickers, but not healthy control subjects, demonstrated interference for words related to social threat (e.g., *stupid*), physical threat (e.g., *fatal*), and separation (e.g., *lonely*). Hope et al. (1990) found that panic patients, but not patients with social phobia, demonstrated interference for physical threat words (e.g., *fatal*), but not for social threats (e.g., *stupid*). McNally et al. (1990) reported that panic patients demonstrated more interference for words relevant to fear (e.g., *panic*), bodily sensations (e.g., *dizzy*), and catastrophe (e.g., *collapse*) than did therapists familiar with the treatment of panic disorder.[1] Interference for threat words was not exacerbated by exercise-induced physiological arousal (McNally, Riemann, Louro, Lukach, & Kim, 1992), and positive words approximately opposite in meaning to threat words failed to produce interference in panic patients (McNally et al., 1994).

---

[1]Clinicians seasoned in the treatment of panic disorder have sometimes been used as control subjects because of their familiarity with the concerns of panickers. Their participation allows one to test the hypothesis that any information-processing bias in the panic group may be attributable to mere familiarity with panic issues rather than with the presence of the disorder.

Panic researchers have applied other paradigms in an effort to capture this bias in the laboratory, such as the dot-probe attention deployment paradigm (MacLeod, Mathews, & Tata, 1986). In this paradigm, subjects execute a neutral response (button press) to a neutral visual stimulus (a dot) that replaces either member of a pair of words that appear on a computer screen. Subjects read aloud the top word of each pair and press a button whenever a dot replaces one of the words. On some trials, one member of the word pair has a threatening meaning. Using this method, MacLeod et al. demonstrated that patients with generalized anxiety disorder, relative to depressed patients and healthy control subjects, were faster at responding to dots that replaced threat words and slower at responding to dots that replaced nonthreat words. MacLeod et al. concluded that an attentional bias for threat in people with generalized anxiety disorder facilitated task performance when dots replaced threat words, but impaired it when dots replaced nonthreat words.

Using the dot-probe paradigm, Asmundson, Sandler, Wilson, and Walker (1992) found that panic patients responded faster to dots that replaced physical but not social threat words. However, there was no evidence that patients shifted attention to threat words. A related paradigm provided some evidence of a similar bias favoring threat versus positive words in panic patients but not in healthy control subjects (McNally, Hornig, Otto, & Pollack, 1997). Yet in a modified version of the MacLeod et al. paradigm, panic disorder patients (ASI: $M = 33.95$) selectively attended to positive words as well as physically threatening words (Beck, Stanley, Averill, Baldwin, & Deagle, 1992). Further puzzling was Asmundson and Stein's (1994/1995) failure to replicate their previous results despite their use of bodily sensation threat words (e.g., *suffocating*), which should have provoked more bias than the general physical threat words (e.g., *cancer*) they had used in the previous experiment (Asmundson et al., 1992) and despite the high ASI score in the panic group ($M = 37.9$).

In summary, most studies indicate that panic patients are characterized by selective processing of threat cues in attentional paradigms. However, there are some failures to replicate, and the specificity of the effect to the predominant concerns of panic disorder patients remains uncertain.

Memory Bias

Panic disorder patients report that threatening thoughts readily flood awareness, especially under conditions of arousal. This implies that cognitive representations of threat may reside in a primed and highly accessible state. Accordingly, panic disorder patients should recall information thematically connected to their concerns more readily than other information and more readily than people who do not share the concerns of these patients.

To test this hypothesis, McNally, Foa, and Donnell (1989) asked panic disorder patients and healthy control subjects to rate the self-descriptiveness of adjectives related to anxiety (e.g., *nervous*) and adjectives unrelated to anxiety (e.g., *polite*) prior to performing either a high-arousal (i.e., exercise step test) or low-arousal (i.e., relaxation) task. Immediately thereafter, subjects were given a surprise free-recall test for the previously rated words. The results reveal that panic patients recalled more anxiety than nonanxiety words, whereas healthy subjects recalled more nonanxiety than anxiety words. This pattern was nonsignificantly enhanced for patients who had undergone the high-arousal induction.

Additional analyses indicate that memory for threat in panic patients could not be attributed to a response bias for outputting anxiety words or to a self-descriptive recall bias. A response bias was ruled out because, had patients merely generated words related to anxiety (rather than specifically recalling the ones they had seen earlier), they would have exhibited elevated false alarm (intrusions) rates for words related to anxiety. Because anxiety words were obviously more self-descriptive for patients than for control subjects, it was possible that enhanced recall for anxiety words might have been an artifact of patients merely recalling those words best that were most self-descriptive. However, this explanation was ruled out because patients recalled more anxiety than nonanxiety words than control subjects did even when McNally et al. confined their analyses to words that patients rated as self-descriptive. The mean ASI scores for the panic patients in the high- and low-arousal groups were 34.46 and 38.25, respectively, whereas the mean scores for the control subjects in the high- and low-arousal groups were 10.42 and 14.00, respectively.

Subsequent studies on explicit memory bias for threat in panic disorder have produced mixed results. Relative to normal control subjects, panic patients demonstrated a free-recall bias for disorder-relevant words (e.g., *madness*) but not for disorder-irrelevant negative words (e.g., *murder*) or positive words (e.g., *sweet*; Becker, Rinck, & Margraf, 1994). In another study, panic disorder patients exhibited better free recall for disorder-relevant threat words (e.g., *collapse*) than for positive (e.g., *pleasure*) and neutral words (e.g., *magazine*), whereas normal control subjects exhibited no differential recall as a function of word type (Cloitre & Liebowitz, 1991). Response bias interpretations were ruled out.

Employing a word-pair association method, Cloitre, Shear, Cancienne, and Zeitlin (1994) exposed panic disorder patients, clinicians who treat panic disorder, and other healthy control subjects to word pairs that were either related or unrelated and of either negative, positive, or neutral valence. Thus, one related threat word pair was *breathless–suffocate*, and one unrelated positive word pair was *cheerful–bureau*. Subjects read aloud and rated the relatedness of word pairs. On a cued recall test, panic patients remembered more threat than neutral or positive word pairs and more neutral than positive word pairs, whereas subjects in the two control groups displayed no such superior memory for threat material.

In addition to recognition tests being insensitive to memory bias for threat in panic disorder (Beck et al., 1992; Ehlers et al., 1988), other studies have sometimes failed to uncover biases for threat on recall tests (Otto, McNally, Pollack, Chen, & Rosenbaum, 1994; Rapee, 1994a, ASI: $M = 31.7$ in panic group). Procedural differences across studies cannot wholly account for the pattern of replications and failed replications. Accordingly, other individual difference variables may influence whether memory biases for threat emerge in panic disorder. For example, Otto et al. (1994) found that auditory perceptual asymmetries associated with relative left hemisphere activation strongly predicted cued recall of threat words in panic patients, but not in normal control subjects. Left hemisphere biases may reflect verbal processing superiority for personally relevant emotional words that becomes evident during recall. Our research group recently found that hemispheric laterality was differentially linked with memory for threat in panic and healthy control groups (McNally, Otto, Yap, Pollack, & Hornig, in press). Free recall of threat words that subjects had been instructed to forget was negatively and significantly associated with greater left hemisphere bias in the control group and positively (but nonsignificantly) associated with greater left hemisphere bias in the panic group. Although the memory tasks in the Otto et al. (1994) and McNally et al. (in press) studies differed, it is nevertheless striking that hemispheric laterality predicted memory performance in both studies. Individual differences in hemispheric laterality may reflect differential abilities to encode and remember verbal material of personal significance.

Several studies have tested the hypothesis that panic disorder is characterized by threat biases in implicit memory. Memory is expressed implicitly when previous experiences influence behavior on a task that does not require subjects to recollect these experiences.

Otto et al. (1994) obtained standard priming (implicit memory) effects on a word-stem completion task, but they did not find greater priming effects in panic patients for items related to threat. In contrast, Cloitre et al. (1994) reported an implicit and an explicit memory bias for threat in panic patients in their word-pair association paradigm. But their unusually large priming effects suggest that the presumptively implicit test may have been contaminated by explicit recollective strategies.

One potential problem with these experiments is that they involved implicit tests that are strongly affected by physical features of the input. For example, priming on visual word-stem completion tasks commonly declines if subjects have heard, not seen, words on the study list (Schacter, 1992). Psychopathologists, however, are interested in the emotional meaning, not physical sensory attributes, of linguistic threat stimuli. Therefore, tests mainly tapping perceptual implicit memory are of uncertain relevance to students of cognition and emotion.

In an effort to test for automatic priming of conceptually complex emotional input, Amir, McNally, Riemann, and Clements (1996) adapted the white noise paradigm devised by Jacoby's group (Jacoby, Allan, Collins, & Larwill, 1988). In this experiment, panic patients and normal control subjects first heard a series of prerecorded threat (e.g., *The anxious woman panicked in the supermarket*) and neutral (e.g., *The shiny apple sat on the table*) sentences presented by a computer. They subsequently heard these same sentences intermixed with new threat and neutral sentences, each embedded in white noise of varying volume levels. They were asked to judge the volume of the white noise accompanying each sentence. In this paradigm, priming for old sentences is indicated when subjects judge the noise accompanying these sentences as less loud than the noise accompanying the new sentences. The results indicate trends for panic patients to exhibit greater priming for threat sentences than for neutral sentences, whereas control subjects tended to exhibit the opposite pattern. A previously conducted, but unpublished, study by A. Ehlers (personal communication, September 8, 1995) did not reveal any such effects among nonclinical panickers.

Pauli et al. (1997) compared panic patients' and healthy subjects' ability to identify somatic (e.g., *suffocating, thirsty*) and nonsomatic (e.g., *decorated*) words, presented tachistoscopically at each subject's threshold for identifying 50% of neutral words. They measured subjects' event-related brain potentials and the proportion of words correctly identified. The results indicate that panic patients identified more somatic than nonsomatic words and the former words elicited larger P300 amplitudes and enhanced positive slow waves (600–800 ms poststimulus presentation) than did the latter words. Neither stimulus identification rates nor electrophysiological responses were affected by word type in the control group. Appealing to previous research on electrocortical responses to affective stimuli, Pauli et al. concluded that somatic words are processed as emotionally salient by panic patients but not by control subjects. Although they referred to their experiment as tapping "recognition" of words related to panic disorder, strictly speaking, their procedures are best characterized as tapping stimulus identification, not recognition memory as such. Moreover, not all somatic words were obviously linked to panic disorder (e.g., *thirsty*). It is unclear whether their results would have been stronger had they confined somatic words to those having negative valence for panic patients.

In summary, panic disorder patients, more than any other anxiety disorder group (McNally, 1996), have exhibited explicit memory biases for threat. Even among panic patients, this bias has occasionally been elusive, and researchers have embarked on the study of other individual difference variables that may interact with diagnostic status to produce the effect.

Interoceptive Acuity Bias

Because people with panic disorder dread certain bodily sensations, an ability to detect them better than other people would likely increase the chances of patients' panicking. That is, just as some individuals have better eyesight than others, so might panic patients have better interoceptive acuity than other people.

Studies have been inconsistent regarding interoceptive acuity bias in panic disorder. Ehlers and her colleagues reported no differences between agoraphobic and control groups in their ability to estimate their respective heart rates (Ehlers, Margraf, Roth, Taylor, & Birbaumer, 1988). In a 24-hour ambulatory monitoring project, Pauli et al. (1991) had panic disorder patients and control subjects rate their anxiety in response to cardiac events (e.g., acceleration in heart rate). The results indicate that patients were no better at detecting these events than were controls, but that the former group became more anxious than the latter when detecting these events. Moreover, only the patient group commonly experienced additional heart rate surges after detection of cardiac events; controls experienced decreases in heart rate. Pauli et al. concluded that panic disorder patients fear these events more than control subjects do, but that they are no better at detecting them.

Ehlers and Breuer (1992) did find that patients with panic disorder exhibited superior interoceptive acuity in a mental tracking paradigm. They recorded subjects' heart rates while having them count their heartbeats for periods of 35, 25, and 45 seconds. Panic patients were better at this task than were healthy control subjects, but not better than patients with generalized anxiety disorder. These results suggest that both syndromes are associated with enhanced interoceptive acuity, but that panic attacks are common only in the group that has an additional fear of the sensations.

Finally, Rapee (1994b) reported that panic patients were no better than healthy control subjects in their detection of increasing concentrations of carbon dioxide in inhaled air. Because carbon dioxide produces dose-dependent increases in bodily sensations, Rapee interpreted his findings as inconsistent with an interoceptive acuity hypothesis.

In summary, evidence is equivocal regarding the association between panic disorder and interoceptive acuity. Merely because a person fears interoceptive cues does not mean that he or she will be especially good at detecting them.

HEALTHY SUBJECTS
WITH HIGH ANXIETY SENSITIVITY

Conclusions about elevated AS and cognitive biases for threat are almost entirely based on inferences from patients with panic disorder. Although panic disorder patients as a group score higher than other anxiety-disorder groups on the ASI (Taylor et al., 1992), they often score higher on other measures as well, rendering it difficult to attribute any cognitive biases to AS as such. Moreover, experimentalists have not always administered or reported ASI scores when they have characterized their study groups; sometimes just the results of diagnostic interviews are reported.

An obvious research direction is to test whether cognitive biases—common in panic disorder—are present in people theoretically at risk for developing panic attacks. In an effort to address this issue, we compared students scoring either high ($M = 31.0$) or low ($M = 15.0$) on the ASI on three cognitive bias tasks (McNally, Hornig, Hoffman, & Han, 1997). Individuals who had experienced a spontaneous panic attack were excluded. Subjects completed McNally and Foa's (1987) interpretation questionnaire—a computerized emotional Stroop task composed of randomized presentations of a series of threat (e.g., *suffocate*), positive (e.g., *affection*), and categorized neutral household (e.g., *doorknob*) words and a surprise free-recall test for words they had seen on the Stroop test.

The results indicate that high AS subjects displayed greater biases favoring the interpretation of threat for both internal and external scenarios than did low AS subjects. That is, high AS subjects exhibited a pattern of bias similar (but less pronounced) to that of McNally and Foa's agoraphobic patients. However, there was no evidence that high AS subjects, relative to low AS subjects, exhibited either attentional or memory biases for threat. Taken together, these data suggest that interpretive biases may be linked to AS premorbidly, but that attentional and memory biases for threat may be correlates of the disorder rather than cognitive risk factors for panic.

Other cognitive bias studies on nonclinical subjects with high AS are scarce. In an unpublished study, Kim (1992) compared high and low AS students on explicit (cued recall) and implicit (stem-completion) tests. The word types were neutral (e.g., *carpet*), threat (e.g., *suffocate*), positive threat relevant (e.g., *safety*), and positive threat irrelevant (e.g., *brilliant*). She found no evidence of either an explicit or implicit memory bias for threat in high AS subjects.

Sturges and Goetsch (1996) found that high AS subjects were better than low AS subjects at a heartbeat-detection task after doing a mental arithmetic task. However, the groups did not differ in their interoceptive acuity after having consumed caffeine. The authors suggest that AS-related enhanced interoceptive acuity may be most evident when subjects experience an increase in heart rate, as triggered by the mental arithmetic task and other anxiety inductions in everyday life.

Finally, Stewart and her colleagues conducted two Stroop experiments indicating that high AS students may, indeed, exhibit biases similar to those exhibited by panic patients (Stewart, Conrod, Gignac, & Pihl, 1998). In the first experiment, high AS subjects exhibited more interference for words related to social-psychological threat (e.g., *embarrass*, *crazy*) and physical threat (e.g., *suffocated*) than for neutral words (e.g., *towel*) relative to low AS subjects. Further analyses indicate that this effect was confined to social-psychological threat words for high AS men and to physical threat words for high AS women. In the second experiment, Stewart et al. tested only men and found that high AS subjects exhibited greater interference than did low AS subjects for social-psychological threat words, but not for physical threat, positive, or neutral words. Appealing to previous studies, Stewart et al. suggested that gender differences in predominant concerns (i.e., physical vs. social-psychological) may affect differential performance in the emotional Stroop paradigm.

It is not entirely clear why Stewart et al. found threat-related Stroop effects in high AS subjects, whereas McNally et al. (1997a) did not. Two explanations are possible. First, McNally et al. excluded any subject who had experienced spontaneous panic. Although Stewart et al. recorded panic history, they did not exclude subjects with such histories. For example, 50% of the male high AS subjects in their first study had a history of panic. Second, the McNally et al. low AS subjects had relatively normal ASI scores ($M = 15$) whereas the Stewart et al. low AS subjects had low ASI scores ($M = 5$). Taken together, these factors may have increased the likelihood of Stewart et al. obtaining significant interference effects for threat words.

CONCLUSION

High scores on the ASI apparently indicate risk for panic attacks and perhaps panic disorder. However, explicit and implicit beliefs about the harmfulness of bodily sensations associated with anxiety provide an incomplete account of how these beliefs influence on-line cognitive processing that presumably generates panic. That is, it is unclear whether AS beliefs affect attention (or acuity) to bodily cues, interpretation of their significance, or enhanced access to memories about harm that influence online interpretation. Therefore, future research should be directed toward further elucidating what cognitive biases are present in people with high AS who have not yet experienced panic attacks and what biases are correlates of the disorder.

ACKNOWLEDGMENT

Preparation of this chapter was supported, in part, by NIMH grant MH51927 awarded to the author.

REFERENCES

Amir, N., McNally, R. J., Riemann, B. C., & Clements, C. M. (1996). Implicit memory bias for threat in panic disorder: Application of the "white noise" paradigm. *Behaviour Research and Therapy, 34*, 157–162.

Asmundson, G. J. G., Sandler, L. S., Wilson, K. G., & Walker, J. R. (1992). Selective attention toward physical threat in patients with panic disorder. *Journal of Anxiety Disorders, 6*, 295–303.

Asmundson, G. J. G., & Stein, M. B. (1994/1995). Dot-probe evaluation of cognitive processing biases in patients with panic disorder: A failure to replicate and extend. *Anxiety, 1*, 123–128.

Beck, J. G., Stanley, M. A., Averill, P. M., Baldwin, L. E., & Deagle, E. A., III. (1992). Attention and memory for threat in panic disorder. *Behaviour Research and Therapy, 30*, 619–629.

Becker, E., Rinck, M., & Margraf, J. (1994). Memory bias in panic disorder. *Journal of Abnormal Psychology, 103*, 396–399.

Burgess, I. S., Jones, L. M., Robertson, S. A., Radcliffe, W. N., & Emerson, E. (1981). The degree of control exerted by phobic and non-phobic verbal stimuli over the recognition behaviour of phobic and non-phobic subjects. *Behaviour Research and Therapy, 19*, 233–243.

Butler, G., & Mathews, A. (1983). Cognitive processes in anxiety. *Advances in Behaviour Research and Therapy, 5*, 51–62.

Clark, D. M., Salkovskis, P. M., Öst, L.-G., Breitholtz, E., Koehler, K. A., Westling, B. E., Jeavons, A., & Gelder, M. (1997). Misinterpretation of body sensations in panic disorder. *Journal of Consulting and Clinical Psychology, 65*, 203–213.

Cloitre, M., & Liebowitz, M. R. (1991). Memory bias in panic disorder: An investigation of the cognitive avoidance hypothesis. *Cognitive Therapy and Research, 15,* 371–386.

Cloitre, M., Shear, M. K., Cancienne, J., & Zeitlin, S. B. (1994). Implicit and explicit memory for catastrophic associations to bodily sensation words in panic disorder. *Cognitive Therapy and Research, 18,* 225–240.

Cronbach, L. J. (1957). The two disciplines of scientific psychology. *American Psychologist, 12,* 671–684.

Ehlers, A., & Breuer, P. (1992). Increased cardiac awareness in panic disorder. *Journal of Abnormal Psychology, 101,* 371–382.

Ehlers, A., Margraf, J., Davies, S., & Roth, W. T. (1988). Selective processing of threat cues in subjects with panic attacks. *Cognition and Emotion, 2,* 201–219.

Ehlers, A., Margraf, J., Roth, W. T., Taylor, C. B., & Birbaumer, N. (1988). Anxiety induced by false heart rate feedback in patients with panic disorder. *Behaviour Research and Therapy, 26,* 1–11.

Harvey, J. M., Richards, J. C., Dziadosz, T., & Swindell, A. (1993). Misinterpretation of ambiguous stimuli in panic disorder. *Cognitive Therapy and Research, 17,* 235–248.

Hope, D. A., Rapee, R. M., Heimberg, R. G., & Dombeck, M. J. (1990). Representations of the self in social phobia: Vulnerability to social threat. *Cognitive Therapy and Research, 14,* 177–189.

Kamieniecki, G. W., Wade, T., & Tsourtos, G. (1997). Interpretive bias for benign sensations in panic disorder and agoraphobia. *Journal of Anxiety Disorders, 11,* 141–156.

Kim, E. (1992). *Implicit and explicit memory biases for threat in high and low anxiety sensitivity subjects.* Unpublished doctoral dissertation, Department of Psychology, University of the Health Sciences/The Chicago Medical School, North Chicago, IL.

Jacoby, L. L., Allan, L. G., Collins, J. C., & Larwill, L. K. (1988). Memory influences subjective experience: Noise judgments. *Journal of Experimental Psychology: Learning, Memory, and Cognition, 14,* 240–247.

MacLeod, C. (1991). Clinical anxiety and the selective encoding of threatening information. *International Review of Psychiatry, 3,* 279–292.

MacLeod, C., Mathews, A., & Tata, P. (1986). Attentional bias in emotional disorders. *Journal of Abnormal Psychology, 95,* 15–20.

McNally, R. J. (1989). Is anxiety sensitivity distinguishable from trait anxiety? A reply to Lilienfeld, Jacob, and Turner (1989). *Journal of Abnormal Psychology, 98,* 193–194.

McNally, R. J. (1996). Cognitive bias in the anxiety disorders. *Nebraska Symposium on Motivation, 43,* 211–250.

McNally, R. J., Amir, N., Louro, C. E., Lukach, B. M., Riemann, B. C., & Calamari, J. E. (1994). Cognitive processing of idiographic emotional information in panic disorder. *Behaviour Research and Therapy, 32,* 119–122.

McNally, R. J., & Foa, E. B. (1987). Cognition and agoraphobia: Bias in the interpretation of threat. *Cognitive Therapy and Research, 11,* 567–581.

McNally, R. J., Foa, E. B., & Donnell, C. D. (1989). Memory bias for anxiety information in patients with panic disorder. *Cognition and Emotion, 3,* 27–44.

McNally, R. J., Hornig, C. D., Hoffman, E. C., & Han, E. M. (1997). *Anxiety sensitivity and cognitive biases for threat.* Manuscript submitted for publication.

McNally, R. J., Hornig, C. D., Otto, M. W., & Pollack, M. H. (1997). Selective encoding of threat in panic disorder: Application of a dual priming paradigm. *Behaviour Research and Therapy, 35,* 543–549.

McNally, R. J., & Lorenz, M. (1987). Anxiety sensitivity in agoraphobics. *Journal of Behavior Therapy and Experimental Psychiatry, 18,* 3–11.

McNally, R. J., Otto, M. W., Yap, L., Pollack, M. H., & Hornig, C. D. (in press). Is panic disorder linked to cognitive avoidance of threatening information? *Journal of Anxiety Disorders.*

McNally, R. J., Riemann, B. C., & Kim, E. (1990). Selective processing of threat cues in panic disorder. *Behaviour Research and Therapy, 28,* 407–412.

McNally, R. J., Riemann, B. C., Louro, C. E., Lukach, B. M., & Kim, E. (1992). Cognitive processing of emotional information in panic disorder. *Behaviour Research and Therapy, 30,* 143–149.

Otto, M. W., McNally, R. J., Pollack, M. H., Chen, E., & Rosenbaum, J. F. (1994). Hemispheric laterality and memory bias for threat in anxiety disorders. *Journal of Abnormal Psychology, 103,* 828–831.

Pauli, P., Dengler, W., Wiedemann, G., Montoya, P., Flor, H., Birbaumer, N., & Buchkremer, G. (1997). Behavioral and neurophysiological evidence for altered processing of anxiety-related words in panic disorder. *Journal of Abnormal Psychology, 106,* 213–220.

Pauli, P., Marquardt, C., Hartl, L., Nutzinger, D. O., Holzl, R., & Strain, F. (1991). Anxiety induced by cardiac perceptions in patients with panic attacks: A field study. *Behaviour Research and Therapy, 29,* 137–145.

Rapee, R. M. (1994a). Failure to replicate a memory bias in panic disorder. *Journal of Anxiety Disorders, 8,* 291–300.

Rapee, R. M. (1994b). Detection of somatic sensations in panic disorder. *Behaviour Research and Therapy, 32,* 825–831.

Reiss, S., & McNally, R. J. (1985). Expectancy model of fear. In S. Reiss & R. R. Bootzin (Eds.), *Theoretical issues in behavior therapy* (pp. 107–121). San Diego, CA: Academic Press.

Reiss, S., Peterson, R. A., Gursky, D. M., & McNally, R. J. (1986). Anxiety sensitivity, anxiety frequency and the prediction of fearfulness. *Behaviour Research and Therapy, 24,* 1–8.

Schacter, D. L. (1992). Understanding implicit memory: A cognitive neuroscience approach. *American Psychologist, 47,* 559–569.

Schmidt, N. B., Lerew, D. R., & Jackson, R. J. (1997). The role of anxiety sensitivity in the pathogenesis of panic: Prospective evaluation of spontaneous panic attacks during acute stress. *Journal of Abnormal Psychology, 106,* 355–364.

Stewart, S. H., Conrod, P. J., Gignac, M. L., & Pihl, R. O. (1998). Selective processing biases in anxiety-sensitive men and women. *Cognition and Emotion, 12,* 105–133.

Stoler, L. S., & McNally, R. J. (1991). Cognitive bias in symptomatic and recovered agoraphobics. *Behaviour Research and Therapy, 29,* 539–545.

Sturges, L. V., & Goetsch, V. L. (1996). Psychophysiological reactivity and heartbeat awareness in anxiety sensitivity. *Journal of Anxiety Disorders, 10,* 282–294.

Taylor, S., Koch, W. J., & McNally, R. J. (1992). How does anxiety sensitivity vary across the anxiety disorders? *Journal of Anxiety Disorders, 6,* 249–259.

Westling, B. E., & Öst, L.-G. (1995). Cognitive bias in panic patients and changes after cognitive-behavioral treatments. *Behaviour Research and Therapy, 33,* 585–588.

Williams, J. M. G., Mathews, A., & MacLeod, C. (1996). The emotional Stroop task and psychopathology. *Psychological Bulletin, 120,* 3–24.

Williams, J. M. G., Watts, F. N., MacLeod, C., & Mathews, A. (1988). *Cognitive psychology and emotional disorders.* Chichester, England: Wiley.

Williams, J. M. G., Watts, F. N., MacLeod, C., & Mathews, A. (1997). *Cognitive psychology and emotional disorders* (2nd ed.). Chichester, England: Wiley.

9

Biological Aspects of Anxiety Sensitivity: Is It All in the Head?

Murray B. Stein
University of California–San Diego
Ronald M. Rapee
Macquarie University

Anxiety sensitivity (AS) is the fear of anxiety-related sensations. It is thought to arise from beliefs that these sensations have harmful conse-quences (Reiss 1991; Reiss & McNally, 1985). This description of AS—as a pathological way of viewing and reacting to anxiety symptoms—certainly sounds like something that must have been learned. However, AS theorists have been careful not to imply that this is the case. In fact, the literature on AS is profoundly bereft of studies of the origins of AS—studies that ask the question, "How does someone develop high AS?" This leaves open the possibility that AS might be a biological characteristic, much like height or intelligence, which may be predominantly inherited rather than learned. This chapter does not directly address this possibility mainly because definitive data are lacking. What it does attempt to do is review studies that sought to examine biological aspects of anxiety sensitivity in the hope that this can inform the discussion and lead to a testable series of questions about the nature of AS.

ANXIETY SENSITIVITY AND THE RESPONSE TO BIOLOGICAL CHALLENGE PROCEDURES IN PANIC DISORDER

A popular technique in the study of panic disorder is to administer a biological challenge agent and then determine the proportion of panic disorder patients and healthy controls that experience panic attacks in response to the provocation. The agent's presumed biological mechanism of action is then used to infer that panic disorder patients and controls differ in their biological responsivity. A wonderful case in point, which arose from the keen clinical observation that panic disorder patients tend to avoid caffeinated beverages (Boulenger, Uhde, Wolff, & Post, 1984), is the series of studies that investigated caffeine sensitivity in panic disorder (Charney, Heninger, & Jatlow, 1985; Uhde, 1990).

Boulenger and colleagues heard from their panic disorder patients that coffee, tea, and sodas tended to make their symptoms worse. Boulenger et al. went on to use dietary questionnaires to confirm that patients with panic disorder did, indeed, consume less caffeine than people without panic disorder. Presumably, patients had learned from experience that caffeine worsened their symptoms so they avoided it (Boulenger et al., 1984). The investigators hypothesized that this tendency for caffeine to exacerbate symptoms in patients with panic disorder might reflect a biologically based sensitivity to caffeine. They went on to test this hypothesis by administering, in a double-blind basis, either caffeine (in doses varying from 240 mg—the equivalent of two to three cups of coffee—to 720 mg) or placebo in oral solution (Uhde, 1990). They found that panic disorder patients were, in fact, more sensitive to the panicogenic effects of caffeine. At the 480 mg dose, for example, 30% to 40% of panic disorder patients experienced panic attacks, as compared with 0% to 10% of healthy subjects without panic disorder.

This was a truly remarkable finding. Here was a psychiatric disorder, a neurosis nonetheless, wherein the response to a biological provocant (in this case, caffeine) was demonstrably different between patients and controls. Similar findings were reported for a drug, yohimbine, which was known to stimulate the sympathetic nervous system (Charney et al., 1985; Uhde et al., 1984). Although it was known for some 20 years that panic disorder patients experienced panic attacks at a rate far greater than that of healthy controls when infused with sodium lactate (Pitts & McClure, 1967), it was—and still is—uncertain what properties of sodium lactate might account for this effect. In contrast, the relatively specific pharmacological effects of caffeine and yohimbine offered the promise of enlightening researchers as to the mode by which these agents invoked panic in susceptible individuals. It was hoped that this would be at a neurotransmitter specific level. This generated considerable excitement in the field, raising hopes that panic disorder might be a biologically based disorder characterized by heightened sensitivity to particular chemical substances, some of which might be endogenous (as in the case of norepinephrine or epinephrine).

The Challenge to Challenge Studies

These stimulating (pardon the pun) studies spawned a cottage industry of investigators who asked patients to swallow (e.g., yohimbine, caffeine, m-chlorophenylpiperazine, fenfluramine), inhale (e.g., 5%, 7%, or 35% CO_2), or be intravenously infused (e.g., isoproterenol, sodium lactate) with a variety of potentially panicogenic challenge agents (see Stein & Uhde, 1995, for review). In most cases, the choice of agent was predicated on the hypothesis that panic disorder patients might be biologically vulnerable to the pharmacological effects of the particular agent (e.g., in the case of caffeine, adenosinergic antagonistic effects; in the case of yohimbine, alpha-2-adrenergic antagonistic effects). In the case of sodium lactate, it was hypothesized that because panic disorder patients were exercise intolerant, they might be producing excessive lactate or be sensitive to its presence in the body (Pitts & McClure, 1967). With few exceptions (e.g., thyrotropin releasing hormone; Stein & Uhde, 1991), panic disorder patients were found to be hypersensitive to the effects of each of these ostensibly pharmacologically specific agents (for reviews, see McNally, 1994; Stein & Uhde, 1995). This posed a problem.

How likely was it that patients with panic disorder have a biological vulnerability to such a diverse group of pharmacologically active substances? Occam's razor would demand that a simpler explanation be sought. One such possibility is that patients with panic disorder are deficient in the functioning of a neurochemical system (such as gamma-amino-butyric acid [GABA]) that has broad inhibitory effects on neural functioning. In fact, patients with panic disorder have been shown to have greater physiological and behavioral reactivity than healthy controls to flumazenil—a substance with antagonistic properties at the GABA-benzodiazepine receptor complex (Nutt, Glue, Lawson, & Wilson, 1990). Panic disorder patients (and perhaps patients with other anxiety disorders; Roy-Byrne, Wingerson, Radant, Greenblatt, & Cowley, 1996) display reduced sensitivity to benzodiazepines' effects on saccadic eye velocity (Roy-Byrne et al., 1990), which also points to a possible defect in GABA-ergic functioning in these patients. These data notwithstanding, a more parsimonious explanation has been proposed for panic patients' tendency to be behaviorally sensitive to the effects of a variety of pharmacological challenge agents.

Pharmacological Challenges Evoke Paniclike Symptoms

What if patients with panic disorder were reacting differentially to these pharmacological challenges on the basis of differences in AS? In other words, what if these chemically diverse agents—which all shared the capacity to evoke physical symptoms—were triggering patients' catastrophic fears and thereby leading to increased anxiety and increased rates of panic attack provocation? Patients with panic disorder have been shown to be particularly prone to misinterpret ambiguous autonomic sensations (e.g., heart pounding) as signs of impending disaster (Clark et al., 1997). Might the panicogenic effects of the challenge agents have little (or nothing) to do with the chemical properties of the agent and more (or all) to do with their propensity to evoke paniclike symptoms in patients with panic disorder?

This hypothesis was first voiced by Margraf and colleagues over a decade ago (Margraf, Ehlers, & Roth, 1986) and has been elaborated on more recently (Rapee, 1995). Yet debate persists (see McNally, 1994). A special case of this argument has been made with reference to a new theory advanced by Klein (1993). As part of this theory, Klein stated that patients with panic disorder might have an oversensitive suffocation alarm, which, when triggered, leads to panic (Klein, 1993). This theory could potentially explain the tendency for patients with panic disorder to panic in response to a variety of respiratory challenges (e.g., CO_2 inhalation, voluntary room-air hyperventilation, and doxapram ingestion). Prior to the development of this theory, it was difficult to explain how two agents with divergent physiological effects could fit into a comprehensive biological model of panic provocation (i.e., inhalation of CO_2-enriched air induces respiratory acidosis, whereas room-air hyperventilation induces some degree of respiratory alkalosis, as does doxapram, which is a respiratory stimulant that induces hyperventilation; Abelson, Weg, Nesse, & Curtis, 1996).

No sooner was Klein's theory advanced than cognitive theorists (e.g., McNally, 1994) took the bait and pointed out that much, if not all, the findings explained by the suffocation alarm theory could also be encompassed by AS theory. Plainly put, if patients with panic disorder were made to feel dyspneic—by whatever the provocant—then AS theory would predict that those who have a tendency to view this as most threatening would become the most fearful and therefore most likely to experience panic attacks. Taylor and

Rachman (1994; see also Rachman & Taylor, 1993) proposed that suffocation fear is a likely marker of the sensitivity of Klein's suffocation monitor. They operationalized the concept of *suffocation fearfulness* to describe the propensity to fear sensations reminiscent of suffocation. Although it is unclear that the suffocation fearfulness construct is anything other than a subset of AS, it is interesting to note that a history of exposure to suffocation in childhood is more common in patients with panic disorder than in nonanxious comparison subjects (Bouwer & Stein, 1997).

As reviewed elsewhere (Rapee, 1995), there may indeed be some variability in the degree to which a particular agent reproduces an individual's typical panic symptoms; this may influence the likelihood that the particular agent will be panicogenic. For example, Lelliott and Bass (1990) conducted a study in which two groups of patients with panic disorder were asked to hyperventilate. One group reported that their typical symptoms during a panic attack were cardiovascular and respiratory in nature, whereas the other group reported predominantly gastrointestinal symptoms. The former group experienced greater distress than the latter group in response to hyperventilation—a challenge procedure that clearly activates respiratory and cardiovascular symptoms.

Two equally plausible explanations can be used to account for these findings. One might conclude that there are two biologically based subtypes of panic disorder: one that is physiologically sensitive to manipulations in the respiratory system and one that is not. However, one might equally well conclude that the likelihood of experiencing a panic attack during a particular biological challenge procedure may depend, at least in part, on the extent to which the symptoms elicited by the challenge match those typically experienced (and feared) by the patient. Following this line of reasoning, in Lelliott and Bass' (1990) study the patients who had few respiratory symptoms during their attacks would not be expected to be frightened by symptoms elicited by hyperventilation (e.g., dyspnea, lightheadedness, paresthesias) and would therefore be unlikely to experience much anxiety during a hyperventilation procedure. To take this further, a challenge that elicited gastrointestinal symptoms (e.g., bloating, flatulence, nausea, diarrhea) would be predicted to make the gastrointestinal panic patients more anxious than the respiratory panic patients. (We are not aware of challenge procedures that have attempted to induce gastrointestinal symptoms, presumably for reasons having to do with patient comfort and esthetics.) Thus, although not directly addressing the relation between AS and challenge studies, Lelliott and Bass' (1990) study exemplified the rather disparate ways in which the same findings can be interpreted to support either a biological or psychological explanation for observed differences in behavioral responsiveness during a challenge procedure.

Physiological Responses to Biological Challenges

What about studies that focus on physiological rather than behavioral responses? Should such studies not provide a cleaner signal of something that can be reasonably interpreted to signify a biological abnormality? Take the response to inhalation of CO_2-enriched air as the best available example.

Papp and colleagues (1997) noted that, "it is now well established that CO_2 inhalation causes more anxiety and panic in patients with panic disorder than in normal volunteers" (p. 1557). This is an irrefutable fact, although the mechanism by which this effect is mediated is not yet known. It could be cogently argued that (some) patients with panic disorder become alarmed by the sense of dyspnea and other bodily sensations arising from CO_2 inhalation; as a result, they experience panic attacks. In other words, it is their level of AS that mediates this effect, at least in part. However, it could be argued that panic-disordered patients are physiologically hypersensitive to elevated arterial CO_2 and that their panic attacks in response to this hypercapneic stimulus are biologically determined. Neither explanation is better supported by the facts than the other.

What about the physiological response to CO_2 inhalation in panic-disordered patients compared with healthy controls? If panic disorder patients and controls were found to differ in the way their bodies respond to or handle a CO_2 load, would this not be indicative of a biological abnormality in patients with panic disorder? Surprisingly, several studies have failed to demonstrate marked differences between patients with panic disorder and normal controls on several physiological measures in response to biological challenges (see Rapee, 1995, for a review). In the largest study to date to examine respiratory psychophysiology in panic disorder, Papp et al. (1997) challenged 59 patients with *DSM–III–R* panic disorder and 39 normal volunteers with 5% and 7% CO_2 inhalation and with room-air hyperventilation. Papp et al. measured respiratory responses to the challenges with continuous spirometry; dependent variables included respiratory rate, tidal volume (the size of breaths), and end tidal CO_2 (which correlates highly with arterial CO_2 levels).

Patients with panic disorder were, as expected, much more likely than normal comparison subjects to experience panic in response to 5% CO_2 (16 of 54 panic disorder patients vs. 0 of 38 comparison subjects) and 7% CO_2 (31 of 51 panic disorder patients vs. 4 of 38 comparison subjects). During the baseline period prior to CO_2 administration, patients with panic disorder had significantly lower end tidal CO_2 levels than the healthy comparison subjects, although the difference between the groups was small (approximately 3 torr). As the authors indicated, this finding should be interpreted "to mean that some degree of respiratory stimulation precedes the induction of panic in the laboratory. It is unclear, however, whether this decrease in CO_2 level is the result of anticipation or represents an ongoing pattern of increased ventilation" (Papp et al., 1997, p. 1563). Given that ambulatory monitoring studies have failed to find that panic disorder patients hyperventilate on a routine basis (Martinez et al., 1996), the Papp et al. data are most consistent with the notion that decreased CO_2 level is the result of anticipation (i.e., anticipatory anxiety).

Physiological data from the inhalation epochs are additionally informative. With 5% CO_2 inhalation, patients who experienced panic attacks during the procedure exhibited an increased respiratory rate compared with nonpanickers and normal comparison subjects. During the recovery period, there was a tendency for panic disorder patients (regardless of whether they panicked during CO_2 inhalation) to maintain their tidal volume at an increased rate for longer than the healthy comparison subjects. Gender effects on several of the respiratory physiological variables were noted, highlighting the need to control or match for gender in these studies.

The authors stated that, "clearly, panic disorder patients exhibit both behaviorally and physiologically abnormal responses to respiratory challenges" (Papp et al., 1997, p.1563). Although the former are robust, the latter are considerably less so. On many respiratory physiological indexes, panic disorder patients and controls were indistinguishable. Moreover, the clearest findings serve to differentiate panic disordered patients who panicked during the challenge from those who did not and from healthy controls. Differences between panic patients as a group and healthy comparison subjects are less clear. This says more about the respiratory physiological accompaniments of panic attacks (i.e., hyperventilation) than about the mechanisms initiating the attacks.

In fact, each and every physiological finding that distinguishes patients with panic disorder in this study (Papp et al., 1997) can be explained most parsimoniously as either a correlate of state anxiety or panic. In other words, persons who become anxious breathe differently than those who do not; because panic disorder patients are made more anxious than healthy comparison subjects by these procedures, their breathing (both before and after the procedures) is different. Does this signify a biological abnormality? Hardly. If data had shown that differences in anxiety do not explain a sizable component of the variance in the respiratory differences between groups, then the biological abnormality hypothesis might be supported. Absent these data, however, a credible case has yet to be made.

Does Anxiety Sensitivity Predict Behavioral
Responding to Biological Challenges?

As indicated earlier, few studies have examined AS as a possible predictor of behavioral responses to biological challenges. Koszycki, Cox, and Bradwejn (1993) administered cholecystokinin tetrapeptide (CCK-4)—a putative panicogenic agent (Bradwejn, Koszycki, Payeur, Bourin, & Borthwick, 1992)—to healthy control subjects classified as having either high, medium, or low scores on the ASI (Peterson & Reiss, 1987). Koszycki et al. (1993) found that subjects with high ASI scores were not more susceptible to CCK-induced panic than the medium or low ASI scorers.

Asmundson and Stein (1994) conducted a study where panic disorder patients, social phobia patients, and nonanxious control subjects were asked to hold their breath for as long as possible. Panic disorder patients held their breath for a significantly shorter time than social phobia patients and control subjects. However, ASI scores did not predict breathholding duration.

The two aforementioned studies might be taken as evidence against the importance of AS as a mediator of behavioral responsiveness in these biological challenge paradigms. However, there are several reasons that this would not be a fair conclusion. First, it must be acknowledged that panic disorder patients, as a group, tend to have markedly elevated ASI scores compared to nonanxiety disordered subjects (Taylor, Koch, & McNally, 1992). Although panic disorder sufferers with relatively low ASI scores can be found, they are relatively rare (Asmundson, Norton, Wilson, & Sandler, 1994). Thus, when the relation between ASI scores and anxious responding to a biological provocant in patients with panic disorder is scrutinized, the range of ASI scores is usually limited and the likelihood of explaining even a small portion of the variance is therefore low. This raises the following question: In studies where a wider range of ASI scores can be found (e.g., using nonpatient populations), to what extent does AS predict anxious responding to biological challenges?

Resorting to Analogue Samples

There are pros and cons to studying AS in nonclinical or analogue samples (i.e., samples of people with high AS but no mental disorder). Each of these must be considered when reviewing the literature on the relationship between AS and biological challenge studies in nonclinical samples. The biggest pro is that, by studying persons from a general population or quasinormative group (e.g., college students), investigators are able to choose from a sample with diverse

AS scores. This enables the selection of groups that are low, high, or somewhere in between on AS. Given a large enough population base, it is possible to find enough healthy persons to fill each of these cells. This contrasts with the limitation encountered when comparing patients with panic disorder and healthy controls, whereas the former subjects are inevitably higher in AS than most, if not all, of the latter.

The biggest con in studying nonclinical samples is obvious. Even the persons highest in AS tend not to be anywhere as high as patients with panic disorder; consequently, the findings must be extrapolated to explain how they might relate to actual panic disorder individuals. This may be a stretch. To use an analogy, it would be like studying people with modestly elevated (but still normal) blood pressure levels and inferring from those studies about the nature of hypertension. Panic disorder may be a distinct condition that is not continuous with either elevated anxiety or, for that matter, nonclinical panic (see chap. 15, this volume). Therefore, it might be a mistake to believe that anything learned from people with high AS is necessarily applicable to people with panic disorder. With this caveat in mind, it is nonetheless informative to review studies that have examined AS as a predictor of response to biological challenges.

Three studies found that healthy people with high AS report more physical symptoms and more anxiety than people with low AS in response to room-air hyperventilation (Asmundson et al., 1994; Donnell & McNally, 1990; Rapee & Medoro, 1994). As shown by Rapee, Brown, Antony, and Barlow (1992), however, although AS generally predicts anxious responding to CO_2 inhalation and room-air hyperventilation, the portion of the variance explained by ASI scores is small (less than 20%). Thus, although AS may be only one factor contributing to the tendency to panic in response to respiratory provocants, there must be others.

McNally and Eke (1996) examined predictors of responses to breathing deeply and rapidly into a paper bag for 5 minutes—a hypercarbic challenge (i.e., one that increases CO_2 levels in the blood)—in 78 college students (39 women and 39 men). They evaluated both the ASI and the Suffocation Fear Scale (SFS; Rachman & Taylor, 1993) as potential predictors of self-reported anxiety and self-reported bodily sensations. Subjects were young (mean age = 19 years, $SD = 3.8$), healthy, and not taking psychotropic medications. Their mean ASI score was fairly low ($M = 19.9$, $SD = 10.4$), as was their mean SFS score ($M = 16.3$, $SD = 10.3$). Using a hierarchical multiple-regression analysis, they found that the ASI accounted for 11% of the variance in self-reported anxiety following the challenge and the SFS predicted an additional 6% of the variance (over and above that accounted for by the ASI). McNally and Eke concluded that, "just as anxiety sensitivity is a better predictor than trait anxiety of the response to bodily sensations in general, fear of suffocation was a better predictor than anxiety sensitivity of the response to a challenge that increases carbon dioxide levels" (p. 148). In their study, ASI and SFS were moderately correlated ($r = .63$, $p < .001$). We agree with the authors' contention that suffocation fearfulness may be a subcomponent of AS.

Like its predecessors reviewed earlier, McNally and Eke's (1996) study showed that AS (and one of its facets—the tendency to fear sensations associated with suffocation) predicts a small amount of the variance in the propensity to experience anxiety in response to respiratory challenge. The key words here, however, are *small amount* and *anxiety*. Most of the variance is left unexplained by AS. More important, the dependent measure is not panic attacks because none of these studies uses provocants that are intense enough (or lack other as yet poorly understood properties necessary) to induce panic attacks in the healthy volunteer subjects. It is unclear at this juncture to what extent inducing and measuring increases in state anxiety is informative about the risk for, or mechanisms involved in, the genesis of panic attacks.

In a pilot study, Taylor and Rachman (1994) administered the SFS to college students and dichotomized respondents into those with high or low suffocation fear based on their responses. Taylor and Rachman used a suffocation provocation test (breathing through a narrow straw for 2 minutes) and found that significantly more students with high suffocation fear experienced panic attacks than subjects with low suffocation fear (18% vs. 2%). Assuming that suffocation fear (fear of dyspnea) is a facet of AS, these results support the role of AS in panic attacks.

If, in future studies, AS scores are found to predict the likelihood of healthy volunteers experiencing panic attacks in response to highly panicogenic doses of agents such as caffeine (e.g., 800–1,000 mg) or yohimbine (0.8–1.0 mg/kg), a stronger claim could be made about the role of AS in panic attacks. Such studies would be difficult to conduct, however, given ethical considerations about the potential deleterious effects of inducing panic attacks in otherwise healthy individuals. However, these arguments must be placed in the context of arguments by some authors that anxiety and panic attacks differ quantitatively rather than qualitatively (Rapee, 1996). If this is the case, then studies using nonclinical populations and demonstrating effects on state anxiety provide a perfectly legitimate analogue by which to study panic disorder.

SLEEP, ANXIETY SENSITIVITY,
AND SUFFOCATION FEARFULNESS

The most convincing evidence in favor of a biologically driven respiratory abnormality in some panic disorder patients comes from studies where these abnormalities can be demonstrated at a time when consciousness—and, presumably, an awareness of one's internal and external environment—is reduced. Sleep has the characteristics of such a state and, at least in the case of nondreaming sleep, further represents a state where anxious cognitions are likely to be less active and accessible than in the waking state. Taking advantage of these special properties of the sleeping state, Koenigsberg and colleagues (1992, 1994) studied respiratory (and cardiac) activity in panic disorder patients while asleep and while they received lactate infusions during sleep. Although limited by their reliance on respiratory rate as the sole measure of ventilation, these studies nonetheless found a tendency for panic patients to hyperventilate when they received sodium lactate during delta sleep (Koenigsberg et al., 1994).

If the ventilatory abnormality in panic disorder is not exclusively a psychological response to respiratory discomfort, it would be expected that this abnormality should be visible during sleep. In fact, in subjective reports of sleep, we found that panic disorder patients were significantly more likely than controls to report awakening with the feeling that they could not breathe (Stein, Chartier, & Walker, 1993). Consistent with these subjective reports, we have noted a tendency for panic disorder patients to breathe more irregularly than healthy controls while asleep (Stein, Millar, Larsen, & Kryger, 1995). We found that patients with panic disorder had more frequent brief breathing pauses (microapneas of 5 to 10 second duration) than controls and that patients with sleep panic attacks tended to have the most pronounced abnormalities. Regretfully, AS was not examined in these studies.

The occurrence of sleep panic attacks (nocturnal panic attacks) was originally thought to represent *prima facie* evidence for the neurobiological nature of panic (Mellman & Uhde 1989a, 1989b; Uhde, 1994). These attacks often arise during non-REM sleep, which is a time when complex cognitive functioning is not thought to occur. However, researchers have observed that sleep panic attacks are somewhat influenced by presleep expectancies (Craske & Barlow, 1989; Craske & Freed, 1995). Hence, the occurrence of panic attacks during sleep provides an excellent opportunity to examine panic from both a psychological and biological vantage point under circumstances (i.e., sleep) where extraneous cues are held to a minimum.

In a new pilot study (Stein et al., unpublished observations), data have been collected using an ambulatory sleep breathing recorder (Nightwatch^{TM}) in 8 subjects with panic disorder, 11 subjects with generalized social phobia, and 4 healthy comparison subjects. Subjects completed two nights of home sleep monitoring, and we conducted a preliminary analysis of the second night's data. Subjects also completed the ASI and SFS. Although the small sample size precludes meaningful statistical analysis, there are several interesting trends in the data that may inform the debate about the psychological versus biological nature of panic.

The following analysis is limited to women because we had only one male panic disorder patient in our pilot study and women and men differ greatly in their rates of sleep-disordered breathing (Strolle & Rogers, 1996). We found that sleep panickers have higher SFS scores than nonsleep panickers and patients with generalized social phobia (see Fig. 9. 1). Given our small sample size, it remains to be determined whether fear of suffocation is a feature of only certain types of panic disorder (e.g., nocturnal panic) or whether it is a component of panic disorder in general.

Some people with breathing disorders such as asthma or chronic obstructive pulmonary disease (COPD) may be at risk for the development of panic disorder (Carr, Lehrer, Rausch, & Hochron, 1994; Smoller, Pollack, Otto, Rosenbaum,

Suffocation Fear Scale (SFS)

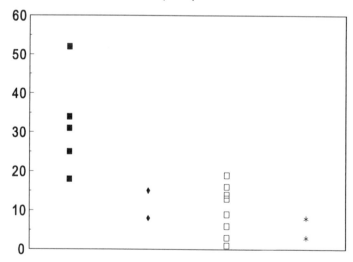

FIG. 9.1. Suffocation Fear Scales scores in five women with nocturnal panic (shaded squares), two women with daytime panic only (shaded diamonds), nine women with generalized social phobia (open squares), and two healthy women (stars).

& Kradin, 1996). These findings, considered along with our preliminary data, suggest that both biological causes (i.e., a physiological basis for actually experiencing difficulty breathing) and psychological causes (i.e., AS or the component of AS better described as the tendency to fear suffocation) may be necessary for the development of panic disorder. To take this a step further, it is possible that the actual experience of difficulty breathing (either from a single exposure to accidental suffocation or from repeated exposure to asthma attacks, COPD, or increased upper airway resistance during sleep) may be a cardinal etiological factor in the development of AS. This hypothesis deserves further testing in prospective, longitudinal studies.

FUTURE DIRECTIONS

In the previous section, we ended with speculation about a role for specific suffocation-type experiences in the development of AS. In the opening paragraph of this chapter, it was posited that AS might be inherited. Are these two notions incompatible?

The Heritability of Panic Disorder: No Mind–Body Dichotomy

Twin studies demonstrate quite conclusively that there is a strong heritable component to panic disorder (Kendler, Neale, Kessler, Heath, & Eaves, 1993; Perna et al., 1997; Skre, Onstad, Torgersen, Lygren, & Kringlen, 1993; Torgersen; 1983). The tendency to experience anxiety in response to CO_2 inhalation runs in families (Perna, Bertani, Caldirola, & Bellodi, 1996; Perna, Cocchi, Bertani, Arancio, & Bellodi, 1995). This has generally been interpreted to support the notion that what is inherited in panic disorder is an alteration in brainstem sensitivity to CO_2—a hard-wired biological abnormality. However, rather than an inherited alteration in CO_2 sensitivity, it may be that what is inherited is an altered tendency to view the somatic sensations associated with this challenge as being physically threatening or dangerous. In other words, what if AS was the risk factor being inherited? This is an equally compelling alternative hypothesis worth considering.

Psychometric research has demonstrated that AS is a subcomponent of a higher order factor commonly referred to as *neuroticism* or *negative affectivity* (Lilienfeld, 1996; Rapee & Medoro, 1994; see chap. 7). Further, a wealth of data exist demonstrating that what is inherited in anxiety disorders is a general tendency toward emotionality, sometimes referred to as the *general neurotic syndrome* (Andrews, 1996). Therefore, it is logical to assume that at least a sizable proportion of the variance in AS is likely to be genetically determined.

Recently, speculation on the origins of anxiety disorders has begun to incorporate genetic vulnerability, family factors, socialization experiences, and specific life events (Hudson & Rapee, in press; Rapee, 1997). AS, a subcomponent of trait anxiety (Lilienfeld, 1996), is likely to be mediated by the same factors. It may be that the heritable component of AS serves as a necessary template for the development of panic disorder and that the experientially derived component of AS serves as the trigger that determines which predisposed individuals will express the disorder. Thus, a home for both biology and psychology could be found within the theoretical framework of panic disorder etiopathology. At present, no data directly address the possibility that AS might be inherited. A clearer understanding of the relationship between AS and the neurobiology of panic disorder awaits the conduct of these studies.

REFERENCES

Abelson, J. L., Weg, J. G., Nesse, R. M., & Curtis, C. G. (1996). Respiratory psychophysiology and anxiety: Cognitive intervention in the doxapram model of panic. *Psychosomatic Medicine, 58,* 302–313.

Andrews, G. (1996). Comorbidity in neurotic disorders: The similarities are more important than the differences. In R. M. Rapee (Ed.), *Current controversies in the anxiety disorders* (pp. 3–20). New York: Guilford.

Asmundson, G. J. G., Norton, G. R., Wilson, K. G., & Sandler, L. S. (1994). Subjective symptoms and cardiac reactivity to brief hyperventilation in individuals with high anxiety sensitivity. *Behaviour Research and Therapy, 32,* 237–241.

Asmundson, G. J. G, & Stein, M. B. (1994). Triggering the false suffocation alarm in panic disorder patients by using a voluntary breathholding procedure. *American Journal of Psychiatry, 151,* 264–266.

Boulenger, J. P., Uhde, T. W., Wolff, E. A. III., & Post, R. M. (1984). Increased sensitivity to caffeine in patients with panic disorders: Preliminary evidence. *Archives of General Psychiatry, 41,* 1067–1071.

Bouwer, C., & Stein, D. J. (1997). Association of panic disorder with a history of traumatic suffocation. *American Journal of Psychiatry, 154,* 1566–1570.

Bradwejn, J., Koszycki, D., Payeur, R., Bourin, M., & Borthwick, H. (1992). Replication of action of cholecystokinin tetrapeptide in panic disorder: Clinical and behavioral findings. *American Journal of Psychiatry, 149,* 962–964.

Carr, R. E., Lehrer, P. M., Rausch, L. L., & Hochron, S. M. (1994). Anxiety sensitivity and panic attacks in an asthmatic population. *Behaviour Research and Therapy, 32,* 411–418.

Charney, D. S., Heninger, G. R., & Jatlow, P. I. (1985). Increased anxiogenic effects of caffeine in panic disorders. *Archives of General Psychiatry, 42,* 233–243.

Clark, D. M., Salkovskis, P. M., Öst, L. G., Breitholtz, E., Koehler, K. A., Westling, B. E., Jeavons, A., & Gelder, M. G. (1997). Misinterpretation of body sensations in panic disorder. *Journal of Consulting and Clinical Psychology, 65,* 203–213.

Craske, M. G., & Barlow, D. H. (1989). Nocturnal panic. *Journal of Nervous and Mental Disorders, 177,* 160–167.

Craske, M. G., & Freed, S. (1995). Expectations about arousal and nocturnal panic. *Journal of Abnormal Psychology, 104,* 567–575.

Donnell, C. D., & McNally, R. J. (1990). Anxiety sensitivity and panic attacks in a nonclinical population. *Behaviour Research and Therapy, 28,* 83–85.

Hudson, J. L., & Rapee, R. M. (in press). The origins of social phobia. *Behavior Modification.*

Kendler, K. S., Neale, M. C., Kessler, R. C., Heath, A. C., & Eaves, L. J. (1993). Panic disorder in women: A population-based twin study. *Psychological Medicine, 20,* 581–590.

Klein, D. F. (1993). False suffocation alarms, spontaneous panics, and related conditions: An integrative hypothesis. *Archives of General Psychiatry, 50,* 306–317.

Koenigsberg, H. W., Pollak, C. P., Fine, J., & Kakuma, T. (1992). Lactate sensitivity in sleeping panic disorder patients and healthy controls. *Biological Psychiatry, 32,* 539–542.

Koenigsberg, H. W., Pollak, C. P., Fine, J., & Kakuma, T. (1994). Cardiac and respiratory activity in panic disorder: Effects of sleep and sleep lactate infusions. *American Journal of Psychiatry, 151,* 1148–1152.

Koszycki, D., Cox, B. J., & Bradwejn, J. (1993). Anxiety sensitivity and response to cholesystokinin tetrapeptide in healthy volunteers. *American Journal of Psychiatry, 150,* 1881–1883.

Lelliott, P., & Bass, C. (1990). Symptom specificity in patients with panic. *British Journal of Psychiatry, 157,* 593–597.

Lilienfeld, S. O. (1996). Anxiety sensitivity is not distinct from trait anxiety. In R.M. Rapee (Ed.), *Current controversies in the anxiety disorders* (pp. 228–244). New York: Guilford.

Margraf, J., Ehlers, A., & Roth, W. T. (1986). Biological models of panic disorder and agoraphobia—a review. *Behaviour Research and Therapy, 24,* 553–567.

Martinez, J. M., Papp, L. A., Coplan, J. D., Anderson, D. E., Mueller, C. M., Klein, D. F., & Gorman, J. M. (1996). Ambulatory monitoring of respiration in anxiety. *Anxiety, 2,* 296–302.

McNally, R. J. (1994). *Panic disorder: A critical analysis.* New York: Guilford.

McNally, R. J., & Eke, M. (1996). Anxiety sensitivity, suffocation fear, and breath-holding duration as predictors of response to carbon dioxide challenge. *Journal of Abnormal Psychology, 105,* 146–149.

Mellman, T. A., & Uhde, T. W. (1989a). Electroencephalographic sleep in panic disorder: A focus on sleep-related panic attacks. *Archives of General Psychiatry, 46,* 178–184.

Mellman, T. A., & Uhde, T. W. (1989b). Sleep panic attacks: New clinical findings and theoretical implications. *American Journal of Psychiatry, 146,* 1204–1207.

Nutt, D. J., Glue, P., Lawson, C., & Wilson, S. (1990). Flumazenil provocation of panic attacks: Evidence for altered benzodiazepine receptor sensitivity in panic disorder. *Archives of General Psychiatry, 47,* 917–925.

Papp, L. A., Martinez, J. M., Klein, D. F., Coplan, J. D., Norman, R. G., Cole, R., de Jesus, M. J., Ross, D., Goetz, R., & Gorman, J. M. (1997). Respiratory psychophysiology of panic disorder: Three respiratory challenges in 98 subjects. *American Journal of Psychiatry, 154,* 1557–1565.

Perna, G., Bertani, A., Caldirola, D., & Bellodi, L. (1996). Family history of panic disorder and hypersensitivity to CO_2 in patients with panic disorder. *American Journal of Psychiatry, 153,* 1060–1064.

Perna, G., Caldirola, D., Arancio, C., & Bellodi, L. (1997). Panic attacks: A twin study. *Psychiatry Research, 66,* 69–71.

Perna, G., Cocchi, S., Bertani, A., Arancio, C., & Bellodi, L. (1995). Sensitivity to 35% CO_2 in healthy first-degree relatives of patients with panic disorder. *American Journal of Psychiatry, 152,* 623–625.

Peterson, R. A., & Reiss, S. (1987). *Test manual for the Anxiety Sensitivity Index.* Orland Park, IL: International Diagnostic Systems.

Pitts, F. N., Jr., & McClure, J. N. (1967). Lactate metabolism in anxiety neurosis. *New England Journal of Medicine, 277,* 1329–1336.

Rachman, S., & Taylor, S. (1993). Analyses of claustrophobia. *Journal of Anxiety Disorders, 7,* 281–291.

Rapee, R. M. (1995). Psychological factors influencing the affective response to biological challenge procedures in panic disorder. *Journal of Anxiety Disorders, 9,* 59–74.

Rapee, R. M. (1996). Information-processing views of panic disorder. In R. M. Rapee (Ed.), *Current controversies in the anxiety disorders* (pp. 77–93). New York: Guilford.

Rapee, R. M. (1997, July). *Big boys don't cry: The origins of anxiety disorders.* Keynote address presented at the national conference of the Australian Association for Cognitive Behaviour Therapy, Brisbane, Australia.

Rapee, R. M., Brown, T. A., Antony, M. M., & Barlow, D. H. (1992). Response to hyperventilation and inhalation of 5.5% carbon dioxide-enriched air across the DSM-III-R anxiety disorders. *Journal of Abnormal Psychology, 101,* 538–552.

Rapee, R. M., & Medoro, L. (1994). Fear of physical sensations and trait anxiety as mediators of the response to hyperventilation in nonclinical subjects. *Journal of Abnormal Psychology, 103,* 693–699.

Reiss, S. (1991). Expectancy theory of fear, anxiety, and panic. *Clinical Psychology Review, 11,* 141–153.

Reiss, S., & McNally, R. J. (1985). The expectancy model of fear. In S. Reiss & R. R. Bootzin (Eds.), *Theoretical issues in behavior therapy* (pp. 107–121). New York: Academic Press.

Roy-Byrne, P. P., Cowley, D. S., Greenblatt, D. J., Shader, R. I., & Hommer, D. (1990). Reduced benzodiazepine sensitivity in panic disorder. *Archives of General Psychiatry, 47,* 534–538.

Roy-Byrne, P., Wingerson, D. K., Radant, A., Greenblatt, D. J., & Cowley, D. S. (1996). Reduced benzodiazepine sensitivity in patients with panic disorder: Comparison with patients with obsessive-compulsive disorder and normal subjects. *American Journal of Psychiatry, 153,* 1444–1449.

Skre, I., Onstad, S., Torgersen, S., Lygren, S., & Kringlen, E. (1993). A twin study of DSM-III-R anxiety disorders. *Acta Psychiatrica Scandinavica, 88,* 85–92.

Smoller, J. W., Pollack, M. H., Otto, M. W., Rosenbaum, J. F., & Kradin, R. L. (1996). Panic anxiety, dyspnea, and respiratory disease. *American Journal of Respiratory and Critical Care Medicine, 154,* 6–17.

Stein, M. B., Chartier, M., & Walker, J. R. (1993). Sleep in nondepressed patients with panic disorder: I. A systematic assessment of subjective sleep complaints. *Sleep, 16,* 724–726.

Stein, M. B., Millar, T. W., Larsen, D. K., & Kryger, M. H. (1995). Irregular breathing patterns during sleep in patients with panic disorder. *American Journal of Psychiatry, 152,* 1168–1173.

Stein, M. B., & Uhde, T. W. (1991). Endocrine, cardiovascular, and behavioral effects of intravenous protirelin in patients with panic disorder. *Archives of General Psychiatry, 48,* 148–156.

Stein, M. B., & Uhde, T. W. (1995). The biology of anxiety disorders. In C. B. Nemeroff & A. F. Schatzberg (Eds.), *American Psychiatric Press Textbook of Psychopharmacology* (pp. 501–521). Washington, DC: American Psychiatric Press.

Strolle, P. J., Jr., & Rogers, R. M. (1996). Obstructive sleep apnea. *New England Journal of Medicine, 334,* 99–104.

Taylor, S., Koch, W. J., & McNally, R. J. (1992). How does anxiety sensitivity vary across the anxiety disorders? *Journal of Anxiety Disorders, 6,* 249–259.

Taylor, S., & Rachman, S. (1994). Klein's suffocation theory of panic. *Archives of General Psychiatry, 51,* 505–506.

Torgersen, S. (1983). Genetic factors in anxiety disorders. *Archives of General Psychiatry, 40,* 1085–1089.

Uhde, T. W. (1990). Caffeine provocation of panic: A focus on biological mechanisms. In J. Ballenger (Ed.), *Clinical aspects of panic disorder* (pp. 219–242). New York: Wiley-Liss.

Uhde, T. W. (1994). The anxiety disorders. In M. H. Kryger, T. Roth, & W. C. Dement (Eds.), *Principles and practice of sleep medicine* (2nd ed., pp. 204–211). Philadelphia, PA: Saunders.

Uhde, T. W., Boulenger, J. P., Post, R. M., Siever, L. J., Vittone, B. J., Jimerson, D. C., & Roy-Byrne, P. P. (1984). Fear and anxiety: Relationship to noradrenergic function. *Psychopathology, 17 (Suppl. 3),* 8–23.

10

Prospective Evaluations
of Anxiety Sensitivity

Norman B. Schmidt
Uniformed Services University of the Health Sciences

Maller and Reiss (1992) concluded their longitudinal study of anxiety sensitivity (AS) by rhetorically raising the question, "With all the recent advances in the biological aspects of panic disorder, what could demonstrate better the continued importance of basic psychological research than evidence of cognitive risk factors?" (p. 246). Only 5 years later, AS appears to be one of the most promising cognitive risk factors in any area of psychopathology as well as one of the best researched risk factors for panic disorder. Prospective studies have played an important role in establishing AS as a risk factor. This chapter focuses on longitudinal studies of AS in both nonclinical and anxiety disordered populations.

ANXIETY SENSITIVITY
AS A COGNITIVE RISK FACTOR

Anxiety sensitivity is distinguished from most other cognitive conceptualizations of anxiety and panic because AS is believed to be a stable, traitlike characteristic that may precede the development of panic attacks. Individual differences in AS are hypothesized to emerge from a variety of experiences that ultimately lead to the acquisition of beliefs about potentially aversive consequences of arousal. Such experiences may include hearing others express fear of such sensations, receiving misinformation about the harmfulness of certain sensations, witnessing a catastrophic event such as the fatal heart attack of a loved one, and so forth. Thus, AS constitutes a disposition to develop anxiety and does not require the experience of clinically significant anxiety or panic in its own development (Reiss, 1991).

One of the important and unique predictions of the AS conceptualization is that AS should act as a risk factor for the development of panic attacks as well as related anxiety disorders. Laboratory-based experimental studies and prospective quasiexperimental studies have supported this prediction. Experimental studies using nonclinical samples with no history of panic attacks have shown that AS is predictive of fearful responding in the context of a variety of biological challenge procedures, including hyperventilation, caffeine, and carbon dioxide inhalation (Donnell & McNally, 1990; Harrington, Schmidt, & Telch, 1996; Rapee & Medoro, 1994; Schmidt & Telch, 1994; Telch, Silverman, & Schmidt, 1996; also see chap. 9, this volume). Prospective evaluation of nonclinical samples has also determined that AS is a risk factor for the development of anxiety pathology (Maller & Reiss, 1992; Schmidt, Lerew, & Jackson, 1997). Taken together, laboratory and prospective studies provide converging evidence for AS as a risk factor in the development of anxiety pathology. Longitudinal investigations of AS, including reviews of both published reports and data from several of our unpublished studies, are the focus of the following sections.

MERITS OF PROSPECTIVE STUDIES

Only a small percentage of all empirical studies employ a longitudinal design (Visser, 1982). This is not surprising given the expense and logistical problems involved in prospective studies. The area of anxiety is no exception. There are only a handful of studies that have prospectively examined nonclinical samples for the development of anxiety pathology (Balon, Pohl, Yerigani, Rainey, & Berchou, 1988; Breslau & Davis, 1993; Eaton & Keyl, 1990). Similarly, only a few published studies have longitudinally examined the role of AS in the development of anxiety (Ehlers, 1995; Maller & Reiss, 1992; Schmidt et al., 1997). Despite the limitations regarding causal inferences in nonexperimental prospective studies, this study design provides an important complement to laboratory-based studies, especially with respect to ecological validity, because it adds a more naturalistic view of the development of panic and anxiety pathology outside of laboratory settings.

LONGITUDINAL EPIDEMIOLOGICAL STUDIES
OF RISK FACTORS FOR ANXIETY

Before examining AS specifically, it is useful to consider the relative risk conferred by other documented risk factors for anxiety. Prospective epidemiological studies of anxiety pathology have focused on the relation between sociodemographic factors and the development of panic (Breslau & Davis, 1993; Keyl & Eaton, 1990). These studies have identified several risk factors including gender, age, negative life events, and nonpsychiatric medical conditions.

Epidemiological catchment area (ECA) data indicate that gender is a risk factor for panic, panic disorder, and agoraphobia (Eaton & Keyl, 1990; Keyl & Eaton, 1990). ECA data indicate that females have approximately twice the lifetime risk for panic disorder, with risk for agoraphobia being even higher. Young adults appear to be at highest risk for the development of anxiety pathology. The ECA study suggests that for onset of initial panic attacks and panic disorder the median age is 24 years. Young adults have approximately 1.5 to 2.0 times greater relative risk compared with other age groups after adjusting for gender. Negative life events, particularly losses such as the death of a loved one, also appear to confer significant risk for anxiety. ECA data suggest that a major loss resulted in approximately eight times greater risk for panic disorder (Odds Ratio: OR = 8.1, 95% Confidence Interval: CI = 2.9 - 22.6) and four times greater risk for spontaneous panic (OR = 4.2, CI = 2.2 - 8.0).[1] In addition, medical conditions appear to substantially increase risk for the development of anxiety pathology. Breslau and Davis (1993) reported that individuals with a history of migraine, compared with those without, were almost 13 times more likely to develop panic disorder during a 14-month follow-up interval (OR = 12.8, CI = 4.1 - 39.8).

In summary, demographic factors such as age and gender confer approximately 1.5 to 2.5 greater risk for anxiety, whereas loss events and specific medical conditions (i.e., migraine) appear to confer much higher risk for panic disorder and panic attacks. However, it is unclear why medical conditions such as migraines increase an individual's risk for panic disorder. This risk may be related to an underlying pathophysiological factor specific to migraine. Alternatively, medical conditions that produce unpleasant and potentially fear-provoking sensations may increase the risk of developing high AS which, in turn,

---

[1]Logistic regression models compute the odds of an event occurring. The *odds* of an event are defined as the ratio of the probability that it will occur to the probability that it will not (e.g., cases of panic disorder vs. cases of no panic disorder).

mediates the development of panic. Schmidt and Telch (1997) found that the presence of co-occurring, nonpsychiatric medical conditions in patients with panic disorder was not related to increased AS. However, the general perception of poor physical health among patients with panic disorder was significantly related to AS prior to treatment ($r = .28$) and six months following treatment ($r = .29$).

LONGITUDINAL STUDIES OF AS

There are few longitudinal studies of AS. Four published reports have evaluated the relationship between AS and the development of anxiety in nonclinical samples (Ehlers, 1995; Harrington et al., 1996; Maller & Reiss, 1992; Schmidt et al., 1997). Our laboratory recently completed a replication of our initial prospective study (Schmidt et al., 1997) that is yet unpublished (Schmidt, 1997). There are also published studies that have prospectively evaluated AS in clinical anxiety disorder samples (Bruce, Spiegel, Gregg, & Nuzzarello, 1995; Ehlers, 1995).

Longitudinal Outcome in Nonclinical Samples

An important advantage of evaluating nonclinical samples with no history of significant anxiety pathology (such as spontaneous panic attacks) is that AS cannot simply be a concomitant or consequence of the development of anxiety pathology. Each of the longitudinal studies of AS using nonclinical subjects is consistent in indicating that individuals with higher levels of AS are at greater risk for the development of anxiety pathology over time (see Table 10.1 for a summary).

In the first follow-up study of AS, Maller and Reiss (1992) evaluated 48 college students approximately 3 years after completion of the AS Index (ASI; Peterson & Reiss, 1987). On entering the study, those in the high AS group

TABLE 10.1
Studies Longitudinally Evaluating the Role of Anxiety Sensitivity
in the Development or Maintenance of Anxiety Pathology

Study	Incidence			Maintenance	
	PA	PD	Anx Sxs	PA	PD
Maller & Reiss (1992)	+	?	NA	+	+
Ehlers (1995)	+	NA	?	+	+
Harrington et al. (1996)	+	-	NA	NA	NA
Schmidt et al. (1997)	+	NA	+	+	NA
Schmidt (1997)	+	NA	+	+	NA

Note. + = support, - = no support; NA = not assessed; ? = assessed but data equivocal or not presented; PA = panic attacks; PD = panic disorder, Anx Sxs = anxiety symptoms.

initially had a mean ASI score of 33, compared with a mean of 11 for the low AS group. Follow-up evaluations were based on structured diagnostic interviews and self-report measures. Evaluation of test–retest scores on the ASI indicated a high level of stability ($r = .71$) over the 3-year period suggesting that AS is a relatively stable disposition. High levels of AS were associated with about a five times greater risk for the development of anxiety disorders. Approximately 50% of the high AS group received a diagnosis of an anxiety disorder (with panic disorder being the most frequent diagnosis), compared with only about 10% for the low AS group. The ASI was also associated with the occurrence of panic attacks. Four subjects experienced spontaneous panic attacks for the first time during the follow-up interval; three of these subjects came from the high AS group. It is unclear whether any of these four individuals also met diagnostic criteria for an anxiety disorder.

It appears that AS was also associated with a maintenance of anxiety pathology during the follow-up interval. Maller and Reiss (1992) reported that, of 18 subjects experiencing panic attacks during the follow-up, only 4 reported panic for the first time; thus, 14 individuals had a history of panic. Of those 18 subjects experiencing panic, 11 had high ASI scores, whereas 25 of the 30 subjects who did not experience panic had low ASI scores. High AS was also associated with greater frequency of panic and more intense panic attacks.

Maller and Reiss (1992) evaluated whether state or trait anxiety was associated with panic attacks during the year preceding the follow-up evaluation (state and trait anxiety were assessed at follow-up). Both measures of state and trait anxiety were not found to be associated with the development of panic attacks. Moreover, the association between AS and panic remained significant even after statistically controlling for both state and trait anxiety. These analyses offer an important demonstration that AS possesses unique variance above and beyond the effects of trait or even state anxiety in its association with anxiety pathology.

This initial prospective study offered evidence for an association between AS and the later development of panic attacks. Unfortunately, the small sample size, low incidence of spontaneous panic, and uncertainty about preexisting psychiatric conditions at the initiation of the study precludes definitive conclusions about the role of AS in the genesis of clinical anxiety conditions. At the very least, these data suggest that AS is associated with the maintenance of anxiety pathology. The maintaining influence of AS is inferred from the fact that most individuals with high AS and a history of panic (and possibly an anxiety disorder) continued to experience panic attacks during the follow-up period.

Ehlers (1995) conducted a 1-year follow-up study of panic attacks and other anxiety-related symptoms in a sample consisting of patients with panic disorder ($n = 39$), patients with panic disorder currently in remission ($n = 17$), infrequent panickers (i.e., individuals experiencing panic attacks who do not meet criteria for panic disorder; $n = 46$), patients with simple phobias ($n = 22$), and nonclinical controls with no history of spontaneous panic attacks or psychiatric disorders ($n = 45$).

AS was a significant predictor of the first reported occurrence of spontaneous panic. One nonclinical control and four individuals diagnosed with simple phobia reported their first spontaneous panic attack during the follow-up period. These individuals had significantly higher levels of AS ($M = 16.2$) compared with nonpanicking individuals ($M = 10.0$). The development of anxiety syndromes was not assessed at follow-up so it is unclear whether any of these individuals met *DSM* criteria for an anxiety disorder.

Ehlers' (1995) study represented a methodological improvement over the Maller and Reiss (1992) study because psychiatric diagnoses and trait anxiety were determined at the initial assessment. Consistent with Maller and Reiss, AS predicted the occurrence of new panic attacks during the follow-up period, but trait anxiety was not a significant predictor. However, the same cautions raised with the Maller and Reiss study must be reiterated. Small sample size and the incidence of panic attacks ($n = 5$) are clear limiting factors of Ehler's study.

Harrington et al. (1996) followed a small group ($N = 62$) of nonclinical subjects completing a CO_2 challenge for 1 year to determine whether exposure to this biological challenge would potentiate panic attacks or anxiety disorders. Subjects were screened and none had a history of spontaneous panic or a diagnosable anxiety disorder prior to completing a single vital capacity inhalation of 35% CO_2/65% O_2. Participants were contacted by phone and completed the anxiety disorders section of the Structured Clinical Interview for the *DSM–III–R* (SCID; Spitzer, Williams, Gibbon, & First, 1990). Thus, one methodological improvement of the Harrington et al. study was the utilization of structured diagnostic interviews at baseline and follow-up.

AS predicted fearful responding when the challenge was administered. Findings at follow-up are also consistent with AS, conferring risk for panic attacks, but fail to reach statistical significance. Of the six individuals experiencing spontaneous panic, four were originally classified in the high AS group (ASI scores one standard deviation above the mean score for the entire nonclinical sample surveyed for the study; high AS group: ASI $M = 26.5$, $SD = 5.6$) and two were in the low AS group (one standard deviation below the nonclinical sample mean; ASI $M = 6.5$, $SD = 3.3$). Logistic regression using AS status (high, low) as the predictor indicated that high AS subjects were at twice the risk for experiencing spontaneous panic ($OR = 2.0$, $CI = 0.39 - 11.8$). AS was not predictive of the development of panic disorder or any anxiety disorder because there was no incidence of anxiety disorders during the follow-up period.

The effects of the challenge procedure and the combined effects of AS status and challenge-induced panic on the later development of panic were also evaluated. It was concluded that the occurrence of spontaneous panic did not appear to be linked with undergoing the challenge procedure; there was no clear temporal relationship between the procedure and reported panic attacks as would be predicted by a survival analysis (e.g., the most proximal panic attack occurred 4 months after the experiment). The interaction between AS status and challenge-induced panic also did not predict the ensuing development of panic attacks during the follow-up period.

Exposure to the challenge procedure represents one potential confound in interpreting results from this study. It is possible that the experience of the biological challenge accompanied by a debriefing procedure may have affected the later development of anxiety pathology. For example, potentially vulnerable high AS subjects were allowed to experience a controlled panic attack (or at least an experience that may closely mimic the sensations that occur during a panic attack) along with the provision of corrective information about the benign nature of these symptoms. Theoretically, this type of procedure may yield the same benefit as does interoceptive exposure for patients with panic disorder. Interoceptive exposure (i.e., repeated exposure to internal bodily perturbations that elicit a fear response) essentially provides corrective information regarding the benign nature of the unpleasant sensations that patients have learned to fear. In fact, level of AS may have been dramatically altered both positively or negatively as a result of the biological challenge procedure. Unfortunately, AS was not reassessed postchallenge or at follow-up.

Consistent with the two previous reports, Harrington et al. (1996) provided evidence that AS is associated with the development of panic attacks over time. In contrast to the inferences drawn from Maller and Reiss (1992), the Harrington et al. report, which employed appropriate controls for assessing *DSM* anxiety conditions, did not find any increased risk for the development of clinical anxiety syndromes. Yet the small sample size and unknown effects of exposure to the challenge procedure must temper conclusions about these study findings.

Schmidt et al. (1997) completed a prospective study of AS that is unique in several respects. This study evaluated whether AS is associated with the development of anxiety pathology in a large sample of nonclinical subjects during a relatively brief (i.e., 5 weeks) but highly stressful period of time. The U. S. Air Force Academy (USAFA) provided an opportunity to evaluate incoming first-year students during their initial 5 weeks of training. This period, called Basic Cadet Training (BCT), consists of highly regimented training in the context of fairly extreme psychosocial (e.g., isolation from friends and family, constant monitoring and evaluation of behavior) and physical (e.g., intense exercise, limited sleep) stressors. These BCT specific factors, in conjunction with the general stressors associated with entering college (e.g., first period away from home for many of these young adults), make BCT an ideal environment for engendering anxiety.

This study evaluated more than 1,000 cadets during the first and last weeks of BCT to determine whether AS predicted the development of anxiety pathology. It was hypothesized that AS, independent of a history of panic attacks and trait anxiety, would predict the development of spontaneous panic and other anxiety symptoms as well as impairment and disability.

Participants were somewhat different from typical undergraduate populations. All USAFA cadets receive congressional or presidential nominations. They can have no criminal record, must be in good health and pass a Department of Defense medical screen, and are required to be young (ages 17–22) and single with no dependents. Approximately 85% of the subjects were White males. Despite self-selection into an occupation that involves higher than average risk (i.e., flying high-performance military airplanes), the average ASI score ($M = 19.8, SD = 8.0$) for this sample was comparable with other nonclinical college samples.

At the beginning of BCT, 14% of cadets reported experiencing at least one "out of the blue" panic attack at some time during their lives. During the 5-week BCT, approximately 6% ($n = 74$) of the sample reported experiencing at least one spontaneous panic attack. Of these 74 cases, 34 had reported no prior history of panic. As predicted, the ASI was significantly associated with the development of spontaneous panic. This was true both for new cases of panic as well as for those cadets with a history of panic attacks. ASI scores for those experiencing panic ($M = 24.5, SD = 8.1$) were elevated relative to the remaining sample ($M = 19.4, SD = 7.8$). These scores are relatively similar to the average scores reported for nonclinical samples (Taylor, Koch, & McNally, 1992). This demonstrates that panic attacks can be induced in individuals with relatively few arousal-related fears when substantial stressors are involved. When the sample is divided into quartiles based on ASI scores, approximately 13% of those in the highest quartile experienced a panic attack compared with less than 3% for those in the lowest quartile. Those in the highest quartile ASI group showed almost twice the risk for developing panic compared to the remainder of the subjects ($OR = 1.7$, $CI = 1.04$ - 2.75). In a similar comparison of the top decile of the sample, approximately 20% of the highest decile ASI group experienced a panic attack with a three times greater risk for experiencing spontaneous panic compared with all others ($OR = 2.9$, $CI = 1.5$ - 5.3).

Because a history of spontaneous panic may confer a risk for additional panic attacks, we also evaluated the unique contributions of a history of panic and AS in predicting panic during BCT. When history of panic and ASI were simultaneously regressed on panic occurrence both were found to be uniquely predictive of panic. The association between trait anxiety and the development of panic was also assessed. Trait anxiety did not predict panic occurrence; when trait anxiety and the ASI were simultaneously regressed, only the ASI significantly predicted panic. Lilienfeld, Turner, and Jacob (1993) suggested that trait anxiety and AS may act synergistically to predict the development of panic. Schmidt et al. used the interaction between the ASI and trait anxiety to predict panic attacks but found it not predictive.

Although Schmidt et al. (1997) did not utilize diagnostic interviews, they did assess for additional anxiety symptoms that allow for tentative conclusions about the development of anxiety disorder diagnoses. Of those reporting spontaneous panic attacks during BCT, 22% ($n = 16$) reported three or more such attacks and 28% ($n = 21$) reported significant worry about having additional attacks or the consequences of panic. Many of these individuals also endorsed symptoms on the Beck Anxiety Inventory (BAI) and Beck Depression Inventory (BDI) in the clinically significant range. Cadets reporting three or more panic attacks had mean BAI scores of 21 and a mean BDI scores of 18; cadets endorsing panic-related worry had mean BAI scores of 20 and mean BDI scores of 14 compared with mean scores of 9 (BAI) and 6 (BDI) for cadets not experiencing panic. Cadets experiencing multiple panic attacks or panic-related worry generally reported that anxiety had created moderate levels of impairment in their ability to function during BCT. Moreover, these cadets reported approximately twice as many meetings with peer counselors and twice as many days on sick call. Approximately 18% of this group of cadets had visited the counseling center compared with less than 2% for cadets as a whole.

The ASI was highly predictive of classification into one of these disabled groups even after controlling for a lifetime history of panic attacks and trait anxiety. Based on a median split of the ASI, cadets showing higher levels of AS were over five times more likely to experience multiple panic attacks ($OR = 5.2$, $CI = 1.9$ - 16.5) and were approximately three times more likely to experience panic-related worry ($OR = 3.0$, $CI = 1.3 - 7.2$). Although endorsement of symptoms and impairment on self-report measures is clearly limited, some of the cadets reporting multiple panic attacks, high levels of anxiety and depression symptoms, and significant impairment were likely to have met diagnostic criteria for panic or other anxiety disorders. Thus, higher levels of AS are not only predictive of the incidence of spontaneous panic but are associated with the development of a broader range of clinically significant anxiety symptoms and possibly formal anxiety disorders.

Schmidt and colleagues recently completed a replication of the initial USAFA study on another cohort of more than 1,000 cadets (Schmidt, 1997). The replication study is essentially the same except that cadets were assessed at three time points during BCT (beginning, middle, and end). In general, findings from the replication study closely match the initial report. Approximately 15% of the sample reported a history of at least one spontaneous panic attack. Once again, approximately 6% of the cadets reported a spontaneous panic attack during the 5-week training period. AS significantly predicted the incidence of panic during BCT even after controlling for trait anxiety and history of panic. Cadets scoring in the upper half of a median split of the ASI, compared with those in the lower half of the distribution, were approximately three times ($OR = 2.8$, $CI = 1.6 - 4.8$) more likely to experience a panic attack during BCT. More than 9% of the high ASI group experienced a spontaneous panic attack compared with around 3% of the low ASI group. The replication study also indicated that AS was predictive of some of the broader indexes of anxiety pathology, including panic-related worry, anxiety symptoms as indexed by the BAI, and anxiety-related impairment and disability in functioning.

The Schmidt et al. USAFA studies provide an important test of whether AS acts as a risk factor for anxiety during acute stress. However, these studies are limited in several respects. The somewhat unique sample population and unusual environmental stressors may limit the generalizability of the findings. Reliance on self-report measures has been found to create an overreporting bias (Wilson et al., 1992), which raises issues regarding the validity of the clinical findings. However, findings across both studies are remarkably consistent both in terms of the incidence of psychopathology as well as the relative associations of AS and other predictor variables such as trait anxiety.

Longitudinal Outcome in Clinical Samples

Prospective studies of AS in nonclinical samples permit the evaluation of the initial incidence of anxiety pathology. Longitudinal studies of clinical populations allow for the examination of the role of AS in the long-term course of anxiety pathology. The AS conceptualization of anxiety and panic emphasizes that high levels of AS should be associated with, and maintain, pathological anxiety among those already afflicted with an anxiety disorder (see chap. 1). Similarly, reductions in AS due to treatment should be associated with clinical improvement and may also predict long-term outcome (see chap. 14).

There have been two published reports evaluating the longitudinal relation between AS and outcomes among clinical anxiety disorder samples (Bruce et al., 1995; Ehlers, 1995). Unpublished data from treatment outcome studies conducted through our laboratory are also reviewed to examine the role of AS in the outcome of patients with panic disorder. These reports are consistent in suggesting that high levels of AS negatively impact the long-term course of anxiety symptoms among both treated and untreated patients with anxiety disorders (see Table 10.1).

As noted earlier, Ehlers (1995) conducted a 1-year follow-up study of patients with panic disorder, infrequent panickers, and remitted panickers (i.e., individuals with a history of panic disorder but no current diagnosis). Higher levels of AS did not predict maintenance or relapse among panic disorder patients receiving treatment during the follow-up, but did predict poorer outcome among untreated patients. Similarly, AS predicted poorer outcome in terms of the frequency of spontaneous panic among untreated infrequent panickers. Moreover, after controlling for history of panic attacks, AS incrementally predicted panic disorder status ($\beta = .27$) and panic attacks ($\beta = .17$) during follow-up. Infrequent panickers who were untreated during the follow-up period were more apt to continue to experience panic attacks if they had higher levels of AS ($M = 21.7$) compared with infrequent panickers with lower levels of AS ($M = 16.4$). AS did not predict outcome for remitted panickers.

Consistent with studies evaluating nonclinical samples with a history of panic (e.g., Maller & Reiss, 1992), Ehlers (1995) also found that AS was associated with the maintenance of anxiety pathology among individuals with a clinical or subclinical anxiety pathology. Ehlers' study suggests that higher levels of AS are associated with poorer outcomes among untreated individuals suffering from clinical or subclinical anxiety pathology. In addition, AS predicted the maintenance of panic disorder and panic attacks in the total sample even when statistically controlling for the effects of previous panic attack frequency and other predictor variables. Failure to find an association among treated individuals may be partly due to low power because most comparisons included only 10 to 20 subjects. However, the small sample size and the liberal levels of significance ($p < .10$) should lead to caution in interpreting these findings in isolation.

Bruce et al. (1995) evaluated predictors of successful benzodiazepine discontinuation among patients with panic disorder who completed either a flexible drug taper schedule plus standard medical management or the same taper schedule with cognitive behavior therapy (CBT). Ten patients were assigned to each group and followed for 6 months after the taper procedure was completed. Nine of 10 patients receiving CBT, compared with only 4 of 10 patients receiving standard medical management, were still medication free at follow-up. Baseline to posttaper change in ASI scores was the only variable of several evaluated that predicted medication status at follow-up. Nonsignificant predictors included severity of withdrawal symptoms, pretreatment dose, duration of previous benzodiazepine treatment, and level of phobic avoidance. Changes in ASI scores correctly classified 85% of all successful outcomes (i.e., successful discontinuation vs. relapse). Therefore, reductions in AS were associated with receiving CBT, which in turn was associated with maintaining benzodiazepine discontinuation. The single subject receiving CBT who relapsed during the follow-up period evidenced no change in ASI scores during the treatment.

The Bruce et al. (1995) study indicates that posttreatment assessments of change in AS may be extremely important clinically in predicting adverse outcomes of benzodiazepine taper particularly among those patients who have not received skill-based interventions (i.e., CBT) for dealing with their anxiety. The study also suggests that it is both possible and beneficial, in regard to keeping patients off benzodiazepines, to lower AS in anxiety-disordered populations. Unfortunately, the authors did not provide data as to the clinical status, other than medication use, at follow-up, which would allow us to determine the effects of changes in AS and other measures of end-state functioning.

Using data collected as part of ongoing treatment outcome studies of panic disorder, we evaluated the relationship between AS and outcome among patients who had received 12 sessions of CBT (see Schmidt, Staab, Trakowski, & Sammons, 1997, for a description of the treatment protocol). Participants included 37 patients with a principal *DSM–IV* diagnosis of panic disorder based on a SCID interview (First, Spitzer, Gibbon, & Williams, 1994). All patients assigned to receive the group-administered treatment protocol were used in the present analyses. Patients were reassessed at posttreatment and 3 months following treatment.

Two posttreatment measures that correspond to somewhat different aspects of the patient's AS status were used as predictor variables: (a) absolute level of AS (i.e., posttreatment ASI scores), and (b) change in AS during treatment (i.e., pre–post residualized ASI change scores). Consistent with AS conceptualizations, the absolute level of AS should be predictive of the development, and therefore redevelopment, of anxiety pathology. However, as is evident in the Bruce et al. (1995) report, significant reductions in AS, regardless of the specific posttreatment level, may also predict long-term outcomes.

This particular group of patients had a mean pretreatment ASI score of 29.3 (SD = 11.3), a mean posttreatment score of 12.1 (SD = 10.1), and mean follow-up score of 11.1 (SD = 9.7). The mean level of reduction based on a pre–post change score was 17 points, suggesting that the treatment exerted a substantial effect on AS. In fact, this particular protocol exerted a substantially greater impact on AS than the treatment reported by Bruce et al. (1995), which produced an average ASI reduction of approximately nine points for patients assigned to the CBT group. In addition, the levels of AS at posttreatment are actually somewhat lower than might be expected in nonclinical populations (Taylor et al., 1992; Telch, Shermis, & Lucas, 1989). This suggests that patients undergoing this treatment were supernormalized in regard to their AS. The follow-up score is comparable to the posttreatment levels suggesting good maintenance of these substantial AS reductions.

Table 10.2 indicates the level of association (Pearson r) between the ASI posttreatment variables and symptoms at follow-up. Both ASI change and ASI

TABLE 10.2

Role of Anxiety Sensitivity in Predicting Symptoms and Impairment 3 Months Following Cognitive-Behavioral Therapy for Patients With Panic Disorder (N = 37)

	Pearson Correlations	
Follow-up Variable	Posttreatment ASI Score	Pre- to Posttreatment Change in ASI
Panic frequency (no. attacks in past month)	.12	.05
Anxiety (Sheehan patient-rated Anxiety Scale)	.39**	.24*
Phobic avoidance (FQ Agoraphobia subscale)	.43***	.44***
Overall disability (Sheehan Disability Scale)	.45***	.41***
Depression (Beck Depression Inventory)	.45***	.35**
Impairment (clinician-rated global impressions)	.33**	.21

Note. The correlations in the second column are positive because ASI change scores are residualized (pretreatment scores regressed on posttreatment scores). Thus, reductions in ASI scores represent negative residualized change scores, with greater reductions corresponding to higher negative change scores. Accordingly, positive correlations indicate that greater reductions in AS are correlated with lower levels of psychopathology at follow-up.

ASI = Anxiety Sensitivity Index; FQ = Fear Questionnaire.

*p < .05. **p < .01. ***p < .001.

level predicted anxiety symptoms, phobic avoidance, depression, patient-rated disability, and clinician-rated level of impairment ($p < .05$). At follow-up, 71% of patients were classified as fully recovered based on clinician ratings. Recovery status was significantly predicted by ASI level as well as ASI change. Based on a median split of the ASI at posttreatment, patients scoring in the lower half of the distribution were approximately 13 times more likely to be recovered at follow-up ($OR = 13.0$, $CI = 1.8 - 26.9$). Similarly, those patients showing ASI reductions greater than 15 points were about nine times more likely to be recovered at follow-up ($OR = 9.1$, $CI = 1.5 - 17.7$). These findings suggest that the malleability of AS as indexed by the change score as well as its absolute level at post-treatment predict the course of the pathology over time.

GENERAL DISCUSSION AND FUTURE DIRECTIONS FOR PROSPECTIVE STUDIES

Comparisons between the reviewed studies and prospective epidemiological studies of anxiety pathology suggest that AS confers a relative risk similar to well-documented demographic factors such as sex, but perhaps somewhat less risk than other parameters such as comorbid medical conditions. Although there have been relatively few longitudinal studies that have evaluated the role of AS in the genesis of anxiety pathology, these studies are largely consistent in indicating that AS is a risk factor for the development of anxiety pathology, particularly the development of panic attacks, and that AS may act as a maintaining factor for those individuals possessing clinical or subclinical anxiety symptoms.

The onset of clinical anxiety phenomena such as panic attacks and anxiety disorders is a relatively rare occurrence in the general population. Data from the ECA study suggest annual incidences of approximately 2% for panic disorder and 10% for panic attacks (Keyl & Eaton, 1990). The low base rates pose one of the biggest problems for longitudinal studies. With the exception of the two studies of air force cadets, all of the longitudinal reports are seriously underpowered for the detection of such low base rate phenomena. As noted previously, outside of the Schmidt et al. studies, the total incidence of new panic attacks totals only 15 cases across all other studies reviewed. However, most of these studies did find an association between AS and panic despite the low incidence of panic attacks. Taken as a whole, the relative consistency across studies as well as the substantial number of initial cases of panic attacks during the USAFA studies should significantly bolster our confidence regarding the association between AS and panic attacks.

The association between AS and the development of full-blown clinical syndromes is not clearly confirmed by longitudinal studies. Although Maller and Reiss (1992) suggested a strong association between AS and anxiety disorders, the lack of diagnostic assessment at the initiation of the study limits our ability to determine whether high levels of AS preceded the development of these conditions. Unfortunately, the Harrington et al. (1996) study, which better controlled for a history of psychiatric conditions, failed to find an association. Perhaps the most compelling evidence that high AS contributes to the development of anxiety syndromes comes from the air force data. A small number of cadets appeared to develop clinically significant symptoms, including multiple panic attacks, panic-related worry, high levels of anxiety symptoms, and anxiety-related impairment. Such symptoms are likely to be associated with clinically significant impairment and the constellation of symptoms is consistent with a panic disorder diagnosis. Several cadets reported multiple panic attacks with panic-related worry, BAI scores in the *severe* range (i.e., mid-40s), and composite impairment ratings in the *extreme* range. It is highly likely that these individuals (each of whom possessed AS scores in the upper half of the distribution) would meet diagnostic criteria for an anxiety disorder.

Expectancy theory describes AS as an amplification factor in fear responding such that individuals with high AS are more likely to worry about anxiety resulting from a stressor (Reiss & McNally, 1985; see chap. 2). It is apparent that AS should act as a cognitive diathesis that places the individual at risk in the context of stressors. Evaluation of the pathogenesis of panic within a diathesis–stress framework is consistent with the typical history of onset for those developing panic disorder. Often panic attacks and the formal panic disorder syndrome emerge during highly stressful times (Pollard, Pollard, & Corn, 1989) or when stressors are perceived as relatively uncontrollable (Roy-Byrne, Geraci, & Uhde, 1986). For example, Faravelli and Pallanti (1989) reported that panic disorder patients, compared with nonclinical controls, experienced significantly more negative life events during the year preceding the development of panic and that the majority of these negative stressors occurred in the month preceding panic.

A diathesis–stress model of AS is strongly supported by the two USAFA studies in which vulnerable individuals were evaluated during exposure to high stress. Despite the limited follow-up interval, it was expected that the 5-week BCT period would be ideal for evaluating the development of anxiety pathology as cadets experienced high levels of generally uncontrollable and unpredictable stressors. The relatively high incidence of anxiety pathology during this brief period bears this out; the lifetime prevalence of spontaneous panic prior to BCT was approximately 14% across the two samples, but almost half of this number (6%) reported a panic attack during the 5-week period of BCT.

Although the prediction of the first occurrence of anxiety pathology has clear importance, longitudinal evaluations also indicate that AS is an important variable for predicting the maintenance of anxiety pathology in clinical and nonclinical populations. For example, high levels of AS predict continued pathology in untreated patients with anxiety disorders. Similarly, reductions in AS predict positive end-state functioning (i.e., remission of panic attacks, panic-related anxiety, and phobic avoidance) during follow-up for patients completing cognitive behavioral treatment (Schmidt et al., 1997) and successful discontinuation of anxiolytic medications (Bruce et al., 1995). These studies also demonstrate that AS is malleable and that these positive reductions can be maintained following treatment. Clinically, these findings indicate that assessments and treatment interventions should be specifically focused on the reduction of this risk factor.

Researchers continue to debate the distinctiveness of AS and trait anxiety (Lilienfeld, 1996; McNally, 1996). Lilienfeld et al. (1993) argued that data linking AS to panic may be accounted for by the shared variance between AS and trait anxiety. To address this issue, several of these longitudinal studies have used trait anxiety as a covariate in relevant statistical analyses. Findings across all studies are completely consistent in indicating that the ASI accounts for a significant proportion of the variance even when the effects of trait anxiety were partialed out. Conversely, trait anxiety does not appear to be a predictor of the outcomes of interest. These data are also consistent with experimental studies that have evaluated the incremental validity of AS compared with trait anxiety. For example, Rapee and Medoro (1994) found that AS accounted for variance beyond the effects of trait anxiety in a series of biological challenge studies. In summary, these studies provide further evidence for the uniqueness of AS relative to other anxiety constructs such as trait anxiety (Reiss, 1997).

The observed level of association between AS and panic across studies clearly indicates that there are other factors involved in the pathogenesis of panic. These factors may independently contribute or interact with dispositional variables such as AS to predict the development of panic. Epidemiological reports indicate that gender, age, negative life events, and medical conditions will contribute to the development of anxiety. Biological challenge studies have implicated a variety of contextual parameters that affect fearful responding and the development of panic. There is a growing literature to suggest that cognitive factors—such as predictability, perceived control, and perceived safety—influence anxious responding in both clinical (Carter, Hollon, Carson, & Shelton, 1995; Rapee, Mattick, & Murrell, 1986; Sanderson, Rapee, & Barlow, 1989) and nonclinical populations (Schmidt & Telch, 1994; Telch et al., 1996). Evaluation of other dispositional variables (e.g., sex, medical comorbidity), contextual factors (e.g., perceived control), and their interaction with AS may more fully elucidate the relation between psychological parameters and panic.

These longitudinal studies consistently implicate AS in the psychopathogenicity of panic and strongly suggest that AS is a risk factor instead of merely an epiphenomenon of developing panic. Because cognitive behavioral therapy can significantly reduce AS (Bruce et al., 1995; Schmidt et al., 1997), this offers an exciting possibility for the implementation of a primary prevention intervention that can effectively anticipate and prevent anxiety and panic reactions among high-risk individuals.

ACKNOWLEDGMENTS

This research was supported by USUHS Grant RO72CF. The opinions or assertions contained herein are the private ones of the authors and are not to be construed as official or reflecting the views of the Department of Defense, the Uniformed Services University of the Health Sciences, or the U. S, Air Force Academy.

REFERENCES

Balon, R., Pohl, R., Yerigani, V. K., Rainey, J. M., & Berchou, R. (1988). Follow-up study of control subjects with lactate- and isoproterenol-induced panic attacks. *American Journal of Psychiatry, 145*, 238–241.

Breslau, N., & Davis, G. C. (1993). Migraine, physical health and psychiatric disorder: A prospective epidemiologic study in young adults. *Journal of Psychiatric Research, 27*, 211–221.

Bruce, T. J., Spiegel, D. A., Gregg, S. F., & Nuzzarello, A. (1995). Predictors of alprazolam discontinuation with and without cognitive behavior therapy in panic disorder. *American Journal of Psychiatry, 152*, 1156–1160.

Carter, M. M., Hollon, S. D., Carson, R., & Shelton, R. C. (1995). Effects of a safe person on induced distress following a biological challenge in panic disorder with agoraphobia. *Journal of Abnormal Psychology, 104*, 156–163.

Donnell, C. D., & McNally, R. J. (1990). Anxiety sensitivity and panic attacks in a nonclinical population. *Behaviour Research and Therapy, 28*, 83–85.

Eaton, W. W., & Keyl, P. M. (1990). Risk factors for the onset of diagnostic interview schedule/DSM-III agoraphobia in a prospective, population-based study. *Archives of General Psychiatry, 47*, 819–824.

Ehlers, A. (1995). A 1-year prospective study of panic attacks: Clinical course and factors associated with maintenance. *Journal of Abnormal Psychology, 104*, 164–172.

Faravelli, C., & Pallanti, S. (1989). Recent life events and panic disorder. *American Journal of Psychiatry, 146*, 622–626.

First, M. B., Spitzer, R. L., Gibbon, M., & Williams, J. B. (1994). *Structured clinical interview for DSM-IV Patient Edition (SCID-N/P, Version 2.0)*. New York: Biometrics Research Department.

Harrington, P. H., Schmidt, N. B., & Telch, M. J. (1996). Prospective evaluation of panic potentiation following 35% CO_2 challenge in a nonclinical sample. *American Journal of Psychiatry, 153*, 823–825.

Keyl, P. M., & Eaton, W. W. (1990). Risk factors for the onset of panic disorder and other panic attacks in a prospective, population-based study. *American Journal of Epidemiology, 131*, 301–311.

Lilienfeld, S. O. (1996). Anxiety sensitivity is not distinct from trait anxiety. In R. M. Rapee (Ed.), *Current controversies in the anxiety disorders* (pp. 228–244). New York: Guilford.

Lilienfeld, S. O., Turner, S. M., & Jacob, R. G. (1993). Anxiety sensitivity: An examination of theoretical and methodological issues. *Advances in Behaviour Research and Therapy, 15*, 147–182.

Maller, R. G., & Reiss, S. (1992). Anxiety sensitivity in 1984 and panic attacks in 1987. *Journal of Anxiety Disorders, 6*, 241–247.

McNally, R. J. (1996). Anxiety sensitivity is distinguishable from trait anxiety. In R. M. Rapee (Ed.), *Current controversies in the anxiety disorders* (pp. 214–227). New York: Guilford.

Peterson, R. A., & Reiss, S. (1987). *Test Manual for the Anxiety Sensitivity Index*. Orland Park, IL: International Diagnostic Systems.

Pollard, C. A., Pollard, H. J., & Corn, K. J. (1989). Panic onset and major events in lives of agoraphobics: A test of contiguity. *Journal of Abnormal Psychology, 98*, 318–321.

Rapee, R. M., Mattick, R., & Murrell, E. (1986). Cognitive mediation in the affective component of spontaneous panic attacks. *Journal of Behavior Therapy and Experimental Psychiatry, 17*, 243–253.

Rapee, R. M., & Medoro, L. (1994). Fear of physical sensations and trait anxiety as mediators of the response to hyperventilation in nonclinical subjects. *Journal of Abnormal Psychology, 103*, 693–699.

Reiss, S. (1991). Expectancy model of fear, anxiety, and panic. *Clinical Psychology Review, 11*, 141–153.

Reiss, S. (1997). Trait anxiety: It's not what you think it is. *Journal of Anxiety Disorders, 11*, 201–214.

Reiss, S., & McNally, R. J. (1985). The expectancy model of fear. In S. Reiss & R. R. Bootzin (Eds.), *Theoretical issues in behavior therapy* (pp. 107–121). New York: Academic Press.

Roy-Byrne, P. P., Geraci, M., & Uhde, T. W. (1986). Life events and the onset of panic disorder. *American Journal of Psychiatry, 143*, 1424–1427.

Sanderson, W. C., Rapee, R. M., & Barlow, D. H. (1989). The influence of illusion of control on panic attacks induced by 5.5% carbon dioxide enriched air. *Archives of General Psychiatry, 46*, 157–162.

Schmidt, N. B. (1997). *Anxiety sensitivity predicts anxiety pathology during acute stress: A replication*. Unpublished data, Uniformed Services University of the Health Sciences.

Schmidt, N. B., Lerew, D. R., & Jackson, R. J. (1997). The role of anxiety sensitivity in the pathogenesis of panic: Prospective evaluation of spontaneous panic attacks during acute stress. *Journal of Abnormal Psychology, 106*, 355–364.

Schmidt, N. B., Staab, J. P., Trakowski, J. H., & Sammons, M. (1997). Efficacy of a brief psychosocial treatment for panic disorder in an active duty sample: Implications for military readiness. *Military Medicine, 162,* 123–129.

Schmidt, N. B., & Telch, M. J. (1994). The role of safety information and fear of bodily sensations in moderating responses to a hyperventilation challenge. *Behavior Therapy, 25,* 197–208.

Schmidt, N. B., & Telch, M. J. (1997). Non-psychiatric medical comorbidity, health perceptions and treatment outcome in patients with panic disorder. *Health Psychology, 16,* 114–122.

Spitzer, R. L., Williams, J. B., Gibbon, M., & First, M. B. (1990). *Structured clinical interview for DSM-III-R Non-Patient Edition (SCID-N/P, Version 2.0).* New York: Biometrics Research Department.

Taylor, S., Koch, W. J., & McNally, R. J. (1992). How does anxiety sensitivity vary across the anxiety disorders? *Journal of Anxiety Disorders, 6,* 249–259.

Telch, M. J., Shermis, M. D., & Lucas, J. A. (1989). Anxiety sensitivity: Unitary personality trait or domain-specific appraisals? *Journal of Anxiety Disorders, 3,* 25–32.

Telch, M. J., Silverman, A., & Schmidt, N. B. (1996). The relationship between anxiety sensitivity and perceived control in a caffeine challenge. *Journal of Anxiety Disorders, 10,* 21–35.

Visser, R. A. (1982). *Analysis of longitudinal data in behavioral and social science research: An exploratory survey.* Leiden, The Netherlands: DSWO Press.

Wilson, K. G., Sandler, L. S., Asmundson, G .J. G., Ediger, J. M., Larsen, D. K., & Visser, R. A. (1982). *Analysis of longitudinal data in behavioral and social science research: An exploratory survey.* Leiden, The Netherlands: DSWO Press.

Walker, J. R. (1992). Panic attacks in the nonclinical population: An empirical approach to case identification. *Journal of Abnormal Psychology, 101,* 460–468.

IV

NEW DIRECTIONS IN ANXIETY SENSITIVITY RESEARCH

11

Anxiety Sensitivity in Children

Wendy K. Silverman
Carl F. Weems
Florida International University

Age does not make us childish, as they say. It only finds us true children still.
—Goethe, from *Faust*
[*The First Part. Prelude on the Stage*], 1808–1852

Meaning, other than practical, there is for us none.
—William James, from *Pragmatism*, 1907

That we are contributing a chapter to an edited volume on anxiety sensitivity (AS) is evidence enough for the intense attention that this construct has drawn among researchers and theorists since Reiss and his colleagues first started writing about it not too long ago (Reiss, 1991; Reiss & McNally, 1985; Reiss, Peterson, Gursky, & McNally, 1986). Although there continue to be more questions than answers about AS, the research findings are impressively consistent. They show that adults with high AS, compared with those with low AS, are more likely to respond negatively to challenge procedures and stress tasks (e.g., Shostak & Peterson, 1990) and are more likely to develop either panic attacks, panic disorder, or other anxiety disorders (e.g., Maller & Reiss, 1992; Schmidt, Lerew, & Jackson, 1997; see chaps. 6, 9, and 10). These findings are all the more amazing when one considers that they have been obtained across different research laboratories, sampling different populations, and using different methodologies. One would be hard-pressed to identify another psychological construct in adult anxiety psychopathology research (and perhaps in all adult psychopathology research) that has proved so promising in the prediction of pathology.

However, unlike the intensity with which AS has been studied in adults, the construct has been relatively understudied in children. At the time of writing this chapter, we could identify no more than 16 research articles on child psychopathology in which AS was either the prime focus of investigation or assessed as an additional variable. The discrepancy in the amount of attention paid to AS in adults versus children partly reflects the greater attention paid to all adult psychological and psychiatric disorders relative to the amount paid to child disorders. That there exists a long history in psychology and psychiatry in which insufficient attention was paid to childhood problems is nothing new and comes as no surprise. This history is in part a reflection of the general societal attitudes of the times regarding children and the nature of childhood (e.g., children are like miniature adults, children should be seen but not heard, childhood problems are fleeting and transitory phenomena).

Fortunately, children (and childhood) are no longer being ignored. Whether the reason for the increased attention to children is due to political expedience (i.e., it is good policy to show one's concern about children) or genuine understanding of and appreciation for children and childhood, we do not attempt to analyze here. The fact is that we currently hear policymakers speak frequently about their concerns about children (and families). Moreover, professional and academic specializations in child clinical psychology, child psychiatry, child development, developmental psychopathology, etc., have fully come into their own.

If general apathy toward children and the problems of childhood does not completely account for the relatively small amount of attention paid to AS in children, what else might? There probably were two main things operating in the years past that might help account for it. One pertains to the considerable controversy stirred by the construct of AS among adult anxiety researchers. The second pertains to the considerable controversy stirred among child anxiety researchers by the *DSM–III*'s classification of anxiety disorders.

The other chapters in this volume cover the first controversy, which was largely elicited by Lilienfeld et al. (1989, 1993) questions about whether AS is distinguishable from trait anxiety. The subsequent burgeon of research that Lilienfeld's criticisms evoked helped tremendously in yielding additional, high-quality empirical evidence for the construct of AS, including a clarification of its nature and structure. While all this work was ongoing, we believe that many researchers and theorists with interests in childhood anxiety were sitting on the sidelines, waiting to see how the dust would settle. "Why get started with this construct with children if it turned out not to pan out with adults?" probably sums up the general sentiment of many child anxiety investigators at the time that the adult AS controversy and debate were in progress.

Moreover, investigators with interests in child anxiety had their own set of controversies and debates going on that were keeping them well occupied and, thus, distracting them from becoming too involved with the construct of AS. Keep in mind that the systematic study of anxiety disorders in youth got underway only when it was introduced as a main category of child and adolescent disorders in the *DSM–III* (American Psychiatric Association, 1980). Recall, too, that in *DSM–II* there was only one specific childhood anxiety category, referred to as *Overanxious Reaction*. *DSM–III* introduced and *DSM–III–R* retained a new, broad category entitled *Anxiety Disorders of Childhood and Adolescence*. Within this category, three subcategories were introduced: (a) Separation Anxiety Disorder, (b) Overanxious Disorder, and (c) Avoidant Disorder. In addition to these childhood disorders, children could receive, as appropriate, diagnoses of other anxiety disorders classified under the adult disorders, with identical criteria being used for children and adults.

Early critical essays (e.g., Achenbach, 1980; Rutter & Shaffer, 1980) charged that the majority of the new *DSM–III* childhood categories and sub-categories, including those relating to the anxiety disorders, were overrefined, untested, and excessive in number. The essays also charged that the evidence for using similar diagnostic criteria for children and adults flies in the face of what is known about development.

These were serious charges, and investigators with interests in childhood anxiety were thus faced with the challenge of providing empirical data that would either support or refute the charges. Accordingly, investigators devoted a great deal of time and energy in attempting to show that the most basic requirements of a taxonomy, such as reliability, coverage, descriptive validity, and predictive validity (Blashfield & Draguns, 1976), could be met with the *DSM–III*, and its successor, *DSM–III–R*. In light of the enormity of this task, interesting theoretical issues about anxiety, such as the role of AS, were put on the back burner as researchers set out to answer more basic, descriptive questions such as the following: Can anxiety disorders in children be reliably diagnosed? Do diagnostic criteria for adult disorders (e.g., criteria for panic disorder) apply to children? Are some of the subcategories, such as Overanx-ious Disorder, even worth having as separate childhood diagnostic entities?

As the data pertinent to these and other questions came in, the realization set in that there was merit to some of the early charges that had been launched against the *DSM–III*. For example, reliability of anxiety diagnoses was indeed poor (see Silverman, 1991, 1994). This spurred concentrated efforts at developing and evaluating structured interviewing procedures as ways of improving diagnostic reliability (e.g., Herjanic & Reich, 1982; Rapee, Barrett, Dadds, & Evans, 1994; Silverman & Eisen, 1992; Silverman & Nelles, 1988; Silverman & Rabian, 1995).

It was speculated that children could not even experience the phenomenon of panic because children were viewed as being too cognitively underdeveloped to be capable of making the interpretations and attributions needed for the panic experience (Nelles & Barlow, 1988). Reviews of studies on panic attacks in early adolescence revealed that this literature contained numerous and profound methodological limitations(see Kearney & Silverman, 1992). Moreover, at the time, there were virtually no studies of panic in children. Thus, to draw any conclusions about panic in children and adolescents would have been premature. All this spurred increased efforts to study the phenomenology and prevalence of panic attacks and panic disorder in youth (e.g., Bradley & Hood, 1993; Kearney, Albano, Eisen, Allan, & Barlow, 1997).

Relatedly, problems with coverage and discriminant validity emerged with respect to some of the childhood anxiety disorders subcategories as described in *DSM–III* and *DSM–III–R*. For example, with respect to Overanxious Disorder, research showed that not only did the reliability of diagnoses of Overanxious Disorder vary considerably across studies, but high prevalence rates of Overanxious Disorder in epidemiological studies suggested that the threshold (i.e., the number of symptoms required to be present to receive the diagnosis) was too low. Because of the nonspecific nature of its symptoms, Overanxious Disorder was found to be too frequently co-occurring or too highly comorbid with other *DSM* disorders (Silverman, 1992; Werry, 1991).

The upshot of these findings was that dramatic changes were made in the *DSM–IV*, which was published by the American Psychiatric Association in 1994. Specifically, the broad category, *Anxiety Disorders of Childhood and Adolescence*, as well as its subcategories (Overanxious Disorder and Avoidant Disorder), that had appeared in *DSM–III* and *DSM–III–R* were eliminated. Only one subcategory, Separation Anxiety Disorder, continued to be listed as a distinct child anxiety disorder subcategory, appearing under the broad category *Other Disorders of Childhood and Adolescence* (American Psychiatric Association, 1994). Thus, with the exception of Separation Anxiety Disorder, the same set of diagnostic criteria and subcategories of anxiety disorders are currently applicable for children and adults in *DSM–IV*.

The reader should not infer from this ending that all went completely happily ever after. *DSM–IV* decisions regarding some anxiety disorders in children were made in the absence of hard empirical data (Silverman, 1993; Spence, 1997).

More work is needed to develop and evaluate methods for reliably making *DSM–IV* diagnoses (e.g., Silverman & Albano, 1996). Nevertheless, the main aim in relaying this history is to help the reader appreciate why a construct as intriguing as AS was insufficiently investigated by child anxiety researchers during the past decade, especially in light of the flurry of activity among adult anxiety researchers. It largely had to do, we believe, with the controversies that were ongoing about the construct in the adult area, coupled with the controversies that were ongoing about the DSM classification of anxiety disorders in children. The former kept researchers wary about examining the construct in children until the issues were better sorted out with adults; the latter kept researchers preoccupied with matters that appeared to be more pressing at the time.

WHERE DO THINGS STAND NOW?

We noted in the preceding paragraph that complete satisfaction about how to classify anxiety disorders in children did not come with *DSM–IV* and that work lies ahead to show that *DSM–IV* diagnoses can be made as reliably as *DSM–III–R* diagnoses via structured diagnostic interviewing procedures. Although work in these areas is needed, we think it is equally important (and timely) for researchers to turn their attention toward improving our understanding about the nature of anxiety in children, including its etiology, maintenance, treatment, and prevention. Indeed, researchers have begun to shift their attention in this direction, as suggested by recent research such as that conducted on behavioral inhibition (e.g., Kagan, 1989), attachment (e.g., Manassis & Bradley, 1994), family processes (Dadds, Barrett, Rapee, & Ryan, 1996), and cognitive-behavioral treatments (e.g., Kendall, 1994; Silverman & Kurtines, 1996) and prevention programs (Dadds, Spence, Holland, Barrett, & Laurens, 1997). However, even more progress can be made in furthering knowledge about etiology, maintenance, treatment, and prevention of anxiety disorders in children if eyes turn toward AS—as a construct in and of itself—and as a construct in relation to these other areas of study (e.g., behavioral inhibition, attachment). More is said on this later.

The two quotes cited in the beginning of this chapter sum up our main reasons for believing that AS may be potentially important for child anxiety researchers to study, and why it deserves to be studied. The quote by Goethe speaks to a developmental perspective and the growing evidence that, despite the differences that exist between anxiety as manifested by children and adults, there also appears to be a great deal of overlap (see Silverman, 1993). That is, much of what we see in anxious adults is seen in anxious children (including elevated AS). Even more similarities are likely to be seen (e.g., AS as a predictor of anxiety and panic disorder in youth)—if we look.

The quote by James speaks to a pragmatic perspective and the growing recognition among investigators and practitioners that, despite the utility of holding a particular theoretical perspective (and embracing its constructs, concepts, etc.), there also is utility in recognizing that all types of knowledge (i.e., other theoretical perspectives and their constructs and concepts, such as AS) may have practical significance or importance (Silverman & Kurtines, 1996, 1997). That is, if we find AS to operate in a similar fashion in children as it operates in adults (e.g., as a risk factor for panic disorder), this is important knowledge that has potential practical relevance (e.g., designing prevention programs). This knowledge is important regardless of what one's theoretical perspective may be—if we are willing to look at it as such.

Thus, the two interwoven themes of this chapter are that (a) similarities exist between AS in children and adults and this construct has the potential to inform us about the nature of anxiety disorders in children and adults (e.g., etiology); and (b) AS is thereby a construct that is likely to have practical significance for all researchers and practitioners with interests in anxiety and its disorders. We hastily add, however, that we have drawn these two themes more from our looking to the future rather than from our looking to the past (which, as noted, contains only a relatively small amount of research). Nevertheless, this chapter shows how these themes make sense in light of the research that has been conducted to date and if the same type of trajectory occurs with respect to future research findings. Although the latter remains an *if*, our hope is that the present chapter serves to stimulate research that will provide empirical evidence to thereby obliterate this as an *if*.

Before we begin summarizing the research on AS in children, we provide background information about two important issues. The first concerns the epidemiology and course of anxiety disorders in children. The second concerns the tenets of developmental psychopathology.

EPIDEMIOLOGY AND COURSE

Published epidemiological studies vary considerably in their estimates of the prevalence of childhood anxiety disorders. This is likely due to the studies' methodological differences (e.g., differences in the types of informants used, assessment method, sample, age of participants, specific disorder assessed, and whether an impairment index was included as part of the definition; see Silverman & Ginsburg, 1998, for details). Also, few studies sampled ethnically diverse populations. Keeping these methodological differences and sampling limitations in mind, the literature to date suggests that the most prevalent disorders are Overanxious/Generalized Anxiety Disorder, Separation Anxiety Disorder, and Specific Phobia and that, overall, anxiety disorders in children are highly prevalent in children and adolescents, with overall estimates ranging from 5% to 12% (e.g., Anderson, Williams, McGee, & Silva, 1987; Fergusson, Horwood, & Lynskey, 1993; see also Silverman & Ginsburg, 1998, for a review).

With respect to the course of anxiety disorders in children, research on the retrospective reports of anxiety-disordered adults reveals that most anxiety disorders have an onset in childhood or adolescence (see Silverman & Ginsburg, 1998, for a review). To illustrate, Pollack et al. (1997) examined the relation between childhood anxiety and adult panic disorder in a clinical sample of 194 panic-disordered adults. Pollack et al. found that 54% of participants had a history of childhood anxiety disorders. Further, adults with a history of childhood anxiety disorders, compared with adults without childhood anxiety disorders, had higher rates of comorbid anxiety disorders in adulthood.

Unfortunately, there have been few longitudinal studies of the course or stability of anxiety disorders in youth (Ollendick & King, 1994). Findings to date (based on *DSM–III* and *DSM–III–R*) are inconsistent probably because of the same methodological differences noted for epidemiological studies (e.g., informant, sample). Also, the amount of time that passed between initial evaluation and follow-up differed across studies and, again, few studies sampled ethnically diverse populations. Keeping these methodological differences and sampling limitations in mind, the literature shows that approximately 4.3% to 68% of anxiety disorders diagnosed in childhood are stable over time and that, for many children, anxiety disorders are chronic (e.g., Keller et al., 1992; Last, Hansen, & Franco, 1997; Last, Perrin, Hersen, & Kazdin, 1996; March, Leonard, & Swedo, 1995).

TENETS OF DEVELOPMENTAL PSYCHOPATHOLOGY

Although this chapter has as its primary focus the single construct of AS, it is important to keep in mind that AS is just that—a single construct. Recall, however, that AS was, and continues to be, conceptualized as a construct that operates within Reiss' broader expectancy model, along with other constructs or variables (Reiss, 1991; also see chaps. 2 and 3). In this frame, it is important to consider AS within an even broader context involving a host of other constructs or variables.

Considering a broad context of variables—to take a big picture perspective—is an important tenet of developmental psychopathology (Lewis & Miller, 1990; Silverman & Ollendick, in press). This tenet states that the same end-state (e.g., pathological anxiety) may be reached from different initial conditions and through different processes (i.e., *equifinality*; Cicchetti & Rogosch, 1996). It also states that a particular adverse condition (e.g., high AS) may not necessarily lead to the same outcome (e.g., pathological anxiety) in every individual (i.e., *multifinality*; Cicchetti & Rogosch, 1996). The concepts of *equifinality* and *multifinality* serve to remind us that the development of psychopathological conditions, including anxiety disorders, is complex, not simple; the causes are multivariate, not univariate. An important challenge for researchers is to disentangle the thorny relations among AS and other risk factors (e.g., behavioral inhibition, patterns of attachment) in an effort to improve our understanding about the development and prediction of pathological anxiety.

RESEARCH ON ANXIETY SENSITIVITY IN CHILDREN

The Childhood AS Index (CASI; Silverman, Fleisig, Rabian, & Peterson, 1991) is the main research instrument for assessing AS in youth. This section reviews studies using and evaluating this scale. The section is divided into three parts. The first section describes the development of the CASI and reviews studies of its factor structure and incremental validity. The second section reviews research on the CASI's ability to discriminate among diagnostic groups and predict panic attacks. This section also examines the relationship between the CASI and measures of depression and worry. The third section reviews the use of the CASI in treatment outcome research.

The CASI: Development, Factor Structure, and Incremental Validity

Development. To study AS in children and adolescents, it was necessary to develop a suitable measure. The CASI was developed by Silverman and colleagues (1991) as a down-scaled version of the Adult Anxiety Sensitivity index (ASI; Peterson & Reiss, 1987). Designed for use with school-age children (ages 6–17 years), the CASI is an 18-item self-rating scale that requires children to rate their fear of anxiety-related sensations. The CASI assesses fears of the same types of anxiety-related sensations that are assessed in the ASI. The CASI uses a 3-point scale (*none* = 1, *some* = 2, *a lot* = 3), which is the same scale that Ollendick (1983) used in his revision of the Fear Survey Schedule for Children (FSSC–R). The CASI uses this scale because Ollendick found it was readily understood by children as young as 7 years. CASI total scores range from 18 to 54. CASI items and instructions are presented in Table 11.1.

TABLE 11.1
Childhood Anxiety Sensitivity Index

Directions: A number of statements that boys and girls use to describe themselves are given below. Read each statement carefully and put an X in the box in front of the words that describe you. There are no right or wrong answers. Remember find the words that best describe you.

1. I don't want other people to know when I feel afraid.	——None	——Some	——A lot
2. When I cannot keep my mind on my schoolwork, I worry that I might be going crazy.	——None	——Some	——A lot
3. It scares me when I feel "shaky."	——None	——Some	——A lot
4. It scares me when I feel like I am going to faint.	——None	——Some	——A lot
5. It is important for me to stay in control of my feelings.	——None	——Some	——A lot
6. It scares me when my heart beats fast.	——None	——Some	——A lot
7. It embarrasses me when my stomach growls (makes noise).	——None	——Some	——A lot
8. It scares me when I feel like I am going to throw up.	——None	——Some	——A lot
9. When I notice that my heart is beating fast, I worry that there might be something wrong with me.	——None	——Some	——A lot
10. It scares me when I have trouble getting my breath.	——None	——Some	——A lot
11. When my stomach hurts, I worry that I might be really sick.	——None	——Some	——A lot
12. It scares me when I can't keep my mind on my schoolwork.	——None	——Some	——A lot
13. Other kids can tell when I feel shaky.	——None	——Some	——A lot
14. Unusual feelings in my body scare me.	——None	——Some	——A lot
15. When I am afraid, I worry that I might be crazy.	——None	——Some	——A lot
16. It scares me when I feel nervous.	——None	——Some	——A lot
17. I don't like to let my feelings show.	——None	——Some	——A lot
18. Funny feelings in my body scare me.	——None	——Some	——A lot

In the initial evaluation study, Silverman et al. (1991) administered the CASI to a nonclinical sample of school-age children ($n = 72$; mean age = 13.3 years) and a small clinical sample ($n = 33$; mean age = 10.6 years). Internal consistency as measured by Cronbach's alpha was .87 for both samples, which is similar to the internal consistency of the ASI (Peterson & Reiss, 1987). Test–retest reliability was assessed by readministering the CASI after a 2-week interval. Test–retest correlations were .76 for the clinical sample and .79 for the non-clinical sample. The CASI's incremental validity was assessed by determining the proportion of additional variance it accounted for in the FSSC–R after scores on the Child Anxiety Frequency Checklist (CAFC) had been entered into the regression equation. The CASI, but not the CAFC, significantly predicted scores on the FSSC–R. The CASI accounted for an additional 48% and 35% of variance in the non-clinical and clinical samples, respectively. In all, the results of Silverman et al. provided strong initial support for the reliability and validity of the CASI similar to that of the ASI. Recently, Sandin (1997) developed a Spanish version of the CASI, which has been shown to have similar psychometric properties to the English-language version.

Factor Structure.   Chapter 5 in this volume provides an excellent sum-mary of the factor analytic studies of the ASI, as well as the controversies. In essence, some advocated a unidimensional model (e.g., Taylor, Koch, McNally, & Crockett, 1992) as originally defined by Reiss and colleagues (1986), whereas others advocated a multidimensional model of four orthogonal factors (e.g., Peterson & Heilbronner, 1987; Telch, Shermis, & Lucas, 1989). Between these two models was a third model, which described a multidimensional structure of three or four oblique factors with substantial factor intercorrela-tions. That model can be viewed as solving the controversy between the advocates of the first two because the oblique structure points to a single, higher order factor. Cox, Parker, and Swinson (1996) tested the proposed models by using confirmatory factor analysis. They found strong support for the third model with four oblique factors. Lilienfeld et al. (1993) and Zinbarg, Barlow, and Brown (1997) have since advocated a hierarchical version of that model: It consists of three correlated first-order factors that load on a single higher order factor (see also chap. 15). However, the main function of the higher order factor is to affirm the oblique structure of the three-factor solution, therefore the hierarchical and oblique multidimensional structure model may be seen as the same general model.

With these thoughts in mind, the first author, along with Drs. Golda Ginsburg and Arnold Goedhart, has begun to develop and test various factor models of the CASI. The findings are as yet unpublished because they are literally "hot off the computer print-out" at the time of writing this chapter. Although tentative, we think the findings are useful to share with the reader because they provide a picture of what the CASI's factor structure is emerging to look like. As a consequence, they have the potential to spur further inquiry and analyses by other investigators.

The findings are based on two samples. The patient sample consisted of 248 anxiety-disordered children (ages 7–16) who presented to the Child Anxiety and Phobia Program, which is housed in the Child and Family Psychosocial Research Center at Florida International University, Miami, Florida. The nonpatient sample consisted of an unselected group of 250 children (ages 7–12) enrolled in a public elementary school in Miami.

Data from the patient sample were used to develop and select the factor models. Principal components analysis of the CASI items was used to extract solutions consisting of two, three, and four factors. Factors were rotated using an oblique (Oblimin) transformation. As expected (Gorsuch, 1983), results were similar to those obtained from an orthogonal (Varimax) rotation. The three-factor oblique solution for the CASI was similar to the three-factor ASI solution reported by Zinbarg and colleagues (see chap. 5). Using data from the patient sample, the oblique factor models were then subjected to confirmatory factor analyses (CFA) using LISREL 7.16 (Jöreskog & Sörbom, 1989). The purpose of the CFA was to evaluate and improve the goodness-of-fit. Fit was improved with the aid of model modification indexes (Jöreskog & Sörbom, 1989). We also tested the goodness-of-fit of a CASI model that was based on Peterson and Heilbronner's (1987) four-factor oblique solution for the ASI. In addition, a unifactorial model was also tested to see whether the multifactor models provided a better fit to the data.

Goodness-of-fit was assessed by the following indexes: the χ^2 statistic, the goodness-of-fit index (GFI), the adjusted goodness-of-fit index (AGFI), and the root mean square residual (RMS). To facilitate interpretation of the χ^2 statistics we used Mueller's (1996) rule of thumb, in which adequate fit is indicated when $\chi^2 (< 2)$. For the other goodness-of-fit indexes, adequate fit is indicated by GFI .90, AGFI .85, and RMS .08. These criteria are between the more lenient ones used by Cox et al. (1996) and the stronger ones used by Zinbarg et al. (1997).

To assess the replicability of the results, factor models derived from the patient sample were tested on data from the nonpatient sample. Models were considered to be successfully replicated if they had an acceptable goodness-of-fit in both samples. Such models were then compared to one another by testing the significance of the difference between chi square statistics (this difference score is a chi square statistic). Finally, for the best fitting model, we computed Cronbach's alpha for each factor and the intercorrelations among factors.

What were our main findings? For data from the patient sample, only the oblique multifactor models passed the goodness-of-fit criteria. The oblique two-factor model met all of these criteria: $\chi^2(134)= 253.31, p<.001; \chi^2 = 1.890$; GFI = .901; AGFI = .874; RMS = .040. The oblique three-factor model also met all criteria: $\chi^2(130)= 186.42$' $p < .001$; $\chi^2 = 1.434$; GFI = .903; AGFI = .872; RMS = .039. The oblique four-factor model, derived from Peterson and Heilbronner (1987), met criteria for some fit indexes: $\chi^2(129) = 204.16$, $p < .001; \chi^2 = 1.583$; RMS = .043. However, it failed to meet criteria for the GFI (.890) and the AGFI (.845). The oblique four-factor model (derived from the CASI exploratory factor analysis) met all criteria: $\chi^2(129) = 150.68, p < .093$ (n.s.); $\chi^2 = 1.168$; GFI = .919; AGFI = .893; RMS = .033. The unidimensional model failed to meet criteria for adequate goodness-of-fit: $\chi^2(132)= 305.01, p < .0001; \chi^2 = 2.259$; GFI = .879; AGFI = .846; RMS = .043.

These results lead us to select the oblique factor models (all derived from the CASI exploratory factor analyses) for the replication analyses using data from the nonpatient sample. The oblique three-factor model met all goodness-of-fit criteria: $\chi^2(132) = 248.16$, $p < .0001$; $\chi^2 = 1.880$; GFI = .904; AGFI = .876; RMS = .039. The three factors were labeled *Physical Concerns, Mental Incapacitation Concerns,* and *Social Concerns.* For each factor, we computed factor scores by summing the scores of all items having a salient loading on the factor. Product-moment correlations between these factors are shown in Table 11.2.

The oblique four-factor model also met all goodness-of-fit criteria: $\chi^2(129) = 222.16, p < .0001$; $\chi^2 = 1.722$; GFI = .913; AGFI = .884; RMS = .035. The first three of the four factors resembled the factors of the three-factor model

TABLE 11.2
Product-Moment Correlations Among the Three Factor Scales
of the Childhood Anxiety Sensitivity Index

Factor Scales	1	2	3
1. Physical Concerns	—	.64	.63
2. Incapacitation Concerns	.59	—	.45
3. Social Concerns	.56	.50	—

Note. Patients below the diagonal and nonpatients above. For all correlations, $p < .01$.

and may be given the same names: Physical Concerns, Mental Incapacitation Concerns, and Social Concerns. The fourth factor may be called *Control*. The oblique three- and four-factor models were compared by assessing the significance of the difference in the goodness-of-fit chi-squares, with the difference in degrees of freedom as the degree of freedom (Jöreskog & Sörbom, 1989). The four-factor model was found to offer a better fit than the three-factor solution; the difference in the chi-squares was $5 = 22.10, p < .01$.

Cronbach's alpha for the factor scales three-factor model ranged from .62 to .85 for both the patient and nonpatient samples. Using the usual cutoff of .60, these results indicate acceptable internal consistency. In comparison, for the four-factor model, the Control factor scale had an alpha of only .33 in the nonpatient sample. Our results, in conjunction with the fact that the Control scale was composed of only two items, led us to prefer the three-factor model above the four-factor model.

Incremental Validity. The findings reviewed so far make it plain that the CASI appears to operate in a very similar manner with children as the ASI does with adults. The initial study on the development of the CASI had virtually identical patterns of results as those found in the initial studies on the ASI— in terms of internal consistency estimates, retest reliability estimates, and amount of variance accounted for in fear inventory scores. In addition, the factor structure that is beginning to emerge looks very much like the oblique multidimensional structure model of Cox et al. (1996) and the hierarchical model of Zinbarg et al. (1997).

However, the construct of AS has been questioned on the basis of parsimony (Lilienfeld et al., 1989). Hence, it has been argued that measures of AS should not just correlate with measures of fear or panic symptoms, but should also make predictions that existing measures of anxiety do not. That is, AS measures should display incremental validity. Numerous studies have now documented the incremental validity of the ASI. What about the CASI?

Chorpita, Albano, and Barlow (1996) examined the incremental validity of the CASI with 112 clinic-referred children and adolescents diagnosed with anxiety disorders. Chorpita et al. hypothesized that the incremental validity of AS would be weaker in young children because young children lack the ability to make "the attributions that are integral to the AS process" (p.78). Using product-term multiple regression with age as a continuous moderator, the authors reported that the CASI lost incremental validity as age decreased in a curvilinear fashion. Specifically, with trait anxiety as the criterion variable, the CASI-by-age[2] interaction was found to account for significant variance beyond that predicted by the Physiological factor subscale of the Revised Children's Manifest Anxiety Scale (RCMAS; Reynolds & Richmond, 1978), CASI scores, age, CASI-by-age interaction, and age^2. Also with trait anxiety as the criterion variable, the CASI-by-age^2 interaction was found to account for significant variance beyond that predicted by the Fear Survey Schedule for Children-Revised (FSSC–R), CASI scores, age, CASI-by-age interaction, and age^2. (Trait anxiety was measured by the Trait version of the State–Trait Anxiety Inventory for Children, STAIC–T; Spielberger, 1973.)

Chorpita et al. (1996) also performed hierarchical multiple linear regression, dividing their sample into two groups. The first group consisted of children ages 7 to 11 (n = 43) and the second group consisted of adolescents aged 12 to 17 (n = 69). Trait anxiety was the criterion variable. The predictors were the Physiological subscale of the RCMAS (i.e., the RCMAS–P), the Fear Survey Schedule for Children–Revised (FSSC–R), and the CASI. Chorpita et al. found that adding the CASI to separate regression equations (containing either the RCMAS–P or FSSC–R) only accounted for a significant amount of variance in trait anxiety for the older group of children. The authors concluded that the incremental validity of the CASI drops around ages 11 to 12; thus, measuring AS in children may not be useful.

Before embracing the conclusions drawn by Chorpita et al. (1996), the study's conceptual basis and its methodology warrant closer attention. Chorpita et al. proposed that only children over the age of 12 are capable of making the attributions necessary for AS. Thus, they concluded that "it appears that the existence of AS, as measured by the CASI, is not supported in children under 12 years" (p. 81). Yet AS is conceptually thought of as beliefs about the consequences of anxiety symptoms, not as attributions about what brought these symptoms about (see McNally, 1989; Reiss, 1991). Further, the Chorpita et al. (1996) findings were based on a fairly small sample of younger children (n = 43). In addition, trait anxiety was used as the criterion variable when, actually, to examine the issue of the CASI's incremental validity, trait anxiety should be used as a predictor variable (along with AS), with FSSC–R scores used as the criterion variable. This would be more in line with how investigators have examined the incremental validity of the ASI (e.g., Reiss et al. 1986).

With the conceptual and methodological limitations of the Chorpita et al. study in mind, Weems, Hammond-Laurence, Silverman, and Ginsburg (1998) tested the incremental validity of the CASI in a larger sample of young children (n =202) and adolescents (n = 78). Weems et al. investigated whether the CASI could account for variance in fears beyond that accounted for by trait anxiety and anxiety frequency in both younger and older children. Weems et al. found that the CASI predicted unique variance in fears for both children ages 6 to 11 and those ages 12 to 17. Specifically, regression analyses using the FSSC–R as the dependent variable and the STAIC–T, anxiety symptom frequency (CAFC), and the CASI as predictors produced significant increases in R^2 when the CASI was added into the equation for both age groups. These results suggest that the CASI can be validly used with younger groups of children and that the CASI measures something distinct from anxiety (i.e., AS) in both younger and older children. Further, the CASI was tested against both the FSSC–R and the RCMAS-P in the prediction of STAIC–T scores, as in the Chorpita et al. (1996) study. Weems et al. found that the CASI predicted variance beyond both measures for each age group.

Weems et al. (1998) also found that the incremental validity of the CASI did not seem to drop off with age in a linear or curvilinear fashion as suggested by Chorpita et al. (1996). Because AS is thought of as a pathological process and an individual difference variable (Reiss, 1991), its development in children may not perfectly correspond with normal development. That is, the development of AS may not be a normal developmental process, and so studies that attempt to correlate the ability for AS beliefs simply with age are likely to be indexing a tenuous relation. More detailed analyses in terms of cognitive processing, the child's experience with the consequences of anxiety, and/or the child's negative affective states, all in relation to AS, are needed if a full understanding of the development of AS in children is to be realized.

At this juncture, like the ASI, the evidence strongly suggests that the CASI shows good incremental validity in both children and adolescents. This is important news for anyone interested in assessing AS in children using the CASI.

Examining the CASI in Relation to Panic, Depression, and Worry

Based on the conceptualizations of AS and findings in the adult literature (see Taylor 1995a, 1995b), measures of AS should distinguish children with anxiety disorders from children with no anxiety disorders; they also should distinguish children with panic disorder from children with other anxiety disorders. Rabian, Peterson, Richters, and Jensen (1993) provided an initial examination of CASI scores among children meeting diagnostic criteria for anxiety disorders, children with externalizing disorder diagnoses, and children who did not meet diagnostic criteria for any psychological disorder. Rabian et al. found the mean CASI scores were highest for children with anxiety disorder diagnoses ($n = 18$;

$M = 30.56$), next for children with externalizing disorder diagnoses ($n = 31$; $M = 28.84$), and lowest for children who did not meet criteria for any diagnosis ($n = 62$; $M = 26.40$). Mean CASI scores were significantly different in pairwise comparisons between the children with anxiety disorder diagnoses versus the children with no disorders. Although somewhat disappointing that the CASI did not significantly distinguish children with anxiety disorder diagnoses from the children with externalizing disorder diagnoses, Rabian et al. noted that this was probably because comorbid diagnoses were not considered in their study. That is, children with anxiety disorder diagnoses were likely to have had comorbid diagnoses of externalizing problems and children with externalizing diagnoses were also likely to have had comorbid diagnoses of anxiety problems. This might explain why no differences were observed between these two groups.

In a study of biased attention in childhood anxiety disorders, Vasey, Daleiden, Williams, and Brown (1995) also found significant differences in mean CASI scores between children meeting diagnostic criteria for anxiety disorders ($n = 12$; $M = 32.4$) and control subjects (matched on age, gender, and intellectual ability) who did not meet diagnostic criteria for a psychological disorder ($n = 12$; $M = 26.0$). Scores on the RCMAS and STAIC–T did not distinguish the two groups. Unfortunately, CASI scores were not examined in relation to the children's performance on the probe-detection task (which measured detection latency toward threat words).

Kearney, Albano, Eisen, Allan, and Barlow (1997) recently found that the CASI distinguished children meeting criteria for panic disorder from children with other anxiety disorders. Kearney et al. (1997) compared children meeting criteria for panic disorder ($n = 20$) with children meeting diagnostic criteria for other anxiety disorders ($n = 20$) on several self-report measures of fear, anxiety, and related variables, including the CASI. CASI scores alone discriminated significantly between the groups (panic disorder: CASI $M = 34.54$; nonpanic anxiety disorder: CASI $M = 28.32$). These results suggest that the CASI differentiates samples of children in a theoretically consistent manner.

In terms of the prediction of panic attacks and panic disorder, several lines of research illustrate the potential utility of the CASI. Lau, Calamari, and Waraczynski (1996) used the CASI to examine the relation between AS and panic symptoms. The latter were measured by the Panic Attack Questionnaire (PAQ; Norton, Dorward, & Cox, 1986). Participants consisted of a community sample of high school adolescents ($N = 77$, age $M = 16.7$ years). Lau et al. found a significant correlation between CASI scores and total number of panic symptoms reported on the PAQ ($r = .42$, $p < .0005$). The CASI was also correlated with other variables assessed by the PAQ, such as the number of panic attacks in the past year and past month, the amount of distress caused by the attacks, and the perceived seriousness of the attacks. Lau et al. also categorized their participants as either *panickers* or *nonpanickers* based on their responses on the PAQ. The mean CASI score for panickers ($n = 30$, $M = 32.20$) was significantly greater than that of nonpanickers ($n = 47$, $M = 27.66$). The Lau et al. study is important because it represents the first attempt to determine whether AS (as assessed by the CASI) predicts panic in youth.

Thus far, the results obtained with the CASI mirror those obtained with the ASI in terms of the ability to distinguish among relevant diagnostic groups. It is now important that researchers begin to conduct behavioral validation studies. Of particular interest is whether a similar pattern of relations between AS and negative emotional responses to stressful tasks, as have been found with adults (see chap. 9), will be found with children.

Unnewehr, Schneider, Margraf, Jenkins, and Forin (1996) recently conducted such a study using another index to assess AS in children, indicating that the CASI was "not yet available at the time of the investigation" (p. 495). Unnewehr et al. constructed a measure of "fear of physical symptoms" (p. 495) for their investigation of children's reactions to exposure to internal and external stimuli. This measure asked children to rate, on a 5-point scale, their degree of fear of the physical symptoms of anxiety. Participants ages 7 to 15 represented three groups. The first group ($n = 27$) was offspring of patients receiving treatment for panic disorder. The second group ($n = 21$) was offspring of patients receiving treatment for animal phobia. The third group ($n = 29$) was offspring of parents who were not in treatment (normal controls). Participants completed two fear-evoking tasks: exposure to a spider and a hyperventilation task. Children who initially reported at least moderate levels of fear of physical symptoms reacted to the hyperventilation task with higher levels of self-reported anxiety, as compared to children with low levels of fear of physical symptoms. For example, they scored significantly higher immediately post-task on the state version of the State–Trait Anxiety Inventory for Children (STAIC). They also were more likely to prematurely terminate the task. These findings suggest that, as with adults, elevated AS may predispose children to react to anxiety sensations in a negative manner and thus illustrates the potential for the construct of AS in predicting negative reactions to anxiety in children.

Another study examining the relation between AS and negative responses to anxiety was conducted recently by Mattis and Ollendick (1997). They investigated cognitive responses to the physical symptoms of panic in a sample of nonreferred third, sixth, and ninth graders. Children listened to a tape describing a panic attack and were asked to imagine that they were experiencing the condition described on the tape. Compared with sixth and ninth graders, children in third grade reported less sophisticated responses to questions regarding panic attacks. (Sophistication was rated in terms of developmental categories of the explanations for panic attacks using the Conceptions of Illness Questionnaire, administered as an interview.) However, among third,- sixth-, and ninth-grade children, no age differences were found in the nature of the internal attributions (e.g., "I'd think I was scared or nervous") or external attributions (e.g., "I'd think I was feeling that way because of the temperature or weather") about the cause of panic attacks, as measured by the Panic Attributional Checklist designed for the study. In other words, there was no difference across grade level in terms of the internal–external nature of attributions for panic attacks.

Most relevant to this chapter was Mattis and Ollendick's (1997) finding that only the children's CASI scores predicted their tendencies to make internal catastrophic attributions (e.g., thoughts of going crazy, losing control, or dying). In terms of the prediction of panic, Mattis and Ollendick concluded that children of all ages were more likely to make internal attributions relative to external attributions, speculating that, "it is possible that high levels of AS and elevated internal attributions in response to negative outcomes set the stage for the development of panic attacks and subsequent panic disorder" (p. 55).

These findings suggest that even if AS were developmentally dependent on the capacity for making internal attributions (Chorpita et al., 1996), children in third grade would be capable of displaying individual differences in AS (the mean age of third graders in Mattis & Ollendick's study was 8.59 years). The findings further suggest that AS in children is not dependent on internal attributions, as Chorpita et al. (1996) suggested. Rather, AS—the belief about the negative consequences of anxious symptoms, in combination with children's internal attributions—influences the later development of panic and other anxiety disorders.

In addition to investigating the relation between AS and panic, recent research has begun to investigate the relation between AS and depression in children. Research findings suggest that similar relations found among adults are found among children. For example, Otto, Pollack, Fava, Uccello, and Rosenbaum (1995) found that depressed adults had lower ASI scores than adults with panic disorder, but comparable to those of adults with other anxiety disorders. Taylor, Koch, Woody, and McLean (1996) also found elevated ASI scores in adults diagnosed with major depression, further suggesting a positive relation between AS and depression.

Similarly, Weems, Hammond-Laurence, Silverman, and Ferguson (1997) used the CASI to examine the relation between AS and depression in a sample of children and adolescents ($N = 209$) referred for anxiety problems. Similar to the findings in adults, Weems et al. found a significant correlation ($r = .52$) between scores on the CASI and the Children's Depression Inventory (CDI; Kovacs, 1981). Correlations between the CASI and CDI were also computed while controlling for several other variables (i.e., each of the RCMAS subscale scores, for combinations of the subscale scores, and for clinician severity ratings). The correlation between the CASI and CDI remained statistically significant ($p < .01$) while controlling for each of these indexes (e.g., partial r = .52 when controlling for clinician severity ratings). Correlations between CASI and RCMAS total scores were also computed while controlling for CDI scores, for RCMAS subscale scores, and for clinician ratings of severity. The correlation remained statistically significant ($p < .01$) while controlling for each of these indexes (e.g., partial $r = .45$ when controlling for the CDI).

The finding that the CASI–CDI correlations remained significant after controlling for the three RCMAS subscales and the CASI–RCMAS total score correlation remained significant after controlling for CDI scores suggests an intriguing avenue for future research in determining why AS and depression are related. For example, Otto et al. (1995) suggested that this relation may be mediated by negative mood (negative affectivity). This is not to say that negative affectivity causes anxiety, AS, or depression, but that negative affectivity is shared by each. Taylor et al. (1996) suggested that it was the items on the ASI that tapped phrenophobia (i.e., fear of going insane assessed by an item such as, "When I am nervous, I worry that I might be mentally ill"), which was associated with depression, and that it was these types of concerns that may mediate the relation between AS and depression.

It is also possible that just as cognitive ruminations and distortions are associated with depression, that AS may be associated with a similar type of cognitive style. The findings obtained in a recent study by Silverman, La Greca, and Wasserstein (1995) provide some support for this view. Although the study was designed to examine children's worries and the relation between worry and various indexes of anxiety (rather than the relation between children's cognitions and AS), relevant here is the finding that CASI scores were significantly related to the number, frequency, and intensity of children's worries. It is possible that children who report worrying about a lot of things (e.g., school, performance, health), and who do so with great intensity, also tend to worry about their anxiety symptoms. Thus, children with high AS, intense depression, or both may tend to worry excessively. Support for this notion comes from

Weems et al. (1997), who found that the correlation between the CASI and CDI, although still significant, was lowest when controlling for the Worry subscale of the RCMAS (partial $r = .21$) as compared with the Physiological subscale (partial $r = .31$) and the Concentration subscale (partial $r = .32$).

Taken together, the studies reviewed in this section highlight a similar set of findings with the CASI as has been found with the ASI. This is true with respect to differentiating among diagnostic groups, predicting panic (including children's internal catastrophic attributions), and in terms of finding a relation among AS, depression, and other negative cognitive states such as worry. Further work is needed to incorporate these findings into a useful theoretical frame. Replication and extension of some of these findings would also be worthwhile, given the importance that the findings of Lau et al. bear on such issues as prevention of psychopathology.

Along these lines, the present authors are about to launch a project that will entail following up on the 273 children who participated in the Silverman et al. (1995) study. The children were administered the CASI in 1991. We are in the process of tracking these children and plan to examine the extent to which their previous CASI scores predict panic and other anxiety disorders—8 years post-initial assessment, when all of these children are now well into adolescence. If the results of this study reveal that children with elevated CASI scores are more likely to report a history of panic attacks than children without elevated CASI scores, it will remain for future researchers to ultimately apply these results in ways that will have pragmatic significance (e.g., in designing prevention intervention programs; Silverman & Kurtines, 1996).

Using the CASI in Intervention Research

Ultimately, we hope that the CASI will be used as a screening tool to identify children who might benefit from prevention trials. Our hope is that the prospective follow-up study just mentioned will provide the necessary data to show that such efforts would be worthwhile. In addition to the potential use of the CASI in prevention trials, the CASI may also have potential use in treatment trials. Although we acknowledge that the current research evidence for this is sparse, we believe that what does exist is suggestive and promising. In the following subsections, we provide a summary of the main ways that the CASI may be used in treatment intervention research—specifically, as (a) an outcome variable, (b) a variable to prescribe specific treatment procedures, and (c) a predictor of treatment response. We provide specific examples from research studies that we are aware of in which the CASI was in fact used in one of these three ways. Four of the five studies summarized next were conducted at the Child and Family Psychosocial Research Center at Florida International University in Miami.

The CASI as an Outcome Variable.   Ollendick (1995) used the CASI in a multiple baseline study of cognitive-behavioral therapy for panic disorder with agoraphobia. Participants were four adolescents ages 13, 14, 16, and 17 (the 17-year-old was the only male). Treatment involved progressive muscle relaxation, breathing retraining, and in vivo exposure; the fourth session was devoted to cognitive coping procedures. The CASI was found to be a sensitive measure of treatment-related change. Pretreatment CASI scores for each adolescent were 34, 48, 43, and 41, respectively. At posttreatment, scores were 31, 35, 32, and 31, respectively. Reductions in CASI scores continued to be maintained at 6-month follow-up; scores were 29, 33, 29, and 29, respectively. These represent substantial reductions. Pretreatment scores for three of the four participants were two standard deviations above the normative mean. In contrast, posttreatment and follow-up were all within the normative range.

Using the CASI to Prescribe Specific Treatment Procedures.   Although randomizing treatments across participants is an excellent experimental method to evaluate treatment efficacy, psychotherapy researchers are beginning to recognize the importance of matching or prescribing treatment to specific patient characteristics (Beutler, 1991; Kazdin, 1993; see Kearney & Silverman, 1990; Öst, Johansson, & Jerremalm, 1982, for examples). Thus, in addition to using the CASI as a treatment outcome measure, what would ultimately be useful is if children's scores on the CASI could be used, in conjunction perhaps with other indexes, to identify those children with elevated AS. Those children could then be assigned to an intervention (i.e., to prescriptive treatment) that specifically targeted AS reduction. To our knowledge, using the CASI in this type of prescriptive way (i.e., where children are prescribed a specific treatment to reduce AS in accordance with their scores on the CASI) has not yet been reported in the research literature.

However, two single case studies speak to the potential use of the CASI in this way (Eisen & Silverman, 1993, 1998). Although these studies did not target AS per se, they did target specific response classes of anxiety and showed that children did better when they received a prescribed treatment in accordance with their specific response classes (or symptom patterns) of anxiety. For example, in the second of these studies (Eisen & Silverman, 1998), a multiple baseline design across subjects was used to examine the efficacy of prescriptive versus nonprescriptive cognitive-behavioral intervention for four boys (ages 8, 11, and two 12-year-olds). All of these boys met *DSM–III–R* criteria for a primary diagnosis of overanxious disorder and *DSM–IV* criteria for Generalized Anxiety Disorder (GAD). Using the CASI in conjunction with other indexes, the children were classified into either a Somatic Response Class (i.e., a lot of somatic complaints, high physiological tension, elevated AS) or a Cognitive Response Class (i.e., a lot of worry, negative cognitions, but not related to anxiety symptoms). Results indicated that, after prescriptive treatment, three of the four participants met criteria for high end-state functioning (i.e., they fell within normal limits on logically related response class measures, one of which was the CASI). These improvements were maintained at the 6-month follow-up. In contrast, nonprescriptive treatment failed to produce sufficient change for participants to satisfy high end-state functioning criteria. For example, one case deteriorated after receiving nonprescriptive treatment and experienced clinically significant levels of distress on the CASI (scores increased from 26 to 34).

In summary, in the two studies by Eisen and Silverman (1993, 1998) the CASI was used in conjunction with other indexes to determine the problematic response classes of anxious children. These data were then used to prescribe specific treatments. As noted, the multiple baseline design methodology used by Eisen and Silverman might be extended for use in research that focuses more closely on the utility of prescribing AS reduction for children reporting elevated AS on the CASI. If a series of multiple baseline design investigations provide further evidence for the utility of prescribing treatment for anxiety disorders in children in accordance with children's response classes, the next step would be to examine its utility in controlled clinical trials using group designs.

The CASI as a Predictor of Treatment Success or Failure.   As evidence accumulates supporting the efficacy of treatments for children with anxiety disorders (e.g., Kendall, 1994), there is a need for investigators to shift their focus to identifying predictors of treatment success or failure. Elevated AS may be one such factor. If research findings bear this out, it would suggest the need to target AS reduction, as discussed in the preceding section, perhaps in addition to giving the child the basic treatment package.

The authors have examined this issue in a preliminary way. We conducted a controlled clinical trial of an exposure-based cognitive-behavioral group therapy for children with social phobia, overanxious disorder, or GAD ($N = 54$; ages 6–17). Treatment was compared with a wait list control. We found that children who did not improve with treatment (i.e., those who still met *DSM* criteria for their presenting problem at posttreatment) tended to have elevated AS at pretreatment compared with children who improved with treatment (i.e., no longer met diagnostic criteria). To illustrate, 7 of 11 cases (64%) still meeting *DSM* criteria at posttreatment started treatment with CASI scores above the mean for the entire sample (the latter was 29.0). This compares with 13 of 30 cases (43%) no longer meeting *DSM* criteria at posttreatment and started treatment with CASI scores above the mean for the sample. Although additional research is needed to more fully examine the utility of the CASI as a predictor and possible moderator of treatment success or failure, particularly in larger samples of children and with children who report experiences of panic, we view these preliminary findings as encouraging.

Taken together, we believe that the studies reported in this section provide preliminary support for the CASI's potential utility as (a) an outcome measure, particularly for panic disorder intervention studies; (b) an index by which to classify participants into particular response class groups for prescriptive treatments; and (c) a predictor or moderator of outcome. As further childhood anxiety treatment research is conducted and the role of AS is examined along the three ways mentioned earlier, the usefulness of including the CASI in treatment outcome studies will become more apparent. Once this is apparent, we would hope that the recommendation of the NIMH consensus conference on the treatment of adult panic disorder patients–that the ASI and other indexes of the *fear of fear* construct be included in all assessment batteries (Shear & Maser, 1994)—will be also applied to child treatment outcome research.

FUTURE RESEARCH DIRECTIONS
AND CONCLUSIONS

As noted in the beginning of this chapter, when it comes to interest in and research on AS in children, we believe, to borrow a line from an old Bob Dylan song, "The times they are a'changing." That is, unlike the insufficient attention that was paid to AS in children in the past, we believe that the tide has shifted. In the late 1990s and into the early 2000s, the field will witness an intensity of attention that will parallel the attention paid to adult AS. It also was noted earlier that the current interest in behavioral inhibition, attachment, and other developmental constructs are reflections of this new Zeitgeist and that future research efforts will focus not just on any one of these constructs, but will begin to focus on integrative models—models that are reflective of the basic tenets of developmental psychopathology (e.g., equifinality, multifinality).

For example, we know that children with elevated behavioral inhibition (e.g., Kagan, Reznick, & Snidman, 1987, 1988; Kagan, Reznick, & Gibbons, 1989) are more likely to develop heightened physiological reactions due to a lower threshold of reactivity in the amygdala and hypothalamus. Does this also lead to a lower psychological threshold to tolerate their reactivity (i.e., elevated AS)?

Similarly, according to attachment theory (e.g., Bowlby, 1973), insecurely attached children may be at risk for later problems including anxiety (see Manassis & Bradley, 1994). Do the cognitive response styles of these children also entail insecurity about the consequences of anxiety symptoms (elevated AS)?

In addition to behavioral inhibition and attachment theory, social learning theory is likely to have a place in obtaining a full understanding about the development of AS in children. That is, AS is likely to develop not just as an interoceptive conditioned response, but also via observation and instruction. Research has shown that such indirect pathways occur in the development of children's fears (e.g., Ollendick, King, & Hamilton, 1991) and that mothers' cognitive triads are predictive of their children's cognitive triads and levels of depression (Stark, Schmidt, & Joiner, 1996). The question is: What about children's AS? Can this also develop through indirect pathways such as observation and instruction? What roles do parents' psychological states and behaviors play? For example, what happens when a child observes a parent showing, not necessarily even a fear of anxious symptoms, but a shortness of breath and complains about it? Are certain children (perhaps the ones with high behavioral inhibition and/or insecure patterns of attachment) likely to develop AS as they think to themselves, "Oh, oh, my mother may die" and thus come to view shortness of breath in him or herself as a potential sign of death? These are intriguing questions that await future study.

Relatedly, we recently examined the relation among parental AS using the ASI, parental depression using the Beck Depression Inventory (BDI) and children's AS using the CASI, and children's depression using the CDI in a sample of children ($N = 144$; ages 6–17) referred to the center (Weems & Silverman, 1998). The results indicated that parental depression was significantly related to child AS and that the relation remained significant after controlling for parental anxiety (partial $r = .22$) and parental AS (partial $r = .17$). The relation between parental depression and child AS was also significant when controlling for child's anxiety frequency (partial $r = .19$). However, a clear relation between ASI scores and CASI scores was not found. These findings highlight the point we have been making throughout the chapter—namely, that whatever the relation between AS in children and their parents is likely to be, it is unlikely to be a simple one. The results suggest the important role that other mediators such as parental depression and child depression is likely to play in understanding the development of AS in children.

In closing, we would like to return to the two, interwoven themes of this chapter, represented by the quotes from Goethe and William James at the beginning of this chapter. We hope we have met the main aim of this chapter, which was to show that both of these quotes provide good reasons for being interested in AS in children. Specifically, when Goethe said that "[age] finds us true children still," we think that he was right (in general) and also specifically in terms of the construct of AS. That is, what has been so well documented among adult participants in AS studies we have shown in this chapter to be slowly but surely being documented among child participants. In other words, many of the adult participants are probably reacting and responding as they did as children when it comes to showing anxiety about their anxious symptoms. Similarly, when James said that "Meaning, other than practical, there is for us none," we think that he was right as well (in general) and also specifically in terms of the construct of AS. That is, the pragmatic significance of AS in children is slowly but surely being documented. As shown in this chapter, evidence is accumulating that anxiety sensitivity has the potential to make a real difference in helping children who suffer from panic and anxiety disorders. For us, there is no better meaning or reason to make use of and study this construct in children than this most important pragmatic one. Our hope is that readers of this chapter will come away with a sensitivity toward AS in children.

ACKNOWLEDGMENT

Support for the writing of this chapter was provided in part by NIMH grant # 54690.

REFERENCES

Achenbach, T. H. (1980). DSM-III in light of empirical research on the classification of child psychopathology. *Journal of the American Academy of Child and Adolescent Psychiatry, 19,* 395–402.

American Psychiatric Association. (1980). *Diagnostic and statistical manual of mental disorders* (3rd ed.) Washington, DC: Author.

American Psychiatric Association. (1994). *Diagnostic and statistical manual of mental disorders* (4th ed.) Washington, DC: Author.

Anderson, J. C., Williams, S., McGee, R., & Silva, P. A. (1987). DSM-III disorders in preadolescent children. *Archives of General Psychiatry, 44,* 69–76.

Beutler, L. E. (1991). Have all won and must all have prizes? Revisiting Luborsky et al.'s verdict. *Journal of Consulting and Clinical Psychology, 59,* 226–232.

Blashfield, R. K., & Draguns, J. G. (1976). Toward a taxonomy of psychopathology: The purpose of psychiatric classification. *British Journal of Psychiatry, 128,* 574–583.

Bowlby, J. (1973). *Attachment and loss: Vol. 2. Separation.* New York: Basic Books.

Bradley, S. J., & Hood, J. (1993). Psychiatrically referred adolescents with panic attacks: Presenting symptoms, stressors, and comorbidity. *Journal of the American Academy of Child and Adolescent Psychiatry, 32,* 826–829.

Chorpita, B. F., Albano, A.M., & Barlow, D. H. (1996). Child anxiety sensitivity index: Considerations for children with anxiety disorders. *Journal of Clinical Child Psychology, 25,* 77–82.

Cicchetti, D., & Rogosch, F. A. (1996). Equifinality and multifinality in developmental psychopathology. *Development and Psychopathology, 8,* 597–600.

Cox, B. J., Parker, J. D., & Swinson R. P. (1996). Anxiety sensitivity: Confirmatory evidence for a multidimensional construct. *Behaviour Research and Therapy, 34,* 591–589.

Dadds, M. R., Barrett, P. M., Rapee, R. M., & Ryan, S. (1996). Family process and child anxiety and aggression: An observational analysis. *Journal of Abnormal Child Psychology, 24,* 715–734.

Dadds, M. R., Spence, S. H., Holland, D. E., Barrett, P. M., & Laurens, K. R. (1997). Prevention and early intervention for anxiety disorders: A controlled trial. *Journal of Consulting and Clinical Psychology, 65,* 627–635.

Eisen, A. R., & Silverman, W. K. (1993). Should I relax or change my thoughts?: A preliminary study of the treatment of Overanxious Disorder in children. *Journal of Cognitive Psychotherapy: An International Quarterly, 7,* 265–280.

Eisen, A. R., & Silverman, W. K. (1998). Prescriptive treatment for generalized anxiety disorder in children. *Behavior Therapy, 29,* 105–121.

Fergusson, D. M., Horwood, L. J., & Lynskey, M. T. (1993). Prevalence and comorbidity of DSM-III-R diagnoses in a birth cohort of 15 year-olds. *Journal of the American Academy of Child and Adolescent Psychiatry, 32,* 1127–1134.

Gorsuch, R.L. (1983). *Factor analysis* (2nd ed.). Hillsdale, NJ: Lawrence Erlbaum Associates.

Herjanic, B., & Reich, W. (1982). Development of a structured psychiatric interview for children: Agreement between child and parent on individual symptoms. *Journal of Abnormal Child Psychiatry, 10,* 307–324.

Jöreskog, K.G., & Sörbom, D. (1989). *LISREL 7 user's reference guide.* Mooresville, IN: Scientific Software.

Kagan, J. (1989). Temperamental contributions to social behavior. *American Psychologist, 44,* 668–674.

Kagan, J., Reznick, J. S., & Gibbons, J. (1989). Inhibited and uninhibited types of children. *Child Development, 60,* 838–845.

Kagan, J., Reznick, J. S., & Snidman, N. (1987). The physiology and psychology of behavioral inhibition. *Child Development, 58,* 1459–1473.

Kagan, J., Reznick, J. S., & Snidman, N. (1988). Biological bases of childhood shyness. *Science, 240,* 167–171.

Kazdin, A. E. (1993). Adolescent mental health: Prevention and treatment programs. *American Psychologist, 48,* 127–141.

Kearney, C. A., Albano, A. M., Eisen, A. R., Allan, W. D., & Barlow, D. H. (1997). The phenomenology of panic disorder in youngsters: An empirical study of a clinical sample. *Journal of Anxiety Disorders, 11,* 49–62.

Kearney, C. A., & Silverman, W. K. (1990). A preliminary analysis of a functional model of assessment and treatment of school refusal behavior. *Behavior Modification, 14,* 340–366.

Kearney, C. A., & Silverman, W. K. (1992). Let's not push the "panic button": A cautionary analysis of panic disorder in adolescents. *Clinical Psychology Review, 12,* 293–302.

Keller, M. B., Lavori, P. W., Wunder, J., Beardslee, W. R., Schwartz, C. E., & Roth, J. (1992). Chronic course of anxiety disorders in children and adolescents. *Journal of the American Academy of Child and Adolescent Psychiatry, 31*, 595–599.

Kendall, P. C. (1994). Treating anxiety disorders in children: Results of a randomized clinical trial. *Journal of Consulting and Clinical Psychology, 62*, 200–210.

Kovacs, M. (1981). Rating scales to assess depression in school aged children. *Acta Paedopsychiatria, 46*, 305–315.

Last, C. G., Hansen, C., & Franco, N. (1997). Anxious children in adulthood: A prospective study of adjustment. *Journal of the American Academy of Child and Adolescent Psychiatry, 36*, 645–652.

Last, C. G., Perrin, S., Hersen, M., & Kazdin, A. E. (1996). A prospective study of childhood anxiety disorders. *Journal of the American Academy of Child and Adolescent Psychiatry, 35*, 1502–1510.

Lau, J. J., Calamari, J. E., & Waraczynski, M. (1996). Panic attack symptomatology and anxiety sensitivity in adolescents. *Journal of Anxiety Disorders, 10*, 355–364.

Lewis, M., & Miller, M. (1990). *Handbook of developmental psychopathology.* New York: Plenum.

Lilienfeld, S. O., Jacob, R. G., & Turner, S. M. (1989). Comment on Holloway and McNally's (1987) "Effects of anxiety sensitivity on the response to hyperventilation." *Journal of Abnormal Psychology, 98*, 100–102.

Lilienfeld, S. O., Turner, S. M., & Jacob, R. G. (1993). Anxiety sensitivity: An examination of the theoretical and methodological issues. *Advances in Behaviour Research and Therapy, 15*, 147–183.

Maller, R. G., & Reiss, S. (1992). Anxiety sensitivity in 1984 and panic attacks in 1987. *Journal of Anxiety Disorders, 6*, 241–247.

Manassis, K., & Bradley, S. J. (1994). The development of childhood anxiety: Toward an integrated model. *Journal of Applied Developmental Psychology 15*, 345–366.

March, J. S., Leonard, H. L., & Swedo, S. E. (1995). Obsessive-compulsive disorder. In J. S. March (Ed.), *Anxiety disorders in children and adolescents* (pp. 251–275). New York: Guilford.

Mattis, S. G., & Ollendick, T. H. (1997). Children's cognitive responses to the somatic symptoms of panic. *Journal of Abnormal Child Psychology, 25*, 47–57.

McNally, R. J. (1989). Is anxiety sensitivity distinguishable from trait anxiety? Reply to Lilienfeld, Jacob, and Turner (1989). *Journal of Abnormal Psychology, 98*, 193–194.

Mueller, R. O. (1996). *Basic principles of structural equation modeling.* New York: Springer.

Nelles, W. B., & Barlow, D. H. (1988). Do children panic? *Clinical Psychology Review, 8*, 359–372.

Norton, G. R., Dorward, J., & Cox, B. J. (1986). Factors associated with panic attacks in nonclinical subjects. *Behavior Therapy, 17*, 239–252.

Ollendick, T. H. (1983). Reliability and validity of the revised Fear Survey Schedule for Children (FSSC-R). *Behaviour Research and Therapy, 21*, 685–692.

Ollendick, T. H. (1995). Cognitive behavioral treatment of panic disorder with agoraphobia in adolescents: A multiple baseline design analysis. *Behavior Therapy, 26*, 517–531.

Ollendick, T. H., & King, N. J. (1994). Diagnosis, assessment, and treatment of internalizing problems in children: The role of longitudinal data. *Journal of Consulting and Clinical Psychology, 62*, 918–927.

Ollendick, T. H., King, N. J., & Hamilton, D. I. (1991). Origins of childhood fears: An evaluation of Rachman's theory of fear acquisition. *Behaviour Research and Therapy, 29*, 117–123.

Öst, L. G., Johansson, J., & Jerremalm, A. (1982). Individual response patterns and the effects of different behavioral methods in the treatment of claustrophobia. *Behaviour Research and Therapy, 20,* 445–460.

Otto, M. W., Pollack, M. H., Fava, M., Uccello, R., & Rosenbaum, J. F. (1995). Elevated anxiety sensitivity index scores in patients with major depression: Correlates and changes with antidepressant treatment. *Journal of Anxiety Disorders, 9,* 117–123.

Peterson, R. A., & Heilbronner, R. L. (1987). The anxiety sensitivity index: Construct validity and factor analytic structure. *Journal of Anxiety Disorders, 1,* 117–121.

Peterson, R. A., & Reiss, S. (1987). *Anxiety Sensitivity Index Manual.* Orland Park, IL: International Diagnostic Systems.

Pollack, M. H., Otto, M. W., Sabatino, S., Majcher, D., Worthington, J. J., McArdele, E. T., & Rosenbaum, J. F. (1996). Relationship of childhood anxiety to adult panic disorder: Correlates and influence on course. *American Journal of Psychiatry, 153,* 376–381.

Rabian, B., Peterson, R.A., Richters, J., & Jensen, P. S. (1993). Anxiety sensitivity among anxious children. *Journal of Clinical Child Psychology 22,* 441–446.

Rapee, R. M., Barrett, P. M., Dadds, M. R., & Evans, L. (1994). Reliability of the DSM-III-R childhood anxiety disorders using structured interview: Interrater and parent-child agreement. *Journal of the American Academy of Child and Adolescent Psychiatry, 33,* 984–992.

Reiss, S. (1991). Expectancy model of fear, anxiety, and panic. *Clinical Psychology Review, 11,* 141–153.

Reiss, S., & McNally, R. J. (1985). The expectancy model of fear. In S. Reiss & R. Bootzin (Eds.), *Theoretical issues in behavior therapy* (pp. 107–121). New York: Academic Press.

Reiss, S., Peterson, R. A., Gursky, D. M., & McNally, R. J. (1986). Anxiety sensitivity, anxiety frequency and the prediction of fearfulness. *Behaviour Research and Therapy, 24,* 1–8.

Reynolds, C. R., & Richmond, B. O. (1978). What I think and feel: A revised measure of children's manifest anxiety. *Journal of Abnormal Child Psychology, 6,* 271–280.

Rutter, M., & Shaffer, D. (1980). DSM-III: A step forward or back in terms of the treatment of child psychiatric disorders? *Journal of the American Academy of Child and Adolescent Psychiatry, 19,* 371–394.

Sandin, B. (1997). *Ansidad miedos y fobias en ninos y adolescentes [Anxiety fears and phobias in children of adolescents].* Madrid, Spain: Dykinson.

Schmidt, N. B., Lerew, D. R., & Jackson, R. J. (1997). The role of anxiety sensitivity in the pathogenesis of panic: Prospective evaluation of spontaneous panic attacks during acute stress. *Journal of Abnormal Psychology, 106,* 355–364.

Shear, M. K., & Maser, J. D. (1994). Standardized assessment for panic disorder: A conference report. *Archives of General Psychiatry, 51,* 346–354.

Shostak, B. B., & Peterson, R. A. (1990). Effects of anxiety sensitivity on emotional response to a stress task. *Behaviour Research and Therapy, 28,* 513–521.

Silverman, W. K. (1991). Diagnostic reliability of anxiety disorders in children using structured interviews. *Journal of Anxiety Disorders, 5,* 105–124.

Silverman, W. K. (1992). Taxonomy of anxiety disorders in children. In G. D. Burrows, R. Noyes, & S. M. Roth (Eds.), *Handbook of anxiety* (Vol. 5, pp. 281–308). Amsterdam: Elsevier Science Publishers.

Silverman, W. K. (1993). DSM and the classification of anxiety disorders in children and adults. In C. G. Last (Ed.), *Anxiety across the lifespan: A developmental perspective on anxiety and the anxiety disorders* (pp. 7–36). New York: Springer.

Silverman, W. K. (1994). Structured diagnostic interviews. In T. H. Ollendick, N. J. King, & W. Yule (Eds.), *International handbook of phobic and anxiety disorders in children and adolescents* (pp. 293–315). New York: Plenum.

Silverman, W. K., & Albano, A. M. (1996). *The Anxiety Disorders Interview Schedule for Children-IV (Child and Parent Versions).* San Antonio, TX: Psychological Corporation.

Silverman, W. K., & Eisen, A. R. (1992). Age differences in the reliability of parent and child reports of child anxious symptomatology using a structured interview. *Journal of the American Academy of Child and Adolescent Psychiatry, 31,* 117–124.

Silverman, W. K., Fleisig, W., Rabian, B., & Peterson, R. (1991). Childhood anxiety sensitivity index. *Journal of Clinical Child Psychology, 20,* 162–168.

Silverman, W. K., & Ginsburg, G. S. (1998). Anxiety disorders. In T. H. Ollendick & M. Hersen (Eds.), *Handbook of child psychopathology* (3rd ed., pp. 239–268).). New York: Plenum.

Silverman, W. K., & Kurtines, W. M. (1996). *Anxiety and phobic disorders: A pragmatic approach.* New York: Plenum Press.

Silverman, W. K., & Kurtines, W. M. (1997). Theory in child psychosocial treatment research: Have it or had it? A pragmatic alternative. *Journal of Abnormal Child Psychology, 25,* 359–366.

Silverman, W. K., La Greca, A. M., & Wasserstein, S. (1995). What do children worry about? Worry and its relation to anxiety. *Child Development, 66,* 671–686.

Silverman, W. K., & Nelles, W. B. (1988). The Anxiety Disorders Interview Schedule for Children. *Journal of the American Academy of Child and Adolescent Psychiatry, 27,* 772–778.

Silverman, W. K., & Ollendick, T. H. (in press). *Developmental issues in the clinical treatment of children.* Needham Heights, MA: Allyn & Bacon.

Silverman, W. K., & Rabian, B. (1995). Test-retest reliability of the *DSM–III–R* anxiety disorders symptoms using the Anxiety Disorders Interview Schedule for Children. *Journal of Anxiety Disorders, 9,* 1–12.

Spence, S. H. (1997). Structure of anxiety symptoms among children: A confirmatory factor-analytic study. *Journal of Abnormal Psychology, 106,* 280–297.

Spielberger, C. D. (1973). *Manual for the State-Trait Anxiety Inventory for Children.* Palo Alto, CA: Consulting Psychologists Press.

Stark, K. D., Schmidt, K. L., & Joiner, T. E. (1996). Cognitive triad: Relationship to depressive symptoms, parents' cognitive triad, and perceived parental messages. *Journal of Abnormal Child Psychology, 24,* 615–621.

Taylor, S. (1995a). Anxiety sensitivity: Theoretical perspectives and recent findings. *Behaviour Research and Therapy 33,* 243–258.

Taylor, S. (1995b). Issues in the conceptualization and measurement of anxiety sensitivity. *Journal of Anxiety Disorders, 9,* 163–174.

Taylor, S., Koch, W. J., McNally, R. J., & Crockett, D. J. (1992). Conceptualizations of anxiety sensitivity. *Psychological Assessment, 4,* 245–250.

Taylor, S., Koch, W. J., Woody, S., & McLean, P. (1996). Anxiety sensitivity and depression: How are they related? *Journal of Abnormal Psychology, 105,* 474–479.

Telch, M. J., Shermis, M. D., & Lucas, J. A. (1989). Anxiety sensitivity: Unitary construct or domain specific appraisals. *Journal of Anxiety Disorders, 3,* 25–32.

Unnewehr, S., Schneider, S., Margraf, J., Jenkins, M., & Forin, I. (1996). Exposure to internal and external stimuli: Reactions in children of patients with panic disorder or animal phobia. *Journal of Anxiety Disorders, 10,* 489–508.

Vasey, M. W., Daleiden, E. L., Williams, L. L., & Brown, L. (1995). Biased attention in childhood anxiety disorders: A preliminary study. *Journal of Abnormal Child Psychology, 23,* 267–279.

Weems, C. F., Hammond-Laurence, K., Silverman, W. K., & Ferguson, C. (1997). The relation between anxiety sensitivity and depression in children referred for anxiety. *Behaviour Research and Therapy, 35,* 961–966.

Weems, C. F., Hammond-Laurence, K., Silverman, W. K., & Ginsburg, G. (1998). Testing the utility of the anxiety sensitivity construct in children and adolescents referred for anxiety disorders. *Journal of Clinical Child Psychology, 27,* 69–77.

Weems, C. F., & Silverman, W. K. (1998). *Child and parent anxiety sensitivity, anxiety frequency, and depression in clinic-referred families.* Manuscript submitted for publication.

Werry, J. S. (1991). Overanxious disorder: A review of its taxonomic properties. *Journal of the American Academy of Child and Adolescent Psychiatry, 30,* 533–544.

Zinbarg, R. E., Barlow, D. H., & Brown, T. A. (1997). Hierarchical structure and general factor saturation of the anxiety sensitivity index: Evidence and implications. *Psychological Assessment, 9,* 277–284.

12

Anxiety Sensitivity and Chronic Pain: Empirical Findings, Clinical Implications, and Future Directions

Gordon J. G. Asmundson
Regina Health District
University of Regina

Most investigations of anxiety sensitivity (AS) have focused on the role that it plays in panic attacks, panic disorder, and the other anxiety disorders. Over the past few years, however, the AS construct has made its way into investigations dealing with other conditions that have close association to panic. For example, AS has been studied in conditions such as asthma (Carr, Lehrer, Rausch, & Hochron, 1994), alcohol abuse (Stewart, Peterson, & Pihl, 1995; chap. 13, this volume), depression (Taylor, Koch, Woody, & McLean, 1996; chap. 6, this volume), and hypochondriasis (Cox, Fuentes, Ross, Borger, & Taylor, 1996). This chapter examines a new and emerging field of investigation that implicates AS in the maintenance of chronic pain and the exacerbation of pain-related suffering.

This chapter sets the stage for this area of study by examining appurtenant background information, critiques recent investigations that address the association between AS and pain, suggests clinical implications of this work, and outlines avenues of future investigation.

SETTING THE STAGE

To explore the relation between AS and chronic pain, it is necessary to have a basic understanding of each of these constructs. This section briefly reviews the defining aspects of each. The general association between anxiety and chronic pain is also addressed.

Definitions

Anxiety sensitivity is defined and comprehensively reviewed in other chapters of this book. Even so, it is important to reiterate a few major points here. Anxiety sensitivity is typically defined as the fear of anxiety symptoms (including thoughts and somatic sensations) arising from beliefs that they have harmful social (e.g., embarrassment), physical (e.g., heart attack), or psychological consequences (e.g., going crazy). It has been proposed that AS is one of several fundamental trait sensitivities that amplifies fear reactions (Reiss, 1987, 1991; Reiss & McNally, 1985; chap. 3, this volume) and that it is distinct from trait anxiety (McNally, 1996; Reiss, 1997; but also see Lilienfeld, 1996). As such, an individual high in AS is more likely to fear and avoid a multitude of other stimuli (e.g., animals, hospitals) and situations (e.g., social gatherings, large open spaces). In short, the generally accepted conceptualization of AS deals with one's tendency to fear the symptoms of anxiety and, in turn, develop many other potentially disabling fears and avoidance behaviors. As mentioned earlier, the study of AS has recently extended from panic and the anxiety disorders to a number of populations, including individuals with chronic pain.

Historically, pain has been conceptualized both as an affective experience and as pure sensation, typically arising from noxious stimulation. Current theory, influenced primarily by the seminal work of Melzack and colleagues (Melzack & Casey, 1968; Melzack & Wall, 1965), holds that pain comprises sensory as well as affective and cognitive components. Thus, pain can be viewed as both a sensory and emotional experience. Pain typically occurs in response to actual or potential tissue damage to motivate (when possible) escape from the source of pain and promote recuperative behavior (see Wall, 1979). Although there is some evidence to suggest that the affective, cognitive, and behavioral experiences of those with acute pain are similar to those with chronic pain (Hadjistavropoulos & Craig, 1994), the latter is the primary focus of this chapter. For our purposes, chronic pain is defined as pain that persists over a period of at least 3 months (International Association for the Study of Pain, 1986).

Anxiety and Chronic Pain

The association between anxiety and chronic pain has been recognized for years (e.g., Large, 1986; Merskey & Boyd, 1978; Spear, 1967). Although the relation is not linear, people with chronic pain tend to be more anxious and fearful than the general population (Craig, 1994). Anxiety responses in people with chronic pain may be related to a variety of factors, including, but not limited to, worries of not regaining lost functional abilities, financial difficulties, feelings of social inadequacy, and uncertainty about the physical consequences of persistent pain.

Catastrophizing over the potential negative consequences of pain appears to be common (Rosensteil & Keefe, 1983; Sullivan & D'Eon, 1990), as does fear (Asmundson, Norton, & Jacobson, 1996) and avoidance (e.g., Letham, Slade, Troup, & Bentley, 1983). Numerous investigations also indicate that, relative to the general population, the prevalence of anxiety disorders is elevated in individuals with chronic pain (see Asmundson, Jacobson, Allerdings, & Norton, 1996). Recently there has been an increase in empirical efforts to delineate the precise nature of the relationship between anxiety and chronic pain. Although several lines of investigation have been pursued, of particular note here is the work being conducted in the area of fear of pain.

Fear of pain has been proposed as a mechanism through which pain is maintained over time. The writings of Fordyce (1976) detail an operant conditioning model that describes how pain behaviors are maintained by positive and negative reinforcement. In essence, the model posits that pain behaviors (e.g., avoidance, reduced activity) may persist, even after tissue damage has healed, as a consequence of previous successful attempts in escaping pain. A number of investigators (Lethem et al., 1983; McCracken, Zayfert, & Gross, 1992; Philips, 1987; Vlaeyen, Kole-Snijders, Boeren, & van Eek, 1995) have proposed modifications of Fordyce's operant model that incorporate cognitive, behavioral, and physiological influences on avoidance behavior. Although the specific postulates of these models differ, the basic premise of each is similar: Negative expectancies (i.e., unpropitious or catastrophic thoughts and beliefs) about the harmfulness of pain initiates avoidance behavior that, over an extended period of time, contributes to deconditioning (e.g., muscular atrophy, decreased mobility, weight gain). In turn, this leads to further pain experiences, negative expectancies, and strengthened avoidance. In other words, the reciprocal relationship between fear and avoidance is thought to be responsible for maintaining pain behavior and disability over a prolonged period. A general model is presented in Fig. 12.1.

There are some similarities between the pain avoidance models and those proposed to account for avoidance behaviors associated with chronic fear and anxiety (Barlow, 1988; Clark, 1986; Marks, 1969; Reiss, 1991). Indeed, Rachman and Arntz (1991) suggested that, much like avoidance in phobic patients, the avoidance behavior of patients with chronic pain is related to inaccurate expectancies, such as overestimations of the probability of noxious events.

In recent years, a number of empirical investigations stemming from the postulates of the avoidance models have been conducted. In general, the results of these investigations support the thesis that negative expectancies about pain contribute to the maintenance of pain over time (for a review, see Asmundson, Norton, & Norton, in press). To illustrate, the work of McCracken and col-

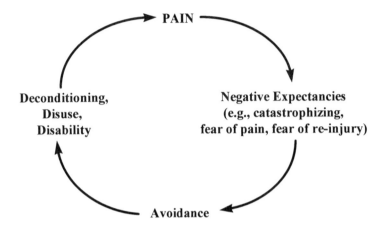

FIG. 12.1. Fear/avoidance model of chronic pain.

leagues indicates that fear of pain is a strong predictor of disability and interference with activities of daily living (McCracken et al., 1992) and predicts restricted range of motion during a passive straight leg raise test (McCracken, Gross, Sorg, & Edmands, 1993). Likewise, Waddell and colleagues (Waddell, Newton, Henderson, Somerville, & Main, 1993) reported that pain-related fear specific to work activities (e.g., fear that work would harm one's back) is a strong predictor of disability. In fact, their results indicate work-specific fear of pain to be a stronger predictor of disability than biomedical indexes such as anatomical pattern, time course, and severity of pain. Similar results have been reported by other investigators working in this area (e.g., Crombez, Vervaet, Lysens, Baeyens, & Eelen, 1998; Hursey & Jacks, 1992; Vlaeyen et al., 1995). Overall, the empirical evidence indicates that fear of pain plays an important role in the maintenance of pain behaviors and related disability.

Summary

Individuals with chronic pain often experience elevated levels of anxiety and, in a significant number of cases, have a diagnosable anxiety disorder. The literature suggests that fear of pain is strongly associated with persistent (i.e., chronic) pain behaviors and disability. Fear of pain also appears to exacerbate general distress and disrupt activities usually found to be pleasurable. This information is useful in advancing our understanding of chronic pain and has contributed to the treatment thereof. Still, there is a need for further investigation of the fear of pain construct. Does fear of pain mediate the association between chronic pain and clinical states of anxiety? What factors impact on one's propensity to be(come) fearful of pain? The next section discusses the theoretical foundation for examining AS in this context and reviews related empirical investigations conducted to date.

THEORETICAL FOUNDATION
AND EMPIRICAL FINDINGS

Reiss (1991) argued, in general terms, that when a person is exposed to an arousal-provoking situation, he or she becomes anxious as the result of (a) expectations about the potential consequences of the situation (e.g., "I expect to panic if I drive my car"), and (b) the reasons he or she fears the consequences (e.g., "People will think I am insane if they see me panicking"). People with high AS, compared to those with low AS, are thought to be more likely to have amplified fear reactions. If AS plays a role in amplifying a number of fears, as suggested by Reiss (1991), then it is plausible that it will be associated with elevated fear of pain. To this end, we (Asmundson & Norton, 1995; Asmundson & Taylor, 1996) have posited that AS plays a critical role in determining the extent to which one will fear pain and attempt to avoid it when it presents itself. Further, we have suggested that AS contributes to the maintenance of pain over time (i.e., chronic pain) and to exacerbation of associated suffering through its effect on fear of pain.

Is AS empirically associated with fear of pain? Emerging evidence from several lines of investigation suggest such a connection. The first line of evidence comes from investigators who, in the context of studying panic disorder, included measures of AS and various aspects of the pain experience. The second line of evidence is based on a series of studies directly targeted toward assessing this relation in patients with chronic musculoskeletal (e.g., low back, cervical) pain.

Evidence From Studies of Panic Disorder

The first study to incorporate measures of both pain and AS was conducted by Kuch, Cox, Woszczyna, Swinson, and Schulman (1991). The study was designed to examine the prevalence and impact of chronic pain complaints in panic disorder. Fifty-four of 141 panic disorder patients reported current pain (most commonly in the shoulders, lower back, and neck) that had persisted for longer than 6 months. In general, patients reporting chronic pain scored significantly higher on measures of psychopathology when compared with those who did not report pain. This pattern of results held true for scores on the AS Index (ASI; Peterson & Reiss, 1992), for which the patients with chronic pain had a mean (and standard deviation) of 42.7 (11.9) versus 36.2 (10.5) for those without pain. Analysis of ASI items selected on the basis of their relationship with somatization/hypochondriasis (i.e., Items 5, 11, and 14) revealed significantly higher item scores on the part of the patients with chronic pain. These data demonstrate a strong association between panic disorder and persistent pain and are the first to suggest that chronic pain (or some aspect of it) and high AS are strongly associated. Whether the association is a function of fear of pain, general hypochondriacal concerns, or some other set of factors cannot be determined from the data collected in that study.

Schmidt and colleagues (Schmidt, 1997; Schmidt & Cook, 1997) also collected some interesting data on pain and AS in patients with panic disorder. In one study (Schmidt, 1997), 45 patients with panic disorder participating in a cognitive-behavioral treatment outcome study completed the General Health Survey (GHS; Stewart, Hays, & Ware, 1988) as part of a larger pretreatment screening battery. The GHS contains six subscales, one of which provides an index of current pain (i.e., during the past 4 weeks) and the extent to which it causes interference with normal work and household activities. Scores on the GHS pain subscale were transformed to a linear scale ranging from 0 to 100, such that higher numbers indicate better functioning. Prior to treatment for panic disorder, these scores were not significantly associated with scores on the ASI ($r = -.14$). This finding is curious in that it suggests a lack of association between current pain and AS. It may simply reflect an artifact of range restriction in pretreatment ASI scores. Following treatment and at 6-month follow-up, the strength of the association between the variables increased to $r = -.27$ and $r = -.25$, respectively. Pretreatment GHS pain subscale scores were found to have a moderate relationship with residualized change in ASI scores at both posttreatment ($r = -.24$) and follow-up ($r = -.19$). This suggests that higher levels of pain in patients with panic disorder may inhibit normalization of AS with cognitive-behavioral treatment. This would occur if pain influences AS through its effects on one's feelings of physical vulnerability to serious illness. Schmidt and Telch (1997) also reported that nonpsychiatric medical comorbidity (e.g., chronic back problems, hypertension) and perceptions of poor health are related to poorer response to cognitive-behavioral treatment. As with the Kuch et al. (1991) study, these data shed some light on the interplay between AS and persistent pain, but they do not speak directly to the issue of pain-related fear and avoidance.

In a second study, Schmidt and Cook (1997) exposed panic disorder patients ($n = 36$) and healthy control subjects ($n = 23$) to a 2-minute cold pressor challenge. This most often involves immersing one's hand in ice water. Progressive aching in the submersed area is typical. To control for the potential confound that anxiety may produce on peripheral vasoconstriction, Schmidt and Cook modified the procedure such that a flexible ice pack was placed across the participant's throat. Baseline levels of AS, again measured using the ASI, were significantly predictive of (a) maximally reported discomfort/pain at both 1 and 2 minutes (rs = .34 and .45, respectively), and (b) peak anxiety (after controlling for baseline anxiety) at 1 and 2 minutes (partial rs = .39 and .25, respectively). Important, scores on the ASI were not significantly correlated with self-reported discomfort/pain tolerance (r = .19), but were significantly related to a measure of discomfort/pain avoidance (r = .51).

Other studies have failed to demonstrate that individuals with high AS report greater discomfort/pain than do those with lower levels following either loud noise bursts (Stewart & Pihl, 1994) or unavoidable electric shock (Conrod, Pihl, & Vassileva, 1997). These studies did not measure discomfort/pain tolerance or avoidance. However, Stewart and Pihl (1994) did find that subjects with high AS reported significantly more emotional arousal in anticipation of noise bursts than did the subjects with lower AS.

Together, the Kuch et al. (1991) and Schmidt (1997) studies suggest that the comorbid occurrence of panic disorder and persistent pain may be related to a more serious clinical condition (e.g., elevated scores on measures of psychopathology) for which a more negative response to treatment (i.e., poorer outcome) may be expected. The results of the challenge studies are mixed and, consequently, do not allow for any firm conclusions regarding the relation between AS and acute pain. The mixed pattern of results may be a function of the different challenge techniques used in these studies (e.g., cold pressor, noise bursts, electric shock). Moreover, investigators used a variety of pain measures, thereby making it even more difficult to draw comparisons across studies. Even so, the relatively strong association between AS and acute discomfort/pain avoidance observed by Schmidt and Cook (1997) is consistent with the strong relation between AS and avoidance observed in our investigations of patients with chronic musculoskeletal pain.

Evidence From Studies of Patients With Chronic Pain

The investigation of AS in patients referred for assessment and treatment of chronic pain is in its initial stages. Preliminary results support that AS plays a critical role in pain-related fear and avoidance responses.

Kuch and colleagues (Kuch, Cox, Evans, & Schulman, 1994) were, again, the first group of investigators to administer the ASI to patients with chronic pain. The ASI and a number of other measures were given to 55 individuals who had survived a motor vehicle accident and presented to the clinic with a primary complaint of chronic pain. Results indicate that the chronic pain patients who were accident phobic (i.e., a simple phobia beginning after an accident with fear related to the accident) scored significantly higher on the ASI ($M = 29.1$, $SD = 14.3$) than those who were not phobic ($M = 20.8$, $SD = 10.9$). Phobic patients, compared with nonphobics, reported pain in more locations of their body and exhibited more frequent utilization of health care services. These results, although preliminary, are intriguing because they suggest that elevated AS in the presence of chronic pain is related to a more serious clinical condition and greater health care utilization. Important, these data suggest that AS, rather than biomedical indexes (e.g., severity) of pain, influence the patient with chronic pain through its association with phobic avoidance (in this case, avoidance of accident related themes that may or may not include pain).

Asmundson and Norton (1995) recently assessed 70 patients with chronic back pain using a self-report battery comprising a number of questionnaires including the ASI and Pain Anxiety Symptoms Scale (PASS; McCracken et al., 1992). The latter is a 40-item self-report measure designed to assess pain-related fearful appraisals (e.g., *I think that if my pain gets too severe, it will never decrease*), cognitive anxiety (e.g., *I can't think straight when in pain*), and physiological anxiety (e.g., *I become sweaty when in pain*). The PASS also assesses pain-specific escape and avoidance behaviors (e.g., *I avoid important activities when I hurt*). Patients were classified as having high ($n = 14$), medium ($n = 44$), or low ($n = 12$) levels of AS as a function of the sample mean and standard deviation (i.e., $M = 15.2$, $SD = 8.6$). Based on conservative univariate follow-up analyses (i.e., $\alpha = .005$) of an overall significant multivariate analysis of variance (MANOVA), we found that patients with high AS, compared to those with lower levels of AS, scored higher on measures of negative affect (i.e., the Beck Depression Inventory: Beck, Ward, Mendelson, Mock, & Erbaugh, 1961; the negative affect subscale of the Multidimensional Pain Inventory: Kerns, Turk, & Rudy, 1985) as well as on subscales of the PASS that assessed cognitive anxiety and fearful appraisals. However, the three AS groups did not differ on measures of pain severity.

Asmundson and Norton (1995) further observed that the ASI and subscales of the PASS were moderately correlated (see Table 12.1). Simple correlations with cognitive anxiety were strongest ($r = .62$), followed by fear of pain ($r = .48$), physiological anxiety ($r = .38$), and escape/avoidance ($r = .32$). Anxiety Sensitivity was also significantly correlated with feelings of self-control ($r = -.29$) and negative affect ($r = .41$), but not with perceptions of social support or the interference that pain caused in performing activities of daily living. Controlling for pain severity, partial correlations did not differ significantly

TABLE 12.1

Comparison of Simple and Partial Correlations (Controlling
for Pain Severity) Between Anxiety Sensitivity
and Pain-Related Cognitive/Affective Variables

	Anxiety Sensitivity	
Variable	Simple r	Partial r
Cognitive anxiety[a]	.62***	.61***
Physiological anxiety[a]	.38***	.36**
Escape/avoidance[a]	.32*	.30*
Fear of pain[a]	.48***	.46***
Social support[b]	.04	.02
Self-control[b]	-.29*	-.29*
Pain interference[b]	.18	.12
Negative mood[b]	.41***	.39***

Note. [a] = measures from the Pain Anxiety Symptom Scale; [b] = measures
from the Multidimensional Pain Inventory. From "Anxiety Sensitivity in
Patients With Physically Unexplained Chronic Back Pain: A Preliminary
Report" by G. J. G. Asmundson and G. R. Norton, 1995, *Behaviour Research
and Therapy, 33*(7), p. 775. Copyright © 1995 by Elsevier Science Ltd.
Reprinted with permission.

*p < .02; **p < .005; ***p < .001. All p values two-tailed.

from the simple correlations. These results indicate that cognitive, physiological, and behavioral dimensions of fear of pain, as well as perceptions of
self-control and negative mood, are significantly related, albeit to different
degrees, to AS. Important, the associations among these variables appear to be
independent of pain severity.

Asmundson and Norton (1995) also found that 71% of patients with high AS,
compared with 34% and 25% of patients with medium and low AS, reported
current use of analgesic medication to relieve pain symptoms. This finding is
intriguing given that groups did not differ in the severity of pain they reported
experiencing. Kuch et al. (1994) similarly observed high levels of analgesic use in
the precence of high AS. About 25% of their panic-disordered patients with chronic
pain reported daily use of analgesics. Panic patients with chronic pain had higher
ASI scores than panic patients without pain. High AS has been associated with the
use of substances that reduce arousal (McNally, 1996; Norton et al., 1997). It may
be that the higher rate of analgesic consumption in patients with high AS represents
an attempt to alleviate and/or avoid aversive aspects of pain and other benign
somatic sensations. At present, the relationship between analgesic use and AS
warrants closer empirical and clinical attention.

On the basis of these initial results, we concluded that pain-related fear and avoidance, as well as other aspects of distress associated with chronic pain, may be significantly influenced by AS. Norton, Hutton, Asmundson, and Cruickshank (1995) found further evidence to support this notion. They administered the ASI and a number of other questionnaires to 87 consecutive patients presenting to a pain clinic with a variety of pain complaints. Regression analysis revealed that scores on the ASI and the Neuroticism scale of the NEO-Five Factor Inventory (Costa & McCrae, 1989) were the best predictors of pain-specific distress, accounting for 21.2% and 22.1% of the variance, respectively. However, pain severity ratings and the specific nature of pain complaint did not add significantly to the prediction of pain-related distress.

Using structural equation modeling, Asmundson and Taylor (1996) recently tested several predictions regarding the role of AS in fear of pain. We tested the predictions that AS directly exacerbates fear of pain and indirectly exacerbates pain-related avoidance via its effects on fear of pain (see Fig. 12.2 for the hypothesized paths). Fear of pain was defined by PASS fear, cognitive anxiety, and physiological anxiety subscales. Pain-related avoidance was assessed by three variables: the PASS escape/avoidance subscale, self-reported analgesic use, and the extent to which the patient's lifestyle had changed as a result of pain. We tested additional predictions to control for the direct effects of pain severity on pain-specific fear and avoidance. Participants in this study were 259 patients with complaints of chronic pain related to musculoskeletal injury, primarily involving the back. The results of the final model (in which nonsignificant paths were deleted) are shown in Fig. 12.2. The findings support the predicted direct and indirect influences of AS on fear of pain and avoidance, even after controlling for the direct influences of pain severity on these variables. (The direct path from pain severity to pain-related escape and avoidance was nonsignificant and therefore deleted from the final model.) It should be noted that the findings of this study are limited by the constraints of structural equation modeling. That is, the predictions were not tested by experimental manipulation, but by the extent to which the predictions were consistent with the data. Still, the findings support the hypothesis that high AS exacerbates fear of pain and thereby promotes avoidance behavior.

Is AS generally elevated in patients with chronic pain? The mean ASI score across the 55 patients in the Kuch et al. (1994) study was 25.0. This is lower than mean ASI scores reported for patients with panic disorder (with or without agoraphobia) and posttraumatic stress disorder, which typically exceed 30, but is similar to values reported for generalized anxiety disorder, obsessive–compulsive disorder, and social phobia (Peterson & Reiss, 1992; Taylor, Koch, &

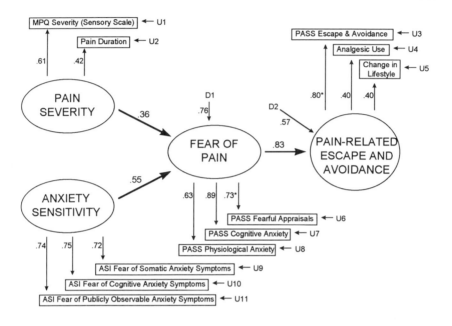

FIG. 12.2. Path diagram for final model showing standardized path coefficients for significant paths (all *ps* < .001). Coefficients marked with an asterisk were fixed to identify the model. D = disturbance terms. U = uniqueness terms. From "Role of Anxiety Sensitivity in Pain-Related Fear and Avoidance" by G. J. G. Asmundson and S. Taylor, 1996, *Journal of Behavioral Medicine, 19*(6), p. 582. Copyright © 1996 by Plenum Publishing Corporation. Reprinted by permission.

McNally, 1992). Data collected from 399 patients with chronic musculoskeletal pain, including those from Asmundson and Norton (1995) and Asmundson and Taylor (1996), indicate a mean ASI score (and *SD*) of 16.6 (11.0). This value is similar to that reported by Peterson and Reiss (1992) for nonclinical samples (i.e., *M* = 19.0, *SD* = 9.1). Overall, these data suggest that there is not a general elevation of AS in patients with chronic musculoskeletal pain. Further investigation is needed to establish whether this holds true across various chronic pain syndromes.

Summary

The current literature obtained from studies of both panic disorder and chronic pain patients indicates that the combination of a dispositional tendency toward being fearful (i.e., high AS) in the context of chronic pain may create a set of conditions that promotes an exaccerbation of overall clinical severity. In the absence of elevated AS there still may be clinically signficant impairment and distress, but may represent a better prognosis for treatment. Also supported is the notion that elevated AS influences those with current and persistent pain, both with and without comorbid panic disorder, through its effects on fear (of pain) and associated avoidance behavior. These effects appear to be independent of pain severity.

CLINICAL IMPLICATIONS

It is beyond the intent and scope of this chapter to provide a comprehensive summary of assessment and treatment of patients with chronic pain or panic disorder. There are, however, several noteworthy clinical implications that stem directly from the information reviewed herein.

For patients with chronic pain, a multimodal assessment of physical, social, behavioral, cognitive, and affective components should be conducted whenever possible (e.g., Turk & Rudy, 1987). The current literature suggests that measures of AS may represent a valuable addition to multimodal assessment batteries. An assessment of AS will (a) provide the clinician with valuable information regarding patients' tendency to respond with fear and avoidance of a number of stimuli, including their pain (Asmundson & Taylor, 1996); (b) serve as a factor useful in predicting those patients at increased risk for developing undesirable and persistent pain behaviors, such as increased reliance on analgesic medication (Asmundson & Norton, 1995); and (c) in cases where high levels of AS are observed, indicate that a structured assessment of anxiety disorders may be warranted. To date, the only measure of AS that has been evaluated in patients with chronic pain is the ASI. Measures that remain to be evaluated with pain patients include the various modified versions (i.e., expansions and abbreviations) of the ASI (see chap. 4), as well as related measures such as the Body Sensations Questionnaire and Agoraphobic Cognitions Questionnaire (Chambless, Caputo, Bright, & Gallagher, 1984) and the Anxiety Symptoms and Beliefs Scale (Kenardy, Evans, & Oei, 1992).

Assessing AS in the patient with chronic pain may provide the clinician with valuable information about how to tailor treatments. Recognition of the heterogeneous nature of chronic pain has led to efforts geared toward tailoring treatments to meet the needs of specific categories of patients (Asmundson, Norton, & Allerdings, 1997; Turk, Rudy, Kubinski, Zaki, & Greco, 1996). Individuals with chronic pain who have concomitant high AS may benefit considerably from treatment regimens geared toward the reduction of AS. These interventions, based primarily on treatments developed for panic disorder (e.g., Craske & Barlow, 1989), are discussed in chapter 14. As applied to those with chronic pain, it is expected that the reduction of AS will reduce the likelihood that individuals will catastrophically misinterpret sensations of arousal associated with pain and thereby minimize their fear of pain and avoidance behavior. It should be noted that no controlled clinical trials of this treatment approach have been conducted in individuals with chronic pain. As such, it is recommended that this treatment approach be combined with other appropriate modalities of treatment (e.g., physical therapy, occupational therapy, physical exercise).

Recall that current and persistently bothersome pain appears prevalent in patients with panic disorder (Kuch et al., 1991; Schmidt & Telch, 1997) and that comorbid panic disorder and chronic pain may worsen the clinical condition and diminish responses to panic treatment. These observations underscore the importance of including simple measures of analgesic use and of pain duration and influence on daily activities (including avoidance) in the assessment of patients with panic disorder. This would, at minimum, provide the clinician with a general view of the impact of pain on the patient and may indicate whether more detailed pain assessment and, perhaps, targeted treatment are warranted.

FUTURE DIRECTIONS

As noted previously, the study of AS in the context of chronic (and experimentally induced) pain is in its infancy. Consequently, there are numerous questions that await empirical scrutiny. The following questions are presented to stimulate thinking and, ultimately, lead to further investigation in this area:

1. What is the precise nature of the relationship between panic disorder and chronic pain? Does it have something to do with AS, fear of pain, hypochondriacal concerns, or some other set of factors not yet identified?

2. What is the most parsimonious explanation of the relationship between AS and fear of pain? Does the ASI simply provide a measure that is correlated with and indicative of the catastrophic thinking that often accompanies chronic pain? Does AS represent a general predisposition toward emotionality whereby exposure to an arousal provoking stimulus, such as pain, promotes a cascade of negative cognitive, physiological, and behavioral responses?

3. What impact does fear of pain have on AS and which, if either, is the more basic fear? Related to this, it is vital to confirm whether high AS precedes persistent pain conditions or if it develops as a consequence of painful experiences.

4. Are high levels of AS associated with analgesic abuse and dependency, guarding (i.e., a defensive posture or motion) or inactivity, and overreliance on others? How can we assess the impact of AS on physical impairment?

5. How do the findings obtained from samples of patients with chronic musculoskeletal pain generalize to those with other pain syndromes (e.g., headache, gastrointestinal pain, temporomandibular joint dysfunction)?

These are but a few salient questions that remain unaddressed at present. As a final point, it is important to consider how the studies reviewed in this chapter impact on the generally accepted conceptualization of AS. The literature indicates that the experience of pain sensations, when accompanied by negative expectancies and persistent avoidance behaviors, can lead to a vicious cycle that mires an individual into a chronic course of pain and suffering (Figure 12.1). The experience of pain, in addition to its influence on affect and behavior, often provokes considerable activity in the autonomic, visceral, and musculoskeletal systems. In other words, pain can provoke somatic arousal akin to anxiety. Consequently, it may be that people come to initially fear pain because they fear the consequences of the affective and somatic arousal that it produces (Asmundson & Taylor, 1996). Alternatively, AS may denote a fear of somatic sensations and perturbations that may not necessarily be identified with anxiety (also see Cox, Kuch, Parker, Schulman, & Evans, 1994). That is, the ASI may be tapping fear of anxiety symptoms as well as fears of other atypical, unpredictable, or aversive somatic sensations and associated emotional reactions. Therefore, the AS construct may reflect a set of fears that is more basic than fear of anxiety. This is an important theoretical question that warrants further attention. Indeed, Taylor (1995) previously noted that further research is needed to determine whether AS can be logically reduced to more basic fears. One likely candidate is the fear that is associated with a sensory and emotional experience that many humans spend a considerable amount of time trying to avoid—pain.

ACKNOWLEDGMENTS

The author acknowledges the helpful comments of Heather D. Hadjistavropoulos, PhD, G. Ron Norton, PhD, and Peter J. Norton, MSc.

REFERENCES

Asmundson, G. J. G., Jacobson, S. J., Allerdings, M. D., & Norton, G. R. (1996). Social phobia in disabled workers with chronic musculoskeletal pain. *Behaviour Research and Therapy, 34*, 939–943.

Asmundson, G. J. G., & Norton, G. R. (1995). Anxiety sensitivity in patients with physically unexplained chronic back pain: A preliminary report. *Behaviour Research and Therapy, 33*, 771–777.

Asmundson, G. J. G., Norton, G. R., & Allerdings, M. D. (1997). Fear and avoidance in dysfunctional chronic back pain patients. *Pain, 69*, 231–236.

Asmundson, G. J. G., Norton, G. R., & Jacobson, S. J. (1996). Social, blood/injury, and agoraphobic fears in patients with physically unexplained chronic pain: Are they clinically significant? *Anxiety, 2*, 28–33.

Asmundson, G. J. G., Norton, P. J., & Norton, G. R. (in press). Beyond pain: The role of fear and avoidance in chronicity. *Clinical Psychology Review*.

Asmundson, G. J. G., & Taylor, S. (1996). Role of anxiety sensitivity in pain-related fear and avoidance. *Journal of Behavioral Medicine, 19*, 577–586.

Barlow, D. H. (1988). *Anxiety and its disorders*. New York: Guilford.

Beck, A. T., Ward, C. H., Mendelson, M., Mock, J., & Erbaugh, J. (1961). An inventory for measuring depression. *Archives of General Psychiatry, 4*, 561–571.

Carr, R. E., Lehrer, P. M., Rausch, R. L., & Hochron, S. M. (1994). Anxiety sensitivity and panic attacks in an asthmatic population. *Behaviour Research and Therapy, 32*, 411–418.

Chambless, D. L., Caputo, G. C., Bright, P., & Gallagher, R. (1984). Assessment of fear of fear in agoraphobics: The Body Sensations Questionnaire and the Agoraphobic Cognitions Questionnaire. *Journal of Consulting and Clinical Psychology, 52*, 1090–1097.

Clark, D. M. (1986). A cognitive approach to panic. *Behaviour Research and Therapy, 24*, 461–470.

Conrod, P. J., Pihl, R. O., & Vassileva, J. (1997). *Differential sensitivity to alcohol reinforcement in groups of men at risk for distinct alcohol syndromes*. Manuscript under review.

Costa, P. T., & McCrae, R. R. (1989). *NEO five-factor inventory*. Odessa, FL: Psychological Assessment Resources.

Cox, B., Fuentes, K., Ross, L., Borger, S., & Taylor, S. (1996, May). *Anxiety sensitivity, hypochondriasis, and the somatoform disorders*. Poster presented at the conference on Pain, Disability, and Personal Injury: Scientific and Applied Aspects, Regina, Saskatchewan, Canada.

Cox, B. J., Kuch, K., Parker, J. D. A., Schulman, I. D., & Evans, R. J. (1994). Alexythymia in somatoform disorder patients with chronic pain. *Journal of Psychosomatic Medicine, 38*, 523–527.

Craig, K. D. (1994). Emotional aspects of pain. In P. D. Wall & R. Melzack (Eds.), *The textbook of pain* (pp. 261–274). Edinburgh: Churchill Livingstone.

Craske, M. G., & Barlow, D. H. (1989). *Therapist's Guide for Mastery of Your Anxiety and Panic (MAP) Program*. New York: Graywind.

Crombez, G., Vervaet, L., Lysens, P., Baeyens, F., & Eelen, P. (1998). Avoidance and confrontation of painful, back straining movements in chronic back pain patients. *Behavior Modification, 22*, 62–67.

Fordyce, W. E. (1976). *Behavioral methods for chronic pain and illness*. St. Louis, MO: Mosby.

Hadjistavropoulos, H. D., & Craig, K. D. (1994). Acute and chronic low back pain: Cognitive, affective and behavioral dimensions. *Journal of Consulting and Clinical Psychology, 62*, 341–349.

Hursey, K. G., & Jacks, S. D. (1992). Fear of pain in recurrent headache sufferers. *Headache, 32*, 283–286.

International Association for the Study of Pain. (1986). Classification of chronic pain. *Pain (Suppl. 3)*, S1–S226.

Kenardy, J., Evans, L., & Oei, T. P. S. (1992). The latent structure of anxiety symptoms in anxiety disorders. *American Journal of Psychiatry, 149*, 1058–1061.

Kerns, R. D., Turk, D. C., & Rudy, T. E. (1985). The West Haven-Yale Multidimensional Pain Inventory (WHYMPI). *Pain, 23*, 345–356.

Kuch, K., Cox, B. J., Evans, R., & Schulman, I. (1994). Phobias, panic, and pain in 55 survivors of road vehicle accidents. *Journal of Anxiety Disorders, 8*, 181–187.

Kuch, K., Cox, B. J., Woszczyna, C. B., Swinson, R. P., & Schulman, I. (1991). Chronic pain and panic disorder. *Journal of Behavior Therapy and Experimental Psychiatry, 22*, 255–259.

Large, R. (1986). DSM-III diagnosis in chronic pain: Confusion or clarity? *Journal of Nervous and Mental Disease, 174*, 295–303.

Letham, J., Slade, P. D., Troup, J. D. G., & Bentley, G. (1983). Outline of a fear-avoidance model of exaggerated pain perception—I. *Behaviour Research and Therapy, 21*, 401–408.

Lilienfeld, S. O. (1996). Anxiety sensitivity is not distinct from trait anxiety. In R. M. Rapee (Ed.), *Current controversies in the anxiety disorders* (pp. 228–244). New York: Guilford.

Marks, I. M. (1969). *Fears and phobias.* London: Heineman.

McCracken, L. M., Gross, R. T., Sorg, P. J., & Edmands, T. A. (1993). Prediction of pain in patients with chronic low back pain: Effects of inaccurate prediction and pain-related anxiety. *Behaviour Research and Therapy, 31*, 647–652.

McCracken, L. M., Zayfert, C., & Gross, R. T. (1992). The Pain Anxiety Symptoms Scale: Development and validation of a scale to measure fear of pain. *Pain, 50*, 67–73.

McNally, R. J. (1996). Anxiety sensitivity is distinguishable from trait anxiety. In R. M. Rapee (Ed.), *Current controversies in the anxiety disorders* (pp. 214–227). New York: Guilford.

Melzack, R., & Casey, K. L. (1968). Sensory, motivational and central control determinants of pain. In D. R. Kennshalo (Ed.), *The skin senses* (pp. 423–443). Springfield, IL: Thomas.

Melzack, R., & Wall, P. D. (1965). Pain mechanisms: A new theory. *Science, 150*, 971–979.

Merskey, H., & Boyd, D. (1978). Emotional adjustment and chronic pain. *Pain, 5*, 173–178.

Norton, G. R., Hutton, M., Asmundson, G. J. G., & Cruickshank, L. (1995, July). *Personality, coping styles, and chronic pain.* In G. J. G. Asmundson & G. R. Norton (Chairs), "Emotional distress in the chronic pain patient: Emerging themes and strategies for successful intervention." Symposium conducted at the World Congress of Behavioural and Cognitive Therapies, Copenhagen, Denmark.

Norton, G. R., Rockman, G. E., Ediger, J., Pepe, C., Goldberg, G., Cox, B. J., & Asmundson, G. J. G. (1997). Anxiety sensitivity and chemical abuse. *Behaviour Research and Therapy, 35*, 859–862.

Peterson, R. A., & Reiss, S. (1992). *Anxiety Sensitivity Index Manual* (2nd ed.). Worthington, OH: International Diagnostic Systems.

Philips, H. (1987). Avoidance behaviour and its role in sustaining chronic pain. *Behaviour Research and Therapy, 25*, 273–279.

Rachman, S., & Arntz, A. (1991). The overprediction and underprediction of pain. *Clinical Psychology Review, 11*, 339–355.

Reiss, S. (1987). Theoretical perspectives on the fear of anxiety. *Clinical Psychology Review, 7*, 585–596.

Reiss, S. (1991). Expectancy theory of fear, anxiety, and panic. *Clinical Psychology Review, 11*, 141–153.

Reiss, S. (1997). Trait anxiety: It's not what you think it is. *Journal of Anxiety Disorders, 11*, 201–214.

Reiss, S., & McNally, R. J. (1985). The expectancy model of fear. In S. Reiss & R. R. Bootzin (Eds.), *Theoretical issues in behavior therapy* (pp. 107–121). New York: Academic Press.

Rosensteil, A., & Keefe, F. J. (1983). The use of coping strategies in chronic low back pain patients: Relationship to patient characteristics and adjustment. *Pain, 17*, 33–43.

Schmidt, N. B. (1997). *The relationship between anxiety sensitivity and pain variables in panic disorder patients receiving cognitive-behavioral treatment*. Unpublished data, Department of Medical and Clinical Psychology, Uniformed Services University of the Health Sciences.

Schmidt, N. B., & Cook, J. (1997). *Psychological parameters affecting fearful responding to a cold pressor challenge in patients with panic disorder*. Manuscript under review.

Schmidt, N. B., & Telch, M. J. (1997). Nonpsychiatric medical comorbidity, health perceptions, and treatment outcome in patients with panic disorder. *Health Psychology, 16*, 114–122.

Spear, F. H. (1967). Pain and psychiatric patients. *Journal of Psychosomatic Research, 11*, 187–193.

Stewart, A. L., Hays, R. D., & Ware, J. E., Jr. (1988). The MOS short-form General Health Survey: Reliability and validity in a patient population. *Medical Care, 26*, 724–735.

Stewart, S. H., Peterson, J. B., & Pihl, R. O. (1995). Anxiety sensitivity and self-reported alcohol consumption rates in university women. *Journal of Anxiety Disorders, 9*, 283–292.

Stewart, S. H., & Pihl, R. O. (1994). Effects of alcohol administration on psychophysiological and subjective-emotional responses to aversive stimulation in anxiety-sensitive women. *Psychology of Addictive Behaviors, 8*, 29–42.

Sullivan, M. J. L., & D'Eon, J. L. (1990). Relation between catastrophizing and depression in chronic pain patients. *Journal of Abnormal Psychology, 99*, 260–263.

Taylor, S. (1995). Anxiety sensitivity: Theoretical perspectives and recent findings. *Behaviour Research and Therapy, 33*, 243–258.

Taylor, S., Koch, W. J., & McNally, R. J. (1992). How does anxiety sensitivity vary across the anxiety disorders? *Journal of Anxiety Disorders, 7*, 249–259.

Taylor, S., Koch, W. J., Woody, S., & McLean, P. (1996). Anxiety sensitivity and depression: How are they related? *Journal of Abnormal Psychology, 105*, 474–479.

Turk, D. C., & Rudy, T. E. (1987). Towards a comprehensive assessment of chronic pain patients. *Behaviour Research and Therapy, 25*, 237–249.

Turk, D. C., Rudy, T. E., Kubinski, J. A., Zaki, H. S., & Greco, C. M. (1996). Dysfunctional patients with temporomandibular disorders: Evaluating the efficacy of a tailored treatment protocol. *Journal of Consulting and Clinical Psychology, 64*, 139–146.

Vlaeyen, J. W. S., Kole-Snijders, A. M. K., Boeren, R. G. B., & van Eek, H. (1995). Fear of movement/(re)injury in chronic low back pain and its relation to behavioral performance. *Pain, 62*, 363–372.

Waddell, G., Newton, M., Henderson, I., Somerville, D., & Main, C. J. (1993). A fear-avoidance beliefs questionnaire (FABQ) and the role of fear-avoidance beliefs in chronic low back pain and disability. *Pain, 52*, 157–168.

Wall, P. D. (1979). On the relation of injury to pain. *Pain, 6*, 253–264.

13

Anxiety Sensitivity
and Substance Use and Abuse

Sherry H. Stewart
Sarah Barton Samoluk
Alan B. MacDonald
Dalhousie University

Behavioral models maintain that substance use and abuse are learned behaviors. The most widely researched behavioral model is the tension-reduction hypothesis (Conger, 1956), which proposes that states of tension (anxiety, fear, conflict, or frustration) are aversive motivational states and drug consumption is a rewarding activity because it reduces such states (Cappell & Greeley, 1987). The tension-reduction hypothesis includes two central postulates. First, alcohol and other drugs are capable of reducing tension. Second, substance-induced tension reduction serves to increase the likelihood of future drug use through the operant learning mechanism of negative reinforcement (Cappell & Greeley, 1987). Due to inconsistencies in the experimental support for each of these postulates, reviews have been quite pessimistic about the utility of the tension-reduction hypothesis as a global explanation for all drug use behavior and substance disorder development (Cappell & Greeley, 1987; Poherecky, 1991; Wilson, 1988). Criticisms leveled at the traditional tension-reduction hypothesis include its: (a) failure to consider motivations for drug use other than tension reduction, (b) failure to recognize that different drugs have different effects, (c) relatively narrow definition of *tension*, (d) failure to consider the situational context in which drug use occurs (e.g., relaxed vs. stressed state; in anticipation of, or following, stress), and (e) failure to consider relevant cognitive and individual difference variables (Cappell & Greeley, 1987; W. Cox, 1987; Poherecky, 1991; Wilson, 1988).

More recently, it has been argued that the tension-reduction hypothesis may be most applicable in explaining the development of substance use disorders in populations exhibiting certain anxiety-related traits (McNally, 1996; Welte, 1985), certain anxiety disorders (Cappell & Greeley, 1987; Kushner, Sher, & Beitman, 1990), or strong sensitivity to substance-induced dampening of their responses to stress (Sher, 1991). Such revisions are consistent with the increased recognition that substance abuse and dependence are heterogeneous disorders with multiple etiological pathways (Pihl & Peterson, 1995; Sher, 1991).

Consistent with the notion that certain types of individuals might be more susceptible to developing drug use disorders, early research focused on identification of the addictive personality. Although attempts to identify a single predisposing personality type proved unsuccessful, the interest in identifying potential personality risk factors for substance disorders has continued unabated (W. Cox, 1987). A common notion (e.g., Welte, 1985) holds that substance abuse is linked to trait anxiety, which is the tendency to experience anxiety in stressful contexts (Spielberger, Gorsuch, Lushene, Vagg, & Jacobs, 1983).

A model of substance abuse risk involving the individual difference variable of anxiety sensitivity (AS) is slightly different than high-risk models involving trait anxiety (Welte, 1985); it relates to the often debated conceptual distinction between AS and trait anxiety (Lilienfeld, 1996; McNally, 1996; see also chap. 7, this volume). Trait anxiety models of substance abuse risk (e.g., Welte, 1985) assume that anxiety experiences are inherently aversive and individuals who experience more frequent anxiety (i.e., high trait anxious individuals), compared with those who experience less frequent anxiety (i.e., low trait anxious individuals), are more motivated to abuse drugs as a way of avoiding anxiety. In comparison, the expectancy model of anxiety (Reiss, 1991) argues that anxiety experiences are not inherently aversive. Just as people vary in the degree to which they experience anxiety when under stress, so may they vary in the degree to which they fear the occurrence of anxiety symptoms. As an anxiety-amplifying factor (Reiss, 1991), AS could be a strong motivator for use of any drug with the capacity to reduce, control, or eliminate arousal, fear, or the tendency to catastrophize about arousal sensations.

ANXIETY SENSITIVITY
AND ALCOHOL USE AND ABUSE

Studies of Alcoholics

Kaspi and McNally (cited in International Diagnostic Systems, 1989) and Karp (1993) have shown that people diagnosed with *DSM–III–R* alcohol abuse or dependence (American Psychiatric Association, 1987) are characterized by significantly higher than average Anxiety Sensitivity Index (ASI) scores when compared with nonclinical ASI norms (Peterson & Reiss, 1992). This finding held regardless of whether the alcoholic subjects were diagnosed with a comorbid anxiety disorder and may be interpreted in several ways. First, high AS could represent a premorbid vulnerability factor related to the motivation to drink to excess. Alternatively, rather than AS leading to alcohol abuse, chronic heavy drinking might increase bodily arousal (e.g., via heightened autonomic reactivity associated with alcohol withdrawal; American Psychiatric Association, 1994). This could in turn lead to elevated concerns with bodily arousal (i.e., high AS). Consistent with this, it has been suggested that high levels of autonomic reactivity may be one of the origins of high AS (Reiss & McNally, 1985). This possibility underscores the point that studies of alcoholics in treatment may confound cause with consequence (Pihl & Stewart, 1991). Research with high AS young adults who do not yet show signs of alcohol dependence (e.g., relatively few withdrawal experiences) helps circumvent such interpretive problems inherent in studies with chronic alcoholics (Stewart, 1995).

Studies of Nonalcoholic Young Adults: Self-Report Studies

Do high levels of AS represent a personality risk factor for the development of alcohol problems? Self-report studies with young adults support an association between high AS and a potentially maladaptive pattern of drinking that may prove to be associated with increased risk for the future development of alcohol disorders.

Self-Reported Drinking Motives. A series of studies exploring the relationships between AS and self-reported drinking motives (i.e., reasons for alcohol use) has demonstrated that high AS young adults report more drinking to cope with negative affect than low AS controls (Stewart, Karp, Pihl, & Peterson, 1997; Stewart & Zeitlin, 1995). Stewart and Zeitlin used the Drinking Motives Questionnaire (DMQ; Cooper, Russell, Skinner, & Windle, 1992; Stewart, Zeitlin, & Samoluk, 1996), which assesses relative frequency of drinking for each of three motives: (a) coping (to reduce or avoid negative affect), (b) enhancement (to increase pleasurable affect), and (c) social-affiliative motives (to increase affiliation with others). The significant positive relation between scores on the ASI and relative frequency of drinking to cope on the DMQ (Stewart & Zeitlin, 1995) has recently been replicated in a study with nonclinical young adults by Novak, Burgess, Clark, and Brown (1997). High AS young adults' more frequent coping-related drinking may place them at heightened risk for future heavy drinking and drinking problems as they learn over time to drink more and more to cope with negative affect (Novak et al., 1997).

High AS college students, compared with low AS students, are more likely to report that their major reason for drinking is to cope with negative affect and less likely to report that their major reason for drinking is to socialize (Stewart, Karp, et al., 1997; Stewart & Zeitlin, 1995). To illustrate, Stewart and Zeitlin (1995) found that over 50% of high AS students, but less than 5% of low AS students, reported drinking primarily to cope. Only about 20% of high AS students reported drinking primarily to socialize, compared with approximately 80% of low AS students. Of the various motives for alcohol consumption, coping-related drinking appears highly associated with excessive levels of alcohol use and is most highly associated with drinking alone and with risk for alcohol problems (Cooper et al., 1992). In contrast, social-affiliative drinking motives appear to be a more protective set of reasons for drinking, in that it is associated with lower alcohol consumption levels and lower risk for alcohol problems than coping-related consumption (Cooper et al., 1992).

Self-Reported Drinking Situations.   Samoluk and Stewart (in press) recently conducted a study examining potential relations between AS and self-reported drinking situations in a nonclinical (student) sample of 396 young adult drinkers. Participants completed the ASI and a well-validated measure assessing the relative frequency of drinking in a variety of specific drinking situations—namely, the short form of the Inventory of Drinking Situations (Annis, Graham, & Davies, 1987; Carrigan, Samoluk, & Stewart, 1998). Analyses supported the predicted correlation between AS and drinking in negative affect situations (i.e., unpleasant emotions, conflict with others, physical discomfort) and not in positive affect situations (e.g., pleasant times with others, pleasant emotions). In other words, students with higher levels of AS reported relatively more frequent drinking in potentially negatively reinforcing drinking contexts than students with lower AS. These findings demonstrate a risky pattern of context-dependent drinking among high AS individuals, specifically in situations that do not necessitate the presence of others. This pattern has been suggested to be risky in that solitary drinkers cannot regulate their drinking levels in comparison with others (Cooper et al., 1992).

Self-Reported Alcohol Expectancies.   *Expectancies* refers to the beliefs that individuals hold about the effects of alcohol. These beliefs are the product of the persons' learning history (Goldman, Brown, & Christiansen, 1987).

Research has shown that alcohol expectancies are formed early in life—prior to actual experiences with alcohol (Goldman et al., 1987). Factor-analytic work has demonstrated that there are several reliable sets of positive alcohol expectancies, including expectations that moderate doses of alcohol lead to relaxation and tension reduction (Goldman et al., 1987). Positive alcohol expectancies in general (as measured by the Alcohol Expectancy Questionnaire [AEQ]; Brown, Christiansen, & Goldman, 1987), and relaxation and tension-reduction expectancies in particular, strongly predict drinking levels, risk for alcohol abuse problems, and relative recovery from alcohol disorders (Goldman et al., 1987).

Few studies have examined whether characterological factors are related to certain patterns of alcohol expectancies. In one study using a large sample of subjects diagnosed with *DSM–III–R* alcohol abuse or dependence, AS was significantly positively related to levels of a variety of positive AEQ alcohol expectancies, including expectations for relaxation and tension reduction (Karp, 1993). Whether these significant positive relationships would be evident in less experienced drinkers from the non-clinical population remains to be determined.

Self-Reported Drinking Levels. Results on the relationship between AS and rates of drinking have been somewhat inconsistent. Stewart, Peterson, and Pihl (1995) chose women from a larger sample of young adults to fill three AS groups (high, moderate, and low) based on their scores on the ASI. The high AS women reported drinking significantly more alcohol on a weekly basis than the low AS women ($M = 7.4$ vs. 2.2 alcoholic beverages per week, respectively). In addition, on a validated index of excessive drinking (Conrod, Stewart, & Pihl, 1997), the high AS women tended to drink to the point of legal intoxication more frequently than the low AS women ($M = 77.0$ vs. 16.2 excessive drinking occasions per year, respectively). The means of the moderate AS group fell between those of the high and low AS groups on both drinking measures, but failed to differ significantly from the means of the other groups. Stewart, Peterson, and Pihl (1995) suggested that their more frequent heavy alcohol consumption may place high AS young adults at greater risk for adverse health and social consequences given the previously demonstrated relationship between excessive consumption and risk for alcohol problems (Sher, 1991).

The significant positive relationship between ASI scores and self-reported drinking rates in young adult women reported by Stewart, Peterson, and Pihl (1995) has been similarly demonstrated in people with panic disorder and agoraphobia (Cox, Swinson, Shulman, Kuch, & Reichman, 1993). However, Novak et al. (1997) failed to replicate these results with their nonclinical sample of young adults. They found that ASI scores did not significantly predict levels of alcohol consumption when the ASI was entered in a regression equation after the inclusion of demographic variables of income, gender, and age at first drink.

These inconsistent findings might have been due to relative differences in the range of ASI scores, age of samples, or data analytic strategies. First, Stewart, Peterson, and Pihl (1995) had greater mean differences between high and low AS groups (mean ASI scores = 37.1 and 7.3, respectively) compared with the high and low AS groups formed by Novak et al. (1997; mean ASI scores = 29.2 and 11.5, respectively). Second, students assessed by Novak et al. (1997) tended to be younger than the Stewart, Peterson, and Pihl (1995) students and much younger than the Cox et al. (1993) panic patients. It may be that relationships between AS level and rates of drinking exist only when comparing extreme groups of high and low AS individuals or only among relatively more experienced drinkers. Finally, Stewart, Peterson, and Pihl (1995) and Cox et al. (1993) examined relationships between ASI scores and drinking rates per se. In contrast, Novak et al. (1997) examined whether ASI scores added any additional information in predicting drinking rates over and above the prediction possible from significant demographic variables. A stepwise multiple-regression approach could be used in future research to evaluate the relative contributions of ASI and other relevant variables in predicting levels of alcohol use across a range of ASI scores and age ranges.

Self-Reported Drinking Problems.   A recent study by Conrod, Pihl, and Vassileva (1998) compared self-endorsed drinking problems on the brief version of the Michigan Alcoholism Screening Test (Brief MAST; Pokorny, Miller, & Kaplan, 1972) among groups of high and low AS young adult males with no family history of alcoholism. All subjects were selected for nonalcoholic status according to scores on the Brief MAST (i.e., scores of 10 or less). A greater proportion of the high AS than the low AS males (i.e., 55% vs. 15%, respectively) reported at least one drinking-related problem on the Brief MAST (i.e., legal, social, physical, occupational). Thus, even at a relatively young age, differences may be seen between high and low AS individuals in terms of emerging drinking problems (Conrod et al., 1998).

Summary of Self-Report Studies

The self-report studies to date on relations between AS and aspects of drinking behavior indicate a potentially maladaptive style of drinking among high AS young adults. Studies consistently show a strong positive relation between AS and frequency of drinking to cope with negative affect (Novak et al., 1997;

Stewart, Karp, et al., 1997; Stewart & Zeitlin, 1995). Similarly, AS has been associated with more frequent drinking in potentially negatively reinforcing drinking contexts (e.g., unpleasant emotions; Samoluk & Stewart, in press). ASI scores are also related to alcohol tension-reduction expectancies among alcoholics (Karp, 1993)—an area that deserves investigation in nonclinical samples. Finally, some evidence suggests that AS may also be associated with self-reported drinking rates among young adult women (Stewart, Peterson, & Pihl, 1995), and panic disorder patients (Cox et al., 1993). However, the failure to replicate this finding in a relatively young nonclinical sample (Novak et al., 1997) suggests that the conditions under which AS and drinking rates are associated need to be more fully investigated.

In summary, high AS young adults may be at increased risk for the future development of alcohol problems. Indeed, preliminary data suggest that high AS young adults (at least high AS men) may already be experiencing more problems as a consequence of their drinking than young adult low AS controls (Conrod et al., 1998). Future studies involving in vivo, prospective self-monitoring of drinking behaviors and situations would complement existing studies by controlling for the many potential biases (e.g., memory) inherent in retrospective self-reports.

Studies of Nonalcoholic Young Adults: Lab-Based Studies

Lab-based investigations can also complement the existing questionnaire studies by controlling for the limitations inherent in self-report methods and allowing for direct examination of predictions made by the tension-reduction hypothesis with respect to high AS individuals' drinking behavior. More specifically, lab-based alcohol administration studies can examine the first tenet of the hypothesis—that alcohol is capable of reducing tension among high AS individuals. Also, lab-based ad libitum alcohol consumption studies can examine the second tenet of the hypothesis—that alcohol-induced tension reduction motivates increased drinking among high AS individuals.

Alcohol Administration Studies. A set of lab-based studies has been conducted to compare the responses to alcohol of nonclinical young adults varying in levels of AS. These studies were designed to investigate whether the differences in self-reported drinking characteristics of high and low AS individuals might be explained by high AS individuals' unique responses to alcohol administration. These studies have consistently shown that high AS individuals appear more sensitive to certain consequences of drinking that may prove to be negatively reinforcing.

Our first alcohol administration study showed that, when sober, high AS subjects were more emotionally and electrodermally reactive to a loud noise burst stressor than low AS controls (Stewart & Pihl, 1994). ASI scores were more strongly related to sober degree of subjective-emotional responding to the stressor (i.e., degree of anxiety, worry, fear, tension) than to sober degree of physiological response to the stressor. Administration of a moderately intoxicating dose of alcohol was shown to eliminate AS group differences in the subjective-emotional and electrodermal stress response measures, specifically by dampening high AS students' degree of reactivity in response to the noise bursts (Stewart & Pihl, 1994).

Stewart and Pihl (1994) identified several limitations to their alcohol administration study. First, the study used a within-subjects design, where each subject was tested both before and after consuming alcohol. Hence, it could be argued that, rather than representing alcohol stress-response dampening effects, the reduced reactivity to the stressor observed in the high AS subjects may have represented an habituation effect (Stewart & Pihl, 1994). Although the findings of Stewart and Pihl argued against a habituation interpretation of the findings (e.g., reactivity levels in the sober testing condition increased, rather than decreased, across noise burst trials in the high AS group), the habituation interpretation still needs to be definitively ruled out. Second, Stewart and Pihl used a moderately intoxicating dose of alcohol resulting in blood alcohol levels in the legally intoxicating range. Thus, it is unclear whether dampening of high AS subjects' responses to a stressful challenge occurs only at relatively high doses of alcohol. Finally, exposure to signaled noise bursts to induce stress constitutes an indirect method of producing arousal-related bodily sensations. This method may lack appropriate theoretical relevance in the study of the AS construct. Instead, biological challenge tests such as voluntary hyperventilation and carbon dioxide (CO_2) inhalation may be more relevant stressors in AS research (Stewart & Pihl, 1994). These methods directly provoke anxiety-related bodily sensations feared by high AS individuals (McNally, 1996).

Research using voluntary hyperventilation and CO_2 challenges with non-clinical young adults has shown that sober high AS participants, compared with low AS controls, report more anxiety in response to the challenge (see chap. 9, this volume). This occurs regardless of panic history or trait anxiety levels (Asmundson, Norton, Wilson, & Sandler, 1994; Donnell & McNally, 1989; Holloway & McNally, 1987; Rapee & Medoro, 1994; Telch & Harrington, 1994). A recent alcohol administration study with panic disorder patients (a diagnostic category associated with high levels of AS; Stewart, Knize, & Pihl, 1992; Taylor, Koch, & McNally, 1992) used a CO_2 inhalation challenge as a stressor (Kushner et al., 1996). Patients who consumed a moderately intoxicating dose of alcohol reported less anxiety and fewer panic attacks in response to the challenge, compared with those who consumed a placebo (Kushner et al., 1996). These results support the notion that alcohol use may be promoted in panic disorder patients (i.e., individuals with clinically elevated levels of AS) through its negatively-reinforcing consequences (Kushner et al., 1996).

Given the limitations to the original Stewart and Pihl (1994) study outlined previously, and the results of the alcohol administration- CO_2 challenge study with panic disorder patients (Kushner et al., 1996), Baker, MacDonald, Stewart, and Skinner (1998) designed an alcohol administration study that used a between-subjects design. High and low AS subjects were administered one of three beverages: a placebo, a mildly intoxicating alcohol dose, or a moderately intoxicating alcohol dose. Arousal was induced by voluntary hyperventilation. Consistent with the results of previous hyperventilation and CO_2 challenge studies with sober nonclinical participants (Asmundson et al., 1994; Donnell & McNally, 1989; Holloway & McNally, 1987; Rapee & Medoro, 1994; Telch & Harrington, 1994), high AS placebo subjects reported significantly greater affective and cognitive reactivity to voluntary hyperventilation (greater increases in fear and catastrophization about the induced physical sensations) than low AS placebo subjects. Moreover, alcohol dampening effects on affective and cognitive reactivity to hyperventilation were observed only among high AS participants. In contrast, all subjects (high and low AS alike) administered alcohol exhibited strongly somatic reactivity to the hyperventilation challenge compared with subjects administered placebo. Results also indicated clear alcohol dose effects relative to placebo among the high AS participants.

These results suggest that nonclinical high AS subjects are similar to clinical high AS people (i.e., panic disorder patients; Kushner et al., 1996): Both appear particularly sensitive to certain potentially negatively reinforcing effects of alcohol (i.e., to alcohol-induced dampening of fear and catastrophization about experienced physical sensations). Moreover, it appears that these reinforcing consequences are most strongly apparent at relatively high alcohol doses (i.e., a dose in the legally intoxicating range). This may explain why high AS individuals drink to the point of legal intoxication more frequently than low AS individuals (Stewart, Peterson, & Pihl, 1995). Interestingly, the pattern of affective reactivity was much more similar to the pattern of cognitive reactivity, than to the pattern of somatic reactivity, across AS groups and beverage conditions (Baker et al., 1998). Thus, alcohol's dampening of catastrophization, rather than alcohol's somatic reactivity dampening effects, may be a better explanation for high AS subjects' sensitivity to alcohol-induced reductions in fear (cf. Stewart & Pihl, 1994). Finally, Baker et al. (1998) provided important information (in addition to Kushner et al., 1996) by including a control group (low AS students) and using nonclinical high AS individuals with no history of panic disorder.

Stewart, Conrod, Gignac, and Pihl (1998) recently conducted a study demonstrating a tendency for high AS people to selectively process threatening information. Numerous studies have shown that anxiety disorder patients and nonclinical samples of anxious individuals are characterized by a selective attentional bias favoring the semantic processing of disorder-specific threat stimuli (see review by Williams, Mathews, & MacLeod, 1996). Most often this bias is assessed using a modification of the traditional Stroop color-naming task in which participants are asked to name the color of ink in which a variety of words are printed. Delays in color naming of threatening as opposed to neutral words have been repeatedly observed in anxious participants—a finding that reflects a tendency to selectively process threat cues. The selective attentional bias toward threat cues has been proposed as an anxiety-maintaining factor (Williams et al., 1996).

To investigate the relationships among AS, attentional bias, and alcohol consumption, Stewart, Achille, Dubois-Nguyen, and Pihl (1992) used an alternative to the Stroop to assess selective processing in nonclinical young adult women with either high or low AS. Women were asked to indicate the location of a series of words (i.e., above or below a central fixation point) as quickly and accurately as possible. Sober high AS women took significantly longer to identify the location of threatening as compared with neutral control words, whereas sober low AS women showed no such tendency to selectively process threatening stimuli. Administration of a moderately intoxicating dose of alcohol was shown to eliminate high AS women's tendency to selectively process threatening words. This preliminary study suggests that alcohol may have negatively reinforcing consequences for high AS individuals in that it eliminates their sober tendency to be hypervigilant toward threat cues in their environment. Given that more recent research indicates that high AS young adults selectively process threat cues on the Stroop (Stewart et al., 1998; see also chap. 8, this volume), future work should attempt to replicate the Stewart, Achille, et al. (1992) alcohol–AS findings using the Stroop task.

Other alcohol administration studies have examined differences between high and low AS young adults in terms of susceptibility to alcohol's baseline stimulating properties. Research has repeatedly shown that alcohol administration induces an increase in resting heart rate (Stewart, Finn, & Pihl, 1992; Peterson, Pihl, Seguin, Finn, & Stewart, 1993; Peterson et al., 1996), which high AS individuals might theoretically find aversive. However, compared with low AS controls, high AS individuals may actually experience lower increases in resting heart rate in response to administration of a mildly intoxicating dose of alcohol (MacDonald & Stewart, 1996). MacDonald and Stewart (1996) suggested that, given their relative insensitivity to the stimulating properties of low alcohol doses, initial heart rate increases may fail to act as a deterrent to high AS individuals' continued drinking.

Ad Libitum Alcohol Consumption Studies.   An unobtrusive lab-based measure of alcohol consumption—the alcohol taste-rating task (Higgins & Marlatt, 1975)—has also been used to validate high AS individuals' self-reports of their typical drinking levels (Cox et al., 1993; Stewart, Peterson, & Pihl, 1995), their reported motives for drinking (Stewart, Karp, et al., 1997; Stewart & Zeitlin, 1995), and the contexts in which their drinking is most likely to occur (Samoluk & Stewart, in press). The taste-rating task involves the presentation of beverages, including drinks containing alcohol, with instructions for subjects to rate the taste of each beverage. The dependent variable of interest is the amount of alcohol consumed in response to the experimental manipulation in question (Higgins & Marlatt, 1975). The taste-rating task has well-established validity as a measure of actual (naturally occurring) drinking levels (George, Phillips, & Skinner, 1988).

One ad libitum drinking study conducted by our research group (Samoluk, Stewart, Sweet, & MacDonald, 1998) has shown that, consistent with their self-reports, high AS students do not appear particularly motivated to drink in pleasant social contexts. A group of high AS students consumed significantly more alcohol on the taste-rating task than a group of low AS controls in a solitary environment, but not in a relatively pleasant social environment. Moreover, high AS subjects in the solitary drinking environment consumed more alcohol than high AS subjects in the social drinking environment. Because high AS is associated with social anxiety (Ball, Otto, Pollack, Uccello, & Rosenbaum, 1995), one possible explanation for these alcohol consumption findings is that the high AS subjects felt more comfortable in the solitary than the social situation and drank most in the situation in which they felt most comfortable. However, affect ratings did not support this latter interpretation. Although negative affect was not directly manipulated, self-reported negative affect (i.e., a combination of depression, anxiety, and anger scores) was higher among those in the solitary situation (high and low AS alike) than among those in the social situation (high and low AS alike). A positive correlation between measures of negative affect and drinking quantity was seen only among high AS subjects. This finding supports the notion of increased coping-related drinking in a high AS population (i.e., drinking in response to negative affect; Samoluk et al., 1998). This is consistent with self-reports that coping, rather than social affiliation, is a primary motive for high AS students' drinking (Novak et al., 1997; Stewart, Karp, et al., 1997; Stewart & Zeitlin, 1995).

Results of a second ad libitum drinking study are more ambiguous. Samoluk and Stewart (1996) found that, contrary to expectation, high AS young adults who were anticipating an anxiety-relevant (AR) interview about their anxiety symptoms failed to drink significantly more alcohol than low AS controls anticipating the AR interview. Rather, high AS young adults who were anticipating an anxiety-irrelevant (AI) interview about their favorite foods drank significantly more alcohol during the taste-rating task than low AS controls anticipating the same interview. Several possible interpretations were offered by the authors to explain this unexpected AS group x drinking situation interaction.

For example, only participation in (but not anticipation of) the interviews significantly affected anxiety levels as predicted (Samoluk & Stewart, 1996; cf. Maller & Reiss, 1987). Thus, the authors suggested that conducting the taste test following the interviews, rather than in anticipation of the interviews, might prove to be a better manipulation for motivating increased coping-related alcohol consumption among high AS individuals in subsequent research. Another possibility is that enhanced interoceptive acuity combined with physical discomfort due to prior food deprivation may have unexpectedly increased alcoholic beverage consumption among high AS subjects in the AI condition, who may have been primed to attend to their physical discomfort given the AI interview's focus on food. This second explanation involves a modified tension-reduction notion, where *tension* is defined as any aversive motivational state including physical discomfort due to hunger. In fact, distress about gastrointestinal sensations is one of the defining features of the AS construct as tapped by the ASI (Peterson & Reiss, 1992), and research has shown that physical discomfort is dampened by even relatively low doses of alcohol (Stewart, Finn, & Pihl, 1995).

In support of this latter explanation, Samoluk and Stewart (1995) found that physical discomfort induced by a short period of food deprivation resulted in greater selective attention for alcohol cues in high versus low AS individuals. In contrast, no AS-related differences in degree of selective attention toward alcohol cues were found when subjects were not in a state of physical discomfort.

Summary of Lab-Based Investigations

Results of the lab-based investigations conducted to date are largely consistent with the findings of the self-report studies discussed earlier. Clear support for the first tenet of the tension-reduction hypothesis (i.e., that alcohol is capable of reducing tension among high AS individuals) has been obtained in several studies. High AS individuals appear particularly sensitive to certain reactivity-dampening properties of alcohol. Moreover, it appears important to consider situational context (i.e., examining alcohol's effects on the response to stress, rather than alcohol-induced tension reduction in the baseline state; Sher, 1991), to observe AS-related differences in responses to alcohol administration. Additionally, it appears important to assess multiple aspects of anxious responses to stressful challenges (i.e., affective, cognitive, and somatic). High AS subjects appear consistently more sensitive to alcohol's cognitive and affective, rather than somatic, reactivity-dampening effects when compared with low AS subjects.

Less support has been obtained thus far regarding the second tenet of the tension-reduction hypothesis (i.e., that alcohol-induced tension reduction actually motivates increased alcohol consumption among high AS individuals). High AS individuals have been shown to drink more alcohol in a solitary than in a relatively pleasant social context and to drink more alcohol than low AS individuals only in the solitary context (Samoluk et al., 1998). However, the findings of the ad libitum drinking study by Samoluk and Stewart (1996) are more ambiguous in terms of support for a tension-reduction interpretation of high AS individuals' drinking: High AS individuals unexpectedly drank more than low AS individuals when preparing for an anxiety-irrelevant interview, but not when anticipating an anxiety-relevant interview as predicted. Future research must give attention to explaining the types of circumstances that promote increased drinking among high AS individuals.

ANXIETY SENSITIVITY
AND OTHER DRUG USE AND ABUSE

McNally (1996) suggested that high levels of AS should be positively associated with the use and abuse of alcohol as well as with the use and abuse of other substances with anxiolytic or arousal-dampening properties (e.g., benzodiazepines, analgesics, heroin) and negatively associated with use and abuse of substances with anxiogenic or arousal-enhancing properties (e.g., cocaine, caffeine). The following sections review the growing literature on the relations between AS and use and abuse of drugs other than alcohol.

Benzodiazepines. Benzodiazepines have many properties in common with alcohol. For example, both drugs exert their anxiolytic effect by facilitating GABA-ergic neural transmission (Deitrich, Dunwiddie, Harris, & Erwin, 1989; Engel & Liljequist, 1983). Benzodiazepine dependence has been shown to be a major problem in patients with anxiety disorders characterized by high levels of AS, such as panic disorder (Bruce, Speigel, Gregg, & Nuzzarello, 1995; Otto, Pollack, Meltzer-Brody, & Rosenbaum, 1992). In addition, high AS college students report higher levels of use of medications for stress (including benzodiazepines) than low AS college students (Telch, Lucas, & Nelson, 1989).

Norton et al. (1997) found that high AS substance abusers were more likely to indicate depressant drugs (i.e., alcohol and benzodiazepines) as their drug of choice (52%) as compared with low AS substance abusers (32%). When drug choice was further broken down for the most commonly endorsed substances of choice (alcohol, cocaine, and marijuana), it was found that a greater proportion of high AS subjects reported alcohol as their substance of choice (69%) compared with the low AS group (46%). The proportion of high and low AS subjects indicating benzodiazepines as their substance of choice was not reported.

Recent evidence also suggests that AS is related to the degree of success of benzodiazepine discontinuation efforts in medicated anxiety disorder patients. Bruce et al. (1995) discontinued the alprazolam treatment of 20 patients with panic disorder who had or had not been treated concurrently with cognitive behavior therapy. The only significant predictor of relapse to benzodiazepine use at 6 months posttaper was the baseline-to-posttaper change in ASI scores. The results suggest that panic patients who maintain high levels of AS after active treatment are more vulnerable to relapse to benzodiazepine use if their feared anxiety symptoms reemerge (Bruce, 1996).

Analgesics. Asmundson and Norton (1995) found that AS was related to use of analgesic medications among a sample of 70 patients with physically unexplained chronic back pain. Specifically, the proportion of high AS patients reporting current use of analgesic medication (71%) was significantly greater than in patients with moderate AS (34%) and low AS (25%), although the three AS groups did not differ in reported pain intensity. The authors suggested that heightened levels of AS in chronic pain patients could motivate the increased use of analgesic medications as a form of pain escape or avoidance behavior. A subsequent study by Asmundson and Taylor (1996) included self-reported current analgesic medication use (coded as present or absent) as one of three pain-related escape and avoidance dependent measures in a sample of 259 patients with chronic musculoskeletal pain. Structural equation modeling supported the prediction that AS promotes pain-related escape and avoidance behavior (including analgesic medication use) by way of its influence on fear of pain (see chap. 12 for further discussion of AS and pain). Findings such as these led Cox (1996) to suggest that AS may be part of a broader set of beliefs about the harmfulness of unusual or strong internal sensations that may or may not be identified as anxiety symptoms. As such, AS may be related not only to the use and abuse of anxiolytic (anxiety-dampening) drugs such as alcohol and benzodiazepines, but also to the use/abuse of any drug that dampens physical sensations such as analgesics.

These findings suggest some interesting avenues for future research (Stewart, 1996b). First, alcohol is a drug that has anxiolytic effects as well as analgesic effects at certain doses (Stewart, Finn, & Pihl, 1995). Future research might investigate whether AS predicts not only the use of prescription analgesic medications in chronic pain patients, but also the use of other drugs with analgesic properties such as alcohol. In addition, it would be useful to extend the study of relations between prescription analgesic medications in chronic pain patients beyond the examination of the simple dichotomous user versus nonuser classification. It is possible that, among chronic pain patients, AS may be related to (a) levels of analgesic use (quantity or frequency), (b) patterns of use (regularly scheduled vs. as needed medication use), and (c) analgesic dependence (e.g., difficulties discontinuing prescription analgesics; Stewart, 1996b; Stewart, Westra, & Thompson, 1996).

Heroin.   Heroin, a drug belonging to the opiate class, produces a powerful sense of relaxation and well-being and also possesses pain-dampening properties. The only study to date to examine McNally's (1996) hypothesis that high levels of AS should be associated with the abuse of heroin was a study by McNally et al. (1987). In this study, groups of heroin-dependent inpatients (Vietnam combat veterans and noncombat veterans) were tested on the ASI and were compared to Vietnam combat veterans with posttraumatic stress disorder (PTSD). The three groups failed to differ significantly in AS, suggesting that heroin-dependent inpatients are similar to PTSD patients (cf. Taylor et al., 1992), in that both score much higher than average on the ASI. Future research on heroin-dependent patients should include matched control groups to allow for firmer conclusions on the association between AS and heroin use and abuse. Additionally, if future research does confirm a relationship between AS and heroin abuse/dependence, it would be interesting to investigate whether heroin's anxiolytic and analgesic effects promote heroin use in high AS people.

Cocaine and Other Psychostimulants.   Norton et al. (1997) found that high AS substance abusers were less likely than moderate AS substance abusers to report stimulants (e.g., cocaine, amphetamines) as their primary drug of choice (i.e., 17% vs. 35%, respectively). However, low AS substance abusers were similar to high AS substance abusers in terms of rates of endorsement of stimulants, including cocaine, as their primary drug of choice (i.e., 18%). Results were similar when proportions of patients specifically preferring cocaine (as opposed to alcohol or marijuana) were examined across AS groups. These results provide only partial support for McNally's (1996) predictions regarding relationships between AS and use of stimulants such as cocaine.

Norton et al. found that high AS substance abusers were relatively unlikely to prefer stimulants compared with substance abusers with moderate AS levels. Contrary to McNally's (1996) hypotheses, low AS substance abusers were not particularly likely to prefer stimulants over other types of drugs. This finding may be an artifact of the classification method of primary drugs of choice in the Norton et al. study. Specifically, a forced-choice procedure was utilized in which participant responses were classified into one of three mutually exclusive primary drug choice categories: *depressants* (alcohol and benzodiazepines), *stimulants* (cocaine and amphetamines), and *other* (marijuana, steroids, etc.). Although alcohol is primarily a depressant drug, it also possesses psychostimulant properties (e.g., induction of positive mood states, baseline heart rate increases; Pihl & Peterson, 1995). Thus, low AS substance abusers who prefer alcohol primarily for its psychostimulant effects may have been misclassified as primarily depressant drug abusers.

Future research designed to examine McNally's (1996) hypotheses regarding relation between AS and drug choice (i.e., stimulant vs. depressant) would benefit from simultaneous measurement of individuals' motives for drug use (e.g., coping vs. enhancement; Stewart & Zeitlin, 1995). Such research could test the hypotheses that low AS substance abusers would be most likely to choose drugs with psychostimulant properties specifically for their euphoric or arousal-enhancing effects; and that high AS substance abusers would be most likely to choose drugs with depressant properties specifically for their anxiolytic or arousal-dampening effects.

Caffeine.   Stewart, Karp, et al. (1997) examined the relation between use of a variety of commonly used legal and illicit drugs (i.e., alcohol, caffeine,

nicotine, and marijuana) among a large nonclinical sample of young adults. Contrary to predictions made on the basis of McNally's (1996) hypotheses, high AS students were no less likely to report use of caffeine (coded as *user* vs. *nonuser*) than low AS students. Future research on the potential relations between AS and use of drugs with stimulating or arousal-enhancing properties, such as caffeine, might examine relations between AS and quantity or frequency of caffeine use. It still may be that high AS individuals are less likely than low AS individuals to be heavy coffee drinkers.

As a drug with arousal-enhancing properties, caffeine has been employed in panic provocation research using a rationale similar to that of studies employing other arousal-induction challenges, such as CO_2 inhalation and voluntary hyperventilation (McNally, 1994). Affective responses to caffeine challenge have previously been shown to distinguish panic disorder patients from normal controls (Uhde, 1990). Future placebo-controlled research might focus on determining whether high AS young adults (with no panic disorder history) are more sensitive to caffeine-induced affective, cognitive, and somatic reactions than low AS young adults, as would be predicted by McNally's (1996) hypotheses. A placebo-controlled study by Sturges and Goetsch (1996) suggested that high and low AS individuals show equivalent levels of heart rate increase to caffeine challenge. However, Sturges and Goetsch did not assess levels of fear and catastrophization to the challenge—variables that have previously been shown to be more consistent discriminators of high and low AS individuals' reactivity to arousal-induction challenges (Baker et al., 1998; Rapee & Medoro, 1994).

Marijuana.   Two studies have investigated potential relations between AS and marijuana use. Stewart, Karp, et al. (1997) found that self-reported marijuana users ($n = 63$) had significantly lower ASI scores than marijuana nonusers ($n = 156$). Similarly, in a sample of 113 individuals seeking outpatient treatment for substance abuse, a greater proportion of low AS patients reported marijuana as their substance of choice (42%) as compared with high AS patients (14%; Norton et al., 1997). People with low AS, compared with those with high AS, may be more tolerant to the physical and mental sensations produced by marijuana (e.g., derealization, feelings of loss of control, heightened resting autonomic arousal; Norton et al., 1997; Stewart, Karp, et al., 1997).

These findings suggest several interesting directions for future research. First, given that several retrospective clinical reports link the use of cannabis with the onset of panic attacks in certain patients diagnosed with panic disorder (McNally, 1994; Roy-Byrne & Uhde, 1988), future studies could examine the role of marijuana use in the acute onset of panic attacks in high AS individuals (because AS is an established personality risk factor in the development of panic attacks and panic disorder; Maller & Reiss, 1992; Schmidt, Lerew, & Jackson, 1997; also see chap. 10, this volume). Second, future research could investigate the suggestion by Norton et al. (1997) that people with high ASI scores should be less tolerant than low AS individuals of the unusual bodily and mental sensations produced by marijuana as well as by hallucinogens. Finally, the findings of Norton et al. (1997) and Stewart, Karp, et al. (1997) suggest that people with very low AS may be at risk for cannabis abuse. In fact, people with very low AS and those with high AS may be vulnerable to different types of disorders (Shostak & Peterson, 1990; see chap. 6, this volume).

Nicotine.   McNally's (1996) suggestions regarding relation between AS and substance use are more ambiguous when considering nicotine. This substance may act as either a stimulant or an anxiolytic depending on the smoking situation (Pomerleau, Turk, & Fertig, 1984). Novak et al. (1997) found that ASI scores were not significantly related to rates of cigarette use among young adults. Similarly, Stewart, Karp, et al. (1997) found that self-reported smokers did not differ from nonsmokers in terms of overall ASI scores. However, in terms of smokers' reported primary motives, ASI scores were positively correlated with the use of cigarettes primarily to cope with negative affect. As mentioned earlier, people with high AS appear to use alcohol in a similar manner (Stewart & Zeitlin, 1995).

Findings by Novak et al. (1997) on the relation of ASI scores to smoking motives have produced a somewhat different picture. These researchers found that smoking for mood-related reasons—both indulgent motives (smoking for pleasure) and sedative motives (smoking in response to negative affect)—predicted the amount of cigarette use among low but not high AS students. These results thus appear to contradict the findings of Stewart, Karp, et al. (1997) that AS is positively associated with smoking primarily to cope with negative affect. As noted by Novak et al., these diverging results might be due to methodological differences. Novak et al. used a continuous measure of smoking motives (i.e., the modified Smoking Motives Questionnaire; Tate, Pomerleau, & Pomerleau, 1994), whereas Stewart, Karp, et al. (1997) used a forced-choice option where smokers were required to indicate the primary reason for their smoking behavior. Given these methodological differences, it may be that when high AS individuals do smoke, they are more likely to do so primarily to cope with negative affect. This possibility was not examined by Novak et al. Also, their findings may indicate that high AS individuals do not smoke heavily when stressed due to the stimulating effects of nicotine, which they might find unpleasant, aversive, or frightening. Perhaps low AS individuals, compared with those with high AS, are better able to achieve both anxiolytic and pleasurable effects from heavier smoking (Novak et al., 1997).

Further research is required to verify whether any consistent relations exist between AS and smoking behavior. One area of interest for future research would be to investigate the impact of AS in addicted smokers and the relation between AS and attempts to quit smoking. A nicotine-dependent person with high AS, compared with a similarly dependent person with low AS, would be expected to find the arousal sensations of nicotine withdrawal to be highly aversive. This may make it more difficult for high AS people to quit smoking (cf. Bruce et al., 1995).

Summary of Relations Between AS and Other Drug Use and Abuse

Available research suggests a particular pattern of relationships between AS and the use and misuse of substances with abuse potential. Much of the accumulating evidence is consistent with McNally's (1996) suggestion that AS is associated not only with the use/misuse of alcohol, but also with the use/misuse of other drugs with anxiolytic or arousal-dampening properties (e.g., benzodiazepines, heroin). Moreover, it appears that AS may be positively related to the use and misuse of drugs with analgesic properties at least in chronic pain patients. Less support is currently available for McNally's (1996) second suggestion—that high AS should predict avoidance of substances with anxiogenic or arousal-enhancing properties (e.g., cocaine, caffeine). Finally, high AS may be related to the avoidance of marijuana, but the research on nicotine remains ambiguous. Clearly, more work is needed on the potential relations between AS and the use or abuse of a variety of substances. This relatively recent research area could benefit from a movement away from simple dichotomous measures of use/nonuse of particular substances to examination of the potential relations between AS and rates or patterns of use of a variety of drugs with arousal-enhancing, arousal-dampening, or other relevant properties. Moreover, the AS–drug use/misuse research area could benefit from the use of the experimental paradigms currently being used with alcohol. These paradigms could be used to examine potential differences between high and low AS people in their responses to various drug challenges and to determine the contexts in which high AS individuals are more or less likely to use or abuse particular substances.

THEORETICAL AND METHODOLOGICAL
CONSIDERATIONS FOR FUTURE RESEARCH

Anxiety Sensitivity as a Distinct Predictor of Substance Misuse

Although the studies presented thus far suggest that AS is related in various ways to substance use and misuse, there needs to be further research on whether it is AS per se or whether some other related variable(s) are responsible for these associations. People with high AS differ in a variety of ways from people with low AS. For example, people with high AS tend to have higher trait anxiety (see chap. 7, this volume).

Karp (1993) found that ASI scores were significantly positively related to expectations for relaxation and tension reduction from drinking, as measured on the Alcohol Expectancy Questionnaire (AEQ). In contrast, trait anxiety levels as measured by the trait version of the State–Trait Anxiety Inventory (STAI–T; Spielberger et al., 1983) were unrelated to AEQ expectations for relaxation and tension reduction. This suggests that, at least for alcoholics, it is the fear of anxiety symptoms rather than the frequency of these symptoms that best predicts expectations that alcohol will produce relaxation and tension reduction (Karp, 1993). Norton et al. (1997) found that AS, but not anxiety (as assessed by the Beck Anxiety Inventory; Beck & Steer, 1990), was related to drug choice among their sample of clients seeking treatment for substance-related disorders. Similarly, in their regression analyses, Novak et al. (1997) found that, even after the effects of trait anxiety (STAI–T) had been statistically controlled, ASI scores were significant predictors of young adults' frequency of coping-related drinking. Consistent with these findings, Sher (1991) observed that trait anxiety is not a particularly good predictor of self-reported alcohol use or for risk of developing alcohol problems.

Rather than trait anxiety per se, it may be the combination of high levels of AS and high trait anxiety that best predicts use and abuse of arousal-dampening drugs (McNally, 1996). Stewart and Zeitlin (1995) found some support for this suggestion. A weighted linear combination of scores on the ASI and STAI–T was found to be the best predictor of DMQ coping motives scores in their nonclinical sample of young adult drinkers. Just as researchers in the anxiety disorders area are beginning to consider the potential interactions of AS and trait anxiety in predicting relevant anxiety-related outcomes (e.g., Orsillo, Lilienfeld, & Heimberg, 1994), researchers in the AS and substance abuse area should also be mindful of such potential interactions. Perhaps people who frequently experience anxiety (high trait anxiety) and greatly fear their anxiety symptoms (high AS) are at greatest risk of abusing arousal-dampening drugs such as alcohol and benzodiazepines (Stewart & Zeitlin, 1995).

In addition to assessing the relative contributions of AS and trait anxiety, researchers in the AS–substance abuse field should be careful to include other negative affectivity measures such as panic history, depression, and social anxiety. Measures of panic symptoms (e.g., the Panic Attack Questionnaire; Norton, Doward, & Cox, 1986) should be included given evidence that AS is related to clinically diagnosed panic disorder (Taylor et al., 1992) and the frequency of nonclinical panic attacks (Donnell & McNally, 1990), and given the high degree of comorbidity of panic disorder and alcohol abuse/dependence (Cox, Norton, Swinson, & Endler, 1990). Measures of depressive symptoms (e.g., the Beck Depression Inventory; Beck, Ward, Mendelsohn, Mock, & Erbaugh, 1961) should be included given recent evidence that (a) AS is elevated in clinical depression (Otto, Pollack, Fava, Uccello, & Rosenbaum, 1995), (b) there is considerable comorbidity of depression and alcohol abuse/dependence diagnoses (Merikangas, Leckman, Prusoff, Pauls, & Weissman, 1985), and (c) it is necessary to consider relationships among anxiety-related variables, depression, and alcohol abuse simultaneously (Leckman, Weissman, Merikangas, Pauls, & Prusoff, 1983).

Finally, measures of social anxiety (e.g., the Social Anxiety Scale of the Revised Self-Consciousness Scale; Scheier & Carver, 1985) should be administered given recent evidence that AS is elevated in social phobia (Ball et al., 1995) and given the strong comorbidity of social phobia and alcohol abuse/dependence diagnoses (Kushner et al., 1990). Scores on these measures may be used in regression analyses to ensure that any observed relations between the substance-related dependent variables of interest and AS levels are actually due to differences in AS per se, as opposed (or in addition) to trait anxiety, panic history, depression, or social anxiety. As an alternative to regression designs, experimental studies may wish to cross AS levels with levels of these other related variables (see Donnell & McNally, 1989, for sample methodology). Studies to date that have included measures of depression (e.g., Norton et al., 1997), social anxiety (e.g., Karp, 1993), or panic-disorder history (e.g., Baker et al., 1998) do provide preliminary evidence that the relations between substance use/misuse and AS are as strong or stronger than the relations between substance use/misuse and other related variables. Clearly, scores on these related measures should continue to be assessed in AS–substance abuse research.

Research should also focus on placing AS within the broader context of other personality and psychopathology variables that are theoretically unrelated to the construct of AS but that are known to be associated with drug use/misuse (e.g., impulsivity or sensation seeking). Conrod, Pihl, Stewart, and Dongier. (1997) represents the first such study. A sample of 293 substance-abusing women recruited from the community were administered a battery of self-report personality inventories (including the ASI) in an attempt to identify subtypes that might differ in comorbid psychopathology and substance dependence profiles. Five subtypes were identified using factor analyses of the personality inventories followed by cluster analysis. A cluster referred to as *Sensation Seekers* was characterized primarily by high scores on the Sensation Seeking Scale (Ridgeway & Russell, 1980). A second cluster, labeled *Impulsives*, was characterized primarily by high scores on the Impulsiveness subscale of the I.7 Impulsivity Scale (Corulla, 1987). A *Hopeless/Introverted* cluster was identified primarily by low self-worth on the Self-Esteem Scale (Rosenberg, 1965) and low scores on the Extraversion subscale of the NEO Five Factor Inventory (Costa & McCrae, 1992). An *Anxiety Sensitive* cluster displayed primary elevations on the ASI (Peterson & Reiss, 1992). The fifth cluster, labeled *Low Personality Risk,* displayed relatively low scores on all identified personality dimensions. The AS subtype, compared with the other subtypes, reported more frequent daily use of benzodiazepines and higher rates of *DSM–III–R* anxiolytic dependence. Similarly, the AS subtype was characterized by significantly higher levels of self-reported levels of monthly alcohol use than two of the other four subtypes (i.e., Hopeless/Introverted and Low Personality Risk). The results of this study are consistent with Pihl and Peterson's (1995) contention that AS represents one of several distinct personality variables that may motivate some people to engage in particular patterns of drug abuse.

Expectancies

Karp's (1993) work suggests that significant positive relations exist between AS and positive alcohol outcome expectancies. Because expectancy-related variables have proved highly predictive of risky drinking practices, future research should place increased focus on determining the degree to which beliefs about the relaxing and tension-reducing properties of alcohol account for the risky drinking behavior and increased sensitivity to alcohol-induced fear dampening observed among high AS individuals. To date, the alcohol-administration studies conducted with high versus low AS people have either compared responses pre- and postconsumption (Stewart & Pihl, 1994; Stewart, Achille, et al., 1992) or compared alcohol administration to a placebo control (Baker et al., 1998). Use of the placebo control has established that sensitivity to alcohol-induced dampening of responses to stress among high AS individuals cannot be accounted for solely by expectancy-related factors (Baker et al., 1998).

However, further research must be conducted to determine any additional influences of expectancy. For example, the balanced placebo design (Marlatt & Rohsenow, 1980) permits one to examine the relative contributions of the pharmacological properties of alcohol- versus belief-related variables. In this design, the instructions to participants regarding the content of their assigned beverage is crossed factorially with the actual content of the beverage. This yields four experimental conditions: (a) told alcohol-administered alcohol (pharmacology plus expectancy), (b) told alcohol-administered placebo (expectancy alone), (c) told placebo-administered alcohol (pharmacology alone), and (d) told placebo-administered placebo (control). Based on the results of a meta-analytic review by Hull and Bond (1986), it is predicted that relatively automatic aspects of the fear response (e.g., somatic responses to stress) would be most influenced by alcohol's pharmacological properties, whereas aspects of the fear response, which are under a larger degree of volitional control (e.g., self-reported affective responses to stress), would be most influenced by high AS subjects' alcohol-related expectancies.

FUNCTIONAL RELATIONS BETWEEN ANXIETY SENSITIVITY AND SUBSTANCE USE AND MISUSE

Correlational studies on relations between AS and substance-related dependent variables do not address issues of causality. For example, in a study of patients diagnosed with a DSM–IV anxiety disorder, Stewart and Westra (1996) found that current benzodiazepine users scored significantly higher on the ASI than medication nonusers. If a causal relation exists between high AS and benzodiazepine use, then either (a) physician or patient decisions to prescribe/use benzodiazepines may be related to the patients' level of fear of anxiety symptoms, and/or (b) benzodiazepine use, as a subtle form of anxiety avoidance behavior, may actually serve as a factor in maintaining high levels of AS (Stewart & Westra, 1996; Westra & Stewart, 1998).

Support for the latter hypothesis comes from a study by Fava et al. (1994). Benzodiazepines were discontinued in 16 patients who had previously undergone exposure treatment for panic disorder with agoraphobia. Drug discontinuation yielded a significant decrease in AS in these long-term users. The authors suggested that, although treatment of panic disorder with benzodiazepines may lower anxiety symptoms in the short term, long-term use of benzodiazepines to suppress and prevent anxiety symptoms might increase a patient's levels of AS (Fava, 1996; Fava et al., 1994).

This latter interpretation appears inconsistent with the notion that high AS is a risk factor for the development of abuse of arousal-dampening drugs (McNally, 1996; Stewart, 1995). However, it is unlikely that research will support a simple, unidirectional, causal relationship between AS and substance use/misuse. More likely, a bidirectional relationship exists—where heightened AS promotes the use of arousal-dampening drugs (or the avoidance of arousal-enhancing drugs) to cope with feared anxiety experiences. In turn, the repeated use of arousal-dampening drugs (or avoidance of arousal-enhancing drugs) over time may serve to maintain or even increase AS in the longer term by suppressing and preventing anxiety symptoms, thereby creating a vicious cycle between heightened AS and drug misuse.

Comorbidity

Some anxiety disorders commonly co-occur with alcohol abuse and dependence (Cox et al., 1990; Kushner et al., 1990; Pihl & Stewart, 1991; Stewart, 1996a, 1997). AS may be one common underlying factor contributing to the high degree of overlap between these diagnoses (Stewart, 1995). There does exist some encouraging, albeit indirect, evidence to support this contention. First, research suggests that there are higher AS levels in overlapping conditions of alcoholism and anxiety disorders than in either alcoholism or anxiety disorder diagnoses alone (Kaspi & McNally; cited in International Diagnostic Systems, 1989).

Second, an increased risk for alcoholism appears to be specifically associated with the anxiety disorders characterized by high levels of AS, such as panic disorder (Cox et al., 1990; Kushner et al., 1990), PTSD (Stewart, 1996a, 1997), and social phobia (Kushner et al., 1990). In contrast, anxiety disorders such as specific phobia, and obsessive–compulsive disorder, which are characterized by comparatively lower levels of AS (Taylor et al., 1992), do not appear to be associated with an increased risk for alcoholism (Kushner et al., 1990; Riemann, McNally, & Cox, 1992). Moreover, benzodiazepine dependence appears to be a particular problem in patients with panic disorder (Otto et al., 1992). The potential role of AS in mediating (Baron & Kenny, 1986; Sher, 1991) the relation between anxiety disorders and alcohol abuse/dependence and benzodiazepine dependence merits further study.

Impact of Gender

Stewart, Karp, et al. (1997) found that when their sample was broken down by gender, the positive relationship between AS and the tendency to drink primarily for coping-related motives was significant only for young adult females.

Stewart and Zeitlin (1995) similarly found that the relation between AS and frequency of drinking to cope with negative affective states on the DMQ (Cooper et al., 1992) was stronger among women than men. These findings are consistent with much previous research suggesting that anxiety-related variables are more strongly associated with alcohol abuse in women than in men (W. Cox, 1987; Sher, 1991). However, Novak et al. (1997) failed to find an interaction with gender in the ASI's prediction of DMQ coping motives scores in a nonclinical young adult sample. Moreover, in two studies with clinical samples, Cox et al. (1993) found that the relation between ASI scores and drinking levels was significant only among the male panic disorder patients, and Norton et al. (1997) found that when samples were broken down by gender, the relation between ASI scores and substance of choice was significant only among their male substance abusers.

Additionally, using a male sample, Conrod et al. (1998) recently replicated Stewart and Pihl's (1994) findings of increased sensitivity to the electrodermal stress-response dampening properties of alcohol among high versus low AS females. Other studies on the relation between AS and substance use/misuse have either used female-only samples (e.g., Conrod, Pihl, et al., 1997; Stewart, Achille, et al., 1992; Stewart, Peterson, & Pihl, 1995; Stewart & Pihl, 1994), male-only samples (e.g., Conrod et al., 1998; Karp, 1993), or have contained sample sizes too small to permit reliable gender comparisons (e.g., Baker et al., 1998; Samoluk & Stewart, 1996; Samoluk et al., 1998).

Thus, the inconsistent findings with respect to gender differences in AS–substance abuse relationships require further investigation. In studies in which gender differences were found (e.g., Norton et al., 1997; Stewart & Zeitlin, 1995; Stewart, Karp, et al., 1997), a relatively larger proportion of one gender may have influenced the findings (Novak et al., 1997). Thus, future research should ensure inclusion of adequate sample sizes to provide sufficient power to detect effects in each gender before any firm conclusions can be reached regarding the impact of gender on AS–substance use/abuse relations.

Recent research indicating gender differences in facets of AS (i.e., fears of anticipated physical, psychological, and social consequences of anxiety experiences; Stewart, Taylor, & Baker, 1997; Stewart et al., 1998) should also be considered in future AS–substance abuse research. More specifically, women have been found to be most concerned with anticipated physical consequences and men most concerned with anticipated social and psychological consequences of anxiety experiences (Stewart, Taylor, & Baker, 1997). Given these gender differences in AS facets, the ways in which AS is related to substance use/abuse might also be expected to vary as a function of gender. For example, high AS males, whose predominant anxiety-related concerns include fears of social consequences of anxiety experiences, might be most motivated to use arousal-dampening drugs when encountering social situations in which they fear displaying their anxiety publicly. In contrast, they may rarely use alcohol/drugs when alone, independent of how anxious they may feel.

Longitudinal Research

The findings with nonalcoholic young adults outlined earlier appear to suggest that high levels of AS may be an important risk factor for the long-term development of substance abuse problems, particularly for abuse of arousal-dampening/anxiolytic substances such as the benzodiazepines and alcohol. However, the associations between AS and a potentially maladaptive pattern of drinking in young adulthood and increased sensitivity to alcohol-induced dampening of responses to stress only indirectly suggest increased long-term risk for the development of alcohol-related disorders in high AS young adults. The next logical step in this line of research would be to conduct a large-scale longitudinal study with high versus low AS nonclinical young adults; this study could test Stewart's (1995) hypothesis that high AS individuals are at heightened risk for the future development of alcohol problems and alcohol use disorders.

Clinical Implications

Another important future research direction will be to develop and evaluate interventions for high AS young adults to reduce risky drinking and drug use behavior in the short term and possibly prevent the development of substance problems and substance-related disorders in the longer term. Research on the mechanisms underlying risk in high AS individuals can assist in providing further information on the functional relations between AS and substance use/misuse. Such research can thereby contribute to the development of appropriate targets for preventative interventions. Although a review of literature on the efficacy of behavioral anti-anxiety treatments for alcoholic clients was not optimistic (Klajner, Hartman, & Sobell, 1984), such approaches may be more effective when directed toward specific subtypes of substance abusers or high-risk individuals. In fact, a recent study demonstrated that cognitive-behavioral interventions matched to the specific motivational profile of substance-abusing women (e.g., providing cognitive restructuring and anxiety management training to the Anxiety Sensitive substance-abusing woman) is more effective in reducing substance abuse/dependence symptoms than the same cognitive-behavioral strategies provided in a generic (mismatched) manner (e.g., providing cognitive restructuring and anxiety management training to the Impulsive substance-abusing woman; Conrod, Cote, et al., 1997).

Cognitive behavior therapy has been shown to effectively reduce AS in panic disorder patients (McNally & Lorenz, 1987) and high AS nonclinical young adults (Harrington & Telch, 1994; see chap. 14, this volume). Such interventions have focused both on training in self-control of somatic arousal symptoms (e.g., controlled breathing) and in reducing high AS individuals' tendency to catastrophize about the meaning of anxiety symptoms (e.g., cognitive restructuring). The experimental work of Baker et al. (1998), on the effects of alcohol on various aspects of response to hyperventilation challenge in high and low AS young adults, suggests that eliminating high AS subjects' tendency to catastrophize about the meaning of arousal-related bodily sensations (e.g., through cognitive restructuring) may be more effective in preventive interventions than providing training in control of somatic arousal symptoms (e.g., through training in controlled breathing). Reducing the motivation for excessive drinking and arousal-dampening drug use among high AS young adults could be achieved by providing cognitive behavioral interventions that reduce AS.

Such AS-focused interventions may prevent the development of alcohol disorders. Alternatively, preventive interventions may have to utilize techniques focused on high AS young adults' aberrant drinking behaviors and/or beliefs. For example, training in controlled drinking (Sanchez-Craig, Annis, Bornet, & MacDonald, 1984) and challenging positive alcohol outcome expectancies (Darkes & Goldman, 1993) may prove useful as alternatives or supplements to AS-focused treatment to effectively reduce current risky drinking and possibly prevent the development of alcohol abuse in this population. Future studies in this area should be designed to determine which combination of AS and/or drinking-focused interventions is most effective in reducing high AS young adults' current alcohol misuse and possible longer term risk for alcohol abuse. The detection of the risk factor of high AS in the early stages represents a unique and cost-effective opportunity for targeting a subgroup of individuals for preventive interventions that thus far has not been exploited.

REFERENCES

American Psychiatric Association. (1987). *Diagnostic and Statistical Manual of Mental Disorders* (3rd ed., rev.). Washington, DC: Author.

American Psychiatric Association. (1994). *Diagnostic and Statistical Manual of Mental Disorders* (4th ed.). Washington, DC: Author.

Annis, H., Graham, J., & Davis, C. (1987). *Inventory of Drinking Situations (IDS) User's Guide*. Toronto, ON: Addiction Research Foundation.

Asmundson, G. J. G., & Norton, G. R. (1995). Anxiety sensitivity in patients with physically unexplained chronic back pain: A preliminary report. *Behaviour Research and Therapy, 33,* 771–777.

Asmundson, G. J. G., Norton, G. R., Wilson, K. G., & Sandler, L. S. (1994). Subjective symptoms and cardiac reactivity to brief hyperventilation in individuals with high anxiety sensitivity. *Behaviour Research and Therapy, 32,* 237–241.

Asmundson, G. J. G., & Taylor, S. (1996). Role of anxiety sensitivity in pain-related fear and avoidance. *Journal of Behavioral Medicine, 19,* 577–582.

Baker, J. M., MacDonald, A. B., Stewart, S. H., & Skinner, M. (1998). *The effects of alcohol on the response to hyperventilation of participants high and low in anxiety sensitivity.* Manuscript submitted for publication.

Ball, S. G., Otto, M. W., Pollack, M. H., Uccello, R., & Rosenbaum, J. F. (1995). Differentiating social phobia and panic disorder: A test of core beliefs. *Cognitive Therapy and Research, 19,* 473–482.

Baron, R. M., & Kenny, D. A. (1986). The moderator-mediator variable distinction in social psychological research: Conceptual, strategic, and statistical considerations. *Journal of Personality and Social Psychology, 51,* 1173–1182.

Beck, A. T., & Steer, R. A. (1990). *Manual for the Beck Anxiety Inventory.* San Antonio, TX: Psychological Corporation.

Beck, A. T., Ward, C. H., Mendelsohn, M., Mock, J., & Erbaugh, J. (1961). An inventory for measuring depression. *Archives of General Psychiatry, 4,* 561–571.

Brown, S. A., Christiansen, B. A., & Goldman, M. S. (1987). The Alcohol Expectancy Questionnaire: An instrument for the assessment of adolescent and adult alcohol expectancies. *Journal of Studies on Alcohol, 48,* 483–491.

Bruce, T. J. (1996). Predictors of alprazolam discontinuation with and without cognitive behavior therapy in panic disorder: Reply to Fava (1996). *American Journal of Psychiatry, 153,* 1109–1110.

Bruce, T. J., Speigel, D. A., Gregg, S. F., & Nuzzarello, A. (1995). Predictors of alprazolam discontinuation with and without cognitive behavior therapy in panic disorder. *American Journal of Psychiatry, 152,* 1156–1160.

Cappell, H., & Greeley, J. (1987). Alcohol and tension reduction: An update of research and theory. In H. T. Blane & K. E. Leonard (Eds.), *Psychological theories of drinking and alcoholism* (pp. 15–54). New York: Guilford.

Carrigan, G., Samoluk, S. B., & Stewart, S. H. (1998). Examination of a short form of the Inventory of Drinking Situations in a young adult university student sample. *Behaviour Research and Therapy, 36,* 789–807.

Conger, J. J. (1956). Alcoholism: Theory, problem and challenge: II. Reinforcement theory and the dynamics of alcoholism. *Quarterly Journal of Studies on Alcohol, 12,* 1–29.

Conrod, P. J., Cote, S., Fontaine, V., Stewart, S. H., Pihl, R. O., & Dongier, M. (1997). The efficacy of brief interventions matched to the motivational basis of substance abuse [Summary]. *Proceedings of the 31st Annual Meeting of the Association for Advancement of Behavior Therapy* [CD-ROM].

Conrod, P. J., Pihl, R. O., Stewart, S. H., & Dongier, M. (1997). *Subtypes of female substance dependents.* Manuscript submitted for publication.

Conrod, P. J., Pihl, R. O., & Vassileva, J. (1998). Differential sensitivity to alcohol reinforcement in groups of men at risk for distinct alcoholic syndromes. *Alcoholism: Clinical and Experimental Research, 22*(3), 585–597.

Conrod, P. J., Stewart, S. H., & Pihl, R. O. (1997). Validation of a measure of excessive drinking frequency. *Substance Use and Misuse, 32,* 587–607.

Cooper, M. L., Russell, M., Skinner, J. B., & Windle, M. (1992). Development and validation of a three-dimensional measure of drinking motives. *Psychological Assessment, 4,* 123–132.

Corulla, W. J. (1987). A psychometric investigation of the Eysenck Personality Questionnaire (Revised) and its relationship to the I.7 Impulsiveness Questionnaire. *Personality and Individual Differences, 8,* 651–658.

Costa, P. T., & McCrae, R. R. (1992). *The Revised NEO Personality Inventory (NEO PI-R) and NEO Five Factor Inventory (NEO-FFI) Professional Manual.* Odessa, FL: Psychological Assessment Resources.

Cox, B. J. (1996). The nature and assessment of catastrophic thoughts in panic disorder. *Behaviour Research and Therapy, 34,* 363–374.

Cox, B. J., Norton, G. R., Swinson, R. P., & Endler, N. S. (1990). Substance abuse and panic related anxiety: A critical review. *Behaviour Research and Therapy, 28,* 385–393.

Cox, B. J., Swinson, R. P., Shulman, I. D., Kuch, K., & Reichman, J. R. (1993). Gender effects and alcohol use in panic disorder with agoraphobia. *Behaviour Research and Therapy, 31,* 413–416.

Cox, W. M. (1987). Personality theory and research. In H.T. Blane & K. E. Leonard (Eds.), *Psychological theories of drinking and alcoholism* (pp. 55–89). New York: Guilford.

Darkes, J., & Goldman, M. S. (1993). Expectancy challenge and drinking reduction: Experimental evidence for a mediational process. *Journal of Consulting and Clinical Psychology, 61,* 344–353.

Deitrich, R. A., Dunwiddie, T. V., Harris, R. A., & Erwin, V. G. (1989). Mechanisms of action of ethanol: Initial central nervous system actions. *Pharmacology Review, 41,* 489–537.

Donnell, C. D., & McNally, R. J. (1989). Anxiety sensitivity and history of panic as predictors of response to hyperventilation challenge. *Behaviour Research and Therapy, 27,* 325–332.

Donnell, C. D., & McNally, R. J. (1990). Anxiety sensitivity and panic attacks in a nonclinical population. *Behaviour Research and Therapy, 28,* 83–85.

Engel, J., & Liljequist, S. (1983). The involvement of different central neurotransmitters in mediating stimulatory and sedative effects of ethanol. In L. A. Pohorecky & J. Brick (Eds.), *Stress and alcohol use* (pp. 153–169). Amsterdam: Elsevier.

Fava, G. A. (1996). Anxiety sensitivity [letter]. *American Journal of Psychiatry, 153,* 1109.

Fava, G. A., Grandi, S., Belluardo, P., Savron, G., Raffi, A. R., Conti, S., & Saviotti, F. M. (1994). Benzodiazepines and anxiety sensitivity in panic disorder. *Progress in Neuro-Psychopharmacology and Biological Psychiatry, 18,* 1163–1168.

George, W. H., Phillips, S. M., & Skinner, J. B. (1988). Analogue measurement of alcohol consumption: Effects of task type and correspondence with self-report measurement. *Journal of Studies on Alcohol, 49,* 450–455.

Goldman, M. S., Brown, S. A., & Christiansen, B. A. (1987). Expectancy theory: Thinking about drinking. In H. T. Blane & K. E. Leonard (Eds.), *Psychological theories of drinking and alcoholism* (pp. 181–226). New York: Guilford.

Harrington, P. J., & Telch, M. J. (1994). Lowering anxiety sensitivity in non-clinical subjects [Summary]. *Proceedings of the 28th Annual Meeting of the Association for Advancement of Behavior Therapy,* p. 23.

Higgins, R. L., & Marlatt, G. A. (1975). Fear of interpersonal evaluation as a determinant of alcohol consumption in male social drinkers. *Journal of Abnormal Psychology, 84,* 644–651.

Holloway, W., & McNally, R. J. (1987). Effects of anxiety sensitivity on the response to hyperventilation. *Journal of Abnormal Psychology, 96,* 330–334.

Hull, J. G., & Bond, C. F. (1986). Social and behavioral consequences of alcohol consumption and expectancy: A meta-analysis. *Psychological Bulletin, 99*, 347–360.

International Diagnostic Systems. (1989). *ASI Annual Update, No. 1.* Worthington, OH: Author.

Karp, J. (1993). The interaction of alcohol expectancies, personality, and psychopathology among inpatient alcoholics [Summary]. *Dissertation Abstracts International, 53*, 4375-B.

Klajner, F., Hartman, L. M., & Sobell, M. B. (1984). Treatment of substance abuse by relaxation training: A review of its rationale, efficacy and mechanisms. *Addictive Behaviors, 9*, 41–55.

Kushner, M. G., MacKenzie, T. B., Fiszdon, J., Valentiner, D., Foa, E., Anderson, N., & Wangensteen, D. (1996). The effects of alcohol consumption on laboratory-induced panic and state anxiety. *Archives of General Psychiatry, 53*, 264–270.

Kushner, M. G., Sher, K. J., & Beitman, B. D. (1990). The relation between alcohol problems and the anxiety disorders. *American Journal of Psychiatry, 147*, 685–695.

Lilienfeld, S. O. (1996). Anxiety sensitivity is not distinct from trait anxiety. In R. M. Rapee (Ed.), *Current controversies in the anxiety disorders* (pp. 228–244). New York: Guilford.

Leckman, J. F., Weissman, M. M., Merikangas, K. R., Pauls, D. L., & Prusoff, B. A. (1983). Panic disorder and major depression: Increased risk of depression, alcoholism, panic, and phobic disorders in families of depressed probands with panic disorder. *Archives of General Psychiatry, 40*, 1055–1060.

MacDonald, A. B., & Stewart, S. H. (1996). Coping-related drinking in high anxiety sensitive individuals [Summary]. *Psychophysiology, 33 (Suppl. 1),* S57.

Maller, R. G., & Reiss, S. (1987). A behavioral validation of the Anxiety Sensitivity Index. *Journal of Anxiety Disorders, 1*, 265–272.

Maller, R. G., & Reiss, S. (1992). Anxiety sensitivity in 1984 and panic attacks in 1987. *Journal of Anxiety Disorders, 6*, 241–247.

Marlatt, G. A., & Rohsenow, D. J. (1980). Cognitive processes in alcohol use: Expectancy and the balanced-placebo design. In N. K. Mello (Ed.), *Advances in substance abuse: Behavioral and biological research* (Vol. 1, pp. 159–199). Greenwich, CT: JAI.

McNally, R. J. (1994). *Panic disorder: A critical analysis.* New York: Guilford.

McNally, R. J. (1996). Anxiety sensitivity is distinct from trait anxiety. In R. M. Rapee (Ed.), *Current controversies in the anxiety disorders* (pp. 214–227). New York: Guilford.

McNally, R. J., & Lorenz, M. (1987). Anxiety sensitivity in agoraphobics. *Journal of Behavior Therapy and Experimental Psychiatry, 18*, 3–11.

McNally, R. J., Luedke, D. L., Besyner, J. K., Peterson, R. A., Bohm, K., & Lips, O. J. (1987). Sensitivity to stress-relevant stimuli in posttraumatic stress disorder. *Journal of Anxiety Disorders, 1*, 105–116.

Merikangas, K. R., Leckman, J. F., Prusoff, B. A., Pauls, D. L., & Weissman, M. M. (1985). Familial transmission of depression and alcoholism. *Archives of General Psychiatry, 42*, 367–372.

Norton, G. R., Dorward, J., & Cox, B. J. (1986). Factors associated with panic attacks in non-clinical subjects. *Behavior Therapy, 17*, 239–252.

Norton, G. R., Rockman, G. E., Ediger, J., Pepe, C., Goldberg, S., Cox, B. J., & Asmundson, G. J. G. (1997). Anxiety sensitivity and drug choice in individuals seeking treatment for substance abuse. *Behaviour Research and Therapy, 35*, 859–862.

Novak, A., Burgess, E. S., Clark, M., & Brown, R. A. (1997). *Anxiety sensitivity, self-reported motives for alcohol and nicotine use, and level of consumption.* Manuscript submitted for publication.

Orsillo, S. M., Lilienfeld, S. O., & Heimberg, R. G. (1994). Social phobia and response to challenge procedures: Examining the interaction between anxiety sensitivity and trait anxiety. *Journal of Anxiety Disorders, 8,* 247–258.

Otto, M. W., Pollack, M. H., Fava, M., Uccello, R., & Rosenbaum, J. F. (1995). Elevated Anxiety Sensitivity Index scores in major depression: Correlates and changes with antidepressant treatment. *Journal of Anxiety Disorders, 9,* 117–123.

Otto, M. W., Pollack, M. H., Meltzer-Brody, S., & Rosenbaum, J. F. (1992). Cognitive behavioral therapy for benzodiazepine discontinuation in panic disorder patients. *Psychopharmacology Bulletin, 28,* 123–130.

Peterson, J. B., Pihl, R. O., Gianoulakis, C., Conrod, P., Finn, P. R., Stewart, S. H., LeMarquand, D. G., & Bruce, K. T. (1996). Ethanol-induced change in cardiac and endogenous opiate function and risk for alcoholism. *Alcoholism: Clinical and Experimental Research, 20,* 1542–1552.

Peterson, J. B., Pihl, R. O., Seguin, J. R., Finn, P. R., & Stewart, S. H. (1993). Alcohol-induced heart rate change, family history, and prediction of weekly alcohol consumption by non-alcoholic males. *Journal of Psychiatry and Neuroscience, 18,* 190–198.

Peterson, R. A., & Reiss, S. (1992). *Anxiety Sensitivity Index Manual* (2nd ed.). Worthington, OH: International Diagnostic Systems.

Pihl, R. O., & Peterson, J. B. (1995). Alcoholism: The role of different motivational systems. *Journal of Psychiatry and Neuroscience, 20,* 372–396.

Pihl, R. O., & Stewart, S. H. (1991). Substance abuse and behavioral pathology: A commentary. *Annual Review of Addictions Research and Treatment, 1,* 153–156.

Poherecky, L. A. (1991). Stress and alcohol interaction: An update of human research. *Alcoholism: Clinical and Experimental Research, 15,* 438–459.

Pokorny, A. D., Miller, B. A., & Kaplan, H. B. (1972). The brief MAST: A shortened version of the Michigan Alcoholism Screening Test. *American Journal of Psychiatry, 129,* 342–345.

Pomerleau, O. F., Turk, D. C., & Fertig, J. B. (1984). The effects of cigarette smoking on pain and anxiety. *Addictive Behaviors, 9,* 265–271.

Rapee, R. M., & Medoro, L. (1994). Fear of physical sensations and trait anxiety as mediators of the response to hyperventilation in non-clinical subjects. *Journal of Abnormal Psychology, 103,* 538–552.

Reiss, S. (1991). Expectancy model of fear, anxiety, and panic. *Clinical Psychology Review, 11,* 141–153.

Reiss, S., & McNally, R. J. (1985). The expectancy model of fear. In S. Reiss & R. R. Bootzin (Eds.), *Theoretical issues in behavior therapy* (pp. 107–121). New York: Academic Press.

Ridgeway, D., & Russell, J. A. (1980). Reliability and validity of the Sensation-Seeking Scale: Psychometric problems in Form V. *Journal of Consulting and Clinical Psychology, 48,* 662–664.

Riemann, B. C., McNally, R. J., & Cox, W. M. (1992). The comorbidity of obsessive compulsive disorder and alcoholism. *Journal of Anxiety Disorders, 6,* 105–110.

Rosenberg, M. (1965). *Society and adolescent self-image.* Princeton, NJ: Princeton University Press.

Roy-Byrne, P. P., & Uhde, T. W. (1988). Exogenous factors in panic disorder: Clinical and research implications. *Journal of Clinical Psychiatry, 49,* 56–61.

Samoluk, S. B., & Stewart, S. H. (1995). Attentional bias for alcohol cues as a function of food deprivation and anxiety sensitivity [Summary]. *Proceedings of the 29th Annual Meeting of the Association for Advancement of Behavior Therapy,* p. 246.

Samoluk, S. B., & Stewart, S. H. (1996). Anxiety sensitivity and anticipation of a self-disclosing interview as determinants of alcohol consumption. *Psychology of Addictive Behaviors, 10,* 45–54.

Samoluk, S. B., & Stewart, S. H. (in press). Anxiety sensitivity and situation-specific drinking. *Journal of Anxiety Disorders.*

Samoluk, S. B., Stewart, S. H., Sweet, S., & MacDonald, A. B. (1998). *Anxiety sensitivity and social affiliation as determinants of alcohol consumption.* Manuscript submitted for publication.

Sanchez-Craig, M., Annis, H. M., Bornet, A. R., & MacDonald, K. R. (1984). Random assignment to abstinence and controlled drinking: Evaluation of a cognitive-behavioural program for problem drinkers. *Journal of Consulting and Clinical Psychology, 52,* 390–403.

Scheier, M. F., & Carver, C. S. (1985). The Self-Consciousness Scale: A revised version for use with general populations. *Journal of Applied Social Psychology, 15,* 687–699.

Schmidt, N. B., Lerew, D. R., & Jackson, R. J. (1997). The role of anxiety sensitivity in the pathogenesis of panic: Prospective evaluation of spontaneous panic attacks during acute stress. *Journal of Abnormal Psychology, 106,* 355–364.

Sher, K. J. (1991). *Children of alcoholics: A critical appraisal of theory and research.* Chicago, IL: University of Chicago Press.

Shostak, B. B., & Peterson, R. A. (1990). Effects of anxiety sensitivity on emotional response to a stress task. *Behaviour Research and Therapy, 28,* 245–259.

Spielberger, C. D., Gorsuch, R. L., Lushene, R. E., Vagg, P. R., & Jacobs, G. A. (1983). *Manual for the State-Trait Anxiety Inventory.* Palo Alto, CA: Consulting Psychologists Press.

Stewart, S. H. (1995). Anxiety sensitivity and risk for alcohol abuse in young adult females [Summary]. *Dissertation Abstracts International, 55,* 4615–B.

Stewart, S. H. (1996a). Alcohol abuse in individuals exposed to trauma: A critical review. *Psychological Bulletin, 120,* 83–112.

Stewart, S. H. (1996b, November). Discussant's remarks in the symposium *"New research on the psychopathology of anxiety sensitivity"* presented at the 30th annual meeting of the Association for Advancement of Behavior Therapy, New York.

Stewart, S. H. (1997). Trauma memory and alcohol abuse: Drinking to forget? In D. Read & D. S. Lindsay (Eds.), *Recollections of trauma: Scientific evidence and clinical practice* (pp. 461–467). New York: Plenum.

Stewart, S. H., Achille, M. A., Dubois-Nguyen, I., & Pihl, R. O. (1992). The effects of alcohol on attention to threat in anxiety sensitive women [Summary]. *Pharmacology, Biochemistry, and Behavior, 38,* 309.

Stewart, S. H., Conrod, P. J., Gignac, M. L., & Pihl, R. O. (1998). Selective processing biases in anxiety sensitive men and women. *Cognition and Emotion, 12,* 105–133.

Stewart, S. H., Finn, P. R., & Pihl, R. O. (1992). The effects of alcohol on the cardiovascular stress response in men at high risk for alcoholism: A dose-response study. *Journal of Studies on Alcohol, 53,* 499–506.

Stewart, S. H., Finn, P. R., & Pihl, R. O. (1995). A dose-response study of the effects of alcohol on the perceptions of pain and discomfort due to electric shock in men at high familial-genetic risk for alcoholism. *Psychopharmacology, 199,* 261–267.

Stewart, S. H., Karp, J., Pihl, R. O., & Peterson, R. A. (1997). Anxiety sensitivity and self-reported reasons for drug use. *Journal of Substance Abuse, 9,* 223–240.

Stewart, S. H., Knize, K., & Pihl, R. O. (1992). Anxiety sensitivity and dependency in clinical and non-clinical panickers and controls. *Journal of Anxiety Disorders, 7,* 119–131.

Stewart, S. H., Peterson, J. B., & Pihl, R. O. (1995). Anxiety sensitivity and self-reported alcohol consumption rates in university women. *Journal of Anxiety Disorders*, *9*, 283–292.

Stewart, S. H., & Pihl, R. O. (1994). The effects of alcohol administration on psychophysiological and subjective-emotional responses to aversive stimulation in anxiety sensitive women. *Psychology of Addictive Behaviors*, *8*, 29–42.

Stewart, S. H., Taylor, S., & Baker, J. M. (1997). Gender differences in dimensions of anxiety sensitivity. *Journal of Anxiety Disorders*, *11*, 179–200.

Stewart, S. H., & Westra, H. (1996). Pattern of benzodiazepine use and anxiety disorder symptoms [Summary]. *International Journal of Psychology*, *31* (3/4), 24.

Stewart, S. H., Westra, H., & Thompson, C. E. (1996). Effects of chronic benzodiazepine use on the selective processing of threat cues among anxiety disorder patients [Summary]. *Proceedings of the 30th Annual Meeting of the 30th Annual Meeting of the Association for Advancement of Behavior Therapy*, p. 169.

Stewart, S. H., & Zeitlin, S. B. (1995). Anxiety sensitivity and alcohol use motives. *Journal of Anxiety Disorders*, *9*, 229–240.

Stewart, S. H., Zeitlin, S. B., & Samoluk, S. B. (1996). Examination of a three-dimensional drinking motives questionnaire in a young adult university sample. *Behaviour Research and Therapy*, *34*, 61–71.

Sturges, L.V., & Goetsch, V. L. (1996). Psychophysiological reactivity and heartbeat awareness in anxiety sensitivity. *Journal of Anxiety Disorders*, *10*, 283–294.

Tate, J. C., Pomerleau, C. S., & Pomerleau, O.F. (1994). Pharmacological and non-pharmacological smoking motives: A replication and extension. *Addiction*, *89*, 321–330.

Taylor, S., Koch, W. H., & McNally, R. J. (1992). How does anxiety sensitivity vary across the anxiety disorders? *Journal of Anxiety Disorders*, *6*, 249–259.

Telch, M. J., & Harrington, P. J. (1994). The role of anxiety sensitivity and expectedness of arousal in mediating emotional response to inhalation of 35% carbon dioxide. [Summary]. *Proceedings of the 28th Annual Meeting of the Association for Advancement of Behavior Therapy*, p. 22.

Telch, M. J., Lucas, J. A., & Nelson, P. (1989). Non-clinical panic in college students: An investigation of prevalence and symptomatology. *Journal of Abnormal Psychology*, *98*, 300–306.

Uhde, T. W. (1990). Caffeine provocation of panic: A focus on biological mechanisms. In J. C. Ballenger (Ed.), *Neurobiology of panic disorder* (pp. 219–242). New York: Wiley.

Welte, J. W. (1985). Alcohol use and trait anxiety in the general population. *Drug and Alcohol Dependence*, *15*, 105–109.

Westra, H. A., & Stewart, S. H. (1998). Pharmacotherapy and cognitive behavioral therapy: Complimentary or contradictory approaches to the treatment of anxiety disorders? *Clinical Psychology Review*, *18*, 307–340.

Williams, J. M. G., Mathews, A., & MacLeod, C. (1996). The emotional Stroop task and psychopathology. *Psychological Bulletin*, *120*, 3–24.

Wilson, G. T. (1988). Alcohol and anxiety. *Behaviour Research and Therapy*, *26*, 369–381.

14

The Impact of Treatment on Anxiety Sensitivity

Michael W. Otto
Noreen A. Reilly-Harrington
Massachusetts General Hospital
and Harvard Medical School

Previous chapters in this volume have made it clear that anxiety sensitivity (AS) can develop independently from panic attacks and that high AS may place an individual at risk for panic disorder (see chaps. 6 and 10, this volume). Furthermore, high AS predicts the maintenance of panic disorder among untreated patients, the prospective emergence of panic attacks among infrequent panickers, the emergence of panic among individuals free of a history of panic (Ehlers, 1995), as well as the average longer term outcome achieved by patients in a clinic setting (Pollack et al., 1996). All of these studies support the hypothesis that AS is central to panic disorder. Consequently, the degree to which successful treatment impacts AS is an important issue for examining the nature of treatment response and the likelihood of maintaining improvement.

This chapter examines the impact of treatment on AS, and addresses the question of whether treatments for panic disorder must directly target fears of anxiety sensations to achieve robust changes in AS. Anxiety sensitivity is considered as both a cause and consequence of panic disorder, with the assumption that a mutually causal cycle may exist between fears of anxiety symptoms and recurrent panic episodes (see Taylor, 1995). Cognitive-behavioral approaches to panic disorder focus on fears of anxiety symptoms as the core maintaining influence on panic disorder. Treatment packages that directly target the modification of these fears have demonstrated clear efficacy for treating panic disorder (for review of outcome studies, see Gould, Otto, & Pollack, 1995). Nonetheless, treatments that do not target these fears directly, such as pharmacological treatments or particular psychosocial interventions, also offer efficacy for panic disorder and, as reviewed herein, reduce AS. Consequently, these studies provide an interesting context for discussing the nature of treatment influences on anxiety sensitivity. Before these studies are examined, it is important to review the theoretical role of fears of anxiety symptoms in maintaining panic disorder and the role of cognitive-behavioral interventions in eliminating these fears.

Cognitive-behavioral accounts of panic disorder propose that catastrophic cognitions and fears of anxiety sensations are central to the development and maintenance of panic disorder (Barlow, 1988; Clark, 1986; Goldstein & Chambless, 1978; McNally, 1994; Otto & Whittal, 1995). An individual's initial panic attack is conceptualized as an unanticipated firing of the emergency fight-or-flight response, often coinciding with a period of stress (cf. Faravelli & Pallanti, 1989; Rapee, Litwin, & Barlow, 1990). Subsequent panic attacks are conceptualized as a refiring of this alarm response in reaction to subjective rather than objective threat. This subjective threat is a result of catastrophic misinterpretations and fears of anxiety sensations (e.g., "I'm going to have a heart attack" or "I am going to lose control"). As repeated attacks occur, individuals with panic disorder may become more and more sensitized to the environmental and somatic cues that signal the panic attacks, providing a wealth of internal and external stimuli to trigger anxious anticipation and hypervigilance. Fears of somatic sensations similar to anxiety may also lead to avoidance of activities associated with such sensations (e.g., avoidance of caffeine intake, exercise, or other activities that may induce feared sensations) as well as avoidance of situations associated with panic attacks (agoraphobic avoidance).

Current cognitive-behavioral treatments (CBT) for panic disorder follow naturally from this model (e.g., Barlow & Craske, 1994; Otto, Jones, Barlow, & Craske, 1996). Greatest emphasis is placed on the elimination of the fears of anxiety sensations and fear of panic episodes that maintain the disorder. These fears are targeted via exposure interventions, cognitive restructuring, and training in arousal reduction. Exposure interventions include both direct exposure to feared internal sensations (via interoceptive exposure) and naturalistic exposures to feared situations. Interoceptive exposure utilizes a variety of exercises designed to induce somatic sensations resembling those encountered during panic attacks.

For example, dizziness may be induced by a head-rolling exercise in which patients swing their heads around in circles with their eyes closed. Lightheadedness, hot flashes, and dry mouth may be induced by having patients hyperventilate for 1 minute. The repeated use of such exercises provides adaptation to the somatic sensations of panic and reduces the probability that such bodily sensations will trigger future panic attacks. Cognitive restructuring interventions target the catastrophic misinterpretations of anxiety sensations. Frequently, these procedures are supplemented with general anxiety management training (e.g., relaxation training or diaphragmatic breathing) to combat the overarousal and vigilance that accompanies panic disorder. Many current treatment packages incorporate all of these interventions, but treatments that emphasize individual elements of this overall package are also common.

ANXIETY SENSITIVITY
AND THE TREATMENT OF PANIC DISORDER

Changes in AS in patients with panic disorder and agoraphobia was first studied by McNally and Lorenz (1987), who examined treatment outcome for a sample of 23 patients with agoraphobia. Treatment consisted of psychoeducation on panic disorder, cognitive restructuring, diaphragmatic breathing training, and in vivo exposure delivered in 10 to 12 individual sessions. Scores on the Anxiety Sensitivity Index (ASI; Peterson & Reiss, 1992) decreased significantly with treatment from the clinical to nonclinical range and remained at this low level at 6-month follow-up assessment. The mean (and standard deviation) ASI scores for this and other studies reported in this chapter are shown in Table 14.1. As a comparison, the mean ASI score for nonclinical samples is 19.0 ($SD = 9.1$; Peterson and Reiss, 1992).

Reductions in ASI scores following CBT also have been reported for treatment in a group format. Telch et al. (1993) examined the outcome of 67 panic disorder patients assigned to either an 8-week CBT program (emphasizing informational, cognitive restructuring, interoceptive exposure, and diaphragmatic breathing interventions) or a delayed treatment control group. Pretreatment means for the ASI were in the mid- to low 30s and remained so across the treatment interval for the wait-list control group (Table 14.1). In contrast, scores for the treatment group decreased dramatically to the nonclinical range at posttreatment and remained at this low level at the 6-month follow-up assessment. Recovery from the panic disorder was observed in 64%

TABLE 14.1

Pretreatment, Posttreatment, and Follow-Up Means (and SDs) of ASI Scores
in Outcome Studies of Patients With Panic Disorder or Relevant Comparison Samples

Study and Treatment	Pretreatment	Posttreatment	6-Month Follow-Up	Acute Tx Change (pre–post)
Controlled Trials of Panic Disorder				
Gould et al. (1993)				
4-week guided coping	46.1	44.3		1.8
(*n* = 9)	(4.4)	(5.2)		
Self-help manual	44.7	34.7		10.0
(*n* = 11)	(2.9)	(2.6)		
Wait-list control	41.4	39.6		1.8
(*n* = 11)	(3.6)	(3.8)		
Telch et al. (1993)				
12-session group CBT	33.7	13.9	14.2	19.8
(*n* = 34)	(11.2)	(8.5)	(10.2)	
Wait-list control	34.5	32.0		2.5
(*n* = 33)	(11.3)	(11.0)		
Shear et al. (1994)				
15-session CBT	30.8	20.7	17.9	10.1
(*n* = 20)	(15.0)	(10.5)	(9.6)	
Nonprescriptive tx.	31.6	21.4	13.7	10.2
(*n* = 21)	(11.2)	(13.8)	(11.8)	
Hazen et al. (1996)				
Therapist-led group	30.2	17.8		12.4
(*n* = 26)	(10.9)	(11.1)		
Self-help group	33.5	23.5		10.0
(*n* = 26)	(10.5)	(13.2)		
Self-help manual	33.7	26.7		7.0
(*n* = 27)	(12.0)	(13.9)		
Wait-list control	36.1	35.1		1.0
(*n* = 27)	(10.9)	(11.6)		
Open Trials of CBT for Panic Disorder				
McNally & Lorenz (1987)				
10–12 sessions CBT	38.3	19.2	15.2	19.1
(*n* = 23)	(11.2)	(12.4)	(8.6)	
Hegel et al. (1994)				
CBT + Alprazolam (taper)	33.7	21.7	20.2	12.0
(*n* = 22)	(9.4)	(8.8)	(9.3)	

(continues)

TABLE 14.1 (continued)

Study and Treatment	Pretreatment	Posttreatment	6-Month Follow-Up	Acute Tx Change (pre–post)
Penava et al. (1997)				
12-session group CBT	35.0	21.5		13.5
(*n* = 26)	(12.5)	(12.9)		
Pharmacotherapy for Panic Disorder				
Otto et al. (1991)				
6-months pharmacotherapy	31.3	22.2		9.1
(*n* = 24)	(10.3)	(9.6)		
Pharmacotherapy for Major Depression				
Otto et al. (1995)				
Fluoxetine treatment	27.1	20.0		7.1
(*n* = 86)	(12.3)	(12.1)		
Preventive Treatment in At-Risk Students				
Harrington et al. (1995)				
3-session CBT	28.0	18.6		9.4
(*n* = 60)	(7.5)	(7.6)		
Control treatment	28.2	23.4		4.8
(*n* = 60)	(7.4)	(8.6)		

CBT = cognitive behavior therapy.

of treated patients and 9% of controls. Computations of a between-group effect size ($M_{control} - M_{experimental}/ SD_{control}$) revealed a large effect size (ES) for the ASI at posttreatment (ES = 1.65), which was larger than the effect size estimates for other outcome scores (overall mean outcome ES = 0.84).

A recent report by Penava, Otto, Maki, and Pollack (1997) also documented significant changes in ASI scores following group CBT for panic disorder. The 12-session treatment program emphasized interoceptive exposure and cognitive restructuring. Rate of response to treatment was examined in 26 patients with a primary diagnosis of panic disorder who were studied as part of ongoing services research. ASI scores decreased from a baseline mean of 35 to a posttreatment mean of 21.5, with evidence that ASI scores decreased consistently across the 3 months of treatment. Overall changes in ASI scores were significantly correlated ($r = .62$) with degree of clinical improvement.

There is also evidence that brief CBT can reduce ASI scores in a nonclinical sample. Harrington, Telch, Abplanalp, and Hamilton (1995) compared a brief, three-session, panic-prevention program of education, interoceptive exposure, and diaphragmatic breathing retraining to a control training condition in a sample of 120 students selected for scores at least one standard deviation above the nonclinical mean on the ASI. Active treatment resulted in significantly lower scores on the ASI for the cognitive-behavioral intervention relative to the control condition.

Perhaps the most direct examination to date of changes in ASI scores following treatment has been provided by Hazen, Walker, and Eldridge (1996). Hazen et al. examined the association between AS and treatment outcome in 106 patients with a primary diagnosis of panic disorder. Active treatment centered on the use of a self-help manual (Clum, 1990) in the context of a therapist-directed group, a self-help group, or individual use. These conditions were compared with each other and with a wait-list control condition. Pretreatment ASI scores for the four groups were in the low to mid-30s, with no significant differences between groups. The wait-list control group demonstrated no pre- to posttreatment changes in AS, with posttreatment scores ($M = 35.1$) remaining almost two standard deviations above the normative mean. Scores in the wait-list condition were highly correlated across the treatment interval ($r = .74$), which is consistent with other data indicating a high test–retest reliability for the ASI (Peterson & Reiss, 1992).

In contrast, ASI scores decreased significantly in the three active-treatment conditions. Posttreatment scores were lowest in the professionally led treatment group ($M = 17.8$) and were in the nonclinical range. Furthermore, reductions in AS were associated with the degree of improvement as assessed by Clinical Global Improvement ratings. The effect size for changes in ASI scores obtained in this study, like those found for the Telch et al. (1993) study, were greater than those of two other measures of outcome—the Fear Questionnaire Agoraphobia subscale and the Sheehan Patient-Rated Anxiety Scale.

Not all outcome studies of CBT have provided such dramatic evidence of reductions of ASI scores. Gould, Clum, and Shapiro (1993) examined the outcome following brief treatment with self-help CBT, brief therapist-directed CBT, or a wait-list control condition. Outcome was examined after 5 weeks. At posttreatment, the groups did not differ in panic attack frequency or severity, depression severity, or avoidance. Significant differences favoring the active treatment groups were found for patient ratings of self-efficacy, ability to cope, perceived likelihood of panic, and catastrophic thoughts during a panic attack. Although there was evidence of overall reductions in ASI scores from the mid- to low 40s to scores in the upper 30s, no significant differences were obtained between groups, perhaps reflecting the absence of significant differences on other core panic measures (i.e., avoidance and panic frequency and severity). The changes in ASI scores obtained for the Gould et al. (1993) self-help group are consistent with the modest changes reported by Hazen et al. (1996) for their self-help program alone (both studies used Clum's [1990] self-help program as the basis for their bibliotherapy conditions). In addition, the relatively limited changes in ASI scores obtained for the Gould et al. guided coping treatment may reflect the short duration of the study period (5 weeks) compared with the longer (e.g., 12–14 week) treatments used in other studies.

THE NATURE OF TREATMENT-RELATED REDUCTIONS IN ANXIETY SENSITIVITY

Overall, data from these studies indicate that when fears of anxiety sensations are directly targeted with exposure and cognitive-restructuring interventions, AS is significantly reduced. Data on the ASI are nicely complemented by findings with other measures of fears of anxiety sensations, such as the Body Sensations Questionnaire (Chambless, Caputo, Bright, & Gallagher, 1984). In their review of the CBT literature, Chambless and Gillis (1993) examined effect sizes for CBT for panic disorder and agoraphobia. Pre- to posttreatment effect sizes provide evidence for significant reductions in fears of anxiety sensations that were similar to the improvement achieved for other outcome variables for panic disorder. However, the success of cognitive-behavioral interventions does not imply that an explicit focus on fears of anxiety sensations is necessary for modification of these fears. Do other treatments—such as pharmacotherapy or relaxation training, which do not explicitly target fears of anxiety sensations— lead to significant AS reductions? Treatment outcome research targeting major depression provides an illustrative context for considering this question.

As a strategy to treat major depression, cognitive therapy focuses directly on the modification of dysfunctional thoughts associated with depression. Dysfunctional cognitions are significantly reduced in cognitive therapy and CBT of depression, with corresponding reductions in severity of depression (e.g., Dobson, 1989; McKnight, Nelson-Gray, & Barnhill, 1992). Nonetheless, significant changes in dysfunctional cognitions associated with depression are commonly found following pharmacotherapy alone (e.g., Fava, Bless, Otto, Pava, & Rosenbaum, 1994; McKnight et al., 1992; Peselow, Robins, Block, Barouch, & Fieve, 1990). This suggests, at least in part, that these dysfunctional attitudes are mood-state dependent (see also Miranda, Persons, & Byers, 1990). However, residual elevations in dysfunctional attitudes remain in some patients (Pava, Nierenberg, Carey, Rosenbaum, & Fava, 1994; see also Eaves & Rush, 1984; Nolen-Hoeksema, Girgus, & Seligman, 1992).

It follows that if fears of anxiety sensations are maintained primarily by the presence of panic attacks, any treatment that controls the panic episodes may correspondingly decrease fears of anxiety sensations. Additionally, reductions in fears of anxiety sensations may result from reattributions about the meaning of these sensations occurring after clinical improvement. When confronted with control of their panic attacks with medications, some patients appear to conclude that "it must have been only anxiety after all." Finally, some changes in ASI scores may occur simply because of reductions in negative affect or affect-laden cognitions.

Otto, Pollack, Fava, Uccello, and Rosenbaum (1995) examined ASI scores in patients with major depression and found elevations—scores in the mid-20s—that decreased moderately (an average of six points) with antidepressant medication (see also Taylor, Koch, Woody, & McLean, 1996). Associations between depression and anxiety-related cognitions are also evident in other disorders. For example, depressed mood appears to increase scores on measures of dysfunctional attitudes characteristic of social phobia (Bruch, Mattia, Heimberg, & Holt, 1993; Ingram, 1989). The association between depression and AS scores may similarly reflect the general contribution of negative affectivity to the negative and catastrophic evaluations of anxiety sensations. Consequently, treatments that significantly reduce negative affect can be expected to have some effect on AS.

Significant reductions in ASI scores have been observed following medication treatment of panic disorder. In a naturalistic study of 24 patients undergoing pharmacotherapy in an outpatient clinic, Otto, Pollack, Sachs, and Rosenbaum (1991) found that ASI scores decreased from a mean of 31.3 at baseline to 22.2 after 6 months of treatment. For 67% of the sample, treatment consisted of benzodiazepines alone; 8% received antidepressants alone, and 25% were taking a combination of benzodiazepines and an antidepressant or other medication. The significant reduction in ASI scores occurring in patients who were not treated with CBT supports the notion that changes in AS may result from clinical improvement alone. It is not clear, however, whether more substantial reductions in AS may have been achieved in this sample with interventions that more directly targeted fears of anxiety sensations.

This issue is more directly addressed by a recent comparative trial of CBT, applied relaxation, and imipramine (Clark et al., 1994). The cognitive-behavioral program utilized a combination of cognitive restructuring, interoceptive exposure, behavioral experiments, and elimination of safety cues. Fears of anxiety sensations were assessed by the Body Sensations Interpretation Questionnaire (BSIQ). At post-treatment, BSIQ scores in the treatment groups were lower than those for the control condition. Moreover, post treatment scores were significantly lower for CBT than for the other two treatments. In addition, for both the total sample and a subsample of patients who achieved panic-free status, the BSIQ at the 6-month assessment period was a significant predictor of subsequent relapse.

The Clark et al. (1994) study supports the hypothesis that changes in fears of anxiety sensations may be related to the mode of treatment, with greater change among treatments that more directly target these fears. However, because patients treated with CBT tended to improve more than those treated with imipramine or relaxation training, changes in fears of anxiety sensations may simply reflect the differential efficacy between the three treatment conditions. Treatments that are similarly effective may result in similar posttreatment reductions in ASI scores regardless of the treatment mode.

A study by Shear and colleagues (1994) provides important data for addressing this issue. Shear et al. examined the outcome differences between a 12-session individual CBT for panic disorder relative to a 12-session nonprescriptive treatment. The non-prescriptive intervention involved reflective listening and focused on the role of stress and reactions to stress in panic disorder. Due to the absence of differential outcome between these treatments, this study is ideal for examining the specific effects of CBT on AS. No specific effects were found. Following the treatment phase (in most cases 10–15 sessions), patients in both treatment conditions achieved similar 10-point reductions in ASI scores, with no evidence of differences between the two treatments (see Table 14.1). Although the nonprescriptive treatment emphasized reflective listening, informational interventions characterized the first three sessions of the nonprescriptive treatment. Unless reductions in ASI are specific to education about the nature of panic attacks and panic disorder, this study—like studies of dysfunctional cognitions in depression—suggests that ASI scores may covary with successful treatment of panic disorder regardless of the treatment mode. As shown in studies of dysfunctional attitudes in depression (e.g., Pava et al., 1994), there is evidence that ASI scores may remain elevated in some subjects despite clinical improvement, perhaps reflecting more traitlike influences on ASI scores (Saviotti et al., 1991; Stoler & McNally, 1991).

EVIDENCE FROM MEDICATION
DISCONTINUATION PROTOCOLS

Difficulty discontinuing psychotropic medication, associated with the emergence of withdrawal effects and reemerging symptoms, is evident for a range of pharmacological treatments, but has received particular attention following benzodiazepine treatment. Benzodiazepine discontinuation is associated with the emergence of a number of withdrawal symptoms reminiscent of panic and anticipatory anxiety symptoms (Tyrer, Murphy, & Riley, 1990). High rates of recurrence of panic attacks and the inability to complete benzodiazepine taper are common among panic patients (Fyer et al., 1987; Noyes, Garvey, Cook, & Suelzer, 1991). Consequently, we have argued that benzodiazepine taper, completed in individuals with high AS, is an effective symptom provocation procedure that should result in increased fear and panic (Otto, Pollack, Meltzer-Brody, & Rosenbaum, 1992).

Given this model of discontinuation difficulties, interventions to facilitate medication discontinuation should treat the tendency to fear and catastrophically misinterpret somatic sensations of anxiety so that the emergence of these sensations during and after discontinuation will not provoke panic episodes (Otto et al., 1992). In other words, a direct focus on eliminating AS may aid benzodiazepine discontinuation and reduce subsequent relapse. To date, three studies have examined the efficacy of CBT to aid benzodiazepine discontinuation. All have reported clear benefit for treatments combining informational and cognitive interventions, interoceptive exposure, and somatic symptom management skills (e.g., diaphragmatic breathing or relaxation training) and, at times, situational exposure (Hegel, Ravaris, & Ahles, 1994; Otto et al., 1993; Spiegel, Bruce, Gregg, & Nuzzarello, 1994).

Two of these discontinuation studies specifically examined changes in AS across treatment. Hegel et al. (1994) provided evidence that ASI scores were still well within the clinical range ($M = 33.7$) in patients treated with medications, primarily benzodiazepines, although these patients were not symptom free. Patients first had their doses of alprazolam adjusted to control panic; then, following a 2-week panic-free stabilization period, patients began 12 weeks of individual CBT, with gradual tapering of alprazolam initiated after Week 4 of CBT. Examination of ASI scores before and after treatment and taper indicated a significant decrease to a mean of 21.7. At 1-year follow-up, 76% of patients remained free of medication; the group as a whole maintained a low ASI score at this assessment (Table 14.1).

Bruce, Spiegel, Gregg, and Nuzzarello (1995) conducted regression analyses to identify patients who were able to discontinue alprazolam treatment in the Spiegel et al. (1994) study and remain medication free during a 6-month follow-up period. Predictor variables were measured after patients were stabilized on alprazolam. The degree of change in ASI scores across treatment and taper was the only significant predictor of relapse; patients who had smaller reductions in AS were more likely to relapse. Together these studies support the hypothesis that AS may be inadequately treated by medications and that short-term cognitive-behavioral treatment can be used to help return fears of anxiety sensations to the nonclinical range. These studies also suggest that the degree of reduction in ASI scores is an important clinical variable for assessing the ability of patients to achieve their goal of medication discontinuation.

Fava and associates (Fava, 1996; Fava, et al., 1994) introduced the idea that benzodiazepines may not only fail to adequately decrease AS, but, because of their suppression of anxiety sensations, may actually increase fears of these sensations over time. This hypothesis was based, in part, on the observation that ASI scores decreased following benzodiazepine discontinuation, completed in the absence of ongoing behavior therapy (Fava et al., 1994; see also Bruce et al., 1995).

Why might benzodiazepine treatment intensify AS? It is possible that fears of anxiety symptoms are intensified by the daily use of benzodiazepine medications to control these sensations. The experience of interdose rebound (a return of anxiety associated with waning medication effects, which is particularly an issue with shorter acting benzodiazepines) may further encourage patients to believe that anxiety sensations are unsafe and must be quickly controlled with the next dose of medication. Although this hypothesis is consistent with observations of decreased AS occurring across the course of benzodiazepine discontinuation, it is difficult to reconcile this hypothesis with evidence of reductions in ASI scores following benzodiazepine treatment (Otto et al., 1991), unless one assumes that resensitization to anxiety symptoms occurs more slowly over time (after a period of acute treatment gains).

An alternative hypothesis is that successful benzodiazepine discontinuation may help reduce AS. As noted, benzodiazepine taper has been likened to biological, symptom provocation procedures (Otto et al., 1992); biological provocation of anxiety and panic symptoms has been used successfully as part of treatment of panic disorder (e.g., Griez & van den Hout, 1983). Likewise, taper of benzodiazepines conducted under conditions in which patients are given at least minimal explanations of the symptoms to be experienced and their origin may help some patients decrease fears of these sensations, at least in the context of a successful taper attempt (consistent with the finding reported by Fava et al., 1994). Although reductions in AS have been observed following benzodiazepine taper in the absence of CBT, greater reductions appear to be achieved when concurrent CBT is delivered (see Bruce et al., 1995). Moreover, the likelihood of successful benzodiazepine discontinuation is much higher with concurrent CBT (Otto et al., 1993).

CONCLUSIONS

Inclusion of measures of fears of anxiety symptoms as part of standardized assessment for panic disorder has been recommended (Shear & Maser, 1994). Results to date suggest that the ASI is sensitive to clinical improvement. As presented in Table 14.1, there is consistent evidence for reductions in ASI scores across cognitive-behavioral treatment of panic disorder. Based on a weighted average of 160 treated subjects from seven studies (Gould et al., 1993; Hazen et al., 1996; Hegel et al., 1994; McNally & Lorenz, 1987; Penava et al,. 1997; Shear et al., 1994; Telch et al., 1993), ASI scores drop an average of 14 points following short-term therapist-directed CBT.

A number of factors may account for ASI reductions following clinical treatment. CBT directly targets fears of anxiety sensations with cognitive-restructuring and exposure interventions, but ASI scores appear to decrease with successful treatment regardless of the treatment mode. This finding is consistent with a reciprocal causation model of the relation between AS and panic (see Taylor, 1995). In some individuals, AS may develop independently of panic attacks and place these individuals at risk for the development of panic disorder (e.g., Donnell & McNally, 1989; Telch & Harrington, 1992). Likewise, panic episodes have long been assumed to increase fears of anxiety symptoms. Treatment of panic disorder appears to reduce AS, perhaps in a manner independent from the original source of these fears.

However, treatment does not always return patients to ASI scores in the normal range (e.g., Saviotti et al. 1991; Stoler & McNally, 1991). Attention to elevated scores in patients who have completed acute treatment appears especially important given the ability of measures of fears of anxiety sensations to predict longer term treatment outcome (e.g., Clark et al., 1994; Ehlers, 1995; Pollack et al., 1996). Attention to AS as a risk factor for the development of panic disorder is also warranted. There is initial evidence that AS in nonclinical samples can be effectively reduced with a brief (three-session) cognitive-behavioral intervention (Harrington et al., 1995).

Studies examining the efficacy of pharmacotherapy for panic disorder typically have not included the ASI as a measure, making it difficult to draw conclusions about the relative impact of psychosocial compared with pharmacological treatments on AS. Pharmacotherapy alone appears to lead to significant reductions in AS. Nonetheless, ASI scores remain elevated in pharmacologically treated patients with residual symptoms, and CBT appears to offer an effective strategy to further decrease ASI scores and aid medication discontinuation in these patients (e.g., Bruce et al., 1995; Hegel et al., 1994).

REFERENCES

Barlow, D. H. (1988). *Anxiety and its disorders: The nature and treatment of anxiety and panic.* New York: Guilford.

Barlow, D. H., & Craske, M. G. (1994). *Mastery of your anxiety and panic: II.* New York: Psychological Corporation.

Bruch, M. A., Mattia, J. I., Heimberg, R. G., & Holt, C. S. (1993). Cognitive specificity in social anxiety and depression: Supporting evidence and qualifications due to affective confounding. *Cognitive Therapy and Research, 17,* 1–21.

Bruce, T. J., Spiegel, D. A., Gregg, S. F., & Nuzzarello, A. (1995). Predictors of alprazolam discontinuation with and without cognitive behavior therapy in panic disorder. *American Journal of Psychiatry, 152,* 1156–1160.

Chambless, D. L., Caputo, G. C., Bright, P. N., & Gallagher, R. (1984). Assessment of fear of fear in agoraphobics: The Body Sensations Questionnaire and the Agoraphobic Cognitions Questionnaire. *Journal of Consulting and Clinical Psychology, 52,* 1090–1097.

Chambless, D. L., & Gillis, M. M. (1993). Cognitive therapy of anxiety disorders. *Journal of Consulting and Clinical Psychology, 61,* 248–260.

Clark, D. M. (1986). A cognitive approach to panic. *Behaviour Research and Therapy, 24,* 461–470.

Clark, D. M., Salkovskis, P. M., Hackmann, A., Middleton, H., Anastasiades, P., & Gelder, M. (1994). A comparison of cognitive therapy, applied relaxation and imipramine in the treatment of panic disorder. *British Journal of Psychiatry, 164,* 759–769.

Clum, G. A. (1990). *Coping with panic: A drug-free approach to dealing with anxiety attacks.* Belmont, CA: Brooks/Cole.

Dobson, K. S. (1989). A meta-analysis of the efficacy of cognitive therapy for depression. *Journal of Consulting and Clinical Psychology, 57,* 414–419.

Donnell, C. D., & McNally, R. J. (1989). Anxiety sensitivity and history of panic as predictors of response to hyperventilation. *Behaviour Research and Therapy, 27,* 325–332.

Eaves, G. G., & Rush, A. J. (1984). Cognitive patterns in symptomatic and remitted unipolar major depression. *Journal of Abnormal Psychology, 93,* 31–40.

Ehlers, A. (1995). A 1-year prospective study of panic attacks: Clinical course and factors associated with maintenance. *Journal of Abnormal Psychology, 104,* 164–172.

Faravelli, C., & Pallanti, S. (1989). Recent life events and panic disorder. *American Journal of Psychiatry, 146,* 622–626.

Fava, M., Bless, E., Otto, M. W., Pava, J. A., & Rosenbaum, J. F. (1994). Dysfunctional attitudes in major depression: Changes with pharmacotherapy. *Journal of Nervous and Mental Disease, 182,* 45–49.

Fava, G. A. (1996). Anxiety sensitivity [letter]. *American Journal of Psychiatry, 153*, 1109.

Fava, G. A., Grandi, S., Belluardo, P., Savron, G., Raffi, A. R., Conti, S., & Saviotti, F. M. (1994). Benzodiazepines and anxiety sensitivity in panic disorder. *Progress in Neuro-Psychopharmacology and Biological Psychiatry, 18*, 1163–1168.

Fyer, A. J., Liebowitz, M. R., Gorman, J. M., Campeas, R., Levin, A., Davies, S. O., Goetz, D., & Klein, D. F. (1987). Discontinuation of alprazolam treatment in panic patients. *American Journal of Psychiatry, 144*, 303–308.

Goldstein, A. J., & Chambless, D. L. (1978). A reanalysis of agoraphobia. *Behavior Therapy, 9*, 47–59.

Gould, R. A., Clum, G. A., & Shapiro, D. (1993). The use of bibliotherapy in the treatment of panic: A preliminary investigation. *Behavior Therapy, 24*, 241–252.

Gould, R. A., Otto, M. W., & Pollack, M. H. (1995). A meta-analysis of treatment outcome for panic disorder. *Clinical Psychology Review, 15*, 819–844.

Griez, E., & van den Hout, M. A. (1983). Treatment of phobophobia by exposure to CO_2 induced anxiety symptoms. *Journal of Nervous and Mental Disease, 171*, 506–508.

Harrington, P. J., Telch, M. J., Abplanalp, B., & Hamilton, A. C. (1995, November). *Lowering anxiety sensitivity in nonclinical subjects: Preliminary evidence for a panic prevention program.* Paper presented at the 29th annual meeting of the Association for Advancement of Behavior Therapy, Washington, DC.

Hazen, A. L., Walker, J. R., & Eldridge, G. D. (1996). Anxiety sensitivity and treatment outcome in panic disorder. *Anxiety, 2*, 34–39.

Hegel, M. T., Ravaris, C. L., & Ahles, T. A. (1994). Combined cognitive-behavioral and time-limited alprazolam treatment of panic disorder. *Behavior Therapy, 25*, 183–195.

Ingram, R. E. (1989). Affective confounds in social-cognitive research. *Journal of Personality and Social Psychology, 57*, 715–722.

McKnight, D. L., Nelson-Gray, R. O., & Barnhill, J. (1992). Dexamethasone suppression test and response to cognitive therapy and antidepressant medication. *Behavior Therapy, 23*, 99–111.

McNally, R. J. (1994). *Panic disorder: A critical analysis.* New York: Guilford.

McNally, R. J., & Lorenz, M. (1987). Anxiety sensitivity in agoraphobics. *Journal of Behavior Therapy and Experimental Psychiatry, 18*, 3–11.

Miranda, J., Persons, J. B., & Byers, C. N. (1990). Endorsement of dysfunctional beliefs depends on current mood state. *Journal of Abnormal Psychology, 99*, 237–241.

Nolen-Hoeksema, S., Girgus, J. S., & Seligman, M. E. P. (1992). Predictors and consequences of childhood depressive symptoms: A 5-year longitudinal study. *Journal of Abnormal Psychology, 101*, 403–422.

Noyes, R., Garvey, M. J., Cook, B., & Suelzer, M. (1991). Controlled discontinuation of benzodiazepine treatment for patients with panic disorder. *American Journal of Psychiatry, 148*, 517–523.

Otto, M. W., Jones, J. C., Barlow, D. H., & Craske, M. G. (1996). *Stopping anxiety medication: Panic control therapy for benzodiazepine discontinuation (Therapist Guide).* New York: Psychological Corporation.

Otto, M. W., Pollack, M. H., Fava, M., Uccello, R., & Rosenbaum, J. F. (1995). Elevated Anxiety Sensitivity Index scores in patients with major depression: Correlates and changes with antidepressant treatment. *Journal of Anxiety Disorders, 9*, 117–123.

Otto, M. W., Pollack, M. H., Meltzer-Brody, S., & Rosenbaum, J. F. (1992). Cognitive-behavioral therapy for benzodiazepine discontinuation in panic disorder patients. *Psychopharmacology Bulletin, 28*, 123–130.

Otto, M. W., Pollack, M. H., Sachs, G. S., Reiter, S. R., Meltzer-Brody, S., & Rosenbaum, J. F. (1993). Discontinuation of benzodiazepine treatment: Efficacy of cognitive-behavior therapy for patients with panic disorder. *American Journal of Psychiatry, 150,* 1485–1490.

Otto, M. W., Pollack, M. H., Sachs, G. S., & Rosenbaum, J. F. (1991, November). *Anxiety sensitivity as a diathesis for panic disorder: Results from a naturalistic, longitudinal study.* Paper presented at the 25th annual meeting of the Association for Advancement of Behavior Therapy, New York.

Otto, M. W., & Whittal, M. L. (1995). Cognitive-behavior therapy and the longitudinal course of panic disorder. *Psychiatric Clinics of North America, 18,* 803–820.

Pava, J. A., Nierenberg, A. A., Carey, M., Rosenbaum, J. F., & Fava, M. (1994). *Residual symptoms in major depressive disorder: I. A comparison with normal controls.* Paper presented at the 147th annual meeting of the American Psychiatric Association, Philadelphia, PA.

Penava, S. J., Otto, M. W., Maki, K. M., & Pollack, M. H. (in press). Rate of improvement during cognitive-behavioral group treatment for panic disorder. *Behaviour Research & Therapy.*

Peselow, E. D., Robins, C., Block, P., Barouch, F., & Fieve, R. R. (1990). Dysfunctional attitudes in depressed patients before and after clinical treatment and in normal control subjects. *American Journal of Psychiatry, 147,* 439–444.

Peterson, R. A., & Reiss, S. (1992). *Anxiety Sensitivity Index test manual* (2nd ed.). Worthington, OH: International Diagnostic Systems.

Pollack, M. H., Otto, M. W., Sabatino, S., Majcher, D., Worthington, J. J., McArdle, E. T., & Rosenbaum, J. F. (1996). Relationship of childhood anxiety to adult panic disorder: Correlates and influence on course. *American Journal of Psychiatry, 153,* 376–381.

Rapee, R. M., Litwin, E. M., & Barlow, D. H. (1990). Impact of life events on subjects with panic disorder and on comparison subjects. *American Journal of Psychiatry, 147,* 640–644.

Saviotti, F. M., Grandi, S., Savron, G., Ermentini, R., Bartolucci, G., Conti, S., & Fava, G. A. (1991). Characterological traits of recovered patients with panic disorder and agoraphobia. *Journal of Affective Disorders, 23,* 113–117.

Shear, M. K., & Maser, J. D. (1994). Standardized assessment for panic disorder research. *Archives of General Psychiatry, 51,* 346–354.

Shear, M. K., Pilkonis, P. A., Cloitre, M., & Leon, A. (1994). Cognitive behavioral treatment compared with nonprescriptive treatment of panic disorder. *Archives of General Psychiatry, 51,* 395–401.

Spiegel, D. A., Bruce, T. J., Gregg, S. F., & Nuzzarello, A. (1994). Does cognitive behavior therapy assist slow-taper alprazolam discontinuation in panic disorder? *American Journal of Psychiatry, 151,* 876–881.

Stoler, L. S., & McNally, R. J. (1991). Cognitive bias in symptomatic and recovered agoraphobics. *Behaviour Research and Therapy, 29,* 529–545.

Taylor, S. (1995). Anxiety sensitivity: Theoretical perspectives and recent findings. *Behaviour Research and Therapy, 33,* 243–258.

Taylor, S., Koch, W. J., Woody, S., & McLean, P. (1996). Anxiety sensitivity and depression: How are they related? *Journal of Abnormal Psychology, 105,* 474–479.

Telch, M. J., Lucas, J. A., Schmidt, N. B., Hanna, H. H., Jaimez, T. L., & Lucas, R. A. (1993). Group cognitive-behavioral treatment of panic disorder. *Behaviour Research and Therapy, 31,* 279–287.

Telch, M. J., & Harrington, P. J. (1992, November). *Anxiety sensitivity and expectedness of arousal in mediating affective response to 35% carbon dioxide inhalation.* Paper presented at the 26th annual meeting of the Association for Advancement of Behavior Therapy, Boston, MA.

Tyrer, P., Murphy, S., & Riley, P. (1990). The Benzodiazepine Withdrawal Symptom Questionnaire. *Journal of Affective Disorders, 19*, 53–61.

V

CONCLUSIONS

15

Anxiety Sensitivity: Progress, Prospects, and Challenges

Steven Taylor
University of British Columbia
Brian Rabian
University of Southern Mississippi
Ingrid C. Fedoroff
University of British Columbia

This book has shown that anxiety sensitivity (AS) appears to play an important role in many forms of psychopathology; it is especially important in identifying people at risk for panic attacks. Given the importance of AS, it comes as no surprise that it is attracting increasingly more attention from theorists, researchers, and clinicians. The construct of AS has become refined and elaborated over time. Herein, details of its structure have been elaborated (chap. 5) and its relationships to related variables have been clarified (chaps. 1, 2, 3, 6, and 7). Thus, AS is not an immutable construct; it is an open concept (cf. Pap, 1958, 1962). That is, it is a *work in progress*, amenable to refinement, elaboration, and other changes. This concluding chapter considers what are seen as some of the most important issues for further research. Our understanding of AS may be enhanced by addressing the following:

- Is AS best regarded as an entirely dimensional construct or are there categorical (taxonic) forms of AS?
- If AS is hierarchically structured with lower and higher order factors (dimensions), how many factors are at each level?

- How is AS related to other sensitivities (e.g., fear of pain; illness/injury/death sensitivity) as described in Reiss' sensitivity theory (chap. 3)? Is AS really a fundamental fear (sensitivity) or the product of more basic fears?
- How is AS related to or distinct from conceptually similar constructs such as trait anxiety or fear of negative evaluation (FNE)? For example, is AS a product of trait anxiety or is there some other relationship among the two constructs (e.g., AS may be a cause of trait anxiety)? Does the fear of publicly observable anxiety reactions belong to the domain of AS or is it part of FNE? Does it consist of a blend of the two?
- Given the recent failures to support the expectancy theory (chap. 2), the question arises as to the nature of the relation between AS and anxiety expectancies. How do these constructs interact to cause or exacerbate anxiety-related phenomena (i.e., fear, anxiety, panic, and related avoidance)?
- AS is correlated with many forms of psychopathology and tends to be elevated in clinical samples relative to normal controls. Does this mean that AS—or some dimensions thereof—are nonspecific vulnerability factors? If so, what are the implications for the expectancy theory (chap. 2) and sensitivity theory (chap. 3)?
- Although AS tends to be elevated in clinical samples (relative to controls), it also varies in particular ways across various disorders (e.g., it is highest in panic disorder and posttraumatic stress disorder [PTSD] relative to other disorders). What causes the differences across disorders?
- What are the environmental (e.g., social learning) and genetic determinants of AS? How important are environmental compared with genetic factors? Does their relative importance differ across the various lower and higher order AS factors?
- If AS is "located" in the brain, what are its neurobiological substrates and how do they produce individual differences in AS? Do environmental factors influence these substrates?
- How does AS unfold over time? At what point in the life span do individual differences in AS generally emerge? What sorts of cognitive operations are required? Do individual differences remain stable once they emerge or do they change in later life?
- What are the major clinical implications of AS?

The remaining sections of this chapter expand on some of these issues and suggest some future directions and challenges for AS research. The answers to these issues could shed light on the etiology, maintenance, treatment, and prevention of several forms of psychopathology.

NATURE AND NUMBER
OF LOWER ORDER CONSTRUCTS

A good deal of evidence suggests that AS is hierarchically structured, consisting of a higher order construct and at least three lower order constructs. The latter can be described as representing (a) fear of somatic sensations, (b) fear of cognitive dyscontrol, and (c) fear of publicly observable anxiety reactions. For the time being, it is assumed that the lower and higher order constructs represent dimensions, although it is possible that taxometric studies will show that some of these define categories or taxa.

A problem with factor analytic studies performed to date is that most have been based on the ASI or other similarly brief scales. Until quite recently, none of these scales was developed to assess the lower order factors and none was developed to investigate the possibility that there may be more than three of these factors. Taylor and Cox (in press-a, in press-b) have begun a series of studies using two expanded measures of AS: the 36-item revised Anxiety Sensitivity Index (ASI–R) and the 60-item Anxiety Sensitivity Profile (ASP). The ASI–R retains the original format of the ASI (along with many of the original items), whereas the ASP has a different format in which respondents are asked to rate the perceived likelihood that each of 60 anxiety-related sensations has harmful consequences.

The ASI–R was administered to 155 psychiatric outpatients (Taylor & Cox, in press-b). Factor analyses using common factor analysis and principal components analysis were conducted. Parallel analysis determined the number of factors to retain and an oblique rotation was used. The ASP was administered to 349 university students (Taylor & Cox, in press-b); data were factor analyzed using the same methods used for the ASI–R. A hierarchical factor structure was obtained for both the ASI–R and ASP, consisting of four lower order factors that all loaded on a single higher order factor.

There were a number of consistencies among the lower order factor solutions. For both the ASP and ASI–R, the following factors were obtained: (a) fear of respiratory symptoms, (b) fear of cognitive dyscontrol, and (c) fear of cardiac symptoms. The solutions differed in terms of the fourth factor; for the ASP, we obtained a factor representing fear of gastrointestinal symptoms, but for the ASI-R we obtained a factor representing fear of publicly observable symptoms. The inconsistencies among results may have been due to differences in scales, samples, or both. The results clearly indicate that further research is required to identify the most robust lower order factors and to determine whether the factor structures vary across populations. However, the results for the ASI–R and ASP are consistent in that they fail to support the three-factor model described by Zinbarg and colleagues (chap. 5). Our results suggest that the three factor model may be an artifact arising from the use of comparatively brief ASI, which was not designed to investigate the multifactorial structure of AS. A challenge for future investigation is to advance our understanding of the number and nature of the lower order factors and to identify their correlates with various forms of psychopathology.

IS ANXIETY SENSITIVITY DIMENSIONAL OR CATEGORICAL?

A common assumption in psychological research is that most variables of interest are dimensional rather than categorical in nature. This assumption is rarely tested. When it is tested, the results can have profound implications for theory and assessment. To illustrate, Waller, Putnam, and Carlson (1996) recently demonstrated that there are two kinds of dissociation: dimensional and categorical. Dimensional dissociation is characterized by traits such as absorption and imaginative involvement, whereas categorical dissociation is characterized by the presence (vs. absence) of pathological features such as dissociative amnesia, derealization, depersonalization, and identity alteration. Categorical dissociation appears primarily due to environmental rather than genetic factors (Waller & Ross, 1997).

An assumption running throughout this book is that AS is dimensional. Is this assumption justified? It may be that AS, or some of its components, are categorical. An important challenge is to determine whether AS is categorical (taxonic) or dimensional (nontaxonic). Evidence of taxonicity would revolutionize the way we think about AS and would call into question all the previous work done on this construct.

We recently began to investigate this issue by focusing on whether the higher order AS construct is taxonic or nontaxonic. (Principal Investigator: Steven Taylor; Co-Investigators, in alphabetical order: Brian J. Cox, Wendy Freeman, Richard J. McNally, Sherry H. Stewart, & Richard P. Swinson.) We began using the taxometric methods developed by Meehl, Waller, and colleagues (e.g., Waller & Meehl, 1998). These are statistical procedures for determining whether a given data distribution represents a single dimensional variable or two latent, nonarbitrary categories. Following the methods used by Meehl, Waller, and colleagues (see Waller et al., 1996, for a recent empirical example), we assembled a data set consisting of ASI scores from 546 people with panic disorder (ASI mean = 35.3, SD = 12.0) and 546 nonclinical controls (university students: ASI mean = 19.3, SD = 9.8).

People with panic disorder tend to have higher ASI scores than people from other populations (see chap. 6). If AS is taxonic, then people falling in one group (high AS) should be at elevated risk for psychopathology (especially panic attacks), whereas people in the other group (low AS) should be at low risk. In other words, most of the people in the panic disorder group should be members of one group (the taxon) and most of the people in the control group should be members of the other group (the complement).

Meehl and colleagues developed several taxometric methods, with the most widely used being maximum covariance analysis (MAXCOV). This method requires three indicators (measures) of a given construct. Call these x, y, and z. For each score on x, one computes the covariance between y and z. Covariance is then plotted as a function of scores on x. Taxonic constructs yield hill-shaped curves, whereas nontaxonic constructs yield flat lines (see the upper two panels of Fig. 15.1 for prototypic examples). Taxonic constructs yield hill-shaped curves because (a) indicators are assumed to be uncorrelated within groups, and (b) the covariance increases as one moves from one group to the next (i.e., the midrange of scores on indicator x represents a mix of scores from the taxon and complement groups). Therefore, midrange scores on x (compared with low or high scores on x) are associated with greater covariance between y and z (see Waller & Meehl, 1998, for details).

MAXCOV works best when the indicators yield a large (1.5–2 SD) separation between the means of the taxon and the complement, and when the base rate of the taxon is close to 50% (Meehl & Yonce, 1996). Our sample consisted of 50% controls and 50% panickers, therefore we estimated that the base rate should be close to 50% (if AS is taxonic). We estimated the separation produced by our indicators (ASI items) by computing the standardized mean separation between controls and panickers as defined by the following equation: ($M_{panicker}$ - $M_{control}$)/SD_{pooled} where $SD_{pooled} = \sqrt{[(SD^2 panicker + SD^2 control)/2]}$. Unfortunately, only eight ASI items produced separation greater than one standard deviation. A further problem was that the ASI items did not contain enough response points to conduct MAXCOV (i.e., each ASI item is rated on a 5-point scale; thus, so for a given item, there are only five different points at which one can compute covariance between two other items). MAXCOV provides more reliable results when there are more (e.g., 20) points (Meehl & Yonce, 1996).

To circumvent these difficulties, we took the eight ASI items yielding more than one standard deviation separation between panickers and controls (mean separation = 1.27 SD units) and combined the items to form four miniscales (labeled *F1–F4*). Items were paired (as far as possible) on the basis of content similarity: F1 (Items 3 and 4 pertaining to fear of feeling shaky or faint), F2

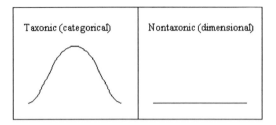

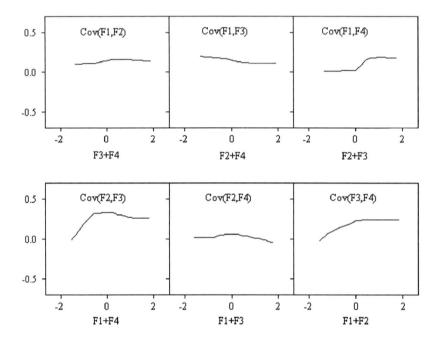

FIG. 15.1. Maximum covariance analyses (MAXCOV) plotting covariance of two measures as a function of scores on a third measure. The upper two panels show the prototypic curves for taxonic constructs (when the base rate of the taxon = 0.5) and for nontaxonic constructs (regardless of base rate). The lower six panels show results of MAXCOV analyses of four pairs of ASI items (F1–F4) used to measure the higher order anxiety sensitivity construct.

(Items 6 and 9 pertaining to fear of palpitations), F3 (Items 10 and 14 pertaining to fears of dyspnea and unusual body sensations), and F4 (Items 15 and 16 pertaining to fear of nervousness). By combining pairs of items, we increased the separation between the means of panickers and controls (mean separation = 1.45 *SD* units, range = 1.25–1.61 *SD* units). The number of response points was increased to 20 by combining miniscales. That is, six MAXCOV's were conducted in which the covariance of a given pair of miniscales (e.g., F1 and F2) was computed across scores on the sum of the combined remaining miniscales (F3 + F4). Figure 15.1 shows the complete set of combinations.

What do these miniscales measure? Chapter 5 revealed that AS is hierarchically structured, consisting of (at least) three lower order factors that load on a single higher order factor. Unfortunately, the ASI contains too few items to perform taxometric analyses on the lower order factors. Accordingly, we confined our analyses to the higher order factor. All of the eight ASI items forming our miniscales had salient loadings on the higher order AS factor. In the study by Stewart, Taylor, and Baker (1997), these items had a mean loading of .64 on this factor (range of .46–.79); in the study by Zinbarg and colleagues (see chap. 5, Table 5.4) the mean loading was .56 (range of .39–.66). Thus, the eight miniscales can be used as markers for the higher order AS construct.

The MAXCOV results are shown in the lower six panels of Figure 15.1. Scores on the x axis were standardized and scores on the y axis represent covariances between the remaining two miniscales. Curves were smoothed using the LOWESS smoothing function (see Waller & Meehl, 1998). Three of the curves are rather flat, suggesting that AS is dimensional. The other three curves tend to slope up toward the right, which suggests that AS is dimensional or that there is a taxon present with a low base rate. Monte Carlo studies by Meehl and Yonce (1996) suggest that these sloped curves could be obtained if a high AS taxon is present in less than or equal to 10% of our combined sample (panickers and students). Further analyses are needed to fully test this possibility. Analyses based on the other taxometric procedures should shed further light on the question of whether a low base-rate taxon is present.

On the basis of our preliminary results, it is more likely that AS is dimensional rather than taxonic. First, although three curves are ambiguous in their interpretation, the other three curves clearly suggest that AS is dimensional. Second, a low base-rate taxon seems implausible because it would mean that most of the panic-disordered sample would not belong to the taxon. Recall that this taxon supposedly represents a group that is at high risk for psychopathology, yet most of our panickers do not fall in this group. If the base rate were 10%, the taxon group ($n = 110$) would have a mean ASI score of 51.8 (range of 43–63). It would consist of 106 panic-disordered people and 4 controls. In other words, only 19% of panic-disordered people would belong to this taxon. The remaining panickers, along with almost all the students, would belong to the complement group. Thus, a low base-rate taxon makes little psychological sense; it does not identify people at high risk for psychopathology. Accordingly, we draw the tentative conclusion that AS (as a higher order construct) is dimensional. It remains to be determined whether this conclusion holds when the other taxometric methods are used and whether this holds for the lower order constructs.

DIFFERENCES IN ANXIETY SENSITIVITY ACROSS DIAGNOSTIC GROUPS: WHAT ARE THE IMPLICATIONS?

AS tends to be elevated in a variety of psychiatric disorders compared with normal controls. There are also differences across disorders (e.g., AS tends to be highest in panic disorder and PTSD, compared with other anxiety disorders; chap. 6). Given the apparent importance of AS in producing Clark's (1986) vicious cycle of panic (chap. 2), Reiss' (1991) theory is consistent with the finding that AS is elevated in panic disorder compared with most other disorders. However, the theory does not explain why ASI scores are almost as high in PTSD ($M = 31.6$) as they are in panic disorder ($M = 36.6$; Taylor, Koch, & McNally, 1992). These scores are higher than ASI scores obtained from people with generalized anxiety disorder (GAD; $M = 26.2$), obsessive–compulsive disorder (OCD; $M = 25.4$), social phobia ($M = 24.9$), and specific phobia ($M = 16.1$; Taylor et al., 1992).

Why should ASI scores be greater in PTSD relative to most other anxiety disorders? The writings of Cox and colleagues (chap. 6) suggest that one dimension of AS—fear of cognitive dyscontrol—increases the risk for disorders characterized by uncontrollable thinking, such as OCD, GAD, and PTSD. However, this does not explain why ASI scores would be higher in PTSD than in GAD and OCD. Neither the writings of Reiss nor Cox et al. answer this question. One possibility is that PTSD, compared with GAD and OCD, is characterized by elevations in more than one dimension of AS. However, this begs the question of why this would be so.

This question could be answered by looking at why AS is elevated in panic disorder. Reiss (1991) proposed a reciprocal relation between AS and panic attacks: Elevated AS may cause panic attacks (as mentioned earlier). In turn, panic attacks may increase AS because these attacks are, by definition, terrifying experiences. If attacks occur repeatedly, the sufferer may become increasingly fearful of anxiety symptoms in general because these symptoms will be seen as signals that a panic attack may occur.

AS may be a risk factor for the occurrence of PTSD, GAD, and OCD. However, we propose that the reason AS is higher in PTSD is that there is a reciprocal relation in PTSD that is less likely to occur in GAD and OCD. That is, we propose that some PTSD symptoms (e.g., flashbacks) increase AS in the same way that panic attacks increase AS. Moreover, we propose that the characteristic symptoms of OCD and GAD typically lack the ability to increase AS. Our rationale is as follows.

Reexperiencing of trauma-related thoughts, images, and memories is a defining feature of PTSD (American Psychiatric Association, 1994). Jones and Barlow (1990) observed a number of similarities between panic attacks and flashbacks. Both are brief, intense events triggered by internal or external stimuli (Davidson & Foa, 1991); flashbacks and panic attacks share many of the same symptoms (Burstein, 1985; Jones & Barlow, 1990; Mellman & Davis, 1985). Mellman and Davis (1985) found that 72% of their PTSD patients experienced flashbacks one or more times per week, which suggests that flashbacks in PTSD may be as common as panic attacks in panic disorder. Mellman and Davis also suggested that flashbacks may, in fact, be a form of panic attack.

If panic attacks increase AS because they are rapid onset, intense, and terrifying events, then flashbacks may increase AS for the same reason (Taylor et al., 1992). In contrast, the characteristic symptoms of OCD and GAD lack the paroxysmal quality of panic attacks and flashbacks and therefore may be less likely to increase AS. This hypothesis, although proposed several years ago (Taylor et al., 1992), remains to be tested.

More generally, an important task for future research is to determine why various disorders differ in their characteristic levels of AS. As noted by Cox and colleagues (chap. 6), it may be useful to look at how the various diagnostic groups compare in terms of the mean scores on measures of the lower and higher order AS dimensions. The challenge is to determine whether AS–or some combination of its dimensions–represent correlates (coeffects), causes, consequences, or perhaps combinations (causes and consequences) of various forms of psychopathology.

DEVELOPMENTAL CONSIDERATIONS

Little is known about the causes of individual differences in AS. How and when in the developmental life span do these differences emerge? Lack of knowledge of this issue stems from the fact that, until recently, theory and research has focused mainly on adults. Fortunately, there is growing interest in AS in children (see chap. 11). As discussed in chapter 11, the study of AS in children and youth may shed light on the development of AS and the development of anxiety disorders, which often emerge during childhood or adolescence (American Psychiatric Association, 1994).

Reiss' theory (e.g., chaps. 2 and 3) suggests that for someone to develop a fear of anxiety, it is necessary for him or her to believe that anxiety sensations are harbingers of threat—indicators that one could die, go crazy, or be ridiculed by others. This led researchers to question whether the fear of anxiety, with its inherent cognitive demands, could exist in young children. Silverman and Weems (chap. 11) present data and arguments to support the view that individual differences in AS can be found in children as young as 7 or 8 years. It is unknown whether individual differences in AS can be found in even younger children. Also unknown is how these differences are related to cognitive development.

It may be that AS in adults is different than AS in young children. Compared with adults, beliefs about anxiety may play less of a role in AS in very young children. If AS is determined, at least partly, by one's genes (see chap. 9), it may be that individual differences in AS may initially start out as innate, reflexive alarm reactions in reponse to anxiety-related sensations. As the child develops, the cognitive component of AS may develop (i.e., beliefs about anxiety may begin to emerge), thereby influencing individual differences in AS.

The possibility that individual differences in AS are (at least partly) innate is consistent with findings suggesting that other fears are innate (Menzies & Clarke, 1995); it also raises the intriguing possibility that individual differences in AS may be found in nonhuman primates and other animals. These possibilities remain to be investigated. One obstacle to studying the origins of AS is that current measures rely on the respondent's self-report. Both the ASI and Childhood Anxiety Sensitivity Index (CASI) are questionnaires, and therefore require the respondent to have sufficient cognitive (e.g., linguistic) abilities to complete these measures. Interview measures of AS could be developed, but these rely on the respondent's verbal and other cognitive abilities. These limitations prevent us from using the ASI or CASI to determine whether individual differences in AS arise in very young children.

New research on anxiety-evoking challenge procedures suggest a way of circumventing these difficulties. Such procedures (e.g., CO_2 inhalation or physical exercise) induce anxiety-related sensations (e.g., shortness of breath, palpitations). Studies of adults show that people with high AS, compared with those with low AS, tend to respond more anxiously to such challenges (see chap. 9). Recently, similar findings have been found with children. In a study of 56 third- and fourth-grade children, Rabian, Embry, and MacIntyre (1997) used a stair-stepping procedure to induce anxiety-related sensations and then examined how well the CASI predicted self-reports of state anxiety and fear following the procedure. After controlling for prechallenge levels of fear and trait anxiety, scores on the CASI were significantly related to fear scores after challenge. The findings raise the possibility that researchers could use fear reactions to these challenges as an index or indicator of the child's level of AS. Fear could be assessed via observational methods, thereby enabling one to assess AS in children too young (or without the requisite cognitive abilities) to complete the CASI. This would enable researchers to determine when individual differences in AS begin to emerge. This possibility merits investigation. An important first step would be to firmly establish whether the challenges are reliable and valid indices of AS in children.

A further important issue concerns the relationship between the development of high AS and other risk factors for anxiety disorders. For example, how is AS related to behavioral inhibition? Is it possible to see the origins of high AS in children with high levels of behavioral inhibition (Kagan, Reznick, & Snidman, 1988)? Currently, Rabian and colleagues are beginning to explore the possibility that early patterns of behavioral inhibition may presage high AS in later childhood. In this research, preschool children attending day care are being exposed to a paradigm similar to Ainsworth's Strange Situation to arouse anxiety, and both verbal and nonverbal behaviors are being coded through an observational measure of anxiety. In addition, behavioral observation of the children are being examined in relation to parental variables (including parental AS) and family variables. Rabian and colleagues plan to follow children over the course of several years until they are old enough to provide self-report data about their functioning, including AS.

CLINICAL IMPLICATIONS
OF ANXIETY SENSITIVITY

Much of the work described in this book has to do with the theory and research on AS. Clinical implications have been described (e.g., chaps. 10 and 14), but much research needs to be done to fully reveal these implications. This final section offers as some of the most important avenues for future investigation. Research using samples of adults suggests that AS predicts the onset of panic attacks and possibly other pathological reactions (chap. 10), but it remains to be seen whether the same applies to children or adolescents. As mentioned, anxiety disorders often arise during childhood or adolescence, so it will be of interest to see whether AS (as assessed by the CASI or other methods) predicts who is at risk for these disorders.

If high AS is found to be a risk factor, this would have profound implications for primary prevention. It may be possible to prevent many anxiety disorders (and possibly other disorders) by screening children or adolescents (e.g., in school settings) to identify those with elevated AS. Their AS could then be reduced by methods used in cognitive-behavior therapy for panic disorder (see chap. 14). Theoretically, this would decrease the risk for anxiety disorders, and possibly other disorders. Although it appears that early screening for elevated AS has great potential for primary prevention, it is important to proceed with caution. If screening for AS is conducted in schools, for example, it is essential to ensure that children with elevated AS are not led to feel stigmatized or abnormal because they have an intense fear of anxiety.

AS has been implicated in a number of psychopathological conditions, including chronic pain, depression, and substance abuse (see chaps. 6, 10, 11, 12, and 13). Therefore, it may be useful to screen for elevated AS in people attending general psychiatric clinics, drug and alcohol treatment centers, and pain management programs. An important question concerns the best way to integrate AS-reduction methods into existing treatment programs, such as programs for depression, chronic pain, or substance abuse. It may be that treatments for these disorders can be improved, at least in some cases, by incorporating AS-reduction methods.

Another important, clinically relevant avenue for further research is to develop appropriate norms for the ASI and CASI, with sensitivity to potential influences of age, gender, and ethnicity on AS scores. The clinical significance of ASI (or CASI) scores also may depend on the population or disorder in question. To illustrate, studies of chronic pain patients found that ASI scores tend to be lower than those found in anxiety-disordered samples. However, when ASI scores were divided into terciles (low, medium, and high), pain patients with high ASI scores tended to respond more poorly to pain management treatment (chap. 12). These findings suggest that even normal or moderately low ASI scores may be of clinical significance if the person has a particular disorder (e.g., chronic pain).

Schmidt (chap. 10) found that the ASI predicted the occurrence of panic attacks in air force cadets, although most cadets had low ASI scores compared with the general population. The cadets were undergoing basic training, and therefore exposed to numerous, unpredictable stressors. This suggests that low ASI scores may be clinically relevant when the person is exposed to high levels of stress.

The findings of Schmidt and colleagues and Asmundson suggest that one needs to proceed cautiously when developing ASI (or CASI) cutoff scores. Cutoff scores for predicting the onset of psychopathology or poor response to treatment may depend on a variety of factors. The cutoff scores may vary with the stressfulness of the person's environment. For example, ASI cutoff scores may be high for people entering low-stress environments and low for high-stress environments. That is, low-stress environments may precipitate psychopathology only in people with high AS, whereas high-stress environments could trigger psychopathology even in people with normal levels of AS. Cutoff scores may also vary with patient population (e.g., the cut-off score for identifying poor response to pain management therapy might be different from the cut-off score for identifying poor response to the behavioral treatment of specific phobia).

A further issue concerns the optimal way of reducing AS. Studies of panic disorder show that numerous interventions are able to reduce AS, including cognitive-behavior therapy (CBT) and some pharmacotherapies (see chap. 14). Little is known about the best way to produce large, rapid, and enduring reductions in AS. Currently popular CBTs consist of a combination of psychoeducation (i.e., information about the harmlessness of anxiety), cognitive restructuring (to correct distorted beliefs about the dangerousness of anxiety), and interoceptive exposure exercises (to show the person that anxiety sensations do not have harmful consequences). Specific exposure exercises may target specific dimensions of AS. Fear of somatic sensations may be best treated by methods that induce these sensations (e.g., palpitations can be induced by physical exercise). Fear of cognitive dyscontrol may be best treated by methods that induce depersonalization or derealization (e.g., staring into a mirror for extended periods of time; see Barlow & Craske, 1994, for descriptions of these methods). Some methods induce a variety of sensations. For example, voluntary hyperventilation can induce somatic sensations (e.g., palpitations, shortness of breath) and cognitive sensations (e.g., derealization, dizziness). It may be that such methods are the most efficient means of treating people who have generally elevated AS (i.e., elevated scores on multiple dimensions of AS). Tailoring treatment may be optimal in other cases, using specific methods to reduce elevations on specific dimensions of AS (e.g., relying mainly on methods that induce cognitive anxiety symptoms in people who only have extreme fear of cognitive dyscontrol).

AS theory and research also have important implications for relapse prevention. CBTs and some pharmacotherapies are often effective in treating panic disorder (chap. 14). However, treatment responders sometimes relapse and elevated posttreatment AS is among the best predictors of relapse (chaps. 10 and 14). This suggests that it would be important to assess AS levels at the end of treatment and provide additional, AS-focused treatment to people with elevated AS. An important question is whether such an intervention is able to substantially reduce the risk of relapse over the long term (i.e., years). A further question is whether elevated posttreatment AS predicts relapse for other disorders, such as substance abuse or dependence, depression, and chronic pain. Answers to these and other questions raised in this section should greatly enhance our understanding of how the assessment and reduction of AS can be used to improve clinical practice.

CONCLUSION

This volume has reviewed the many important developments in the theory and assessment of AS. This construct has been the subject of a good deal of research, and the body of empirical work continues to grow at a rapid pace. AS has been implicated in several disorders, although it appears to be most important in panic attacks and panic disorder. Much remains to be learned about the causes, consequences, and clinical implications of AS. This volume will have served its purpose if it stimulates further research on these important issues.

ACKNOWLEDGMENT

Preparation of this chapter was supported in part by a grant from the British Columbia Health Research Foundation.

REFERENCES

American Psychiatric Association. (1994). *Diagnostic and statistical manual of mental disorders* (4th ed.). Washington, DC: Author.

Barlow, D. H., & Craske, M. G. (1994). *Mastery of your Anxiety and Panic II*. New York: Psychological Corporation.

Burstein, A. (1985). Posttraumatic flashbacks, dream disturbance, and mental imagery. *Journal of Clinical Psychiatry, 46*, 374–378.

Clark, D. M. (1986). A cognitive approach to panic. *Behaviour Research and Therapy, 24*, 461–470.

Davidson, J. R. T., & Foa, E. B. (1991). Diagnostic issues in posttraumatic stress disorder: Considerations for DSM-IV. *Journal of Abnormal Psychology, 100*, 346–355.

Jones, J. C., & Barlow, D. H. (1990). The etiology of posttraumatic stress disorder. *Clinical Psychology Review, 10*, 299–328.

Kagan, J., Reznick, J. S., & Snidman, N. (1988). Biological bases of childhood shyness. *Science, 240*, 167–171.

Meehl, P. E., & Yonce, L. J. (1996). Taxometric analysis: II. Detecting taxonicity using covariance of two quantitative indicators in successive intervals of a third indicator (MAXCOV procedure). *Psychological Reports, 78*, 1091–1227.

Mellman, T. A., & Davis, G. C. (1985). Combat-related flashbacks in posttraumatic stress disorder: Phenomenology and similarity to panic attacks. *Journal of Clinical Psychiatry, 46*, 379–382.

Menzies, R. G., & Clarke, J. C. (1995). The etiology of phobias: A nonassociative account. *Clinical Psychology Review, 15*, 23–48.

Pap, A. (1958). *Semantics and necessary truth: An inquiry into the foundations of analytic philosophy.* New Haven, CT: Yale University Press.

Pap, A. (1962). *An introduction to the philosophy of science.* New York: The Free Press.

Rabian, B., Embry, L., & MacIntyre, D. (1997). *Behavioral validation of the Childhood Anxiety Sensitivity Index in children.* Submitted for publication.

Stewart, S. H., Taylor, S., & Baker, J.M. (1997). Gender differences in dimensions of anxiety sensitivity. *Journal of Anxiety Disorders, 11*, 179–200.

Reiss, S. (1991). Expectancy model of fear, anxiety, and panic. *Clinical Psychology Review, 11*, 141–153.

Taylor, S., & Cox, B. J. (in press-a). Anxiety sensitivity: Multiple dimensions and hierarchic structure. *Behaviour Research and Therapy.*

Taylor, S., & Cox, B. J. (in press-b). An expanded Anxiety Sensitivity Index: Evidence for a hierarchic structure in a clinical sample. *Journal of Anxiety Disorders.*

Taylor, S., Koch, W. J., & McNally, R. J. (1992). How does anxiety sensitivity vary across the anxiety disorders? *Journal of Anxiety Disorders, 6*, 249–259.

Taylor, S., Koch, W. J., Woody, S., & McLean, P. (1996). Anxiety sensitivity and depression: How are they related? *Journal of Abnormal Psychology, 105*, 474–479.

Waller, N. G., & Meehl, P. E. (1998). *Multivariate taxometric procedures: Distinguishing types from continua.* Newbury Park, CA: Sage.

Waller, N. G., Putnam, F. W., & Carlson, E. B. (1996). Types of dissociation and dissociative types: A taxometric analysis of dissociative experiences. *Psychological Methods, 1*, 300–321.

Waller, N. G., & Ross, C. A. (1997). The prevalence and biometric structure of pathological dissociation in the general population: Taxometric and behavior genetic findings. *Journal of Abnormal Psychology, 106*, 499–510.

Author Index

A

Abelson, J. L., 202, *212*
Abplanalp, B., 325, 332, *334*
Achenbach, T. H., 241, *263*
Achille, M. A., 296, 308, *318*
Ackerman, P. L., 175, *175*
Agras, W. S., 77, *81*, 99, *113*
Ahles, T. A., 324, 330, 332, 333, *334*
Ahmad, T., 86, 88, 90, 97, *113*, 118, 120, *148*
Ahrens, A., 132, *148*
Albano, A. M., 242, 243, 251, 252, 253, 254, 256, *264*, 267
Albus, M., 76, *78*
Alford, B. A., 7, *13*
Alkubaisy, T., 100, 101, 104, *112*, 117, 119, 120, *146*
Allan, L. G., 191, *196*
Allan, W. D., 242, 254, *264*
Allen, G. J., 139, *146*
Allerup, P., 76, *78*
Allport, G. W., 150, *175*
Aman, M. G., 47, 49, *56*
American Psychiatric Association, 24, *31*, 47, *56*, 98, 121, *144*, 241, 242, *263*, 289, *313*, 347, 348, *352*
Amir, N., 187, 191, *195*, *196*
Anastasiades, P., 12, *14*, 328, 329, 332, *333*
Ancis, J. R., 117, *147*
Anderson, D. E., 205, *213*
Anderson, J. C., 245, *263*
Anderson, N., 295, 296, *316*
Andrews, G., 212, *212*
Annis, H. M., 290, 313, *318*
Antony, M. M., 117, *144*
Apfeldorf, W. J., 117, 122, *144*
Arancio, C., 211, *214*
Argyle, N., 76, *78*

Arntz, A., 271, *284*
Aronson, T. A., 7, *13*
Arrindell, W. A., 73, 74, 75, *78*, 100, 101, 104, 107, *111*, 156, 157, 161, 171, *175*
Asmundson, G. J. G., 5, *13*, 64, 66, 75, 76, *78*, 118, 119, 126, 134, 135, 138, 139, 141, *144*, *146*, 149, *175*, 188, *195*, 206, 207, *212*, 226, *235*, 269, 271, 273, 276, 277, 278, 279, 280, 282, *283*, 294, 295, 300, 302, 303, 304, 306, 311, *314*, *316*
Assenheimer, J. S., 94, *113*
Atkinson, G., 160, *179*
Averill, P. M., 188, 190, *195*
Ayuso, J. L., 76, *78*

B

Baeyens, F., 272, *283*
Baglioni, A. J., 77, *79*
Baker, J. M., 20, *33*, 64, 65, *80*, 85, 87, 88, 89, 90, 91, 92, 93, 94, 96, 97, 99, 106, 107, 108, *113*, 118, 120, *147*, 295, 296, 303, 307, 308, 311, 313, *314*, *319*, 345, *353*
Baldwin, L. E., 188, 190, *195*
Ball, S. G., 117, 118, *144*, 297, 307, *314*
Balma, D. L., 166, *177*
Balon, R., 218, *233*
Bandelow, B., 76, *78*
Bandura, A., 28, *31*, 38, 39, 40, *56*
Baranyai, G., 117, 136, 138, *144*
Barlow, D. H., 5, 12, *13*, 54, *57*, 67, 68, *81*, 106, 107, 110, *111*, 117, *144*, *147*, 151, 154, 158, 159, *175*, *180*, 209, *213*, 233, *234*, 242, 248, 249, 251, 252, 253, 254, 256, *264*, *265*, *268*, 271,

355

Subject Index

367